THE UNFORGIVING MINUTE

THE UNFORGIVING MINUTE

by

David Sanctuary Howard

with a foreword by
the Reverend Canon John Andrew

The Memoir Club

First published in 2004 by
The Memoir Club
Stanhope Old Hall
Stanhope
Weardale
County Durham

British Library Cataloguing in
Publication Data.
A catalogue record for this book
is available from the
British Library.

ISBN: 1 84104 124 6

Printed by CPI Bath.

For my children
Philippa, Sophie, Jo and Thomas

Other books by the author

Chinese Armorial Porcelain
Faber & Faber, 1974

*

China for the West
(with John Ayers)
Sotheby Parke Bernet, 1978

*

New York and the China Trade
The New-York Historical Society, 1984

*

The Choice of the Private Trader
Zwemmer, 1994

*

A Tale of Three Cities
Canton, Shanghai and Hong Kong
Sotheby's, 1997

*

Chinese Armorial Porcelain, Volume II
Heirloom & Howard, 2003

Contents

Foreword

by

The Reverend Canon John Andrew, OBE, DD

If ever there was an appropriate title for this autobiography, *The Unforgiving Minute* would be it. The man who writes it, the world authority on the particular historical porcelain he has brought to international notice, has literally crammed his life with travel, discovery, recognition, hard-thinking business enterprise and keeping friendships in repair, while meticulously compiling in minute detail the subjects of his seminal work of scholarship on a subject desperately needing an ordered, classifying mind. The profundity of his scholarship is recognised by a university for whom he has examined for doctorates. His reach is global, and like an eagle he misses nothing as he flies above his porcelain firmament.

But he has a reservoir of charitable common sense. He reveals his vulnerabilities. His photographic memory and intellectual energy are harnessed to a loving balance of life's reality and healthy purpose in bringing people together to enjoy what they see, and discern the strengths of historical discipline in what they examine. Underlying all his enthusiasm is a purpose: his eye for detail, the accuracy he drives for, the careful notes he has made of individuals met and enjoyed in the countless visits he has made out of friendship, business and scholarly obligation, have set David Howard apart as a *rara avis*.

However, he is by no means a one-dimensional man, an academic who has intrigued people all over the world with his esoteric historical subject. David's account of his business life, pursued with such energy in the years of his younger adulthood, makes the reader aware of an investigative and determined expertise which took him to far places and away from his family for long periods as he explored market potential and met influential leaders in the enterprises he represented. I am left with the impression that he was well on his way to international stature in the commodities he sought to promote on the world market. It is precisely this single-minded approach to his professional business life that is reflected in his later, fulfilling career as an academic and author.

I have already hinted at David's enthusiasm, but not its link with generosity. Many a student has sought his academic help and has been suprised at the readiness of it, with the length and depth of his replies. Not that this even gets a mention in what he writes. But I know; and this man's willingness to help is as much a part of him as his knowledge.

On reading this book I have on frequent occasions needed to take a breather after absorbing the battering intensity of his travel agendas. Breakfasts with friends and clients are followed by lunches with confrères in the academic discipline, and end with memorable dinners at the tables of his friends, colleagues, students, scholars and collectors, all enjoying sharing his companionship.

I have known David for over forty years. I have met the women he has loved and some of his children. I have lived in a house he had. I have rejoiced with him in important milestones in his life. His capacity for friendship has shown itself in this remarkable story, and I am proud to be a beneficiary of it.

John Andrew
New York, August 2004

Preface

Some years ago my sister and I sorted through my mother's and father's papers. Among them was a diary with my name, dated 1937. On 1st January there was a bold statement: 'Resolved to keep a *dairy*'. It was the only entry that I made that year (or any other).

Now, almost seventy years later, it is time to make amends for that omission, although as I write I am not yet sure whether this is to tell my children their father's story, or whether this book could have an interest for a larger audience.

At various moments throughout my life I have been able to draw great comfort and reassurance from a poem by Rudyard Kipling. I would liken it to a set of secular values which I hope to keep to myself, and which I always admire in friends.

I have frequently turned to this poem when in doubt and have never found it wanting in any line – even in our age which, at times, Rudyard Kipling himself would find hard to understand.

Today, when self-interest is all too often admired over service, and arrogance over modesty, many might glance at this poem and find it 'old-fashioned', but I think that anyone who will read it line by line and consider the implications would have to agree that it is timeless and completely true – as appropriate to a better future as it was to a successful past.

> If you can keep your head when all about you
> Are losing theirs and blaming it on you,
> If you can trust yourself when all men doubt you,
> But make allowance for their doubting too;
> If you can wait and not be tired by waiting,
> Or being lied about, don't deal in lies,
> Or being hated, don't give way to hating,
> And yet don't look too good, nor talk too wise:
>
> If you can dream – and not make dreams your master;
> If you can think – and not make thoughts your aim;
> If you can meet with Triumph and Disaster
> And treat those two impostors just the same;
> If you can bear to hear the truth you've spoken
> Twisted by knaves to make a trap for fools,
> Or watch the things you gave your life to, broken,
> And stoop and build 'em up with worn-out tools:

If you can make one heap of all your winnings
And risk it on one turn of pitch-and-toss,
And lose, and start again at your beginnings
And never breathe a word about your loss;
If you can force your heart and nerve and sinew
To serve your turn long after they are gone,
And so hold on when there is nothing in you
Except the Will which says to them: 'Hold on!'

If you can talk with crowds and keep your virtue,
Or walk with Kings – nor lose the common touch,
If neither foes nor loving friends can hurt you,
If all men count with you, but none too much;

If . . .

These values waste no space in explanation or justification. Their answer is clear. In short, they are values – not just value.

When my coat of arms was granted in 1988, based on my ancestry carefully checked by the College of Arms, it followed my curatorship of the international exhibition in New York marking the 500th Anniversary of the establishment of the College of Arms. As always there were numerous decisions to make and I chose the words from the poem for my motto: 'Trust yourself'.

This book has been written between September 2003 and April 2004 and completed at a time when health problems have begun to make themselves evident. One must acknowledge also, as one looks back at situations long past, that such a book reflects largely the writer's view of events – whereas some of these may be open to other interpretations. But it is written in the hope that my children and grandchildren will enjoy it – and I am spurred on by the last four lines of Kipling's verse:

. . . If you can fill the unforgiving minute
With sixty seconds' worth of distance run,
Yours is the Earth and everything that's in it,
And – which is more – you'll be a Man, my son!

David Sanctuary Howard
West Yatton, October 2004

A blending of the ancient arms of Howard and those of Sanctuary, granted in 1988. The central shield on a lozenge and the lion are as borne by the Howards, the four crosses pattée and cross held in the crest are as borne by Sanctuary.

CHAPTER 1

Cheshire and Belmont

Oakfield, Wellington Road, was exactly what it said. A house built about 1835 of grey brick in fading Georgian style, and in the centre of a large lawn a solitary oak which had probably stood there for at least 300 years. The road, at the end of a long drive, stretched out towards the hamlet of Broad Heath on the outskirts of Altrincham and was undoubtedly one of a great many Wellington Roads that proliferated across England between 1815 and 1850 to honour the Iron Duke.

The four-storey mansion had long broad staircases with additional rooms on each landing – one of which became mine when my mother and father bought the house in 1931. Sleeping in my large oak bed with two long windows and a great marble fireplace (now filled with a gas fire) I remember clearly on more than one occasion waking to see two elderly men sitting in huge chairs before a log fire in the broad grate. One wore a stocking cap – rather like a character from Dickens – and they both spoke, but I was too far away to hear them.

After two or three occasions I asked my mother who they were and why I only saw them when I woke at night. She was reticent and changed the subject, and after another occasion my bedroom was moved to one over the front door which looked down the drive to the lane. It was only thirty years later that she told me about the two old men – the one with the stocking cap had been the son of the builder of Oakfield. She had learned from an elderly lady who helped clean the house that, when she was a girl, he used to sit late into the night before the fire on the first floor playing draughts with an old friend. He had died before the First War – at least twenty-five years before I saw him.

Oakfield was one of six or seven late Georgian or early Victorian houses which stretched about a mile along Wellington Road. When my parents bought it there were fields to the south of us stretching into the distance, the only building in sight being the club house of a golf club of which my mother was a member. It wasn't until many years later that I found a cutting from *The Daily Telegraph* in 1933 about a golf club in Cheshire where the ladies team captain, Mrs Gemma Howard, insisted on wearing 'slacks' at matches although this was against the Committee's rules. To the north of the house beyond a huge wall were our kitchen gardens and in the distance the

Bridgewater Canal, built in the 18th Century by the family of Lord Egerton of Tatton, one of whom was created Duke of Bridgewater. His canal connected the industrial and cotton city of Manchester with the sea south of Liverpool, long before the Manchester Ship Canal was built. It was this vital artery which helped establish Manchester as the third greatest city in Britain at the time of the Industrial Revolution.

When we moved there in 1931 from a home at Whalley Range in the outskirts of Manchester, where my sister Hazel and I had been born in 1929 and 1928, there was considerable building afoot on the fields north of us towards the canal. By 1934 new houses filled those fields and extended the outer boundaries of greater Manchester through Old Trafford and Sale. In 1935 the fields before us were gradually sold, and before we moved again to the country between High Legh and Knutsford, houses were stretching south from Wellington Road so that you could no longer see the golf course. They all had big notices on them saying '£480'. While Wellington Road became increasingly part of suburbia, there were always two important people who continued to use it regularly. One was the Walls ice-cream man who sold from a box on his tricycle and whose bell was an ever welcome sound (cones: a penny; choc bars: two pence). The other was the remarkable trapeze artist, the lamplighter – who cycled the length of this and many other roads with his long, hooked rod to switch on the road gas lights at the top of each pole each night (except on Sundays). He never put his foot on the ground as he peddled from light to light every evening at dusk, and in the morning again to switch them off.

This was our home for six years and the two or more acres of garden were a happy world for us, and the huge spacious rooms and hallways of Oakfield (later to become a private hotel) saw all our relations from the south coming to stay with us, with the lawn turned into a veritable cricket field in summer, while in autumn I remember arranging armies of acorns round the oak tree to fight Napoleonic battles (and my favourite joke was, 'My grandfather's brother died at Waterloo'; – friend, 'Oh, which platform was he on?'; – reply, 'Don't be silly, what does it matter which platform he was on').

Such houses could not possibly be maintained without staff and we were very fortunate that when my mother's father and mother died in 1932 and '33 their cook and butler – Ella and Charles Northover – moved to Cheshire from Dorset. There was another lady for cleaning and our governess, Lidie, came from Hungary and used to sing beautiful songs. Our dogs, too, were an essential part of everyday life and we loved our black Labrador (inevitably 'Simba') while my mother and her sister 'Aunt Bunny' had between them two dachshunds christened about 1928, 'Adolf' and 'Hitler'. I didn't really understand why about 1932 their names were changed to 'Dolfie' and 'Tatler', but they didn't seem to mind and still came running when called to 'din-din'.

My mother was the younger daughter of Campbell Fortescue Stapleton Sanctuary (the Stapletons were cousins and the Fortescues friends of his father at Winchester in the 1850s). His father, Thomas Sanctuary, had lived at Powerstock in Dorset for nearly fifty years – much of the time as Archdeacon of Dorset. At his own expense he had built a new road to Powerstock and it is recorded that on more than one occasion the Archdeacon, a powerful man and descendant of generations of Norfolk farmers and millers, would settle a disagreement with the road builders by a round of fisticuffs. His eldest son was known in the family as 'wicked Uncle Tom' – a local doctor and fly fisherman, and a friend of F. M. Halford in the early days of that art. He christened his daughters alphabetically in reverse: Zoe, Ysobel and Xarifa, but finding his dictatorial wife difficult, he walked out one day in 1904 and was not heard of again by any member of the family until my uncle was walking in Driffield in Yorkshire about 1925 and saw his nameplate on a door. Knocking and entering he found his elderly uncle tying flies for fishing! It was the coming of the railway which changed the centuries-old name of Poorstock to Powerstock when the Archdeacon allowed them to build across his land and the line was extended to Bridport. His mother was Isobel Lloyd, daughter of Charles Lloyd, the Bishop of Oxford, who died unexpectedly of a chill at the very early age of forty-four in 1829.

When the First War broke out my mother, Gemma, with her sister and brothers all wanted to join the Services. After a year working in a munitions factory she was eventually trained as a nurse as soon as she reached the age of eighteen and was posted to Coventry airport to drive an ambulance. She told me that in 1916 she was deeply in love with her second cousin Henry Pownall, but sadly he was killed on the Somme.

Coventry was a principal supply point for the Royal Flying Corps – later the Royal Air Force – and after the sharp but very individual encounters on the western front the damaged planes were patched up and flown to Coventry for repair. The aviators who did this may not always have had the exhilaration of single combat over France but they certainly learned to fly their wounded planes with care, and not infrequently with danger. My father was in the air force and every other day flew a wounded aeroplane to Coventry and the next day a repaired or new one to the front.

Horace Howard, my father, was the youngest of three sons of Frederick Thomas Howard of Bedford who had built up a successful stationery company over the years. He was also for a while proprietor of the *Bedfordshire Times* and *Bedfordshire Standard*. As a younger man, as an artist, he had learned the trade of a professional photographer and had created a thriving business providing the photographs for railway carriages (until the 1950s most railway compartments had three or more photographs of British scenery – many were marked 'Howard, Bedford').

Horace hated his Christian name and always called himself 'Tommy'. His eldest brother, Frederick, was later Assistant Permanent Under Secretary at the Colonial Office, while his brother Mitchell was also in the Flying Corps and, like him, was to set up his own business in the motor trade after the war. His eldest sister, Mabel, married one of the Berry brothers who were wine merchants in St James's; they became missionaries but were both murdered by their cook after living twenty years in India.

My father and mother met at Coventry airport and were married in Dorset in 1923. He had left the air force as a Captain in 1919 and started a garage supply business in Manchester the following year with a partner called Merriman (whom I recall as a formidable man but with a kindly smile). Whalley Range was then a quiet suburban area of Manchester and my father and mother threw themselves into the life of the local golf club and tennis club (my mother had played tennis for Dorset in 1921 and '22).

In January 1928 their only son was born and christened David Sanctuary Howard and in November 1929 their daughter Hazel Elizabeth Gemma. I have only an occasional flash of memory of my life in Whalley Range – a visit from my mother's uncle, Admiral Glossop (who had commanded HMAS *Sydney* when it sunk the *Emden* at the beginning of the First War) and his fascinating sister Allerley ('Aunt Joh') Glossop. Aunt Joh was an artist and had lived in South Africa from 1898, knew Rhodes and General Smuts, and painted the coronation presents of Basutoland to their monarchs in London, George V and George VI. I remember her address, 'Miss Glossop, Lion River, Natal' and am fortunate to have many of her sketch books left in her shed at the time of her death in 1955. I recall the last time I saw her in Bridport a year earlier, and she said, 'Do you know how to build a five-barred gate, young man?' and when I replied, 'No, Aunt Joh,' she said, 'But you should – everyone should know how to build a five-barred gate.'

Occasionally we visited our grandparents – in Bedfordshire at Woburn Sands and in Dorset at Powerstock – but although I have photographs taken in their gardens in the early 1930s, all four of my grandparents had died by the time I was seven in 1935.

*   *   *

Life at Oakfield was organised and comfortable. My father left after an early breakfast to take the train from Altrincham to Knott Mill Station,

Manchester, and his office in Deansgate, while Hazel and I usually walked to school – about twenty minutes. The establishment run by the two Misses Clegg (inevitably 'Big Miss Clegg' and 'Little Miss Clegg') was very well-organised and efficient. Some boys left for their prep school by the age of seven; I was nine before I went in the spring of 1937.

We usually spent our summer in Dorset or at the seaside in north Devon, but there were the occasional other exciting holidays – particularly when my godmother, Ebie Jeeves, came to stay in her gleaming Alvis touring car – or when we went to stay with her in Wimbledon, at the Well House at the top of Arthur Road. In the earlier years it had been a large Georgian house where she lived with her father, the retired Judge Jeeves, a leading expert on the law of divorce, but after his death she pulled down the house and built a luxurious modern home which is still there today.

Aunt Ebie was a long-term friend of my mother's, as was my other godmother, Marjorie Rackham, whose husband Maurice (the brother of the celebrated artist Arthur Rackham) together with others in the party had been killed in an avalanche at Zirst in the Alps about 1930 while my mother and Aunt Marjorie watched helplessly from the terrace of their hotel. Visits to London alternated between the Well House and Marjorie Rackham's home, the drawing room walls covered with her brother-in-law's paintings – not the Rackham who is so well known today as a book illustrator, but of another period: mountain and lakeland landscapes.

A particularly exciting visit was in 1935 when we went up to the Silver Jubilee parade of King George V and spent a day in the crowds in Pall Mall, near where both my godmothers were members of a club – little did I guess that one day I should take part in such a parade.

I can remember clearly one evening in December 1936 calling at the local newspaper shop, which I did most days to collect an evening paper and perhaps some cigarettes for my mother (always in packets of five because in that way I could collect more cigarette cards – there was one per pack whether the pack was five or twenty). On this evening the wireless was on in the shop and the voice of the new King Edward VIII told us that he could not be king without the woman he loved. I didn't really understand that, but at Christmas the most popular carol sung loudly by all of us at school was:

> Hark the herald angels sing –
> Wallis Simpson's pinched our king.

The only practical result was that all the mugs and coronation souvenirs that were given to us at school with the picture of Edward VIII were put away on the back of the shelf and we received new ones of George VI and Queen Elizabeth. (It must have cost someone a good deal of money!)

*   *   *

By 1937 the view from Oakfield across the fields had changed dramatically and my mother and father were thinking of a new move and sending their son to a prep school in Sussex. It was a wrench for Hazel and me because we had grown to enjoy greatly our frequent riding lessons at the stables in one of the other large houses along Wellington Road which were run by a delightful Miss Norbury. I held her elderly father in some awe, for he had been the senior partner of a large cotton-brokering business in 1930 at the time of the great crash and had lost everything – becoming a bankrupt with huge debts.

These debts he was determined to pay back as a matter of honour and had for a number of years worked very long hours carving large letters on linoleum. These in turn were used to print the signs which every bus in the Manchester region had, and which were adjusted on every journey by the driver turning a handle within his cab. The work was very hard and his fingers were covered in calluses by the work he did, but from time to time he would pay off old debts – and I know continued to do so until shortly before his death in the 1940s. It was a type of commercial principle which is often lacking today, but it impressed me greatly, as a boy, as the right thing to do – especially when my father explained that he didn't HAVE to do it.

With Miss Norbury we rode into the country, through Clibrands Nursery and along the lanes to what is today Manchester Airport. The North Cheshire Pony Club was a well-organised affair, particularly as it was backed by Lady Daresbury as its president – indeed as a treat on one or two occasions we were allowed to see her stables.

*   *   *

Moving to a new home in the country south of High Legh in Cheshire took much of the summer of 1937. Everything needed so much to do and my father, over the next few years, turned a field into a garden with a tennis court. Hazel was delighted, for there was a five acre field and we kept two horses, which gave us a lot of independence but also a lot of extra work going to Pony Club gymkhanas. The field was sown and eventually harvested by the local farmer, Mr Simpson, who sometimes let me help in his dairy. The edges of the field were hand-cut by scythe (I learned how it was done from one of Mr Simpson's men). The 'modern' harvesting machine was drawn by two magnificent horses and then the tied corn sheaves were 'stook'd' – stood in threes across the field until collected some weeks later, an exciting time when two men threw the stooks with their pitchforks on to a wagon drawn by the patient horses.

In fact I think my mother enjoyed being in charge of her smaller house. As a girl she had attended a ladies' finishing school in Gloucester for nearly a year in 1914, living with an elderly cousin in The Close. I still have her pre-First War cookery instructions – apple and blackberry tarts – and how to manage household chores, perhaps turning sheets 'sides to middle' when they became worn, or careful instructions for darning socks.

At home life had changed substantially, for there was now no room for the loyal Ella and Charles Northover (and their daughter Diana) who had moved from Dorset to be with my mother. In this smaller house we did much more ourselves. They left and lived in comfort – working for Mr Keeling, whose bulk milk distribution business in Manchester had made him a wealthy man. He was also a friend of my father's.

My father still left every morning early to catch the train to Manchester but as I left for my prep school in the summer of 1937 I entered a new world which was both exciting and would lead to unexpected new directions in my life.

*　　*　　*

Belmont School, Clayton Wickham, Hassocks, Sussex, was one of a considerable number of preparatory schools on the Sussex Downs. Term started by most boys meeting at Victoria Station and catching the train to Hassocks. Goodbyes were said at the station and when we reached Hassocks two small buses took us towards Hurstpierpoint and down the hill to Clayton Wickham and the large house which was the school. The school had been founded in 1904 in Brighton and one of the two headmasters when I joined was Mr Cuthbert Jeffries, who had been with the school since 1910. He was unmarried and had all the appearance of a gentle but firm sergeant-major, and was always known as Mr J.

His financial partner could not have been more different: Max de Wharton Burr (whose kinsman later became a well-known actor, Raymond Burr) had led an adventurous life, travelling much of the world, and had only recently married his wife, 'Nilla, whom I am sure had a calming influence on his mercurial spirit. Of the other masters whom I remember well was Mr Haughton who taught French, Mr Townshend who taught geography (and later lived in Cheshire near Knutsford). There was also Mr Buncher who taught Latin.

The school lay in a gentle valley and the fields round had been converted into cricket grounds, athletics tracks and football fields, and there was a recently-built swimming pool. Both Max Burr and his wife were at times members of the English archery team and increasingly boys learned archery. I was never in the school team but I remember there was one which competed with other schools in Sussex. Afternoon walks when there was no organised sport took us to the foot of Wolstonbury on the South Downs past Danny Park. A chapel had just been completed in the grounds where there were weekday as well as Sunday services, and a long row of buildings which were once kennels had been converted to workshops where lino cutting, glass work, metal work and printing were taught. Long hours setting lead type for printing on paper sheets certainly focused attention. The garden was well kept although certain lawns were reserved for senior boys only.

Looking back after so many years, I cannot remember any time that was wasted. A number of lessons, including poetry, included the need to remember and recite when that lesson was next taught. Max Burr himself taught mathematics and some simple science and woe betide anyone who was not paying attention, for he would at once direct an awkward question to anyone he caught gazing out of the window.

For new boys a system of 'fathers' was used for the first year so that any younger boy could seek support and advice on any subject. This system worked well and I was fortunate to have as my 'father' John Ommaney, who was head boy, and everything one expected of a good prep school. In later years I discovered that his great-grandfather had been an admiral and was related by marriage to my own family – but such thoughts never crossed my mind at this time. Other senior boys included Christopher Page (a powerful and forthright boy who was killed in action in the Coldstream Guards near the end of the war).

There were two Attlee brothers whose uncle was a politician (politics played no part in our curriculum and the fact that he was a socialist was hardly noticed). Their cousin Martin, Clement Attlee's son, was in my form and although quite a friend he was not noted for his scholarship and was usually in a form with boys younger than his age. My particular friends, as the terms wore on, were Colin Sundius-Smith – a notable school cricketer – and Roy Henderson, whose father was a well-known baritone (who sang at the school on a number of occasions, my particular favourite being 'Old Father Thames') and Michael Campling, with whom I kept up a correspondence for many years until we lost touch.

One way of getting to know boys of other ages was when there was an epidemic and one was, perhaps, 'cooped up' in the sanitorium for days with measles or mumps (I had both) and one such friend was Alan Caiger-Smith. Little did I guess that we should both be at the same public school and later both have books on porcelain published by Fabers.

A number of boys at Belmont had links with the East – their parents usually working in India or perhaps Singapore or Africa. Amongst these were John Horwood, Brian Walton, Christopher Willy and Tony Kendall. Most had grandparents or relatives who looked after them in the shorter holidays while they had the adventure of going to the East in the longer summer holidays. (It was later to be almost natural that they formed a sizeable part of the contingent who went to Belmont in the Bahamas during the war.)

There was a 'long weekend' in the summer term but at almost any other time boys were allowed to spend a Saturday night with relatives. On occasions I was able to go to London to stay with Aunt Ebie (it was more fun when she drove down to collect me); sometimes I stayed with my godfather who, I think, lived near Horsham – Arthur Garrard, an estate agent in London – and sometimes with friends like Colin Sundius-Smith or Peter Bibby (whose parents had shipping connections with East Africa).

Discipline was not a matter of much concern but was firmly enforced. In particular there was no talking in dormitories after 8.30 pm and anyone heard doing so usually suffered 'two of the best'. I remember on one occasion the door opening and a voice saying, 'Who is talking besides Howard?' To most of us this was just desserts for having broken a rule, but occasionally there was a complication. Typically of Max Burr, I remember in my last year at Belmont Hassocks the occasion when during a class the headmaster put his head round the door and said, 'Taylor – come to my study.' This was usually an ominous remark, but no-one was surprised for John Taylor, apart from being a delightful cricketer, was also prone to getting into numerous 'scrapes'. On this occasion he left the room and returned shortly after, smiling broadly. In the headmaster's study he had been told to bend over and given two whacks while a new boy stood in the corner crying. As John stood up, wondering which of a number of disciplinary crimes had been spotted, Max Burr said to the new boy, 'Now, he had done nothing wrong and you see how he behaved – that is how you should,' and in a passing remark as John prepared to leave the room, 'Taylor, here's a box of chocolates – well done.' John was well satisfied.

The clear individualism of reward and punishment was well-understood and never abused. We didn't waste time standing as dunces in the corner (as had happened at Miss Clegg's) or writing lines. (If that sort of punishment were needed, it would probably be that one had to learn two extra verses of Kipling for the next poetry lesson, or solve an extra maths problem or translate some extra French.)

Saturdays were usually exciting because there was a match of cricket or football against another school – particularly if it was an away match. We always travelled in two or three of the masters' cars and in the summer it would be twelve boys (the team plus the scorer) and in the winter twelve or sixteen (soccer or rugby and a linesman). The job of scorer or linesman was quite an honour – the linesman, of course, took the school flag in school colours. I still remember the day when I was the newly promoted linesman and arrived at St Peter's Seaford to find I had left my flag behind. I had to run the line with a St Peter's flag and the dishonour I felt at not having 'ours' lives with me still! A particularly interesting day in each annual calendar was 5th November, for a very large bonfire was piled high near the football field and lit by one of the parents – usually those of the head boy. I recall that in 1938 it was lit by Clement Attlee (then Leader of the Opposition in Parliament), but we could not have guessed that this was the last year that it was to happen.

The last week of term in every dormitory saw a ritual known as 'the feast'. Although well known to the staff, every boy had collected some special sweets or chocolate biscuits and hidden away a bottle of ginger beer in his locker. These were surreptitiously produced after lights out and exchanged and eaten with gusto. Of course Matron noticed in the morning but no one said anything – even when a tin of glaxo powdered sugar was accidentally spilled out of a window and, as it had been raining, at least two classroom windows were covered in white powder in the morning.

*   *   *

The later summer holidays of 1939 were interrupted by a new phenomenon. We had all been brought up listening to our parents talking about 'The Great War' – but that was history. Now it was to happen to us, and this time aeroplanes were expected to fly from Germany and drop bombs. I remember standing in the drawing room at home on Sunday 3rd September 1939 and listening to Neville Chamberlain say the fateful words – that as the Germans had not withdrawn their soldiers from Poland '…we are at war with Germany.'

Daily routine altered little at home, but there was a great deal of talk of gas masks and we all stood in queues and were fitted. They were carried at all times, everywhere. The other major effect was the order that all houses must be 'blacked out'. This wasn't just drawing curtains but special boards or black cloth had to be made to fit every window and it was not permitted to open the front door into the night without first turning out the lights. Car lights were reduced to a minimum and fitted with masks and there were no street lights.

At home this was soon routine, but going back to school in September 1939 saw a journey through London and unfamiliar uniforms at the stations and in the streets. For once my godmother decided not to drive up from Wimbledon ('to save petrol') and I had a comfortable lunch with my Aunt 'Bunny' and was put on the train at Victoria. There was more than the usual excitement as we set off to Hassocks and war-time school.

Max Burr was at once spurred into action and beside the school a large hole was dug which at first we thought was a new swimming pool but turned out to be a luxurious air-raid shelter –complete with classroom equipment so that it could double as a much needed classroom. It was approached by lengthy steps downwards from the lawn and exciting double doors 'in case of gas'.

Max Burr himself was soon travelling every day to London to work, we were told, at the Admiralty – quite what this involved we didn't know, but this, with the blackout and occasional air-raid drills, gave us a sense of involvement.

It was a particularly snowy early December and one Saturday the post didn't arrive. A party of sixth formers with a sledge was despatched to collect the mail, but were told to be careful and vigilant 'as it was wartime'. No sooner had they left on their two-hour round trip than Max Burr organised an 'ambush party' so that as the sixth formers returned across the snow-covered fields they were attacked by some twenty other boys who had spent the last hour making piles of snowballs and hiding themselves behind hedges. Such occasions played a considerable part in raising morale to a high level and making us understand the war.

A few days later I fell from a tree in the orchard during a private exercise 'in combat' and broke my arm. It was only a green-stick fracture I was told, but it made for problems getting suitcases home for Christmas. It was, however, a particularly exciting time because the German raider, *Graf Spee*, had just been cornered in Montevideo harbour after causing considerable havoc to Allied shipping in the Atlantic, and her scuttling after the engagement with HMS *Exeter*, *Ajax* and *Achilles* was the only topic of conversation amongst the boys, particularly as Max Burr always insisted on newspapers being available to us all. We felt the war was almost won.

I recall that in 1939 there was, as usual, a poetry competition, with the best poem published in the school magazine. This was won by my friend Morgan. I still recall some lines:

> Hitler said to America, 'I wish you'd be a pal,
> I want a thousand aeroplanes to guard the Kiel Canal'.
> America replied that, 'If you are willing to pay,

You can have a thousand aeroplanes this coming Saturday.'
'What PAY?!' said Adolf, 'some idea of me you sure have got.'
'Of cheek,' replied America, 'you've got a blooming lot.'
Meanwhile a bomb was ticking under Adolf's chair ...
... We're too polite to mention it but we know where Adolf is.

We had official geography lessons which made us well aware of 'The Maginot Line' – an impregnable fortress which was supposed to make it impossible for the Germans to win the war because they could never penetrate it. There was also, we were told, a much inferior line of fortifications on the German side called 'The Siegfried Line'. This was reinforced by the popular song of the day 'We're going to hang out the washing on the Siegfried Line – if the Siegfried Line's still there.' It became clear with hindsight that as the Maginot Line was of a much less powerful nature along the friendly Belgian border, it was tactically possible for the Germans to attack neutral Belgium and use this circuitous route to the coast.

The Easter term in 1940 was not unlike any other Easter term and the war appeared to have ground to a halt, although there was always speculation that Italy under Benito Mussolini might get too friendly with Hitler and join on his side.

My mother joined the Red Cross and for much of the war was an assistant commandant in North Cheshire, spending much time at the hospitals which were set up at Tabley Hall, near Knutsford, and Arley Hall and later Outringham Hall, near Lymm. Later in the war I remember frequent visits to Arley (still the home of the Viscounts Ashbrooke) and always enjoyed the old signpost near the Chester road which read:

This road forbidden is to all,
Unless they wend their way to call
At Church or Green or Arley Hall.

Who could resist such an invitation?

That Easter holiday was enlivened by the fact that my mother was putting into place all sorts of plans to improve our wartime diet. She kept hens who laid eggs which were put into large metal containers in the attic filled with 'water glass' (this allowed the eggs to be preserved for months so there was an ever-growing supply for cakes and other small dwindling delicacies). The kitchen garden, too, took on an added importance with the planting of every form of vegetable and fruit bush. At the end of this an area was cleared for beehives which, although sometimes needing supervision, provided welcome teatime treats when there was no sugar for jam.

My father's spare time became increasingly tied with the LDV (Local Defence Volunteers) shortly to be called the Home Guard. A mile down our road there was a delightful pub and landlord at Bucklow Hill – *The Swan* and Mr Tunstall – where my father's platoon flourished. These headquarters were to last throughout the war and be the centre of much training and local initiative, which by 1944 had expanded into co-operation with American battalions stationed nearby and the training of many of the early parachute regiments at Rostherne Mere.

The Home Guard undoubtedly provided an organisation which would have been able to harass any German troops in the event of an invasion and provided an additional back up where police services were stretched because so many men had joined the forces. At a time, too, when social contact was more difficult because of travel, it provided co-ordinated local contact over a wide area. The North Cheshire Home Guard was commanded by Colonel Edge, a former owner of some Welsh coal fields. By the end of the war he and his family were considerable friends, but I probably remember them best because he had two pretty daughters. (In the later 1940s they moved to Ireland and I remember a delightful party at Rathfarnham, their home near Dublin, at the time of the Dublin Horse Show in 1949.)

*   *   *

The German breakthrough in May 1940 – achieved to a large extent by ignoring Belgian neutrality and thus outflanking the main fortifications of the Maginot Line – was as lethal as it was unexpected. In the course of two weeks the name 'Dunkirk' was to enter the English language both as a noun and an adjective for all time.

The 'Dunkirk spirit' was epitomised by the vast fleet of tiny ships which left their harbours along the south coast of England and brought back an exhausted but still standing army from the French beaches. Although we were at school only eight miles from the Sussex coast at Brighton – with its busy railway line to London – we were hardly able to appreciate what was happening or see the ever-growing number of troops being landed haphazardly along the coast.

Max Burr was, however, quite aware of the potential risk, particularly if Dunkirk was quickly followed (as expected) by a German invasion, and he at once despatched Mr Buncher, who lived in the Midlands and was a keen cyclist, to find at all costs a large house to which the school could be moved. Meanwhile our half term break became the end of a short term and before the southern line to Brighton was taken over for military purposes, or the area was heavily bombed as the preliminary softening up for an expected invasion, we all packed up and set off for home. An exciting but rather pleasant holiday of, as yet, unknown duration.

Mr Buncher was no mean house hunter, despite having only a bicycle, and we had not been at home a week when my parents were told that Belmont was to reopen in the next few days at Stowe House near Lichfield in Staffordshire; a fine old pre-Georgian house within walking distance of the spires of Lichfield Cathedral.

Within two weeks Belmont had opened again and somehow all the staff was still there. The classrooms were different but taught the same lessons, dormitories were rearranged but the principal difference was that the windows opened on to the spires at Lichfield instead of Wolstonbury on the South Downs. I did not appreciate at the time how great an achievement this had been – but achievement it certainly was.

As there were almost no playing grounds for cricket, archery was pursued with new enthusiasm. Max Burr invented a new game which first consisted of creating a veritable metropolitan dockland in wood and plasticine, stretching over an area of perhaps ten feet square on boards, with realistic buildings and shipping of all sorts on the river. This was then placed at the well of a very substantial Georgian staircase and boys, in strict rotation, were allowed to drop darts from the second and third landings in simulation of air attacks, scoring points depending on what they hit. Any serious damage led to more craftwork. I'm glad to say it was the only close-to air attacks I witnessed in the war, but it made us very aware of the problem, although as a game rather than a murderous attack.

To the surprise of many of us, Max Burr continued to spend most days in London, but we were aware that he had various other matters to sort out. As the term wore on, Belmont began to enjoy its new situation – walking to the cathedral along the small lake, and the unaccustomed freedom for senior boys to walk into shops in Lichfield (at Hassocks, Brighton had been too far away). Anyway it would soon be the summer holidays and the Germans hadn't invaded yet.

In the closing weeks of term we learned that a plan was being considered to take the school abroad. Some parents seemed to welcome it while others did not (and clearly it was not appropriate for the most senior boys who were going to their public schools next term or within a year).

We broke up in July as usual, but many of us were not to see our friends again for much longer than the usual summer holidays – if ever.

CHAPTER 2

Nassau in the Bahamas

It was the vision of Max Burr, who had himself led an adventurous life as a younger man, that led to part of Belmont School being evacuated to the Bahamas at the time of the Battle of Britain.

Among the acquaintances he had made as a young man had been the American adventurer Harry Oakes who, having been thrown off a train when 'bumming it' across Canada, had stumbled on what was to prove a major gold field which transformed his life. Aged sixty-six in 1940, Harry Oakes had the previous year been created a baronet and had estates in the Bahamas. At the time of Dunkirk, Max Burr, who as well as being headmaster was still working part-time at the Admiralty in London on scientific matters, particularly magnetic mines, telephoned Sir Harry to ask if he had any spare houses which would be suitable for a preparatory school. Sir Harry replied at once with the offer of a large colonial building on the harbour waterfront in Nassau called Clerihew House, which he said the school could have free of charge as long as they liked if he could bring the school over.

Within days this generous offer had been transmitted to all the school parents, and a majority at first accepted the idea. However, shortly after the sinking in the Atlantic of a ship carrying evacuees with considerable loss of life – particularly among the school children being evacuated to Canada and America – most parents decided to keep their children in England now that the school had found its new home near Lichfield, which seemed to be a pleasantly safe place. In the event only thirteen, joined in four cases by their sisters, were to set out to Nassau on the morning of 11th August 1940 accompanied by Mr Jeffries as headmaster and his niece, Elizabeth. The eldest boy and head of the new 'Belmont Bahamas' School was John Horwood, and I was the 'second head boy' as the second eldest boy – just over twelve and a half years old, my sister Hazel being nearly eleven. The adventure was unfolding and the sadness at leaving our parents was masked by the feeling that the autumn term had just started early and was more fun than usual.

We travelled to Liverpool with a trunk and suitcase each, and boarded RMS *Orduna*, one of three leading cruise ships of the Pacific Steam Navigation Company which plied regularly to South America in peacetime. We were completely unmoved by any possible danger which might lay ahead and

15

At Belmont, Lichfield, 10th August 1940.
Author, no hat, on top step behind Hazel.

At Belmont, Bahamas, 3rd September 1940. The Governor and
Duchess of Windsor visit the school. Author's head by Mr J.'s shoulder.

probably never gave it a thought in the excitement. We sailed down the Mersey on 11th August and although we were two or three decks down, three to each small cabin, it was all excitement as we watched the English coast fade into the dark. We were not to see it again for three and a half years.

The ship had many evacuee children on board, some travelling with their parents, and the excitement of the comfortable dining rooms, the frequent boat drills when we all stood with our life jackets on and the 'holiday' atmosphere as we watched a convoy of some fifty ships assembling, accompanied by perhaps three or four destroyers and sailing north westwards towards Iceland, all kept us very interested.

It was on the fourth or fifth day out that the alarm bells rang with serious intent and we assembled late in the morning at our drill positions on deck, wearing our life jackets. Above us and on the stern, crews manned the light anti-aircraft guns and we waited in anticipation as the convoy moved steadily westwards. Suddenly one of the smaller ships ploughed ever more deeply into the moderate swell, its stern rose up to an angle of 45 degrees and within little more than two minutes it had disappeared beneath the waves. We thought we saw a lifeboat launched but we had not seen any explosion as the German torpedo struck and it was not long before any trace was a mile or two astern. Our interest, however, turned to a ship on the other side which was rapidly settling in the water and also dropping astern. The arrangement of other ships in the convoy had become a regular pattern, with the destroyers moving between us at greater speed and in no regular way. The attack did not alter that and as a third ship was hit, and we saw lifeboats being launched as it slipped out of line astern, we noticed that no vessel slowed or made any attempt to pick up survivors, for it was well known that in spite of this apparent disregard, such action would have led almost certainly to more ships being sunk as they slowed or stopped and thus became easy targets.

Although we were eventually allowed to have lunch, we kept our life jackets with us all day and had them beside us as evening fell – but we were aware that the ship's engines were pulsing much more furiously and we were travelling at much greater speed. When we came on deck at breakfast time we were still travelling at high speed and there was no sign of any other ship on the horizon. The convoy had scattered as a means of making it much more difficult for the U-boats to pick off their victims one by one. We were told that six ships had been lost but we never saw any other maritime traffic from that day onwards.

At no time do I remember any fear, only excitement. It is certain that these matters weighed much more heavily on our parents and exactly a month later, on 17th September, the *City of Benares* was sailing as the leading ship in a slow moving convoy with some four hundred passengers bound for America, including many children, when it was hit by a torpedo and sank in forty minutes with the loss of more than two hundred and fifty, including eighty-one children. We heard it on the daily news during our first few weeks in Nassau but hardly realised that it might as easily have been ourselves.

It was now clear that we were heading south-southwest, while the weather grew warmer and some four or five days later there was great excitement as we entered the harbour of Hamilton at Bermuda on 24th August. It was the first glimpse of the life we were to come to know in the Caribbean.

We anchored in Hamilton harbour and gazed at the white-roofed houses round the port. One bronzed Tarzan-like man who had been travelling first class (and whom we had not seen before) raised gasps of amazement as he dived from the deck into the harbour and swam in what we felt sure must be shark-infested waters. We were told he was Johnny Weissmuller, whom we all knew played Tarzan in the most popular schoolboy films of the late '30s. It was a first introduction to the gallery of interesting people we were to see or meet in the succeeding months in a new, unreal and exciting life.

We did not go ashore in Bermuda but were able to watch the busy roads and lanes round the harbour at Hamilton from the deck. At that time no cars plied the roads of Hamilton (although we were told at some stage that the Governor had a Rolls). We saw many horse-drawn buggies and were told that these had now been replaced by cars in Nassau (to our disappointment). After three days the *Orduna* gathered steam and I remember seeing from fairly close range the fortifications at the end of the harbour that looked very much the same when we visited them fifty years later.

On the morning of 30th August we were almost too excited to have breakfast as the *Orduna* slowed and anchored off the lighthouse and the mouth of Nassau harbour. In those days the larger cruise liners always anchored off the Bar because the channel to the main pier in the harbour was sometimes too shallow, in spite of the busy and almost continuous work of the harbour dredger – the *Lucaya* – which for the next three and a half years we saw almost daily as she ploughed up and down the harbour with piles of sand which I think we were told were offloaded at sea among the islands.

We boarded a tug with our luggage and together with some other children and their mothers, whom we had hardly met because they were travelling first class, we sailed into the harbour below the fort and were shortly at the jetty where on 17th August the new Governor, the Duke of Windsor, and his Duchess had landed in greater state.

Nassau was, it seemed to us, a land of kind-hearted ladies who met us at the gangway and overwhelmed us with talk of swimming from their beachside homes and coming to tea. I remember Mary Moseley (owner of the *Nassau Guardian*), Mrs Solomon, Mrs Burnside and Mrs Sands in particular, and we were later indeed treated to dream-like tea parties at their homes so that the autumnal world of England temporarily faded almost out of sight as the evacuees were spoiled and we adapted quickly to life in Nassau – in particular being made to wear large straw hats for fear of getting sunburn.

As a school under the complete control of a headmaster who himself had been brought up in Victorian times and had been a schoolmaster from 1910, we still abided by the rules so well drummed into us in Hassocks. Whenever we went out we never walked more than two abreast on the pavement and wore our straw hats so that as a school in Bay Street we looked rather like a scaly crocodile. Another rule which was strictly obeyed was that in spite of the temptation of an unheard-of range of ice creams – one should never eat one in the street. It is a rule that has stayed with me.

Clerihew House was a tall, four-storied, 18th Century house with broad verandahs, the front door on the first floor verandah and a wide lawn leading to the harbour wall which looked out on the pier where we had landed. The rooms were tall and a winding staircase led to bedrooms on the upper floors and a basement at garden level below. This was quickly converted into two top floors of dormitories, a first floor of dining room and kitchen and all the lower floors into classrooms.

Our first weekend in Nassau we were all invited to a party at Paradise Beach on Hog Island as the guests of Mr Maura who owned the principal travel agency in Nassau, while later in the week we had a party at Cable Beach as the guest of Arthur S. Vernay, noted traveller, explorer and golf partner of the Duke of Windsor. We reached Paradise Beach in an exciting glass-bottomed boat so that we could see the vegetation, fish and crustacea on the harbour floor as we approached the long, low island running parallel with New Providence – creating Nassau harbour.

Hog Island in 1940, unlike today, was virtually uninhabited apart from its well-known lighthouse, but had a wooden beach hut on a glorious stretch of sand called Paradise Beach which was privately owned. Today a bridge crosses the harbour and the whole island is called Paradise Island and is covered from end to end with hotels and luxury houses. Then there was only one large house, owned by Axel Wennergren, a Swedish millionaire with a large yacht called *Southern Cross*. He was best known, however, as the supplier of strategic material to Hitler and as Goering's brother-in-law, and for this reason did not mix with much of Nassau's anglophile community. I am happy to remember Paradise Beach as I first saw it.

Indeed, the harbour became a daily source of information and interest, and we were seeing it much as Winslow Homer had seen it when he painted the local fishing boats and the visiting sailing craft from America, only two hundred miles away, the largest of which were called 'Chesapeake Bugeyes'. Many of the smaller craft were called 'conchers' and 'spongers' and had for generations provided a living for large numbers of divers – men who dived into the sea, cutting off natural sponges which had abounded in these waters and bringing up a rich catch of conch shells (by the 1930s a blight had affected most sponges, leading the divers to concenrate on conch). The contents of these shells provided both tasty meat and rich soups, while the shells themselves were cleaned and polished and provided a tourist attraction on many stalls in the local market which were swamped by tourists from cruise ships, many of which tied up at the dock in the harbour while their passengers enjoyed a day in busy Bay Street.

All this quickly became part of our life and we watched as the legendary Marion Carstairs' great yacht, *Estelle*, entered the harbour, while J. E. Williamson's Undersea Post Office always excited interest and the *Lucaya* ploughed back and forth with tireless energy and piles of dredged sand. John Williamson, whose daughters joined Belmont for a short spell, had made his name by being in charge of the photography for the first film of Jules Verne's epic story *Twenty Thousand Leagues under the Sea* – inventing a diving bell fixed below a stable boat and attached by a long flexible tube so that photographers could light and photograph underwater scenes. In particular he had fought and knifed a shark in sight of the cameras. I have a signed copy of his own book *20 years under the Sea*.

*   *   *

We started school in early September after a visit from the new Governor, the Duke of Windsor, who toured the house and spoke to us all as English evacuees. Indeed he was to visit us more than once and gave a party each Christmas at Government House for all the children who were not at home.

Lessons themselves were remarkably similar to those in England. Naturally Mr J. taught Latin and history (as he had in Sussex) but he also drew in outsiders who, after a term or two, included Kenneth Brown, the announcer on the local Nassau radio station; Father Holmes, later a Bishop; Baroness Trolle of Sweden, who taught art; and an interesting American, Mr Mitchell, who returned to America after Pearl Harbour. Our French teacher was Mrs Marcelle Goldsmith, whose husband, a director of Claridges, the Savoy, the Scribe in Paris, the King David in Jerusalem and numerous other hotels, had bought a home east of Nassau for the duration, and whose two sons Teddy and

Jimmy joined the school, as did Tommy Sopwith, son of the aircraft designer, and some Americans who lived in Nassau for much of the year.

In fact the Easter term of 1941 was to start with 36 boys and 16 girls (whereas the school in Lichfield had 38 boys at that time). By the end of the year the numbers at Belmont Bahamas had risen dramatically to approaching a hundred, for we had been joined by the children of numerous British families then living in Nassau, including those of an ADC to the Duke of Windsor, two sons and a daughter of Sir Harry Oakes and some Bahamian girls and boys – including Norman Solomon, whose uncle Sir Kenneth Solomon was Speaker of the Bahamian House of Assembly, and who himself became Leader of the Opposition in the Bahamian Parliament for many years and has remained one of my greatest friends.

Shortly after our arrival, the Dean of Nassau discovered that a number of us had sung in the school choir and we were soon co-opted into the Cathedral choir – indeed at one time we formed a major part of the choristers and continued to sing until we left in 1944, although by then there were a number of tenors among the trebles. There was a weekly choir practice and a small crocodile of Belmont boys in their straw hats became a familiar sight. Sunday service was frequently attended by the Governor, who sometimes read the lesson. Government House was just at the top of a steep hill above the cathedral (although he always arrived at a service by car with his ADC) and Sunday afternoon usually saw him playing golf on the course three miles west of Nassau.

Our first Christmas was enlivened not only by a party at Government House but by the taking of a carefully scripted film of life at Belmont Bahamas and a short interview with each English child so that it could be sent home to our parents.

The 'holidays' came as a relief from school work after our normal exams at the end of term, but we continued to live at Clerihew House and were encouraged to follow our own hobbies in the holidays and had longer and more frequent visits to the beach. In particular we used to swim at two beaches towards the west of the island which we reached by cramming up to sixteen children into our veteran Oldsmobile driven by Mr J. At Old Fort (where the ruins of an 18th Century fort had been turned into a beautiful house) a long white beach stretched away to the west, while a secluded natural beach behind the sand dunes known as 'Danger go slow' because this was written on a sign on the road before a sharp corner and three humble cottages as one drove westwards. In spite of its name the beach was safe, and the sand dunes provided perfect 'changing rooms' for boys and girls; there was an area of shallow sea and neither sharks nor barracudas frequented that stretch of coast. Few, if any others, seemed to swim there because it was fairly 'far out' and most of those who had beautiful and expensive homes at Cable Beach used their own private beaches.

Other interests included training for the Red Cross and archery, and most of the boys were able to acquire bows and arrows and used the parade ground before the Fort opposite the mouth of the harbour. The Nassau Red Cross was very strongly supported during the war by Nassau society and the Duchess of Windsor was its active President. We took comprehensive tests and attended occasional parades and a number of us reached a respectable sub-professional level after examinations and duly 'passed out' at a ceremony at which the Duchess gave us our certificates. Some boys were also fortunate enough to be befriended by families who had yachts and at weekends and in the holidays we learned to sail. In spite of the carefree but regular regime which still applied in both term time and holidays, a number of boys spent weekends with local families, particularly where they too had children at Belmont.

We did not understand the social life of Mr J. – he seemed always to be there. He was known by the senior boys to have had an unhappy love affair after the First War and had never married (a photograph of 'Mary' was always beside his desk and went everywhere with him). It was much easier to understand that of Miss J., his niece, who was only three years older than the oldest boy, and who eventually had a local boy friend and still lives in Nassau as Mrs Inglis Sawyer.

Strict rules applied to bed time and all but the senior dormitory (the four oldest boys) had to be in bed with lights out at 8.30 while we were allowed the privilege of 9.15. Mr J. himself would walk round each evening to see that everything was in order and this routine frequently ended with him sitting in a chair with the four eldest boys at about 9.15 when the conversation eventually turned to his experiences in the First War. Had any of us had a mind to do it, I think we could have written a book of his experiences and this included the most gruelling accounts of his life in the Artists' Rifles.

He had refused a commission on egalitarian grounds that I never quite understood, but was soon a Sergeant Major on the Western Front and remained there until 1918. The Artists reached the front in late 1914 and he served on the Somme and at Passchendaele. To this day nothing can erase the knowledge of the appalling sacrifice of the first day of the Somme (on which there were 60,000 casualties) and the detailed descriptions of the duck boards across the water-logged fields of Passchendaele where almost as many drowned as were cut down by enemy fire. Sometimes Mr J. would talk for up to three-quarters of an hour in graphic and minute detail and I know that the stories not only affected him still, but with hindsight they affected my life

The Duke of Windsor gives Brian Archer a Christmas present
at Government House, 1940.

Red Cross certificate passing-out parade. The Duchess of Windsor, President,
faces the author – one of a number of Belmont boys.

afterwards, and the sense of sacrifice and gallantry at that time makes it even more difficult to understand the greed and selfishness so often displayed today.

My father and mother wrote weekly as did we, although occasionally letters went astray (as one which arrived nearly a year late having come by sea by way of Bahrain). My father, too, thought it would be both fun and educational to collect stamps and most weeks sent a different set of 1935 George V Silver Jubilee colonial stamps. One soon learned the name and often the principal industry of every British Colony stretching across the world, including such far-flung outposts as Pitcairn Island. It provided many hours of pleasure arranging and cataloguing, and with a pre-war Stanley Gibbons catalogue one built up a picture of the geography and history of much of the world which was to come in useful later as one studied these subjects at school. Stanley Gibbons painstakingly put a value against each stamp – but this I found of less interest. It was, however, my first collection.

A high spot of our years in Nassau was the annual Belmont play, written by Max Burr for Lichfield while we were his 'overseas touring company'. The first one was played in January 1941, on a stage built before the house in the garden while the audience filled the lawn; the title was *The Scorpion's Gizzard* in which I played the wizard in a tall hat – I remember the first lines as I burst on to the stage to find 'my wife' looking very fed up because supper had been waiting for half an hour. When she asked where I had been I replied in the rhyme I used throughout the play:

> To see a man about a dog
> But can't you see I'm all agog ...

The following January we played a more pantomime-like production called *Grimm but Gay* (when that word only had happiness in mind) and the plot centred round a billeting officer who brought some difficult children to be billeted on a King and Queen. In 1943 the play was very adult and called *The Sagging Hammock* and centred round thriller action in a Devon country pub into which a German spy had somehow found his way in order to aid a seaborne landing and blow up the local harbour defences. He was, of course, foiled by a combination of two or three locals in the pub and a smart detective from London (played by me – complete with rain coat, gas mask and moustache!).

*   *   *

The excitements of the first year in Nassau had given way to the business of daily life. Term time occupied about three-quarters of each year and we followed a routine which we knew would inevitably lead to Common Entrance examinations and a public school in England. One unexpected bonus came in December 1941 when a disastrous fire burned much of the street leading up to the Cathedral and with it the Island Bookshop which was severely damaged. Instead of gazing in awe at the shelves of fine editions, I was able to gather all my resources together and buy over forty volumes: Gibbons' *Decline and Fall ...*, the complete works or plays of many authors, Bullfinch's *Mythology*, *The History of Greece*, and Prescott's *Mexico* and *Peru*, for the enormous sum of £8 – a large amount in those days, but they are all still on my shelves today.

But increasingly as we grew into 'teenagers' (a term not then invented) we developed friendships and interests outside the school – particularly with those who came to Belmont each day, no doubt to give them an English experience. It was natural that we developed a keen interest in swimming from our almost daily trips to a beach only ten minutes' walk from the school (in a quiet corner of the harbour not far from the Nassau boat yard, where later in the war a number of wooden mine-sweeping vessels were built for special service to combat the growing threat of magnetic mines). We were encouraged to join the Nassau Swimming Club and received expert training in all the techniques of competitive racing. Indeed, by 1942 three of us were included in the shortlist for a tour of Florida and other competition venues – but this, alas, never materialised because of Pearl Harbour. (This and our early introduction to water polo were to stand me in good stead in later years.)

Some of us kept large wall maps of the battlefields in the Middle East and later in Russia where we became familiar with the names of Tobruk, El Alamein and Smolensk. It was also of enormous importance to the Bahamas that the 450th anniversary of the landing of Columbus in the New World on 30th October 1942 was remembered and there were celebrations (and a special set of stamps – I still have all mine) to commemorate the landing on San Salvador.

Within the confines of New Providence, an island only twenty miles long, it was easy to forget that it was only one of some two thousand islands and outcrops which were the Bahamas and of which perhaps barely a tenth were populated. The majority of the islanders were of African origin descended from the slaves who had reached the Caribbean in the 17th and 18th centuries. There was no known remnant of the Lucayans who had inhabited the islands when Columbus had landed. They had been needlessly abducted and many perished in the mines which were to produce the wealth of New Spain.

Clerihew House, Bay Street, Nassau, 1941.

Off to the beach in Mr J.'s car
with sixteen on board.

Archery on the beach.

On Mr Maura's boat at the bottom of Clerihew House garden (with Nassau's main pier behind) before setting off on an out-island trip.

As the elder boys reached the age of fourteen and became more aware of the friendship of the sisters and other girls at the school, it was decided that a long shed near the harbour at the end of the garden should be demolished and rebuilt to become a new 'girls wing'. To us this just seemed practical and I doubt that we realised that there could be problems if we all remained in adjacent dormitories in Clerihew House, although Hazel later explained in greater detail some matters of which I was not aware! I believe Sir Harry Oakes financed this and he occasionally visited the school.

The biggest adventure of our Bahamian life so far took place in the summer of 1942 when at the invitation of Father Tanter, the Anglican priest on idyllic Harbour Island, we were invited to stay at his house above Dunmore Town and we all set off in one of Mr Maura's inter-island boats to spend two weeks at the Rectory. Our suitcases were collected at the pier and taken up to the Rectory itself in batches by a very authoritative porter called Napoleon. As we looked from the Rectory windows we could see the long beach on the Atlantic shore – with nothing between us and the Scilly Isles – providing the perfect place to swim and lie in the sun. We slept in Father Tanter's spare bedroom and along the balcony of the Rectory while the girls stayed in two or three houses which kindly provided rooms for them.

The white beach, tinged with pink from the ground coral reef which lay off the island, provided long days of swimming and playing in the sand. Lady (Blanche) Boles was one of the English parents who had come to Nassau, whose son Jeremy grew up at Belmont and who frequently had Jeremy's friends to stay the weekend. She, too, enjoyed the sun on the long beach as did many local children. One little black girl had kicked a ball which landed on Lady Boles' towel and as she went to collect it Jeremy's mother said to her, 'And what is your name?' 'Blanche Boles' came the surprising reply as she darted back into the sea with her ball.

The Solomons, too, had a house on the island where we all had tea one day – Norman was still then at Belmont. In later years he was, for much of his life, the MP for Harbour Island and the neighbouring town of Spanish Wells which had been settled in the late 17th Century, in part by those fleeing after the Monmouth Rebellion of 1685. The settlement had followed strict rules concerning both religion and racial segregation, for from the outset all black people had to leave Spanish Wells by sundown and could only return to work after sunrise next day. So ingrained had this close society become that there were probably no more than twenty surnames at Spanish Wells and almost everyone was closely related. It did not seem strange to us when we visited for a cream tea in 1942, but appeared more so when we stayed in a still white town in 1995 with friends of Norman Solomon.

Pearl Harbour had been greeted in Nassau by the same reaction as it was throughout America. It was barely two days before most cars in Nassau had flags or window stickers reading 'Remember Pearl Harbour'. There was a noticeable feeling that somehow the war had grown much closer. That week the brilliant solo artist Ruth Draper was playing at the local theatre in Nassau and we all went to see her. (She had changed little when I saw her again almost six years later when she played in London on the night of Princess Elizabeth's wedding.)

Closer to home the following summer an event shattered the normal calm of Nassau life. Sir Harry Oakes had purchased large stretches of the barren land in the centre of New Providence and built an airport which was soon to be used increasingly by the military and which encouraged the RAF to have a major staging post in the Northern Caribbean. We had seen him there one day in the summer of 1942 with the Duke of Windsor. Lady Oakes frequently gave parties at their beautiful home at Cable Beach and was always kind to Belmont. Their son, Harry Philip, was still at Belmont although his elder brother Pitt and his sisters had gone to a senior school. The air was full of gossip because his eldest daughter Nancy had married a Mauritian Count called Alfred de Marigny and lived up a palm-fringed avenue not far from Clerihew House.

But nothing was to prepare us for the Nassau news on the local radio which said that Sir Harry Oakes had been involved in a bizarre fight in his bedroom on Cable Beach and was dead. The news was read, as usual, by our maths master, Kenneth Brown, but it was all far more realistic to us than the war, for we knew all the players – both Sir Harry, who owned the house we lived in, and soon the prime suspect, Count de Marigny, who was the brother-in-law of a boy at our school.

Stories abounded of late night drives both by Harold Christie, Sir Harry's financial partner in many respects, and the local police lieutenant, whose record of late night sightings seemed at odds with some other accounts. Most Nassau citizens were surprised (as I believe was Colonel Wanklyn, the head of police at whose home we had been entertained) when the Duke of Windsor, as Governor, brought in two private detectives from America. Vital fingerprints were lost, even forged, and tales of disagreements over collecting evidence were common gossip, as was revealed by his lawyer at the trial.

The following summer Alfred de Marigny, whose blood-stained spanner was supposed to have been discovered in the boot of his car, was arrested and tried for his father-in-law's murder. We knew nothing of the facts, only the local gossip, but it was not too great a surprise when he was acquitted by a jury and we stood in Rawson Square and watched him walk down the steps of

Mr Williamson's 'Undersea Post Office' in Nassau Harbour, with Ann Walton about
to descend. Mr J. stands by Mary Moseley, with author in background.
Mr Williamson kneels, with Mr Maura right.

Sir Harry Oakes and the Governor at Oakes Airfield, Nassau
(an informal Belmont boy photograph).

the Court House, a free man. Contradictorily, he was expelled from the Bahamas by an order announced by the Chief Justice, Sir Oscar Daly, acting for the Governor.

It is unlikely that all the facts of this strange case will ever be known, but I have no doubt that the jury was correct: that the introduction of the private American detectives hindered the case; that the death, some years later, of a woman journalist who announced that she had new evidence but was found dead in a well on the east of the island before it could be published; and conversations I have had with a number of knowledgeable people over the years in Nassau, all point away from Alfred de Marigny. His own book on the subject, and a more recent play and television documentary, suggest financial rather than family links, and it can probably be in no-one's interest to investigate the truth of what happened that night sixty-three years ago in a luxurious bedroom on Cable Beach – a house we had visited for tea on a number of occasions.

*   *   *

As we approached our third year in Nassau, the concept of spending our weekends and holidays in the school relaxed and a number of us were 'adopted'. This was, perhaps, spurred on by the fact that John Horwood, the senior boy, left Nassau to go to school in Canada where his parents felt he would receive a broader and more conventional education with proper holidays. I was, by late summer 1942, the senior boy in Belmont.

Christopher Willy went to live with the Boles' (tragically Jeremy's father was killed in North Africa in 1945). Lady Boles had a delightful house with a garden running down to the harbour to the east of Nassau which she shared with her mother, Mrs Hall Parlby, and an elderly retired Colonial Governor called Sir Hesketh Bell, who was becoming increasingly blind. My sister spent the holidays with the Dean of Nassau, Dean Streatfeild, and his very kind wife, and I found myself staying with Major Frank Goldsmith and his wife Marcelle, who had taught French at Belmont for two years, and their sons Teddy and Jimmy.

It was a very happy time. Teddy was a little younger than I was but I think we found it easy to live under the same roof. Jimmy was rather younger, with a mind very much of his own and I can hear his mother, even today, shouting often in exasperation '*Tais toi*, Jimmie.' There was little to indicate what Sir James would one day become. Marcelle was beautiful and kind, but it was Major Frank Goldsmith who inspired and interested me as a fifteen-year-old boy.

Not only was he a senior director of the Savoy, Claridges and other well-known hotels on both sides of the Atlantic, but he seemed to have assumed control of the Royal Victoria Hotel in Nassau and I sometimes spent an hour or two in his office. More fascinating was his own career, for he had been an MP and political ally of Winston Churchill when they both crossed the floor of the House of Commons in 1904. He would sit back and talk to a wide-eyed fifteen-year-old of moments in Victorian days, of his cousins, the Rothschilds, and allow me to sit quietly behind him as he played bridge in the evenings with other retired colonels, colonial officials or friends, so that, listening to their conversation, one felt that one understood what they, too, had experienced.

By this time my principal hobby was painting in watercolours and in particular scenes of the sea which came easily to me and were endlessly inspired by the colours of the sea in Nassau and the sailing ships which continued to frequent the harbour, for during the war there were no cruise liners after Pearl Harbour although the occasional warship crossed the bar. There were occasions when I glimpsed the adult world as when I gave my best ever painting to Marcelle, but it was 'coolly' received because it depicted the elegant German battle cruiser *Bismarck* – and one didn't want German ships on one's walls at that time! At another time, I walked into her office at the Royal Victoria Hotel and found her in some distress because of the behaviour of a military officer. To my surprise I shouted at him and he hurried away, and she gave me a delightful hug and told her husband that she'd been 'rescued' when she got home.

In a dawning adult world I was lucky to find two jobs in my last year in Nassau. One was a most interesting occupation spending two evenings a week as a volunteer at the desk of the servicemen's club just outside the centre of Nassau. The development of Oakes Field had brought a great many British and American aircrews to Nassau, particularly from Transport Command, and also a large permanent staff to man the growing airfield; with almost no amenities to cater for them the club provided a relaxing evening, good inexpensive meals and a bar.

The other job was much more exciting – at least to me. Sir Hesketh Bell was by now anxious to complete his last book *Glimpses of a Governor's Life* but he could no longer read the diaries he had written since his colonial days which started in the 1880s and ended when his second term as Governor of Mauritius expired in 1928. He had a secretary who could type the manuscript but he wanted to read the diaries carefully and include as many quotations and stories as he could. My task was to read his diaries to him and mark them carefully, often providing linking paragraphs, so that these could be given to

Evening hobbies.
A drawing of the 'Undersea Post Office' by the author.

his secretary. It was a fascinating task and I still have his book with a letter written from the Hotel Windsor in Monte Carlo in February 1947, reading:

> To my friend David Howard, in memory of the happy hours we spent together in Nassau when he helped me so much with this book – affectionately yours, Hesketh Bell.

The book itself started with a quotation:

> Lives of 'small' men all remind us
> We should write our 'Lives' ourselves,
> And, departing, leave behind us
> Two octavos on the shelves.

Sir Hesketh had joined the Colonial Service in the later 19th Century and among his earlier jobs had been Colonial Secretary of the Bahamas in 1902 under the acting Governor, John Spencer-Churchill, and his first Governorship of Dominica in 1898. I remember particularly reading the diaries in which he accompanied others in a small boat as one of the first to land after the catastrophic volcanic eruption which destroyed St Pierre, when the only man found alive in part of the deserted town was a condemned murderer who had had to dance up and down on a red hot floor for two days before being rescued.

In 1906 Sir Hesketh became Governor of Uganda where he was largely responsible for reforms which made it possible to combat sleeping sickness. He wrote of atrocities in the Congo and traces of ancient Egyptian civilisation, and of entertaining the new Parliamentary Secretary for the Colonies, Winston Churchill. He later became Governor of Northern Nigeria where he pioneered the cleansing of water supplies, and was in 1912 Governor of the Leeward Islands and in 1915 Governor of Mauritius before retiring in 1925 to a hilltop home in Cannes, from which he had been driven by the war.

I read his diaries written at the time, and the breadth of information concerning colonial administration over more than forty years was enlightening and warming, for it showed a largely selfless aspect of colonial rule which benefited vast numbers of uneducated people in a way that has conspicuously not been their lot since independence in the 1960s – I witnessed some of the changes myself at that time. Modern political thought has treated with great injustice generations of dedicated work by these colonial administrators. Of course it is easy now to laugh at and caricature a

Belmont boarders and staff in the Spring of 1943.
Staff seated (*left to right*): Baroness Trolle, Dean Streatfeild,
Mrs Marcelle Goldsmith, Mr. J., Miss J., Father Holmes, Nurse Cary.

system whose officers wore solar topees, but it was honest and frequently selfless work which benefited millions in a way that modern political regimes have significantly failed to achieve.

*   *   *

During the latter part of 1943 we became increasingly aware of our own educational problems which lay ahead. A number of us had had arrangements made for us to go to public school by the age of 13 or 14 – and I would be 16 in January 1944. The increasingly fierce Battle of the Atlantic presented its own problems and it became clear that we should have to follow a tortuous route home, including the issue of new passports with Portuguese visas in the United States, for there was no direct route from the Bahamas and a journey via Lisbon seemed most practical.

Not every Belmont pupil took this route home and Miss J. remained in Nassau with those who stayed behind, but on 20th January most of those who had sailed to Nassau in 1940 flew to Miami with our suitcases and took a train to New York where we arrived the following day and, filled with wonder, stayed at the Roosevelt Hotel. Two days in New York, including an exciting day at the Rockefeller Center on my 16th birthday and a necessary visit to the British Consul, ended in us boarding a night train with sleepers for New Orleans.

I suppose this would now be called the 'Chattanooga Choo Choo' but our two journeys by train, up the East coast from Miami and down again to the deep South, provided an opportunity to see America in a way which is much less used today. On the early morning of the second day we gazed from our compartments at English Lookout, the last station before New Orleans, and as we arrived we were met by a bus which took us to the quay and our home for nearly three weeks, the Portuguese liner *Magallanes*.

At that time the only safe way to travel across the Atlantic was on a neutral ship – which sailed with all its lights blazing and special lights illuminating its name on either side. Such vessels reported their routes and largely sailed to and from neutral ports. Two days later we slipped our moorings in the Mississippi and slowly passed down the final miles into the estuary and the Caribbean, bound first for Trinidad and finally to Lisbon.

Life on board the *Magallanes* was pleasant and exciting, and we all tucked into 'huevos fritos' at every opportunity. It was a disappointment, however, that although we anchored close to Port of Spain and remained there for three days we did not have a chance to go ashore. (I was later to enjoy that pleasure on more than one occasion.)

It was by now early February. We left Port of Spain at night and headed out from the warm Caribbean towards the colder winter shores of Europe. The journey was uneventful and nearly two weeks later we entered the Tagus and disembarked in Lisbon. We were only able to get a glimpse of the city for we were taken by coach to Estoril where we spent the night in the most comfortable hotel. We were able to spend the next day wandering round the streets – our first day in Europe for three and a half years.

It was not easy to enter Britain in 1944 from Continental Europe, in fact one of the only routes was via Portugal and Ireland. On the evening of 26th February we were taken down to the Tagus again and boarded a British Short Sunderland flying boat which plied on occasions from Lisbon to Foynes in the Irish Republic. It was on one of these flights the previous year that the actor Leslie Howard (who had recently starred in *Gone with the Wind*) had been lost, but such thoughts didn't enter our minds.

The luxury of huge bed-like seats and dinner were a reassuring experience and after taking off we slept until dawn broke over Galway Bay and our flying boat landed on the Shannon. A bus took us into Galway where we spent a day anticipating the last leg of our journey, most details of which had been unknown to us when we started.

I am not sure how we secured our final flight on 28th February, although I understand it had, in part, been negotiated by my cousin, Michael Brander, who was throughout the war the Aga Khan's personal pilot (although he would have preferred to have stayed with his Squadron). But that afternoon we went to the local airfield and boarded an RAF freighter. We sat in the hold on jump seats with our suitcases and as the doors closed our only view of the outside world was through unfilled rivet holes in the fuselage which gradually darkened as we left Ireland behind. We landed at Northolt at about 9pm in wartime darkness and were driven to a blacked-out warehouse office where beyond a bar stood the parents we hadn't seen since August 1940.

That night, after a blacked-out drive into London, we heard the droning sounds of our first doodlebug raid.

CHAPTER 3

Stowe

My mother always said that her son who came back from Nassau was far more mature and worldly-wise when he and his sister returned, than two years later when he left Stowe to go into the Army. This was not apparent to me and may have been as much the result of becoming part of a family again as any effect of my public school. We all accepted the experience (although one boy's mother – he was later a Colonel in the Army – was so upset at the length of separation that she could hardly bear to speak of Nassau).

In the weeks after our return we spent a short spell at Belmont Lichfield which was enjoying a 'normal' prep school Easter term. This seemed to align our studies with English tuition and assess our learning during our long absence. It speaks wonders, I think, for Mr J. and his team that all the Belmont boys were able to be assimilated at their higher age levels in schools who normally accepted newcomers at the age of thirteen to fourteen. Undoubtedly Max Burr must have worked hard behind the scenes to see that his Nassau boys could start the summer term of 1944, often without common entrance exams.

In my case I travelled to Stowe in late March and met the ever-understanding headmaster – surely one of the greatest headmasters of the 20th Century – J. F. Roxburgh, and my house master, known as 'Fritz' Clifford (who was regarded as a somewhat eccentric and tough martinet by those who crossed his path, but as a kindly disciplinarian by those who wished to conform).

Surprisingly, although long absence of parental control may have given us an adult gloss in everyday life, the fact that we had had to conform to prep school 'norms' and had lived in a school much of the time for three and a half years under the steady and predictable hand of a pre-First War master, made us easily attuned to the rules of our public schools – indeed I found the regime at Stowe very democratic and understandable from the outset. But it was like settling into a luxurious historical mansion, sitting in dining rooms looking down the mile-long view of the South Front beneath portraits of the Dukes of Buckingham and the Prince Regent, while the Library felt that it was still used by the family who had left Stowe earlier in the century. It was exhilarating to walk across the North Front beneath the equestrian statue of George II beside what was now the First Team cricket field and feel the full impact of the magnificent architecture. One could wander at will round the grounds and discover the many monuments and temples with which the Dukes of Buckingham had embellished their estates while walking the long straight drives which the dukes had fondly imagined they might turn one day into private roads to London and Oxford. As JF is recorded as saying, 'Every boy who goes out from Stowe will know beauty when he sees it for the rest of his life.'

JF had always instilled a mistrust of excessive school 'traditions' – partly because it was only twenty-one years since the school had been founded and partly because he believed, I think rightly, that they could lead to a pupil hierarchy of repression and bullying. It was therefore easy for a new boy of sixteen years and three months to fit in without undue initiations.

Fritz, however, did not wish to allow any newcomer to avoid the experience of 'growing up' at Stowe. Each of the eight houses had boys who occupied the position of Head of House (a prefect), three or four monitors and about four 'settlers' (assistant monitors with less authority), while every new boy had to be an 'officer' (or 'fag') for up to two years. I found myself, very fortunately, Desmond Low's 'officer'. He was Head of House and little more than a year my senior – and his principal hobby was heraldry. He had a small display of books on heraldry which it was my duty to dust, but which I read and eventually borrowed when he discovered my own fledgling interest in the subject.

Life in Grafton House was very straightforward and I enjoyed my two years there. It was, for me, easy to conform, and on occasions experiences in Nassau provided one with backup. On the day I first entered Grafton I stopped to gaze at the house photographs in the lobby and saw in the first one 'B. Gadney' and 'D. G. Niven'. I think I was more excited about Bernard Gadney, for he had captained a successful England XV before the war, while David Niven was 'just a film star'. (I was fortunate in being able to play rugby with a contemporary, 'Ricky' Bartlett, who was then only just showing signs that he, too, would captain the England XV in years to come.)

Gradually one was able to commit to memory the names of previous Grafton House prefects and monitors on the houseroom boards. Some would appear at Stowe occasionally on leave from the services while others remained names with reputations only. Had I started when originally planned in 1941, I might just have met Jack Hayward who later developed Freeport in the Bahamas, or Peregrine Worsthorne, the formidable right-wing commentator; but would certainly have known I.G. Butler, chairman of many companies, and John Hillier and Colin Wallis-King as heads of Grafton (the latter of the school as well) although I met the last three later in the

Coldstream. Colin and I saw a lot of each other in Palestine and he was later to become a General.

It would have been difficult to guess from among one's contemporaries throughout the school what they might become – although George Melly in the art school painted pictures which foretold his later career, while stocky Frank Kitson on the rugby field did not yet reveal his distinguished future as Chief of the UK Land Forces, nor did one guess that Roger Chorley, who joined Grafton at the same time as I did, would become Chairman of the National Trust. For a while I so enjoyed working in the art school that I had visions of following my great-aunt Joh as an artist.

But it was the summer term, and I settled into a routine of lessons and games every afternoon and a chance to run in the school sports. There was great excitement as we all heard an exceptional roar of aircraft early on the morning of 6th June and learned by lunchtime that a Second Front had opened on the Normandy beaches.

The war was never too far away, for we read the papers daily and kept our wall maps up to date as the Russians swung back from Stalingrad and the Western Allies rolled across Europe. I was to learn in dramatic fashion just how closely the war affected Stowe at the School Chapel services on each 11th November when, after a traditional service, JF read from the pulpit in a measured tone the names of Stoics who had been killed in the last twelve months. It was a sobering but inspiring experience for us, particularly when the name of someone you had known as a senior boy, perhaps eighteen months earlier, was intoned. One can only imagine what it was like for JF who had been headmaster since the school's foundation and knew them all in person. By the end of 1945 almost one in six Old Stoics who had been at the school since 1923 was on the Roll of Honour. (It was, of course, a matter of intense pride when Leonard Cheshire won his Victoria Cross, but this could hardly compensate for those who didn't come back. He was only one of two Stoics who joined the same house in the same term in 1931 who were awarded a VC – the other being Major John Anderson.)

The summer term had an unexpected bonus for me and that was swimming. Stowe then had no indoor swimming pool and throughout the term we swam in one of the great lakes before the house in an area marked off by floating planks. Nobody drowned (although the weeds were fairly long) and swimming only came fourth in prestige after cricket, tennis and athletics. Nevertheless, I suddenly found that my Nassau experience put me in the swimming team almost at once, and during my two years there I swam against Harrow, St Edward's Oxford, Bedford Modern (where my father had been at school), Rugby and other schools, and played water polo against local RAF teams.

Mr Davis and the Stowe swimming team, 1945 (author seated second right).

A Stowe rugby team, 1945 (author seated third right).

It was a happy summer holidays with my parents in 1944, part of it spent in Cornwall where my mother had just purchased a house on the cliffs at The Lizard called *Tresawle*. Looking across Housel Bay to the lighthouse to the southwest, it had recently been de-requisitioned by the Army and was just a field away from the wooden shed from which Marconi sent his first message across the Atlantic forty years earlier. (I was later to enter the shed in Newfoundland where it had been received.) Hazel, too, had settled at a new school and had new friends in south Staffordshire; already Nassau seemed a world away.

Winter term at Stowe in wartime was a rather sterner affair. Every curtain had to be tightly drawn so that we wouldn't attract 'enemy bombers' (in reality the local air raid wardens). It was, of course, colder but every afternoon the entire school changed into rugby gear and most walked up the Grecian Valley (created by spade by hardworking landscape gardeners in the 18th Century) and to the 'Bourbon Fields' where house teams, juniors and seniors battled their way until it was nearly dark. Occasionally wartime problems took a hand as when one particularly large player, who was not able to buy size 13 rugby boots, was allowed to wear Corps boots – which made him an uncomfortable proposition to tackle. During my two rugby seasons at Stowe I managed to reach the first XV in the second year but was disappointed to have an injury in the Old Stoics match when Bernard Gadney himself was fullback for the Old Stoics and I was just a linesman.

It was not only the games that attracted those who enjoyed sport but the opportunity to travel to away matches at other schools. Petrol rationing made longer journeys (perhaps to Oundle) out of the question by coach, so we got to Buckingham Station by mid-morning and managed by train. There was virtually no transport by car and most parents were only able to visit their sons once a term, if that, and the opportunity to go to a match was a prize in itself. On my second summer half term I thought nothing of cycling the forty miles to Oxford to stay for the weekend with my Uncle Arthur and Aunt Evelyn. He was still then the Administrator of the Radcliffe Infirmary. (When, years later, my nephew Nick was taking a postgraduate degree at Oxford, his girlfriend, Jan – now his wife, but at the time studying to be a midwife – was considerably surprised to discover that one of the nurses' homes, 'Arthur Sanctuary House', was named after her boyfriend's great-uncle.)

When in the Easter term there were only cross country matches – running against Uppingham was always a high point – three of us organised some school chess matches, and by 1945 there was an official school chess team which enabled us to travel two or three extra times in the Easter term and we actually won some matches. Home matches were also a bonus because of the special school tea with extra jam and chocolate cake. It was always the duty of the home team to hand round the sandwiches – that put one in a favourable position for choosing the ones you wanted at a time when more exotic refreshments were hard to come by.

It is difficult to appreciate, today, the effect that rationing had in 1944. Few if any could bring to school more than two pots of jam per term because there wasn't the sugar to make it. When I dropped my precious pot of marmalade on the way into tea early in the Christmas term of 1944, I remember spending almost half an hour (and missing tea) scraping up every bit and then washing every piece of orange before putting it back in a new pot. Oranges, so plentiful in Nassau, were almost unobtainable in England.

In 'Hall' – where we had lunch and dinner every day – tables were occupied by forms with a master at each. The one at which I sat for most of my first year had Mr Ratcliffe ('Ratters') seated at the head for lunch. He intrigued us because he always sat right on the edge of his ample chair. Popular rumour had it that he had had one buttock shot off in the First War and had a silver plate as a replacement – but whether this was so we never knew and no-one dared ask him!

In fact there were a considerable number of older masters and some who had been recalled because so many younger ones were now in the services. My mother's cousin, Jack Le Breton, was one, and he had some difficulty in keeping control having spent much of his life as a farmer in East Africa. Another master's lessons on geography were interesting and very factual. He used numerous slides to illustrate his lectures but no longer saw clearly what was shown on the screen because he had his reading glasses on to read his copious notes. He was, however, very pleased that his lectures were greeted with considerable mirth and applause which he took to be a compliment. The boy using the projector was occasionally putting in transparencies incorrectly and upside down so that when he told us we were seeing a view of Mount Killimanjaro it was in fact sheep in New Zealand upside down. I don't think he ever realised what was happening – nor did we want him to as we didn't like to hurt his feelings.

Learning at Stowe was both a challenge and a pleasure. In my case I was soon able to catch up the year or so of detail that I had missed in Nassau although I was seventeen when I took School Certificate and only had two terms in the upper school instead of two years. This was occupied largely by 18th Century and American history, and statistics, and although leaving just after I was eighteen to join the Army, it was possible, by considerable reading, to reach a standard which I was told would get me to Oxford or Cambridge after the war.

Among my ancestors had been a Reverend William Ackroyd who died in 1485 and left the rents of two villages in Yorkshire to send a descendant of his brother to either Oxford or Cambridge 'in perpetuity'. These villages were Fogathorpe and Heptonstall, and while the former had by the 20th Century only a handful of cottages, the income from Heptonstall was considerably greater. My interest in heraldry, fostered to some degree by Desmond Low's collection of books in his study, led naturally to genealogy, and in my spare time I worked through many ancestors and corresponded with the Ackroyd Foundation in York. Among many descendants, some in very distant lines, was Lord Beveridge – while many other lines included well-known Yorkshire families today.

The 'Founders Kin' Scholarship, finding itself with sufficient income, had divided the funds so that each year two boys would benefit – one, a descendant of the Founder, the other a boy brought up in Heptonstall or Fogathorpe. In some years there was competition, and in the summer of 1945 I stayed in Leeds for five days and took a number of papers to try to win the Ackroyd Foundation Scholarship. I was fortunate and with the help of Stowe found myself with a place at Trinity, Cambridge, on the recommendation of J.F. Roxburgh, and a scholarship to help my parents to pay the fees. But this would all be after National Service.

With the war in Europe over, attention turned increasingly to the Far East. Summer holidays 1945 saw a small group of Stoics, all interested in the 'Cadet Corps', go on a week's camping holiday in the Lake District. I went direct from home in Cheshire and missed the last train at Lancaster, arriving at a wayside station about twelve miles south of Lake Coniston at nearly midnight, so I decided to walk across the fells to reach our camp about dawn. After about six miles in country lanes, I set off across the fells on a track in total darkness using my pre-war map; it was only as I descended to our camp at about 6 am that I came across a locked gate and a large notice which announced that the path I had followed was strictly out of bounds because of live army shells – the area being a training ground.

By then it didn't matter and I made camp by breakfast. One of my friends had bought a newspaper at the village shop: there had been a new sort of bomb which had just been dropped on Hiroshima and there was speculation that the explosion was so great that the Japanese might sue for peace. The rest of our holiday passed off peacefully. We climbed a number of peaks and by the time we reached home we *were* all at peace at last.

*   *   *

The duties of an 'officer' in the senior studies were never too onerous and after Desmond Low the next Head of House was Martin Arnold (whom I got to know very well fifteen years later). By my fourth term in Summer 1945, then over seventeen, I was officially released from those duties and later in the term became a house 'settler'. Promotion is often as much a matter of good fortune as good management, and in the autumn term I was a monitor, and Head of Grafton and a prefect in my last term in Spring 1946. (It was unusual to go from 'officer' to Head of House in less than a year.)

I shared a study in autumn 1945 with two other boys who were to be lifelong friends. Teddy Archibald was for many years Curator of Oil Paintings at Greenwich Museum and later wrote the standard reference *A Dictionary of Sea Painters*, and John Bourdon-Smith was to start a London business in Georgian silver and for half a century, with the help of his wife, Charmian, and later his children, was to occupy a leading place in the world of antique silver. It would seem that the whole ethos of Stowe and its estate lands filled with temples and monuments was, as JF had predicted, to breed an unusual number of men who themselves wished to become involved in one way or another in the world of art and history.

Following our autumn term in the upper school, and a number of rugby matches in the First XV (including a memorable huge loss at Uppingham where their wing three-quarter – Wilkinson – outstripped our best efforts on a number of occasions; we were not to know that one day he would win a gold medal as an Olympic quarter-miler) the first Christmas of peace passed very much as the previous one, with rationing still in full swing but with street lighting and car headlights again.

The journey to and from Stowe usually involved arriving at Bletchley Station and catching a bus twelve miles to Buckingham. As the new Head of Grafton I was expected to arrive a day early in January 1946, but as I walked out of Bletchley Station with two suitcases there were no buses and I couldn't afford a taxi, so I spent two hours in the snow hitchhiking first to Buckingham and then getting a cab three miles to Stowe. But supper with Fritz Clifford and the excitement of the new term made it worthwhile.

In my last term it was inevitable that increasing thought should be given to what would happen after Stowe. A number of leading Stoics had joined the Brigade of Guards and the Coldstream in particular. The three Grafton prefects just before I started (but whom I would have known well had I arrived at a normal age) were no exception. That all of them had visited the school as Coldstream Officers to inspect the Corps made it particularly enticing to try to enter the Regiment.

With another Stoic prefect who was senior to me I visited Birdcage Walk in London and saw the Regimental Colonel, Lionel Bootle-Wilbraham (later Lord Skelmersdale). It was a very nerve-wracking interview with Major John Chandos-Pole, the Regimental Adjutant, present and lasted for twenty to thirty minutes. I was particularly conscious that I had no relatives in the Regiment, but I had managed to dig up a Colonel Charles Howard who had served as a Colonel in the Regiment in 1735 and was a second cousin of a direct ancestor in my *mother's* family! To my delight I received a letter the next day from Birdcage Walk to say that I had been accepted into the Regiment and would join the 23rd Brigade Squad at Caterham at the beginning of May in 1946. My fellow Stoic, in spite of his seniority, had not been so lucky.

The Easter term was normally sparse of sport except for cross-country and hockey and as I had never learned to play the latter (except for a few knock-about games when I am sure that the laws of the game were significant by their absence) I concentrated on trying to win the school cross-country which course took us towards Silverstone (home of another racing sport) and back along a gruelling avenue to end on the North Front before the school. As a private initiative (after the weeks of training) I got up early on the day of the race and spent a long time in a hot bath, to relax before the start. I'm not sure whether this was a good thing or not as in the event I finished second after Michael Binns, the captain of the cross country team. Although I did win the school mile and half-mile in close finishes later in the Easter term, I never thought of pursuing these athletics activities later in life.

Among heart-warming traditions which *had* been allowed to flourish at Stowe was that if one became a school prefect one was allowed to join the Headmaster at dinner in his private dining room once a term. Everything was very elegant, with silver on the table, but as with everything else JF promoted it was all most informal and you felt at home, while the conversation turned to stories of his own education and matters of general or world interest.

JF was also noted for 'happening' on Stoics on their birthdays and to one's great surprise he would happen past a classroom as it emptied and wish a junior boy 'happy birthday'. No doubt this was well organised by his secretary, but this and the fact that almost every boy was taught by him during his time at Stowe (French in particular) meant that there was a strong bond of loyalty. He was a particularly well-dressed man and always wore a silk handkerchief either in his breast pocket or sleeve – bringing it out with a trifle of a flourish. I found these things endearing (and still wear a silk handkerchief myself today more than fifty years on – although it is never flourished!).

Another gentle tradition that had sprung up among those who were leaving Stowe at the end of their last term was that they should collect signatures of all their friends. But these were in no ordinary notebook. Throughout our time we had sung in Chapel from a special collection of hymns called *Cantata Stoica*. Some of these hymns were unusual for standard hymn books, but no doubt had been selected by JF as representing his favourite church music or his tenets in life. So you went to the school shop and bought a copy of *Cantata Stoica* and over the last few weeks gave it to a wide circle of friends so that each could sign his favourite hymn. I sometimes look at those pages today: they remind me of friends of those days or the themes of the excellent hymns in *Cantata Stoica*. My own favourite – No. 83, by Arthur Clough – has the opening lines:

> Say not the struggle nought availeth,
> The labour and the wounds are vain …

and concludes:

> And not by eastern windows only,
> When daylight comes, comes in the light;
> In front the sun climbs slow, how slowly,
> But westwards, look, the land is bright.

Most of the signers I can only remember as they were then, although every name contains a memory, and the signatures include that of J. F. Roxburgh himself, whose organisation, kindness and elegance must have influenced many Stoics in their later lives, as it did mine.

After leaving Stowe I never led a life which kept me in touch with more than a few Old Stoics – particularly John Bourdon-Smith, the Arnolds and Teddy Archibald – although another particular friend had been Michael FitzGerald, with whom I sometimes shared weekends because parents only had the petrol to visit once a term. He had a debonair father who owned a paint factory but was also supposed to be very much more closely related to the FitzGeralds, Dukes of Leinster, than the reference books could report. Mike was a very talented sportsman and would almost certainly have captained Stowe at both cricket and rugby in his last year had he not left early. We continued to meet for a year or two in Cornwall and then lost touch. Almost twenty years later I was at a tennis match on a vicarage lawn in Dorset when someone I hardly knew, who travelled on business in Canada, came up to me and said 'Were you at Stowe?' He had just returned from Arctic Canada where he had met an Englishman to whom he had mentioned he would be staying in Dorset the following week, to which the reply was, 'If you meet

David Howard give him my best wishes.' It had been Mike – but the businessman could give me no address and we haven't met again.

Stowe, for me, was two years filled with much to learn and many happy memories.

CHAPTER 4

The Coldstream

After a rather social Easter holidays (I felt I had a girlfriend, although we only met unofficially at dances and occasional hunt balls, but I did go to tea with her and she had dinner with us twice in the country) I packed up a very sparse suitcase and set off to stay the night with my uncle and aunt in London – (General) Max and Mary Brander – and then caught a train at Waterloo for Caterham.

Caterham Hill was very steep and I arrived at the gates of the Guards Depot in a taxi – the end of luxury for some time. Having been shown our barrack room we were issued with uniform and settled nervously to discover the routine that would be ours for about eight weeks. Each barrack room had a 'trained soldier' – our leader who introduced us to everyday life. We were fortunate to have Trained Soldier Yeomans, who was both careful and fair and of course had seen active service.

Corporal Whitehorn's Brigade Squad consisted of eighteen recruits, some of whom were to become life-long friends. I was the only Stoic but there were more than one Etonian, Harrovian and Wykehamist as well as those from other schools. The Regiments to which we aspired were also evenly spread between the Grenadier, Coldstream, Scots, Irish and Welsh Guards, and while at first those who knew each other already tended to do things together, this lasted only a very short while, after which we seemed to integrate well.

The regime was firm, immediate and hard but not unduly oppressive. Inside our hut we kept warm and scrupulously tidy so that a shoelace out of place merited a fierce reprimand, while our morning kit inspections became a matter of huge importance. Some were much better at this than others, and Nick Elwes, whose company I much enjoyed, usually managed to let a wet sock lie on the red hot circular stove and catch alight, or have something facing the wrong way round or inside out at his kit inspection. It was quite endearing, but raised the ire of Trained Soldier Yeomans. Among those who became friends later were Ted Bonnor-Maurice, Mike Hicks (later a General), Laurie Barrington, 'Pooh' Luard and Tom Wheeler, some of whom took regular commissions with distinction. National Service was still an obligatory two years for us all, but those who sought regular commissions aimed at Eaton Hall or Sandhurst – while the rest of us were bound for OCTU elsewhere.

My last holiday at home before joining the Army, 1946.

Gdsn. R. Windsor-Clive, M. Straker, Sgt. K. Powton (P. T. Instructor), Gdsn. R. Ransford, J. Luard
Gdsn. L. Barrington, P. Whiteley, C. Spencer, M. Hicks, M. Mitchell, S. Meade, D. Loder, D. Howard
Seated: Gdsn. E. Bonnor-Maurice, Sgt. R. Peden (W. T. Instructor), CPL. W. WHITEHORN (Squad Instructor),
Lieut. C. J. Cowlard, Sgt. A. Dear (Supt. Sgt.), Td. S. E. Yeomans, Gdsn. N. Elwes

The purpose of Caterham was to break us in and make us achieve a level of near unquestioning obedience and personal smartness which would be our hallmark for the coming years. Drill parades were physically stretching but provided some amusing moments as we became a unit. The officer in charge was Victor Le Fanu (later Major Sir Victor Le Fanu, Her Majesty's Serjeant-at-Arms) but we were known as Lance Corporal Whitehorn's Squad and although able to mix with other squads not destined to be officers and messed together, we nevertheless kept and enjoyed our own company.

All of us had experienced the Corps at our different schools and while the regime was more professional and harder, it was not entirely unfamiliar. We learned our arms drill and went for route marches – with a degree of 'at the double' – and were easily able to fall asleep early, ready for our early reveille. Perhaps the most novel aspect was the time spent, literally, on spit and polish, and we learned how to turn our sometimes muddy boots into gleaming mirrors, with the aid of such devices as tins of molten shoe polish and 'boning' (the rubbing of the leather surface with a teaspoon to make it shine).

Time passed very quickly and we were soon to 'pass out' and assembled for the train journey to Pirbright Camp – and pre-OCTU – a three-month course intended to turn us from a Brigade Squad into cadets with a preliminary understanding of warfare, the use of the rifle and the Bren gun, and field tactics learned in long and tiring days on Pirbright Heath and various training areas nearer Aldershot.

Our introduction to Pirbright was typical of that day, when young men who had seen action wished to ensure that those who followed them would stand firm as they had. We marched from the station to the Camp office and stood in two sections near the door. A car came round the corner very fast and unexpectedly and slammed on its brakes, ending no more than a foot away from the leading rank. Most jumped sideways when the officer driving leapt out and shouted, 'Who gave you permission to break ranks? Get back in line, you bloody recruits.' This did not typify those in charge of us at Pirbright but was an indication of how close the war still was.

In fact our Commanding Officer was a man I later learned to admire, Colonel Roddy Hill of the Coldstream; while our Company Commander was Major David Butter (whom I met many years later at his home in Scotland and who then, to my amazement, produced a photograph of our pre-OCTU) and Platoon Commander John Swinton – both Scots Guardsmen of distinction. The latter, having lost a leg in action, walked with a stick and pronounced swinging stride and was later to be a distinguished general.

While drill still played an important part of our training, our days were much more varied and barrack rooms slightly more relaxed. We spent many hours with our weapons instructors learning every movement of the rifle, the Bren gun and the newly-introduced Sten gun. The Bren machine gun was a formidable and very successful weapon and we had to learn how to dismantle it for cleaning in any light or weather and very quickly. The order in which this was done – piston, barrel, butt, body – was learned by heart, but all the more quickly because of the sentence we were made to repeat constantly by our arms instructor: 'Piss on the barrel but not on the body' (pelmanism is a formidable aid in one's armoury of remembering, and there are many more important things I have long since forgotten).

Apart from spells on the range there were frequent route marches, some with full kit which stretched us to the limit. But more exciting were the simulated battle experiences when we each took turns to be in charge of a small section and not only were thunderflashes used in abundance, which gave the very real impression of action, but occasionally training officers used their pistols with live rounds to ensure that we were fully alert.

One warm afternoon I was acting as Platoon Commander and beside me was Nick Elwes acting as my platoon runner: 'Nick, run behind those trees and tell Mike that we are going to swing round to the left and advance.' Nick stood up in a nonchalant way and started walking leisurely across the open ground towards Mike's platoon. This wasn't very realistic and a couple of shots rang out from a training officer behind me. I saw Nick fall, no doubt in realistic surprise, but then he called out, 'I've been shot' – and indeed a bullet had shattered his elbow. The exercise was quickly brought to a close and Nick was rushed to hospital.

It was the end of one military career (and very nearly of two, because the officer was severely reprimanded but fortunately escaped dismissal). Many years later I spoke to him about the incident and he said it was almost the most harrowing of a long and successful military career. I kept in touch with Nick for many years, but we met only infrequently.

Pirbright was convenient for going up to London; even more so if one could get to Woking and a fast train. This made a short period of leave, after about six weeks, easy. We frequently visited the outskirts of Woking because one of the more long-term benefits was a driving and motorcycle course. (An added advantage being that if you attained a driving licence in the Army it was never necessary to take any further driving test in civilian life.)

Our driving experience was largely in 18 cwt vans, then the principal workhorse of the Army, and the instruction included a fairly comprehensive maintenance course which stood me in good stead for a number of years until engines became more sophisticated and I gradually forgot what I had learned. Lessons were largely along the Hampshire Hogs Back and we learned to navigate the narrow steep roads – I remember one village in particular: Christmas Pie.

More exciting was our despatch riders' course on formidable Army motorcycles. Near the end of our time at Pirbright we did a week's 'live' training on Dartmoor and drove ourselves down to a training area on the moor above Bridstowe. It was a road I was to use over the decades and I never forgot, as I passed through the village, how on that training course in 1946 a moment of inattention saw my motorbike and I drive through a hedge near the road to Tavistock and both of us end upside down in a cornfield. Fortunately no harm was done and we were both on the road again in twenty minutes (but I never had any later yearning to be a motorcyclist).

The Dartmoor training almost marked the end of three months at Pirbright and our Brigade Squad realised that it was to become irreparably divided, as those who had arrived for a regular career in the Army left for a year or more at Eaton Hall, while those of us who had arrived for a short service commission left for less than eight months OCTU at Trentham Park in Staffordshire. At a final passing-out parade on the square the salute was taken by Colonel Roddy Hill, and I think that we all left Pirbright with mixed feelings of regret and satisfaction.

*   *   *

It was a grey October day when some of us met again at Trentham Park, and it was a very different regime at OCTU than it had been at Pirbright. The dozen of us who had been together since the spring at Caterham were spread across a much larger number of comfortable barrack rooms with a great many other cadets whose training had been with other regiments. For me it was comforting that our Company Sergeant-Major was a Coldstreamer with a voice scarcely less memorable than the famous Regimental Sergeant-Major 'Tibby' Britton, of whose voice it was said that it could be heard at Victoria Station when he gave an order at Wellington Barracks.

Such luxuries as cars were allowed for the few that could afford them and weekend leave was normal, with most going by train to London while I faced a fifty-mile hitchhike in various weathers into North Cheshire. The winter of 1946/7 was a particularly cruel one with considerable snow and this led to some late night adventures – for there was no restriction on when one reached Trentham Camp so long as one was on parade punctually next morning.

A somewhat more academic approach to command and tactics was included and TEWTs (Tactical Exercises Without Troops) were planned and executed in the countryside north of Stafford, including a very realistic two-day exercise. I remember leading a bayonet charge down a hill and having a very physical struggle before being thrown as a prisoner into our 'enemy's' camp which was later overrun by 'our side' leading to our release after an uncomfortable night tied up on a stable floor. Such exercises introduced one, as nearly as they could, to realism and a feeling of challenge.

With Stoke-on-Trent barely over the hill, we sometimes went out in the cars of those who had them, and I remember in particular John Hartigan's vehicle which didn't have a door on the driver's side nor any brakes to speak of. John usually wore a particularly strong boot on his right foot so that if he wanted to slow down, he would put his right foot outside on the road. It was both more comfortable for him (for he was a very tall Irishman with a rather small car) and much safer for those that rode with him because it did enable the car to stop within a reasonable distance. The winter brought with it rugby, although as an ever-changing team the OCTU did not play many games against local clubs.

As the spring eventually turned to summer the occasion of the passing-out parade loomed. This was the end of about ten months of effort designed to turn schoolboys into officers. Had we been two or more years older we would have joined our regiments and almost at once been posted overseas. Now there loomed the possibilities of joining the fast-declining troops in Europe, going to the Middle East where Palestine was an ever more dangerous place, or settling down to less exciting duties in Britain. But some all-important questions needed an answer.

Would we receive our commission? Would we pass well enough to enter the regiment of our choice? (This was particularly relevant in the Brigade and some other regiments where the numbers of their battalions were slowly to be reduced to peace-time levels, and demand was greater than vacancies.) In the event we were told before the passing-out parade, and, with Ted Bonnor-Maurice, I found myself an Ensign in His Majesty's Coldstream Regiment of Footguards.

*   *   *

Posted to the 1st Battalion, newly returned to Pirbright from Germany, the summer and autumn of 1947 proved both busy and interesting. Ted and I were the only officers in the Battalion who had not seen active service and so we felt rather small. Ted joined No. 1 Company (Johnny Baxendale's) and I joined No. 3, of which Bobby Phillips was Company Commander, later to be joined by 'Lump' Windsor-Clive as Second in Command.

Almost at once we learned that we were to provide the square-lining troops for the first Trooping of the Colour since the war. It was not to be in full dress uniform but the degree of practice was still very considerable, taking numerous days of rehearsal on the parade ground at Pirbright. In the event we all went up to Wellington Barracks a day or two before the Trooping and a final rehearsal was on Horse Guards Parade. By comparison with today it might be seen as a rather low-key affair, but it was a first step after the war back to the ceremonials which are still a feature of June in London.

At about that time another incident took place which was never reported but played a role in our lives for a few weeks. A relatively junior officer in the Coldstream Battalion at Wellington Barracks had so infuriated some of his colleagues that two car-loads of officers from Pirbright went up to London one night, entered his room at Wellington Barracks and took him in a car to the lake in St James's Park where they threw him in almost naked. With some aplomb, and a towel, the officer marched back in the early morning into the barracks. The Sergeant of the Guard, recognising him – although in unfamiliar dress – called out the Guard to salute his entry. The episode did not end there, for those involved were confined to barracks at Pirbright for at least a month.

Life at Pirbright at the Mess was a pleasant and relaxing affair where a number of Regimental customs were observed, including one that every officer had to call every other officer by his Christian name. After a few weeks this became second nature, but it was a little daunting at first when one found oneself sitting with senior officers of considerable rank.

The half-sized billiard table in the Mess was frequently the scene of a game which would not have been appreciated by the purists, for 'billiard fives' employed very rapid and skilful hand-swings along the surface of the table with the balls sometimes leaping from the table and through surrounding windows. Many played bridge or backgammon in the evening, games which could come to a sudden end if someone was losing heavily and let off a thunderflash beneath the table. Such amusements came easily to those who were slowly re-adjusting to a more peaceful world.

Frequent visits to London and more than one visit to Eton with friends – on one such occasion I found myself chatting again with Jimmy Goldsmith – led to pleasant moments recalling the past. I had exchanged Christmas cards annually with Mary Moseley, who had for much of her life been editor of the *Nassau Guardian*, and she let me know she was staying at the Savoy in the run up to Princess Elizabeth's wedding. I had lunch with her there and she asked if I'd like to spend the afternoon with her at the *Daily Express* – for she was a very old friend of Max Aitken, then Lord Beaverbrook. We wandered into various offices and had tea with Lord Beaverbrook; he was pleasantly inquisitive and even asked if I was planning a journalistic career when I left

Cambridge after the Army. But four years down the road seemed a long time, although I did say I'd write to him if I wanted a job.

Even more warming was an invitation from Marcelle Goldsmith to have lunch with her at Claridges. Unfortunately Frank Goldsmith could not be there, but I was surprised to find the other guest was Lord Rothschild. It was a happy lunch which continued into the afternoon and I learned something of Teddy and Jimmy's plans and she, too, asked what I was going to do after university. It all passed off as pleasant reminiscing and stargazing, but I have sometimes wondered whether I would have been sensible to take such 'opportunities' more seriously.

The path of duty crossed that of pleasure again at Pirbright when it was decided that the Annual Rifle Competition was to be held again for the first time since the war, and the 1st Battalion was to be in charge of the ranges. It was less of an onerous task than one of discovery, for enthusiasts even from as far as Australia brought their idiosyncratic shooting to fire on the ranges. It was inevitable, I suppose, that one war-hardened officer ignored the flags and drove across the ranges in his landrover during the firing. It hardly raised an eyebrow amongst his friends, but would not happen today.

A totally unexpected bonus was the sale of wine which the Battalion, then part of the Guards 1st Armoured Division, had captured about two years before from the supply column of a German panzer division retreating from France. We were asked to fill in a form as to which wines we would like and I understood that the funds went to the Regimental charity. From memory Chateau Yquem 1929 was £2 per bottle and brandy from the 1870s the same, while early 20th Century chateau-bottled wines were about £1. This, of course, must be compared with the pay of those days, but I remember a weekend spent taking two trunk loads of wine home by train. My father in particular was still enjoying a very occasional bottle in his Cornish home in 1980.

That summer, too, saw a weekend in Dorset staying with my uncle Harry Sanctuary and his wife, Eileen, whose father had been the virtual 'inventor' of sports netting and whose brother Campbell Edwards, was, like Uncle Harry, a director of a new group of netting companies in Bridport, called 'Bridport Industries'. This had amalgamated most of the smaller independent netting firms in the town, which had been the centre of the cordage and netting industry since the 12th Century (when the Bridport cordage trade is recorded as the main supplier of the navy of King John) into one company. The immediate occasion of the weekend was the marriage of my second cousin, Peronelle Le Breton, to Dennis Laskey (later Sir Dennis, and a senior figure in the Foreign Office).

The Le Breton's home at Loders Court near Bridport was the centre of a small Victorian estate, with peacocks wandering about on the terrace. Both Sir Edward (Ted) and Mary Le Breton were cousins of my mother and I have happy memories of visits there during later years. Ted's father was a cousin of Emily Le Breton who married a Mr Langtry, and as 'Lillie Langtry' was the celebrated actress and mistress of King Edward VII – a fact that irritated him immensely. In fact a small portrait of her (which I was later given by Peronelle) was kept locked in an upstairs bedroom so that no-one could see it.

It was the first country wedding of style I had experienced as an adult and it left a lasting impression on me. Of more immediate concern was dinner with Campbell Edwards and his mother that evening when inevitably again the subject of career came up. (I had already told my father that I did not want to follow him into a waiting position in his company in the motor trade.) Harry and Eileen's son, Anthony, had already arranged to start training in Bridport Industries the following year and it was clear that if I were offered a post in the company, it would be on the assumption that I started soon after leaving the Army in the later part of 1948. Another important reason why this opportunity occurred was that the only son of the Chairman of Bridport Industries, Anthony Trenchard-Cox, who had been in Normandy in the Coldstream, had been killed in 1944, and there was almost an emotional reason why I should consider such an offer – but none of this seemed particularly immediate to me and going up to Trinity in 1948 was still very much the official plan.

*   *   *

As the autumn of 1947 wore on, two interesting national and international situations loomed larger. In England, the wedding of Princess Elizabeth was clearly a ceremony of great significance, while in Palestine a deteriorating situation was calling for British troops as boatloads of displaced Jews managed to make their way ashore and strengthened the Jewish voice for a national homeland.

It became clear that most of the duties at the royal wedding would not fall to the 1st Battalion Coldstream which was by now training at Pirbright so I was very surprised when, at the last moment, I was told that John Wills, who was to command the half Company to the right of Buckingham Palace Gate and to the south of the Victoria Memorial, was unwell and I was to take his place. Sleeping at Wellington Barracks, we paraded early and were at our posts perhaps two or three hours before the Princess's carriage left the forecourt of the Palace. I stood with my back to the Palace looking up the Mall. I had for many years (but can no longer find) a copy of the BBC recording of the ceremony in which I can clearly hear my shouted order 'Right half Company; Royal Salute; Present Arms' as the crowd started to roar and the carriages left the Palace.

It was a wait of about two hours before the procession started to return. Standing now with my back to the Victoria Memorial, one had to somehow quickly assess as the various carriages approached and passed from behind whether they contained royalty and merited a Royal Salute. As the many carriages passed, one acted more as an automaton and it was a joke at the time that we almost gave a Royal Salute to the King of Egypt's groom.

That evening Alastair Tower, who had also been on duty that day, told me he had a spare ticket to a London show and having first had drinks with my Uncle Harry, who was staying at the Hyde Park Hotel, we went to watch Ruth Draper. It was a formidable performance which brought back memories of seeing her in Nassau at the time of Pearl Harbour. Emboldened, we decided after the show to go to the stage door and, perhaps because we were still wearing uniform, we were allowed in. She was charming. I told her of the occasion in Nassau, we drank champagne and she signed our programmes. It was a fitting end to a memorable day.

*   *   *

As December approached, the 1st Battalion readied itself for the move to Palestine. In a final training session, on a mortar range, I stepped on an unexploded incendiary mortar shell and was very lucky to survive without serious injury. Losing much of my uniform and with considerable burns to hands and face I was able to throw myself in a deep pool of icy mud and stay there until help arrived. A few days in Aldershot hospital only confirmed that my moustache was largely burned away and had to grow again, but otherwise no lasting harm was done.

It was a short but pleasant Christmas at home, but we left for Southampton a few days later and No. 3 Company were sailing by the beginning of January. After heavy weather in the Bay of Biscay we sailed through the Straits of Gibraltar and then directly to Port Said.

CHAPTER 5

Palestine

Our arrival at Port Said was attended by a swarm of small boats offering a range of fare. We spent only a night in port before gliding slowly down the Canal to Suez, where no sooner had we arrived than we caught a troop train, which during the next night took us up the Canal again by rail and then across the inhospitable Negev desert through Gaza to Tel Aviv. It felt almost like home as No. 3 Company disembarked into a small convoy of three-ton lorries, and we drove north to Nathanya and our camp for the next few months.

I remember brief instructions as to the political situation in Palestine, but unlike today there was no State of Israel, and all the land between Lebanon and Egypt, and east to the River Jordan, was the Protectorate of Palestine; while the land to the east was Trans Jordan, ruled by the eminently sensible King Abdullah. The influx of desperate, displaced European Jews, sometimes in barely seaworthy freighters, landing wherever it was possible from Acre in the north to Tel Aviv in the south, was creating great unrest and many were held in camps if they had not already 'disappeared' into the villages already held by Jewish settlers. All this was part of a continuing process which had been set in train after the defeat of the Ottoman Empire in the First War and the establishment of Palestine as a separate Protectorate under a charter from the League of Nations.

For centuries Jews had lived in this land under the Ottoman Empire and it was unsurprising that some of their race had adopted the Mohammedan religion in order to prosper under Turkish rule, while others had progressively moved to Europe and Russia to preserve a greater (but not absolute) degree of religious freedom. It was therefore an uneasy, but usually peaceful, territory when the gradual increase in Jewish power started after 1920 and Jewish settlements began to grow, as that on the hill above Haifa called 'Ahuzzah Sir Herbert Samuel'.

Tensions during the 1930s had led to an Arab uprising in 1935 and '36, but the world war had overshadowed this and by 1946 three Jewish organisations in particular were trying to establish greater Jewish supremacy. We were briefed on the Haganah, a large and moderate group which could turn itself relatively easily into a Jewish army; the Irgun Zeva'i Le'umi, which adopted harsher, terrorist methods; and a breakaway organisation known as the Stern Gang, which would stop at nothing to achieve its militant ends.

Clearly these were viewed by the British Army, and the still majority of Muslim Arab people, as providing varying focuses of discontent, although they were not the whole problem. During the months before our arrival, militants had blown up the King David Hotel in Jerusalem – then a diplomatic and military focus of British rule – and during 1947 had kidnapped and brutally murdered two British sergeants who were relaxing in the seaside town of Nathanya, where our camp now was.

To a certain extent the 1st Battalion Coldstream was replacing the 3rd Battalion which was leaving as our various companies arrived. Their Commanding Officer was Lt. Col. George Burns and Second in Command 'Buster' Luard (who was Pooh Luard's uncle and had earned a great deal of Regimental – and Army – fame by leading a successful breakout from Tobruk in 1942 when officially the town had been surrendered to the Germans by a South African General). It was no surprise that Colonel George was later to command London District: he was the sort of commanding officer who inspired great loyalty, and I was amazed that when I met him years later he at once knew my name and turned the conversation to Palestine in 1948. (I did not know then, but later learned, that his great-uncle was the American financier, J. P. Morgan, and that he lived until the 1990s at South Mimms Park.)

The accommodation at Nathanya was all tents, well-spaced near a large parade ground, and at first I shared one with Guy Yerburgh (later General Lord Alvingham) and David Somerset (in the 3rd Battalion and later to return to England, who became well known in the art world and eventually succeeded his uncle as Duke of Beaufort). Later, the other occupant of the tent was Mike Parkes – a dedicated career officer who commanded the 'carrier platoon' and who could do almost anything with the tracked carriers including spinning them in the sand.

Although an unpleasant ambush near Bethlehem in which the Battalion suffered a small number of wounded, but no fatalities, took place shortly after our arrival, there were relatively few active duties for the Company unless a particular incident called for action, and as the Battalion assembled we even played rugby on the sandy parade ground. 'Showing the flag' was a frequent operation, in which a number of carriers and vehicles filled with guardsmen drove slowly through local Arab towns – Tulkarm was the nearest – to remind the local population that there was a military force nearby ready for action. Road blocks, also, had to be manned although I was never sure quite who they were meant to stop (but the fact that they could be quickly deployed may have meant that they deterred the movement of potentially hostile groups).

One group, which moved with impunity and were recognisable at once as they travelled rapidly in the hills with three vehicles bristling with Bren guns

Officers of the 1st Battalion Coldstream (and a few of the 3rd Battalion) Nathanya, 1948. Seated 5th and 6th from left: Colonels George Burns and John Chandos-Pole. (Author, back row, 4th from right, next to a 'discussion'.)

The Arab Committee, North Haifa. A friendly meeting with 'The Brigade'. Bobby Phillips right and author standing centre.

and a light anti-aircraft gun, were the staff cars of General Glubb of the Arab Legion – later Glubb Pasha, whose headquarters were just over the Jordan. It would have required far more than one of our road blocks to stop General Glubb!

Those who had a mind to shoot duck at weekends found a perfect place at Lake Hule, while I was very fortunate to find myself involved in a visit to Petra – which was in the hills, far south of the Dead Sea, and seemingly unapproachable. By good fortune, the father of David Whitaker (in later life for long the Rector of Tiverton in Devon) had been a distinguished Coldstream officer and had served in Trans-Jordan. David had a plan, and the friends that would make it possible.

On a Thursday evening David and I, together with a friend in the Grenadiers, set off in a 15 cwt lorry and crossed into Jordan, spending the evening and benefiting from a comfortable bed at the Trans-Jordan Frontier Force station near Irbid. In the morning we drove down to Amman and met at the hotel near the Roman amphitheatre two senior ladies who had served in the WRAC (Women's Royal Army Corps), one being a colonel. We would share the hire of a light aircraft for a weekend – I think for the colossal sum of £240. After a light lunch at the hotel we boarded our plane and flew over the Dead Sea and down the valley towards the Gulf of Aqaba, landing at Ma'an.

At Ma'an a large taxi was waiting and we all crammed in and drove westwards up into the hills for sixty miles. There was no road that we could see on the desert, but our driver navigated by the sun and we reached a long narrow pass through the hills and eventually found ourselves at a Trans-Jordan Frontier Force fort overlooking the rocks which led down through the 3,000 year old deep gully into Petra itself. The taxi parked to await our return nearly two days later (I think he charged us £60 for the weekend). In the gathering darkness we set off down a narrow track to the 'rose red city half as old as time'.

The story of Petra is far better known today than it was sixty years ago. The five of us, with our Arab guide, spent a night in a cave halfway up a precipitous rock face with a wood fire kept burning at the entrance for fear of wolves. We were, I think, one of the first parties to return there after the war and were the only people there that weekend (and I believe since some weeks before).

The Nabatean people who built the city had controlled many of the trade routes across the South Arabian desert from the 5th Century BC and earlier. Their wealth came from the tolls they levied on the trade of the caravans they protected. Our route into Petra passed down the narrowest of tracks, sometimes only five feet across, through a gorge 300 feet high and more than a mile long. Along this ran a channel, cut waist-high into the rock face, down which water once flowed to the city. It had never been captured until the army of Trajan swept into the city in AD 106 and it became part of the Roman Empire, later being called 'Hadriana' by the Emperor Hadrian (so well remembered by his wall in the north of England). This led to a period of some 250 years of growing prosperity until a disastrous earthquake struck in AD 363, and although a much reduced population still lived there, it was taken by the Saracens in AD 636 and much later by the Crusaders for a short period in the 12th Century when it was largely lost to civilisation until rediscovered by the Swiss explorer Burckhardt in 1812. It was only in 1865 that systematic archaeological exploration started.

Both the influence of Roman architecture in the east and the reinforcement of this after Trajan's victory, caused a Roman city with temples, shops and houses with paved streets to be raised up on valley floor of a square mile or so. These were overlooked by the homes of the earlier inhabitants who had lived in a network of caves, many interconnecting and carved and decorated as houses.

Alas, I have not been back to Petra, but know that today it is visited by large numbers of tourists who can stay at a nearby hotel, even arriving by helicopter. In the summer of 1948 one felt that no-one had been there for many years, and as we walked along the lanes between the ruins of some houses near a temple it was possible to find the location of a pottery shop and pick up some twenty pieces of broken Nabatean pottery lying on the ground, including jug handles and other pieces decorated with fine geometric lines and patterns in darker red or the far paler pink/sandy clay. There is little doubt that many had been lying amongst the rubble for up to a thousand years, having probably been ignored as too unimportant by the archaeologists eighty years earlier.

Our guide took us with a torch (of ancient flaming type, not electric) across the floor of the city, followed by the donkey that carried our cases, and we scrambled up a causeway to a cave facing the entrance to the city where he lit a fire and we laid out padded cushions on which we all slept in our clothes in two interconnecting 'rooms'. We slept well because we were exhausted, but woke soon after dawn to a breakfast of tea and freshly-cooked chappatis.

During the day which followed we walked to every corner of the city and explored numerous caves. We were taken to a high point that looked out along a range of rocky hills to the south, but it was clear that the only way in which the city could have been taken was through the narrow rock cleft along which we had come. As the afternoon wore on we reluctantly collected our rucksacks

Our charter plane to Ma'an – David Whitaker right – before return journey.

Cave houses and remaining Roman temple in Petra, 1948.

and walked back up the entrance to our waiting taxi, which drove in the gathering dusk to Ma'an and to our plane, reaching Amman in time for dinner. My memory is that this was all organised by David, and for some years afterwards I used to see him occasionally. I have no memory of the names of the WRAC officers, but perhaps someone may one day recognise them and confirm that it was, for all of us, a most interesting and also breathtaking two days in the distant past, unencumbered by modern tourism.

*   *   *

As summer approached, the 1st Battalion divided into companies and found themselves in strategic houses in Haifa. Company headquarters, under Bobby Phillips, was in a large office building at the end of Hertzel Street, while my platoon was fortunate to be up a winding hill road overlooking Haifa from the north with a view across the plains to the ancient town of Acre, fifteen miles up the coast. Our purpose was to settle that part of Haifa and prevent any local conflicts. We were, however, well aware that a quarter of a mile further up the hill was a Haganah training camp, which was permitted so long as it did not carry out any sorties.

To our surprise, Bobby and I were invited to dinner by the Jewish owner of a luxurious house at the far end of Hertzel Street. We travelled in an army car and wore our pistols throughout dinner, but discovered that our hosts had lived in London during the war. At least two of the guests were, we thought afterwards, staff officers in the Haganah, and we guessed that we were probably there for them to assess whether we were aggressive or balanced in our views. It was a pleasant and unthreatening evening, and after dinner we sat and listened to a talented pianist.

A few days later another officer and I were, to our very great surprise, invited to a hotel and a dinner for the feast of Passover. We made it clear that we had to be armed and, with the agreement of our hosts, laid our pistols above the plates (having removed the pudding spoon and fork to either side). Again it was a pleasant evening and while battalion headquarters had given permission for us to be present, it was made clear that acceptance was entirely a matter of our choice. At one point later in the evening we were both aware that we had been photographed, for a face appeared over a windowsill with a camera and a flash. But we left our Jewish hosts in no doubt that we were honoured to have been invited and that our army presence in central Haifa was intended as entirely peaceful.

Below our platoon headquarters there was a mixed area of Arab and Jewish houses, but it was not conducive to good order that on many nights there was some fierce gunfire and on one morning a cart was called out to remove a number of bodies from the street. We found the leaders of both the Arab and Jewish communities, and after delivering a message I went down to see them to impress on them that such behaviour would not be tolerated. The Arab elders invited us to an elaborate coffee ceremony (complete with hubble-bubble) while the Jewish commander, who had once served in the Palestine Police, told me over one of a number of visits that his grandparents had been Muslims under the Turks but had reverted to their original religion as Jews after 1920. In a gentle 'show of force' I said that we had 'special equipment' which enabled us to fire at night and wouldn't hesitate to use it if we saw from our outpost on the hill that anyone was being aggressive. Our 'special equipment' was nothing more than a 'fixed line' which enabled a Bren gun to be set up with telescopic sights with great accuracy on any target. In this case it was clear that a particular location in a house was always involved. Two nights later, after particularly fierce fire, it was only necessary to pull the trigger on the Bren – and the shooting stopped. When I had tea with the Jewish commander next day I commented on the noisy night. 'I know,' he replied, 'One of our people was badly wounded at a window in his house.' I contented myself with saying that he probably should not have been at the window. From then onwards it was much quieter.

My platoon sergeant, Duxbury, was a well-known Coldstreamer with service from the early 1930s. He had been a Company Sergeant-Major but had blotted his copybook rather badly and had been reduced to the ranks about 1946. I remember the charge in the Battalion record book: 'Whilst on guard at St James's Palace holding a baby in his arms to be photographed.' (He told me the mother was a very pretty girl.) I was very fortunate to have such a knowledgeable sergeant and I found his stories of service in the 1930s both interesting and amusing.

On a night in late May I was called to a hurriedly convened meeting at Company headquarters. From intelligence, as yet unconfirmed, it was thought that the Haganah would launch a full-scale assault on Arab forces at 6 o'clock the following morning and to avoid heavy crossfire we were to withdraw to a warehouse on the harbour side if the intelligence was correct. Later, Sergeant Duxbury and I crept out and, under cover of darkness, approached the Haganah camp above us and about midnight crawled to the wire to see if we could see any special activity. Undoubtedly everyone was awake at the camp but there was no evidence of any breakout. We crawled back out of sight and returned to our platoon house where we completed arrangements to leave at dawn. At 5.30 two carriers and a number of 3-tonners drove up and within half an hour we had completely removed ourselves from our outpost, which had

Platoon Headquarters, Haifa – Platoon Sgt Duxbury.

Platoon Commander.

been so convenient for weeks but would have been completely isolated when hostilities commenced. We were soon at the warehouse by the harbour and at 6 o'clock the Haganah opened a huge offensive on Arab posts in and round Haifa and, we later learned, throughout Palestine.

For some three days heavy house-to-house fighting took place throughout central Haifa and we defended our warehouse and an area south of the harbour known as Peninsula Barracks. We were not directly involved in the conflict although in an effort to regain the initiative our Commanding Officer, John Chandos-Pole, was badly wounded in the arm while patrolling in a carrier in the centre of the town. It was brave but perhaps foolhardy. Some weeks before I had had an interview with Colonel John in which he had asked me whether I would like him to recommend me for a regular commission. I can remember feeling that while life in Palestine was exciting, the thought of years of London duties did not appeal to me. It was popularly believed that 'The War' had brought conflict in the world to an end, and there would be little active service in the future. How wrong we were – although I do not regret my decision. I had considered the matter carefully and told Colonel John that I would not seek a permanent commission.

Following the declaration of the State of Israel, our Battalion withdrew to Peninsula Barracks and it was announced that the Battalion would shortly move to Tripoli where some unrest still persisted in Libya under King Idris after the country's liberation from Italy.

We had little to do of purpose at Peninsula Barracks, and I had to hand over my platoon to my successor, Bill Crossley (later Lord Somerleyton), who had recently come out from England with Richard Gibbs (whose house, Tyntesfield, has recently become a focus of National Trust interest). I had enjoyed a year with my platoon and felt a bond of great loyalty – in particular to my 'batman', Guardsman Bernard Crossland, whom I met again many years later in Leeds.

As luck would have it, the *Strathnaver*, a luxury liner just preparing for its first cruise after the war but still a troopship, was in Haifa and I sailed back to England in cruise-like fashion with a small group of brigade officers including Colonel Hector Bolitho, whom I was to meet again at his delightful home near Penzance in Cornwall (and in whose local village the inn is called 'The Coldstreamer'). We sailed through the Greek Islands, first to Salonica and then via Piraeus to Malta, and docked at Southampton on a warm summer's evening.

Having given a great deal of thought to what I should do next, and with a place at Trinity Cambridge waiting for me, I agonised over the choices. In what may have been the greatest mistake of my life, or possibly guided me to

My parents' everyday view of Housel Bay and The Lizard lighthouse from Tresawle.

Housel Bay at low tide. A painting by the author.

a world which I later enjoyed, I wrote to the Bursar of Trinity to say that I would not be taking up my place there (nor the Ackroyd scholarship). I have often pondered on how different things might have been had I gone up, but I was in part propelled by the thought that after a lifetime of school I didn't want to return to a college having seen life 'outside'. I have only once visited Trinity when, thirty years or more later, I lunched with the Master after a correspondence about his armorial porcelain, and an introduction from his sister Iris, who owned a service inherited from her husband's family, the Portals (and whose brother-in-law, Lord Portal, had been Chief of the Air Staff throughout most of the war). It was an exciting moment to meet Lord Butler.

Filled with the thought of entering industry, particularly one which had a rich history, life seemed poised to move forward successfully: one in which I had been offered an immediate opening to train for management. I wrote to the Chairman, Keith Trenchard-Cox, and accepted the offer to join Bridport Industries in the autumn.

Much of the summer we spent at Tresawle, my mother's house on the cliffs at The Lizard, where the lighthouse on England's most southerly point shone into our bedrooms, but where the only light at home was provided by oil lamps in the days before electricity reached the houses near Housel Bay and it was necessary to pump water with a hand pump each day for half an hour into the tank in the roof. I somehow felt like relaxing and looked forward to the future, for I was now twenty.

CHAPTER 6

Bridport

Arriving in Dorset at the beginning of October 1948, I found myself, for the first time in my life, unbound by rules and free to choose how I lived, how I worked and how I spent my spare time. My salary for the first year as a management trainee in Bridport Industries – a quoted company with about two thousand employees and another three thousand or more outworkers – was £20 per month. Although I had met personally all the directors and was related to two, this was considered a fair salary for such a job.

The first problem was lodgings, and after a short period in the home of a friend I moved to a house in South Street, where I was to live for the next three and a half years. My ground-floor room at Mrs Geeves' was well furnished, with ample breakfast and full evening meal, costing £12 per month. The rest of my salary was mine: it was my only income.

Bridport Industries had been formed from the amalgamation of four of the six principal netting and cordage firms in the town, the oldest dating from 1660. Most had been run until recent years by family dynasties, but the increasing advent of expensive machinery in spinning, rope making and net making had required capital beyond the means of some families.

The momentum with which this had happened was illustrated by the family of the Vice Chairman, Campbell Edwards, whose grandfather in the mid 19th Century sold twine from the back of his wagon (it was always said that the difference between a one penny ball of twine and a two penny ball was that the hole was bigger in the latter).

His son 'WS' was a remarkable man who, after a disagreement at a major football match in the 1880s as to whether the ball had scored a goal (gone under the bar) or missed (gone over), with the help of a Colonel Brodie had designed a net which would put an end to such disputes. Standard tennis nets were also in their infancy, and within thirty years he was to be the leading maker in the world of these now essential sports nets, including a contract at Wimbledon which lasted for decades. It was clear, too, that it was easier to practice cricket with cricket nets, and later golf in golf nets. After the Great War, his friendship with Jack Hobbs saw an annual cricket match in Bridport in which the world's leading batsmen would play.

The rapid development of sports nets between 1880 and 1960 was matched in other parts of Bridport Industries by the huge development of the fishing

71

industry in many areas of the world. Bridport's netting machines tied at least 20 million knots a day and the vast sheets of netting were cut into trawls and drift nets, sprout nets and agricultural netting, and, during wartime, camouflage netting. The outworkers created billiard pockets and lorry nets and hundreds of miles of railway rack netting, while increasingly nets were used for safety on building sites. Markets were in almost every country of the world.

The principal raw materials before the war were hemp and flax; the companies did not usually buy ready-made twine, but thousands of tons of raw hemp and flax which was spun into yarn and then twisted into twine so that it could either be further twisted into cordage or made into netting. Until the 19th Century, flax had grown in the local valleys and been harvested for the local trade.

The sheets of netting themselves were cut and shaped and bound; the flax, hemp and cotton nets preserved in tar or other preservatives. Most were pre-packed into bundles so that, say, Edwards Sports Net Company might have between twenty and fifty thousand nets ready at the beginning of the season to supply to such wholesalers as Slazengers and En-tout-Cas, or the fishing net companies could supply miles of drift netting or finished trawls in many meshes suitable for catching any fish from herring to salmon or North Sea cod – to any market in the world. The mesh was usually crucial, for many countries had strict regulations even then to preserve fish stocks and meshes were measured to one eighth of an inch.

The great majority of all the camouflage nets in the Second World War came from Bridport and the additional work of threading and dying the 'skrim' from sand colour to arctic forest-green provided work for thousands at times of stress like Suez. Nor should the humble fruit cage net or sprout net be forgotten, and these had been used in increasing quantities to protect and pack fruit.

By the early 1950s the advent of artificial fibres – then nylon and terylene – transformed some departments (for instance, doing away with the need for preservatives in some cases) and the old type of nets gave way slowly to new types. Safety nets for building sites, and cargo nets for both lorries and aeroplanes, were soon all made of synthetic fibres.

In Bridport, Joseph Gundry and Company, still a private firm who owned some of the smaller companies, kept rivalry at a high level. This competition stood us in good stead: for honed on competitive sales, Bridport was able to prosper in world markets: always in quality and usually in price.

*   *   *

On joining the company I was one of three management trainees, the others being my cousin Anthony Sanctuary, and Robert Langran, a nephew of Donald Cox, the Managing Director of Hounsells. It was expected that I learn how to work every machine in our four main factories, and I started in Hounsells' spinning mill where the hours were 8 am to 6 pm. Donald Cox impressed on me the absolute need to get to know all the three hundred employees in the mill. Friday afternoons were set aside for him so that he could walk round the mill and talk to everyone, learning of the wife of one spinner or the ill child of another packer. Many of the employees had worked all their lives in the mill: Fred Brake, foreman of the twine bundling shop, was eighty-four and had worked in the same room over the mill's great waterwheel for 76 years. His assistant was a lady in her seventies who had worked with him for some decades; it was before the installation of a loud-speaker system and she sang once popular Victorian songs much of the day as she worked for the benefit of her colleagues.

The mill manager, Fred Baker, had also worked in the mill all his life (and was the son-in-law of a previous manager) and always wore a bowler hat at work. He was particularly incensed one day when he found that in the lunch hour I was reading a well-known book called *The Principles of Scientific Management*, written about 1890 by the American, Frederick William Taylor, who reorganised the Bethlehem Steel Company in the 1880s and introduced a number of more efficient work practices such as rollers for moving steel along (instead of using sixteen men) and overhead hoists to assemble parts (instead of other teams of men carrying pieces from distant stores in the works). He said that such books were 'disruptive' and would introduce entirely alien and unnecessary reorganisation and that I should no longer read the book. 'When I was a boy about 1900,' he said, 'I was working here aged ten and dared to ask the manager for a rise. He looked at me in disbelief and told me to fetch a chair from the opposite corner of the office. "Stand on it, Baker," he said – and I did – "You've had your rise, don't ever dare to ask me again, now get out."' Fred Baker was a kindly man who worked all his life in the mill and as manager rose to live in the pleasant cottage at the gate close to the waterwheel. He was understood and obeyed, and it was a happy mill.

I learned to 'card' by hand and machine, and to operate a spinning machine. The sound of hemp spinning machines roared happily all week, except for lunch time and 'baccy time' when most men went into sheds behind the mill to smoke a pipe for ten minutes. The chief engineer was a highly intelligent Bridport boy who had the misfortune to be assembling a new carding machine when it was accidentally turned on and his sleeve dragged his arm into the rollers; he was lucky to survive. Undeterred, he worked on, now with one arm, and was promoted and sent to Ireland to learn more about spinning machines at James Mackie in Belfast and become an engineer – I was to follow a similar path later.

In the other factories I learned how to work all the different types of netting machines – from the modern multi-shuttled 'Zangs' which were entirely automatic, to the ancient 'Jumpers' where twine was drawn from a single 'ball' by a long shuttle and then the operator jumped on a long lever six or eight feet long which released up to 400 hooks that fell the depth of the mesh to create a new row of netting, being followed by the shuttle again. Such machines had been in use since the 1860s and were frequently 'loaned' to 'jumpers' who would work in sheds at home and produce netting 'piecework' at so much a sheet. Pieceworkers were frequently allowed to claim payment on work started but not completed. This was nice when you were paid but you then had to 'work off a dead horse' before you could earn your next payment – in the 1920s perhaps fifteen shillings per week, but by 1950 as much as £5. Jumpers were considered the elite of the workforce between the wars and many worked all their life until they could jump no longer.

The introduction of the sports net brought many new types of work into the trade – making or fitting football nets, sewing the cotton bands on tennis nets, the invention of new types of tennis posts, the hugely enlarged carpentry shop which made goal posts, and a number of departments who shaped and joined netting for fruit cages, and golf practice nets and cricket nets. Sometimes we were called on to install them at smart cricket or golfing clubs – from Wembley to Wimbledon.

As I worked through all the factories over four years I got to know everyone, particularly when for eighteen months I was asked to take on a newly created post in the office – the costing clerk – which was to introduce a wide measure of piecework and try more 'scientific' management (shades of F. W. Taylor!). There were moments when unexpected problems arose with such innovative ideas as 'work sheets' – and the fact that many older employees could neither read nor write. The senior carpenter, Alf, could enter details on his sheet of the number of football poles he had made in a week, but the first week I was surprised to find it was '200509' poles (more than a year's supply). Discussion about the way numbers were written made it clear that this was intended to mean 'two hundred and fifty-nine'. Alf's assistant, Wilf, had never mastered mathematics at all so he always wrote on his worksheet, 'same as Alf'. (In the days before computers this was quite adequate.)

Other working moments of note were when the foreman of the tarring machine fell into the tar vat. He was pulled out unscathed and insisted on working on (although he never found his glasses) – not for nothing was he known as 'Tarry Harry'.

As many of the factories had once made cordage in open ropeworks, there was a long field between the office and the River Brit. The company's active social club had a new facility in the 1950s when two hard tennis courts were built beside the river. One evening I was playing tennis with friends and a ball fell into the river. Near the courts was a pile of unfinished metal poles (for football net supports) and I seized one and rescued the ball, carrying the heavy pole to the pile near the works upwards above my head. At that point an electricity substation for the Bridport neighbourhood of Skilling had low power lines and I touched two. After a huge flash I was able to drop the pole and run; my brand new rubber tennis shoes had undoubtedly saved my life. I had not a mark on me, but the substation and Skilling were without power all night and in the morning on my desk at the office was a neatly typed note with a black edge from someone who lived in Skilling, reading: 'Oh death, where is thy sting?'

*   *   *

But life was not all work and four areas of social life seemed to blossom in the late 1940s: the Dorchester Rugby Club, the West Dorset Young Conservatives, the Bridport Amateur Dramatic Society, and weekends and evenings with relatives and friends.

It was by chance that I found myself invited to dinner at a hotel in Dorchester in late 1948 which was held with the purpose of forming a Dorchester Rugby Club. Dorchester was fifteen miles from Bridport across the downs and either a bus or hitchhiking made it accessible. The Club was formed and an active committee of enthusiasts soon put together a list of possible matches, stretching from Eastleigh to Exeter and north to Chippenham. We trained keenly on Thursdays, and by the new year every Saturday was filled with matches against other clubs: some newly-created after the war, others with longer histories. In many cases we played the second XVs – Exeter, Taunton, Bath and Bristol, but within two years there was a match list to be proud of and players came from up to thirty miles away. One particular friend was Alan Dalton, whose size and thrust soon made him a candidate for county games. He had been in the Navy and had a delightful girl friend, Peggy, who had broken up with her husband. Alan performed an amazing feat for 1950 by bringing a small naval vessel up the Thames to Tower Bridge in a blacked-out cabin (he had been practising on the Seine). This was made possible by a new type of 'radar' – proving that one could navigate very accurately at night. As he was leaving the Navy I introduced him to my Uncle Harry in the hope that he could persuade him to join Bridport Industries. No – but he did much better and joined English China Clays at St Austel not long after as assistant to the chairman, and was later managing director and chairman himself as Sir Alan Dalton.

Dorchester fielded about six players who at one time or other played for Dorset and Wiltshire, and our matches took us further afield. I was fortunate to establish a permanent place as left wing and later fullback and in the late 1950s was captain for two good years. By then I had a small car and often travelled direct, but until about 1955 I always used the club coach, sometimes deciding to leave an away fixture early and hitchhike home. On one occasion we played at Truro, I think, and as it was about 2.30 in the morning by the time I reached Axminster – still with ten miles to go and no passing cars – I curled up on a triangle of grass beside the A35 and woke about six when there were some milk lorries passing, and one took me to Bridport.

Another winter's night I set out for home from Dorchester about eleven, after the bus arrived back from an away match, but it was snowing hard before I had covered two miles and there was no passing traffic at all. Seeing the lights of the BBC relay station on the downs I knocked on the door and a sympathetic junior manager allowed me to sleep on the floor under a radio transmitter, but made it clear that I had to leave by six because his supervisor was making an inspection then. All this worked smoothly and I soon got a lorry in the daylight.

Nearly twenty years later I was dining with educational friends as the marketing director of a Yorkshire publishing company in the smart new hotel in Lusaka, Zambia, and among the guests was the director of Zambia's radio and television station. The subject turned to football but as yet, he said, there was not the determined enthusiasm that one sometimes saw in Europe. 'I remember a snowy night about eighteen years ago when a mad rugby player, half frozen, came to our radio station because he could no longer walk the last fifteen miles home, and I let him sleep on the floor.' He was astonished when I looked him in the face and said, 'And you had to put him out in the snow again at six o'clock!'

There were many games which one can't recall, but others that one can: a weekend playing Jersey and Guernsey on a Saturday and Sunday about 1960, and a game against Gloucester for a special occasion. Then there was a match against the Bristol second XV, but their fullback had played for England earlier in the year and was rather difficult to run round, and another when I fell on a ball just as someone was about to give it a tremendous kick. The only ball he kicked was my eyeball and I spent ten days in Weymouth hospital and wore a patch for a year. (Patches tend to give one an air of authority – I was almost sorry when it was no longer needed.)

*   *   *

It was not long after I moved to Bridport that Hazel married Bob McKinnel, whose family we had known well in Lymm in Cheshire. It was a happy day and our lawn in Cheshire was covered by a marquee almost the size of the house. They soon moved to Liverpool where Bob took up his first appointment as a dentist but by the 1950s had moved to Bradninch in Devon. Within two years my father decided to retire and he and my mother moved happily to The Lizard in 1951, where we had enjoyed our holidays since returning from Nassau; they were to spend the rest of their lives at Tresawle, and by the time my father died thirty years later, having become much involved with the church, the lifeboat and politics, he almost felt he was a true Cornishman.

In Bridport politics were at first as much a social pleasure as a serious occupation, but joining the Bridport Young Conservatives soon gave one a feeling of understanding and as the agent, Colonel Shirley, and his assistant agent and later wife, Kit Rowe, were very friendly and encouraging, a social occupation became more serious. Helping to organise Young Conservative and later West Dorset Conservative functions was interesting, and the spare time of one whole winter was taken up in writing the questions for a series of quizzes and travelling twice a week by car to different parts of the West Dorset constituency as chairman of the quiz. The member for Dorset was Simon Wingfield-Digby – for some time Civil Lord of the Admiralty – and as one became involved with fetes and dinner dances throughout the constituency, one enjoyed it more; this was made easier because Campbell Edwards was a vice chairman of the Division, which I later became myself.

All this led to more serious politics: to regional conferences and speaking occasions and even dinners at Simon Digby's home, Hayden Gate at Sherborne (on one evening there were only two other members of Parliament present – one being the chairman of the Conservative Backbenchers Committee). It was inevitable that this gave rise to the thought that one day one might try to enter politics professionally oneself; certainly I had discussions with Colonel Shirley along these lines, and during the years from 1958 to '62 attended party conferences in Blackpool, Scarborough, Llandudno and Bournemouth. But other factors were to intervene and it was not to be.

*   *   *

Although all my spare time three or four days a week was taken up with rugby and politics, living in Dorset was almost like going home, for there were many family links stretching back into the past and at least half a dozen houses where cousins and uncles lived, and one increasingly met them and their friends.

It was only a few months after I started at Bridport that my Uncle Harry and Aunt Eileen gave a dinner party at the Bull Hotel and later a dance for my twenty-first birthday; it was to be an occasion with far-reaching consequences in various ways. They had given me as a birthday present a copy of Fox-Davies' monumental book *The Art of Heraldry* – it was to be the starting point of my heraldic library, built over fifty years, which has saved countless hours of time by enabling me to solve problems at home without recourse to public libraries. It also spurred me on to spend any spare cash on reference books.

The guests included most of Harry and Eileen's friends who lived in West Dorset including Sir Philip Colfox (who had, for many years, been MP for West Dorset) and his wife and son John, and Admiral Sir Dudley and Lady North and, I think, two of their daughters, Mary and Elizabeth. Admiral North had been the Commander on HMS *New Zealand* at the Battle of Jutland (when Uncle Harry was a midshipman) and Captain of the *Renown*, which took the Prince of Wales on a tour of Australia and New Zealand in 1920, before commanding the 1st Cruiser Squadron. He had later served as Admiral of the Royal Yachts under George V, Edward VIII (whose naval ADC he was) and George VI, becoming Commander-in-Chief North Atlantic at the outset of the war based at Gibraltar.

It fell to him, on the orders of the Admiralty, to send Admiral Somerville to sink the French fleet in the harbour at Oran – a task which disturbed him greatly because he both knew and liked the French admirals and did not feel that this order by Churchill would have the right long-term effect. This caveat was known to the Admiralty, for he had urged a different plan.

A few months later a powerful French cruiser squadron approached Gibraltar at full speed from Toulon. Sir Dudley signalled both the Admiralty and the British Embassy in Madrid to ask if they wished him to stop their passage. A number of repeated messages went unanswered because the Admiralty coding department was a day or two behind with their work and, in the absence of orders to the contrary, Admiral North allowed them to pass and they sailed southwards out of his area along the African coast. A few days later the French squadron arrived at the Port of Dakar and interrupted a plan by Churchill to seize part of French West Africa. This infuriated Churchill and quite unjustly Admiral North was removed from his command and returned to England where he became a major in the Home Guard. Later in the war he was reinstated as Admiral in charge of air sea rescue in the North Sea.

Uncle Harry and many others knew this well and a group of his fellow admirals had petitioned the Admiralty to put matters right, but it wasn't until Macmillan became Prime Minister in the late 1950s that Admiral North was given an 'Amend Honourable' with the reluctant agreement of Churchill. A number of books were written about it: the first by Noel Monks, *That Day In Gibraltar*. I was there when he met Dudley and stayed the night at his home. The whole affair cast a shadow of sadness over the last twenty years of his life. His wife, Eilean, was a fascinating, kind and broadminded person, brought up as the daughter of a housemaster at Harrow.

But the party in January 1949 was to be a stepping stone to many other occasions in villages near Bridport (I usually employed a bicycle to get there) and usually to Netherbury, five miles north of Bridport, where it was a treat to have lunch or tea and get to know their daughters better – particularly the youngest, Elizabeth.

In my first few years in Bridport I was an active member of the local Amateur Dramatic and Operatic Society which put on either one or two shows a year, the operatic presentation frequently being by Gilbert and Sullivan which played at the local cinema for a week near Easter. Much more exciting was the decision of the Borough to celebrate the 700th anniversary of its incorporation in 1253. Bridport Industries published an illustrated book called *The Bridport Story* which inevitably drew attention to the netting and cordage industry and included numerous illustrations inside their factories which I knew so well. Sports netting was given a prominent place, and there was a 14th Century illustration and a record of a man 'playing a game popular in the south of England' known variously as 'creag' or 'cricce' in which he defended a target against a hurled ball with a 'cryce' – a piece of wood shaped like a broadsword. (The term 'stabbed with a Bridport dagger' meant hanged, for the trade had made hangman's rope since the earliest times.)

In the summer, the Borough held an elaborate pageant enacting a number of episodes in its history and Princess Margaret was present as the guest of honour. I played three parts in different episodes: an ancient Saxon; in the time of King John (who had sent an order in 1213 to make 'as many ropes for ships both large and small and as many cables as you can, and twisted yarns for cordage …'), and in the time of Henry VIII. Undoubtedly the best part I was given was as King John's court jester, for I was able to turn cartwheels and wave my jester's wand near the Princess's face. As she sat in the front row of the stand she said, 'I'm glad we don't have court jesters nowadays.'

*   *   *

The gathering pace of learning the machinery for manufacturing in Bridport's factories saw me posted to Belfast in the summer of 1949 to spend twelve weeks as a trainee at James Mackie & Company. I lodged with Mrs McCracken at the top of the Crumlin Road and caught the tram to work each morning at 7.30. As a management trainee of a customer I was put under the charge of a dynamic director called John Gailey. As I first entered his office overlooking a sea of factory roofs it was impossible not to notice a large painted label: 'There's no fun like work.' Indeed, John Gailey was reputed to start at 6 am and leave at 9 pm each day.

Seeing all the processes which created the machines which were in Bridport, and feeling that I knew the operative purpose of each nut, cog and hook, made every day at Mackies fascinating. Nor did it escape me that the hum of activity was also driven by the Mackie family themselves – there were, I think, five brothers in active management of the company, some of whom had sons. In particular one, Grenville Mackie, was very kind and after a few weeks I was spending weekends on his yacht and sometimes at their estate in the country in Northern Antrim, where I remember they had classical music played to their dairy herd as it was milked because they were certain that the contented cows yielded more and sweeter milk (such progressive ideas were then in their infancy).

With their encouragement I spent a long weekend walking along part of the northern coast of Ulster from Portrush to Ballycastle. It is a fascinating stretch of coastline with fine views and the ruins of a number of castles, not to speak of the Giants' Causeway and villages like Ballintoy. Although by no means the direct route, I kept as near to the sea as possible and the most exciting hours were at Dunluce Castle which, at that time, was not apparently closely monitored and to my surprise I found it possible to climb to the top of one of the ruined gables taking numerous photographs and then clambering down the cliff to the great cavern beneath the castle which joined the sea and had enabled those besieged to be supplied by sea, even when completely cut off by land. Sleeping for two nights at cottages for a few shillings, including an excellent dinner and catching a bus back to Belfast on Monday, was a very pleasant way to spend a weekend.

I returned to London via the ferry from Larne to Stranraer and shared a cabin with a young Coldstream cadet (who also caught the same train to London) called Lord Bingham. We had some friends in common and he invited me to stay with him when I returned to Ireland one day. Although that never came to pass, we were to exchange Christmas cards for a few years and I met him again on the train to Pirbright when I was bound for a 'Retired Officers Course'. In due course he succeeded his father as the Earl of Lucan and I only saw him again once in London in the early 1970s before his disappearance at the time his family nanny was murdered.

Back in Bridport I found myself increasingly drawn to visits to Netherbury. Elizabeth and I went to dances together, and I would sometimes cycle to Netherbury Church on Sunday mornings and inevitably end at Netherbury House with the Norths for lunch. In the spring of 1951 Elizabeth moved to London, taking a secretarial job at the Masonic Hospital, and soon I found more excuses to go there at weekends, sometimes staying with her brother, Roger, who was determined to be a composer, later (and still) living at Strand-on-the-Green in Chiswick. His flat for a while was immediately below an avant-garde writer called John Osborne. (I remember at that time that Roger's father, through an old friendship with Noel Coward, tried to get him a well-paid job, and later Roger was offered a post as assistant music master at Harrow. Such initiatives, however, were firmly rejected as 'musical suicide'. I well understand now, but at the time it seemed to me an opportunity lost!) Roger had been at school at Harrow and that winter acted in a school production of a Shakespeare play. Elizabeth and I were present on the first night and in the seats in front of us were two young Harrovians who were to become King Hussein of Jordan and the ill-fated King Faisal of Iraq.

The Norths kindly invited me to spend Christmas with them in 1951, which I was delighted to do. Elizabeth's sister, Mary, was also there with her boyfriend, John Grigg, whose father, Lord Altrincham, had been a long-time friend of Dudley North and fellow ADC to Edward, Prince of Wales, in the 1930s. John was later to surprise the establishment with articles criticising the role of royalty – but Mary did not marry him.

Shortly after Christmas I proposed, and to my delight Elizabeth accepted me; much of the spring of 1952 was taken up by preliminary planning for a wedding in September. I already knew Elizabeth's relatives well and particularly liked her aunts: Carol Graham, who had been a Deaconess in the Church of South India; Sheila Stewart, who would turn up for a weekend on the back of her son, Jeremy's, motor cycle and had been the first woman announcer in the BBC (she was later to marry again and for many years had her own radio show in Clearwater, near Tampa in Florida), and Elizabeth Bankes, whose husband Michael was a surviving member of the family who had lived at Corfe Castle in the Middle Ages and whose son was Graham Rhys-Jones; their only brother had been killed in the First War, having won a DSO.

In the works at Bridport I was by now a junior manager, with responsibilities for work planning and efficiency. This was a new appointment and rather surprised (and sometimes irritated) the senior works manager, Bill

Captain Dudley North with the Prince of Wales on tour in the East, 1920,
on HMS *Renown*. It was traditional that officers assisted with re-coaling the boilers
– a task not to everyone's liking.

Wedding, September 1952, with parents, bride's brother, Roger North,
and best man Anthony Sanctuary.

Edwards, who was Campbell Edwards' cousin. But it was all the price of progress and was accepted in good heart by all levels of factory management – few were ever in a union as they preferred to trust the time-honoured system of 'talking to Mr Bill' when he was walking round the factory to anything else. The chief engineer, Sid Norman, was another cousin of both Campbell and Bill, and certainly there were many other relationships by marriage throughout the works.

As the summer blossomed and 6th September loomed, more time was spent on planning the wedding at Netherbury and soon presents started to arrive which were stacked in a room on display behind the house. The bridesmaids, all of whom I have loved ever since, were Caroline and Miranda, the children of Elizabeth's eldest sister, Sue, and her husband Basil Watts (who had won a Military Cross after Arnhem and was now a company executive), and Georgina and Euphan, the children of Anne Lockie and Mark Sanctuary, two of my cousins. Georginia is now married to Henry Maude, while Euphan married John Davies, physician to Winchester College. My cousin, Anthony Sanctuary, was my best man, a pleasure I was able to reciprocate when he later married Frances, who still lives in Dorset. Anthony was for many years a director of Bridport Industries and Frances became much interested in the history of the netting and cordage industry and Bridport's museum.

Netherbury Church was the perfect setting and was followed by a delightful party under a tent at Netherbury House with all the usual speeches and the warmest send off from our parents and friends. Elizabeth and I spent the night in a London hotel, then after a train journey to Harwich we took a ferry to the Continent and a long train journey to Austria, spending two very happy weeks on our honeymoon at a hotel above the lake at Millstatt See.

CHAPTER 7

Of Armorials and Ancestry

It was a busy return to Bridport, moving what furniture we had into our new home in a road overlooking North Mills. I think our first overnight guest was John Bourdon-Smith, who by now was touring the country in search of antique silver. Although my antique interests were largely limited to table glasses of which I had collected a very small number, spurred on by Uncle 'Peter' (Campbell) Sanctuary who collected and occasionally wrote on the subject for antiquarian journals, John struck a chord with me when he showed me various coats of arms on pieces of silver he had bought and wondered if, with my meagre knowledge of heraldry, I could discover who they were made for. In fact I even offered to write a letter to each prospective buyer – and the agreed reward was ten shillings per letter plus 5% of the sale price if sold.

John would send a parcel of half a dozen pieces of silver and I would work out the original owners and take a photograph. It soon became a most absorbing spare time occupation with what today would be considered a fortune in antique silver being posted back and forth. My letters were posted in London after being carefully typed by Elizabeth.

We were quite surprised how well this new occupation suited us, and as we never had any money to spare, it paid for a few luxuries and the gradual building of an heraldic library which became more useful and comprehensive as the parcels of silver arrived by post, or on the back of John's motorcycle. One day this was to lead to an even greater surprise.

Among other pieces in one parcel was a George III teapot which I found to have the arms of Trollope impaling Annesley – my own x4 great-grandparents. Their son had been a captain in the army who had died young in 1799 on the Walcheron Expedition leaving a posthumous son. His elder half-brother was later Admiral of the Fleet Sir Henry Trollope, while his uncle was the 4th Trollope Baronet and great-grandfather of Anthony Trollope the novelist. The teapot would have cost £50, a sum I could not possibly afford, but I told my Uncle Harry who could, and some years later he generously gave it to me. This, however, was perhaps the principal trigger in a train of events which was to lead to far-reaching changes in my own life over the next twenty years.

Everyday life in Bridport continued as before. Elizabeth and I enjoyed a pleasant social life and were frequently at Netherbury where her father, now approaching eighty, was increasingly less mobile, and on occasions I was able to drive him on longer journeys to see friends outside Dorset. One such occasion was when he asked me on a Saturday to drive him to Chichester to see a very old friend, Admiral James.

Admiral James was better known to his friends by his nickname 'Bubbles', for as a boy he had been painted by the artist Millais, sitting blowing soap bubbles. The rights for this picture had, in turn, been acquired by Pears Soap and for many years been used in their advertising programme for their soap. It was, perhaps, one of the most successful advertising campaigns of the 1870s and '80s, but Bubbles James had had to live with this story throughout his naval career. We talked over lunch and well into the afternoon of naval operations at the turn of the century and the Mediterranean Fleet in the 1880s and '90s. I was glad that I had a great-uncle in the Navy at that time – Jack Glossop – and so didn't feel completely left out. But it was an interesting day and the last time he and Dudley met.

It was about this time too that Dudley and Eilean decided to leave Netherbury and move to the lodge at the recently sold estate of Parnham near Beaminster (for over a century the home of the Oglander family and much more recently the centre for carpentry excellence run by John Makepiece).

They were able to enclose the lodge and part of the driveway itself with hedges and turn it into a garden. In fact the period-style lodge to the great Elizabethan house made a perfect home and was much more easily managed than Netherbury House. There were comfortable guest bedrooms and a tall flagpole from which Dudley frequently flew his flag in naval fashion. Not only did the Norths move, but Elizabeth and I found Pear Tree House in the village of West Milton near Powerstock. Uncle Peter had lived at the other end of the village since before the war and the old mill was purchased by Aunt Bunny and her retired husband Max Brander, who stocked the swimming pool with trout so that the stream should provide good fishing.

We bought Pear Tree House for £2,800 and the former owners, Mr and Mrs Surtees Lugg, also sold us their car, a 1935 model Hillman with less than 8,000 miles on the clock, for an additional £240 (they had only driven about twenty miles per week throughout the war). We moved in the early summer of 1954, and our eldest daughter, Philippa, was born on my sister's birthday in late November. It was a busy year and I had my first real taste of management as Assistant Manager of the netting factories of Bridport Industries and a first real salary to match: at first £1,000 and later £1,500 per year – we almost felt rich.

*   *   *

Having one's own home and a car to drive into Bridport each day led to many changes. We were able to invite friends to stay and I spent a considerable time tidying the garden and orchard. Although very sound in structure, with its well-laid thatched roof, the house needed some redecorating. There was room to put up more bookshelves and add to the growing heraldic library, and with so many relatives in the village and in Powerstock – where my great-grandfather had been the rector for fifty years – I was anxious to expand my knowledge of my own ancestors while I could consult earlier generations, as well as continuing to provide information on other arms in general, including John's silver.

Among our earlier guests was Mr J., long retired from Belmont School, but somewhat lonely in his home near Petersfield. He was surprised at the considerable library of notes I had built up through working on John's silver, and an idea taking shape of writing a book on armorial silver. 'But it's so much better if the armorials have colour,' he said, 'I know a man in Minehead who has a collection of Chinese porcelain with coats of arms – you ought to go to see him and see if he needs any help.' It sounded rather far-fetched, but a few weeks later I drove over to Minehead and met Cecil and Muriel Bullivant for the first time. It was difficult to take in the scale of his collection of more than a thousand pieces of Chinese armorial porcelain and he asked if I would be interested in coming again soon and staying the weekend. This was quickly agreed, and undoubtedly it changed the course of my life.

At the time I knew nothing of 'famille verte' or 'famille rose' (the painted enamels used on Chinese porcelain, of which the earlier translucent colours, the principal one being green, flourished in the early 18th Century; and opaque enamels, of which pink was the principal hue, after about 1724). But any work I had so far undertaken on heraldry was little more than a hobby, which sometimes provided pocket money. With our family under way it was still essential to provide an adequate standard of living, and as I found myself offered more senior posts at work, I envisaged a time, not too far off, when I might be offered a directorship at Bridport Industries, from which my ambition might take me further. Certainly, in the mid 1950s, Bridport was the centre of my world.

Cecil Bullivant was by then in his seventies and had led a very varied and interesting life. At first a journalist in the 1890s, he had taken to writing what were known at the time as 'Penny Dreadfuls' under the pseudonym 'Mrs Henry Everard'. These were often about damsels in distress in far away lands where the hero would, in the end, 'ride off into the sunset' with his bride. By 1914 he had written over ninety novels, but at the beginning of the First War was sent to the Admiralty as Secretary to the Fifth Sea Lord. A few years ago,

Cecil and Muriel Bullivant, Minehead.

Armorial porcelain cupboard in a guest bedroom in Minehead.

in the late '90s, I found to my surprise in the bookshop at Paddington Station a pile of books for sale called *Boys Own Handbook* by Cecil H. Bullivant (reprinted in Finland in 1994). With his own hand-drawn illustrations he covered in fifty-six chapters such important and fascinating subjects as 'How to make a secret money box'; 'How to make a submarine boat'; 'How to make a flagstaff'; 'Leaf skeletons'; 'How to patent an invention'; 'Advertisement writing'; 'The making of a botanical collection'; 'Out and about with a geological hammer'; 'How to make a fresh-water aquarium' and 'How to keep silkworms'. Every page contained a jewel of advice – the first chapter on carpentry being headed 'Plain talk from the bench'.

During the war he met Algernon, later Sir Algernon, Tudor-Craig who had also spent time at the Admiralty. While Sir Algernon first started to write about Chinese armorial porcelain and made a catalogue of the thousand services of which he knew (published in 1925 as *Armorial Porcelain of the 18th Century*) Cecil Bullivant returned for a time to journalism; but as Sir Algernon opened a shop at 100 Knightsbridge in London, which he called 'Century House', Cecil also decided to become an antique dealer, specialising in furniture and Chinese porcelain.

Sir Algernon retired in 1929 at the time of the Depression and Cecil bought much of his stock of porcelain. Throughout the early 1930s he spent much of the time near Norwich where he built up a large clientele (including the Marquess of Townshend who disposed of a number of armorial services) before moving to Looe in Cornwall, where his business gradually declined and finally closed during the Second World War. His first wife having died during the 1930s, he remarried in 1945 Muriel, the daughter of a wealthy brewer, and with her encouragement he re-established his business in armorials, working from their new home in Minehead.

Cecil was anxious that I should write a new book on armorial porcelain. I said that I understood the armorials but that he would have to write the chapters on the porcelain, about which I knew nothing. When, ten years later, I had completed about half of the then-known services, he said one day, 'David, if you write the chapters, I'll write the foreword.' Later again, shortly before the book was published in 1974, I said to him, 'May I dedicate the book to you, Cecil?' He was delighted. In fact I had written it all.

But in 1955 I was a new father and an ambitious manager in Bridport Industries, and all this was hardly dreamed off. I still identified some things for John and occasionally heard from other London galleries as when, to my surprise, Sparks of Mount Street asked for some advice on a Dutch service of porcelain and later that year I was even more surprised to get a letter from Lord Perth with a number of questions about armorial porcelain and a piece decorated with ships. (He had, I think, bought something at Sparks and they had given him my name.) As a manager I had frequently visited London and one evening was invited to see Lord Perth's collection in Hyde Park Gardens. It was the start of a long acquaintance, turning to a friendship which lasted until his death more than forty-five years later.

Building up information on armorial porcelain required close and repeated reference to each piece, and this was only possible by photography. I created a photographic 'corner' at Pear Tree for any pieces I was fortunate enough to find myself (my first purchase was a plate of the 1737 Chapman service which I found in a shop near Penzance; the honest shopkeeper told me it was 'Samson ware' and reduced the price from £1.18s. to £1.10s.), but most of the work was done during the summer months at Minehead, for during the winter I still played rugby (although sometimes driving from a match straight to the Bullivants to get in a few more hours work). In all I had photographed and identified some 600 pieces with different armorials at Minehead by the late 1950s and then asked Cecil to introduce me to as many collectors as he knew, travelling to see them when there was time.

Sophie arrived safely in 1957, although not without some problems which were greatly helped by the kindness of Campbell and Pauline Edwards, whose only daughter, Amanda, was now my godchild. Everyday life became increasingly complex, but there were high moments – such as when an old warehouse in Bridport was pulled down and I was able to buy the beautiful cut stone to create extensions to our home; there were also low points – as when one day, on a bend on an A-road, (Philippa was still very small and securely wrapped in blankets) the back door of our car flew open and the bundle rolled into the long grass at about twenty-five miles per hour. As we raced back we heard a wail and a completely unharmed daughter was restored to her parents. Not long afterwards we got a (nearly) new car.

*   *   *

Excitement over the growing volume of information about armorial porcelain was still tempered by no clear idea as to how all these illustrations and the copious notes written in long-hand could be turned into a book. But Cecil encouraged me to drive far and wide to see collectors whom he had known well in the past. He now seldom left home, although he had a large old Daimler in the garage, but said to me one day, 'David, what *is* a motorway?' His own dealing days were almost done and although still undoubtedly the largest buyer of armorial porcelain since the war, covering all the sales, his last major auction venture was when in 1959 he bought the early Chinese

Imari Walker service of 61 pieces, with numerous rare bottles and shaped dishes, for £390. A new name was appearing in this field in the London salerooms: the remarkable Mrs Helen Glatz, who had a shop in London and when she rolled up her sleeves to wash dirty porcelain, the printed number that had been tattooed in Ravensbruck was clearly visible. Helen Glatz had no car but travelled country-wide in a London taxi which she often filled with armorial porcelain from Falmouth to Aberdeen. We never knew Mr Glatz, but she had a very pretty daughter who was usually as scared of her as were most other people – but if tough and firm, she was scrupulously honest.

Leaving Elizabeth with the children at summer weekends I would drive furiously with my photographic equipment to visit collectors in Yorkshire or Birmingham, Norwich or Buckinghamshire; or castles in Scotland, Northumberland and Gloucestershire. The kindness I received was heart-warming and many of those who helped me then are still friends today – or now their families are. In particular a journey to Pontefract to see Phil Cooke was a turning point. He had collected all his life, building on a collection started by his father, and I made arrangements to return, not realising that by the time I did so I should be living much nearer.

Clive Rouse in Buckinghamshire was an experienced man in the art field and the world's leading authority on mediaeval (and earlier) paintings on church walls. He knew the details of paintings in remotest Anatolia and frequently discovered new stories in English churches where early mediaeval paintings had been covered up in a later or puritan time and were long forgotten under layers of paint or whitewash. His collection of porcelain numbered nearly a thousand pieces but as a single man (who died just short of a hundred in the 1990s) purchases were often left in wardrobe drawers with a piece of newspaper between, or in a pile on a study table already covered with letters, some dated many years before. On a sideboard in the drawing room stood a photograph of a very pretty girl – Julie Christie was his god-daughter (alas, I never met her!).

Maurice Overton, another exceptional collector of Chinese porcelain, had a large home in Edgbaston, Birmingham. His family had been friends of the Bullivants for two or three generations, for although Cecil's family was well-documented in the reign of Elizabeth I, his immediate ancestors had had links with the Birmingham metal trade, and there had been a company called 'Bullivant Wire Nippers'.

A fascinating long weekend in Norwich introduced me to members of the Levine family who besides collecting Chinese porcelain were leading dealers and restorers of very fine furniture. I spent a day with two of their restorers, who only used Elizabethan or early Georgian type tools and methods, so that any work done was impossible to tell from the production of centuries earlier. This occasionally led to situations where the work was so expert that it became impossible some years later, in a house in East Anglia, to know which was the additional chair that completed Chippendale's set of twelve, although on any larger piece they used their own initials in 17th/18th Century style, carved behind a drawer or leg so that those who knew could tell.

The Grand Hotel at Cromer had belonged to the Willins family since the early 20th Century and part of the collection of Mr Willins was displayed in a great case in the main entrance. His son, John, who had been a prisoner of the Japanese during the Second World War, later had much of it in his house in a village nearby while his sisters had substantial collections in Sussex and Oxfordshire (and some is still the property of his two nieces).

In these, and many more homes, I stayed as a fellow collector (although my own collection was very small and largely confined to duplicate and damaged pieces bought from Cecil, usually for between £3 and £5).

It was exciting, too, to spend a day at Stobhall, while I was travelling for Bridport Industries to rope and netting works in Gourock and Dundee. Lord Perth had recently had the opportunity of recovering a small but ancient Drummond castle and its chapel from his distant cousin Lord Ancaster, who had been asked to repair the near-ruin by the Scottish authorities. Lord and Lady Perth had been looking for a home in Scotland, for their ancestors had lost all their rights after 1745 when the then Duke of Perth and other cousins had fought at Culloden in the army of Prince Charles Edward. David Perth's ancestors were also the Lords Strathallan and the banking Drummonds (whose principal branch was in Trafalgar Square) and his direct ancestor was a successful East India merchant who eventually returned to Scotland after being Chief of Council in Canton from 1802-06. The Viscounty of Strathallan was restored in 1824 and the Earldom of Perth in 1853. Through the death of a by-now very distant cousin, the Duc de Melfort and Earl of Perth in France in 1902, his father, Sir James Drummond, Private Secretary to the Prime Minister and from 1919-33 first Secretary General to the League of Nations, eventually succeeded as 16th Earl of Perth in 1937. David Drummond had married in 1934 Nancy Fincke (the daughter of Reginald Fincke, a very successful New York financier) and having worked in the later 1920s and early 1930s in China himself as a merchant and financier, became Earl of Perth in 1951. He was a long-term partner of Schroders and Minister of State for Colonial Affairs in Macmillan's Cabinet from 1957-62, but dedicated to his faith and the memory of the Stuart Kings.

While this was the most interesting small castle I had come to know, there were others which fascinated me – particularly Alnwick, the home of the

Percys and the Dukes of Northumberland (which had once been the home of 'Hotspur', the Earl killed at the Battle of Shrewsbury in 1403 and an ancestor of my own), and Berkeley, where the grim fate of Edward II (also a direct ancestor) could not easily be forgotten when one saw the well where the King had been kept. On quiet nights it was said that the people of Berkeley could hear the screams of the King as he was brutally murdered in 1327, in a way which would not be visible as he lay in state. I photographed the porcelain of the Berkeley family of Stratton on the mounting block in the castle courtyard.

*   *   *

With the birth of Joanna, our third daughter, in March 1960 and a new board of directors in Bridport, on which I was to sit as an assistant director, life was much busier than ever for both Elizabeth and I.

The last few years of the 1950s and the earlier years of the 1960s had seen many steps taken in my broadening interest of genealogy, history and porcelain, as well as new roles in Bridport, while Philippa, and soon Sophie, were going to their first school. But the library I was now acquiring – and had to acquire to keep pace with my amateur research into the families who had purchased this ware in China – threw open the gates to evenings when I was lost in the families of my mother and father, and indeed those of Elizabeth (although I was probably more interested in this than she was). Perhaps some details are worthwhile recounting here, although this is more for my children than any other reader, but there are various matters of general interest, and it also serves to illustrate the vast volume of Victorian and later work in history and genealogy – which frequently lies unrecognised and unused, but which can reveal so much of interest to those that care to look.

Among the North ancestors of whom I became aware were the Beechings, a banking family in Kent who were ancestors of the Dr Beeching who was the first reorganiser of the British railway network. One had married the father of Walter de la Mare, indeed Dudley was his second cousin and I was later to know well Richard de la Mare, his son, the uncle of Julian Thompson, still a director of Sotheby's.

The Norths themselves came from Walkeringham in Norfolk and were a branch of the family from whom descended Lord North, the Prime Minister, and the Barony of North. After fighting for Parliament in the mid 17th Century, their branch of the family moved to County Westmeath in Ireland (although another branch settled in America) and from the early 19th Century were in the army – Colonel Roger North was the son of Colonel Charles Napier North of the 60th Rifles, who married Fanny Beeching from Tunbridge

In the garden at Pear Tree House, West Milton.
My mother and father with Philippa and Sophie, 1960.

Wells and had five sons and a daughter, of whom Dudley was the fourth. Born in 1881, Dudley first married Eglantine Campbell, daughter of an Australian senator, but she died in 1917 and he married again in 1923 Eilean Graham, the daughter of a well-known Harrow housemaster before the First War, Edward Graham.

Eilean was a sparkling person of great talent and quick thinking whose mind was always running ahead so fast that when she typed letters there were often words missing as her thoughts ran ahead of her fingers. Her father's family were of Gartmore and her mother was the daughter of General Sir Robert McGregor Stewart, the Governor of the Bermudas from 1904-07. The Stewarts of Gortlee were a collateral line of the Earls of Galloway (and bore very similar arms) and they, in turn, stretched back to such legendary ancestors as Banquo (murdered by Macbeth about 1040).

*   *   *

My father's family was, at that time, something of a mystery to me, but over the years I have found information and consulted researchers with some success. It was never assumed that they were from any of the numerous noble families of Howard but by examining more humble records, largely in Buckinghamshire, it was possible to establish a line to about 1650, at which period it became increasingly difficult, for church registers spelled names Haward, Heward and even Hayward, when it was clear they were related. Without a great deal of extra research I could just record all the variations and parish registers and was occasionally pleased when I found another generation, almost all in the neighbourhood of Marlow and Beaconsfield in Buckinghamshire, although there is a particularly interesting graveyard near Burnham Beeches where there are numerous Howard graves going back to 1600 and one mention of a previous generation in London in Elizabethan times in the parish register, which I sought in vain.

They were almost all farmers and I found a will of an ancestor who lived near Gerrards Cross and had quite a substantial holding. It was the grandson of John Howard of Burnham, who married a German governess living in Devon as a schoolteacher, whom I have always understood was in the employ of the Duke of Bedford. Her name was Mary Mickelburg and I believe her father was a Jewish doctor in Germany (but I haven't been able to confirm this). Their son, Frederick Thomas Howard, was my grandfather, who left farming and settled in Bedford where he was first an artist and later a successful businessman and newspaper publisher. His wife was Susan Turpin Mitchell, born about 1850 at Ranscombe House, Berry Head, Brixham in

Frederick Thomas Howard (1850-1933).

Horace 'Tommy' Howard (1890-1981),
David Howard and Thomas in 1968.

Great-grandson Thomas Howard,
1992.

Devon (her neighbour being the Reverend Francis Lyte who wrote, among many other things, 'Abide with me').

Susan Mitchell's father was a modest ship owner at Brixham and his mother was called Baddeley (from which family descended the actress Hermione and later the actor Kenneth Horne). A Baddeley had married in the 18th Century the daughter of a physician to George III, Dr John Colwell, originally from Staffordshire.

But I could not have settled in Dorset among my mother's family without having the greatest curiosity concerning her parents' ancestors, through Archdeacon Thomas Sanctuary and his wife Isobel Lloyd and their daughter-in-law Mary Glossop. Isobel's father was Charles Lloyd, a professor of Mathematics and History and Bishop of Oxford, who died of a chill at the early age of 44 in 1829. On his father's side he descended from John Lloyd, born in 1638, and his wife Jane, daughter of Sir Thomas Gresham, founder of the Royal Exchange, although his father had been a country parson.

The Bishop's mother was the daughter of Nathaniel Ryder, later Baron Harrowby, by a Miss Clarke, the daughter of his father's agent – whom he left unmarried with three children when he married the daughter of the Bishop of London. He certainly did not abandon them entirely, however, and not only paid a dowry of £2,000 when his natural daughter married the country parson, Mr Lloyd, but left each £4,000 in his will, which would have the purchasing power of about half a million pounds today. What was more interesting was that Lord Harrowby was the son of Sir Dudley Ryder, a brilliant and distinguished Lord Chief Justice who died unexpectedly in 1759 before he could accept the peerage offered to him, but is still remembered by Ryder Street, called after him, in St James's, London. It seems likely that the Bishop of Oxford inherited his formidable brain power from Sir Dudley Ryder (the Bishop's elder brother won a triple first at Oxford and died 'of a brain storm' at twenty-one, while his younger brother was Dr Foster Lloyd, an economist, who, in England, was the first man to advance the theory of marginal utility).

The Bishop himself had married Mary Harriet Stapleton, whose sister, Charlotte, married Captain, later Admiral, Frederick William Beechey (the son of Sir William Beechey, the portrait painter). The two sisters were the great-nieces of Lieutenant Governor William Bull II of Charleston, South Carolina. Frederick William Beechey was a brilliant draftsman, and wrote and illustrated a book on the coast of North Africa. In 1825 he sailed to the Pacific as Captain of HMS *Blossom* to map the many coasts and islands for the Admiralty, including the coast of California, and in search of the North-West Passage, where the most easterly point they reached is today known as Beechey Island. By chance he was the first Naval officer to find the last remaining mutineer alive on Pitcairn. He stayed ten days on the island, writing an account (which is the basis of Nordoff and Hall's story of the mutiny) of what happened to the last six mutineers who escaped justice, most dying in jealous quarrels betwen 1805 and 1828. He also did various drawings of the island including one of John Adams, who gave him a small piece of wood from the *Bounty*. This Beechey gave, in the form of a box, to his brother-in-law, the Bishop of Oxford, the inscription inside reading:

This Box
made from the Wreck
of His Majesty's Ship Bounty
is presented to
Charles Lord Bishop of Oxford
as a tribute of respect and esteem
by Fred^k. Willm. Beechey
Captain R.N.

The Stapletons, who descended from an ancient Yorkshire family, had fled Charleston, South Carolina, in 1776. Colonel Stapleton was the ADC to the Lieutenant Governor, William Bull, whose niece, Catherine Beale, he married. The Stapletons settled in Ireland, and he was to loan £2,000 to a somewhat impoverished Major Wellesley from a nearby estate so that he could afford to 'buy' his regiment (an essential route to quicker promotion). I have since inherited some of the correspondence with the Duke of Wellington about this affair. The money was repaid correctly and Colonel Stapleton had breakfast with the Duke in 1816. The Duke also later corresponded frequently with Stapleton's son-in-law, Charles Lloyd, who was then the tutor to the Marquess of Douro – a somewhat unruly undergraduate at Oxford. Again this correspondence survives, as does a letter in my possession in the handwriting of the Duke dated 16th July 1829 to the widowed Mrs Lloyd:

Dear Madam,

I have the pleasure of informing you that the King has been graciously pleased to grant you a Pension on the Civil List of two hundred pounds a year Net.

I have the Honour to be, Dear Madam, your most obedient and faithful Humble Servant.

Wellington

The Beales were an early family in Marblehead, Massachusetts, where they landed in 1621 on the *Fortune*, and Catherine's grandfather, Othniel Beale, was a Charleston ship's captain who in the early 18th Century had been captured by Algerine pirates in the Bay of Biscay, but when a storm followed by a heavy fog enveloped them, the Algerine captain had sought his help to navigate the pirate ship. Three days later the fog cleared and the ship was found to be in the Thames near Gravesend! Captain Beale had an audience with the King and was given a thousand guineas for his boldness.

In fact my American ancestry was one of some interest, for besides a descent from the father of John Winthrop, first Governor of Massachusetts, the family of Othniel Beale (originally from Marblehead in the same State) married into others in South Carolina including the Draytons, and his daughter married William Bull II, the last colonial Lieutenant Governor of the State (whose father had been Lieutenant Governor before him). This story is well told in *The Oligarchs in Colonial and Revolutionary Charleston* by Kinloch Bull, Jr. with whom I later stayed when he worked in the State Department in Washington.

In the task of unmasking my own ancestry I was greatly helped by my growing library and in particular two books: the first, *Stemmata Chicheleana*, being all the descendants of Sir Robert Chichele, Lord Mayor of London, brother of the Archbishop of Canterbury, Henry Chichele, who died in 1443. This book, published in 1765, was of more general importance because the Archbishop had left his estate to All Souls College, Oxford, and by his wish any graduate of that college who was a descendant could also become a Fellow of All Souls. Three hundred years later this had become a problem for the College – the rule eventually being rescinded although not without a struggle. The book, however, was a very accurate record and my descent was through the Shirleys, Onslows and Trollopes, or alternately through the Howards, Earls of Surrey, and the de Veres. By chance, too, (although not in *Stemmata*) there is a descent also from Archdeacon Cranmer, whose brother was also Archbishop of Canterbury.

The other book which provided a great deal of information was the substantial volume of *The Plantagenet Roll of the Blood Royal* (Mortimer-Percy volume) which was published in 1911. This was the fourth volume of a series which aimed to list all the descendants of Edward III (who died in 1377), published by the Marquis de Ruvigny between 1903 and 1911. On page 400 was my mother, and her descent could be followed clearly all the way; by 1911 there were more than 90,000 descendants of Edward III, both male and female, so that such descents are rather more usual than might be believed.

It was like opening a golden book as I was able to follow a path through sometimes devious lines where cousins married cousins. Where better to start than John of Gaunt – to the Staffords, Dukes of Buckingham (more than one of whom was beheaded). The daughter of the 3rd Duke married Thomas, 2nd Duke of Norfolk, while of another line Lady Elizabeth Percy married Henry Percy – 'Hotspur' – who died in 1403 at the Battle of Shrewsbury.

The lines joined again in Henry, Earl of Surrey, who was the victor of Flodden but whose arrogance was displayed by the fact that, as son of the Earl Marshal, he had devised personal arms which put the Royal arms before those of Howard. This suggested his aspirations and so infuriated Henry VIII that he was executed. His son, the 4th Duke of Norfolk, was himself executed in 1572 and *his* third son, Lord William Howard – known in the north as 'Belted Will' – was to marry Elizabeth Dacre 'of the North' and inherit vast Dacre lands across the moors which separate England from Scotland.

Following my mother's line, Belted Will's youngest daughter Margaret Howard married Sir Thomas Cotton, son of Sir Robert (whose collection of books was to provide the foundation for the British Library), while a great-granddaughter, Frances Howard, married Sir George Downing, the architect (and notoriously unpleasant man) who built Downing Street and advised his brother-in-law, Charles Howard, Earl of Carlisle, on the building of Castle Howard. (Sir George Downing's mother was Lucy Winthrop, sister of John Winthrop, the first elected Governor of Massachusetts.)

Their daughter, Frances Downing, married John Cotton, her cousin and son of the 3rd Baronet, and soon the names were ones which I had heard mentioned so often when I was a boy. It was of interest that John Cotton's eventual heir, his daughter Frances, had vested in her the right, by an Act of Parliament in 1752, to appoint independently a 'Cottonian Trustee' to the British Museum and this right remained with our family until 1948 when it was last held by my mother's cousin, Fred Bradburne. Hereditary rights are frequently seen today as an abuse of democracy but they provided, at no cost to the nation, generations of hard work and sound opinions without the intrusion of politics and bureaucracy which so often replace one perceived evil with another more real.

Frances Cotton married William Hanbury of Little Marcle in Herefordshire and their daughter, Mary, the Reverend Martin Annesley whose great-grandfather had been the 1st Viscount Valentia. In 1761 *their* daughter married the Reverend John Trollope whose eldest son was Captain Arthur Trollope of the 40th Regiment, who died of fever while on active service aged 28 in 1799. He had enjoyed a short but interesting career, and, but for an action by his half-brother, later Admiral Sir Henry Trollope, would probably

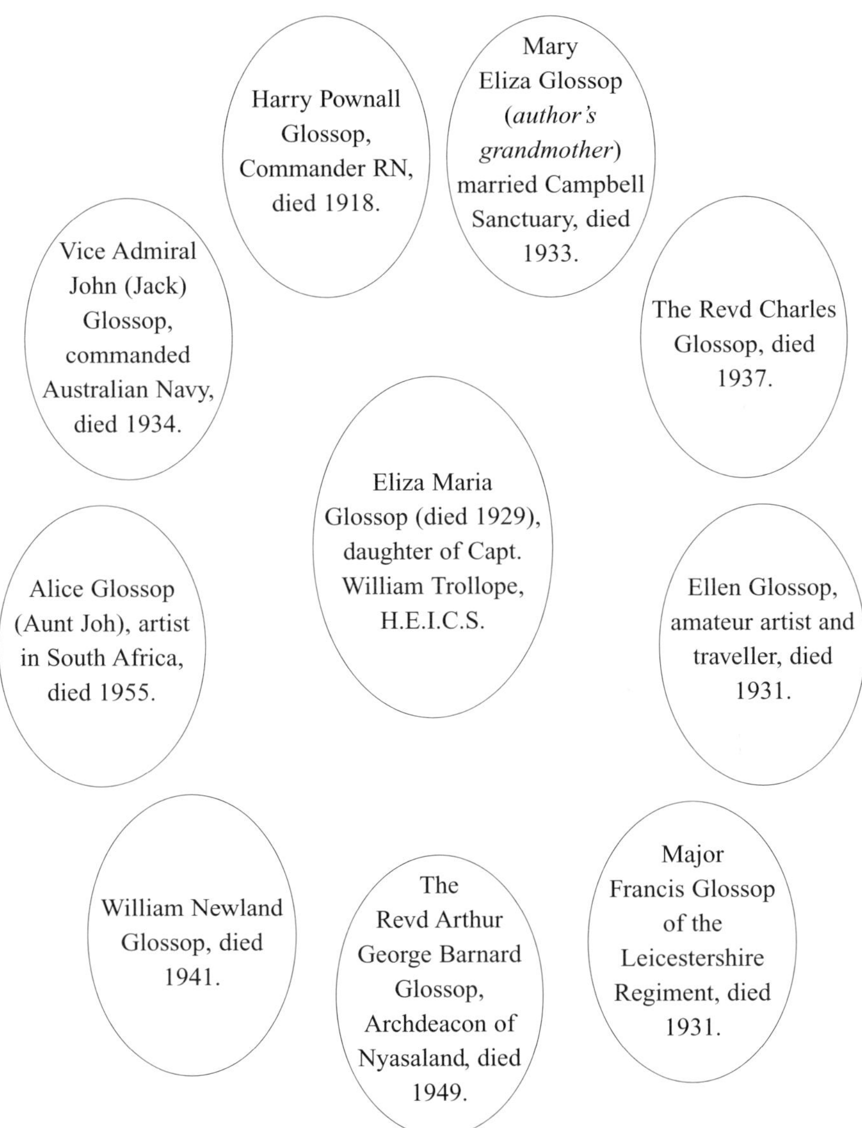

Portraits of the nine children of Great-Grandmama Trollope (*centre*) the second wife of the Revd George Goodwin Pownall Glossop (1827-74), Vicar of Twickenham. (*In order of birth, from top right clockwise.*)

have died unmarried in a French prisoner of war camp (and I would never have existed). Sir Henry had fought as a young naval officer at Bunker Hill in the American War of Independence and had then sailed to 'rescue' Lord Dunmore, the Governor of Virginia, at Williamsburg. Later, as so often happened in peacetime, he retired on half-pay as a captain to a house on the cliffs in South Wales.

One night in the late 1780s a French ship *L'Aimable Martha* on her return from a voyage to Senegal was wrecked on the Carmarthenshire coast below his house, and by dawn the bedraggled crew discovered the house and approached. In the words of Volume II of Rolfe's *Naval Biography,* '… its doors instantly flew open to the strangers, and relief was administered to them in every shape that could be devised; Captain Trollope, his lady, and domestics being all eager to show the utmost attention to those who stood so much in need of it …', all of which was gratefully acknowledged by the French officers in the account which was subsequently published (*Voyage au Senegal, ou Memoires* by Jean-Baptiste-Leonard-Durand, Paris, 1802). It continues, '… After remaining for about three weeks the officers and crew departed for Liverpool, taking with them letters of recommendation …'. Shortly after their return to France, Lord Howe received a message from the French Minister of Marine asking him to convey the thanks of King Louis to Captain Trollope.

But the story does not end there, for after the outbreak of hostilities with France, Henry Trollope again experienced active service, in particular on HMS *Glatton* which, sailing alone but armed by the new carronade, attacked a squadron of seven French ships and dispersed them after a conflict which lasted all night. Shortly before this, he had had the satisfaction of hearing from his brother (my great-great-grandfather) a heart-warming story. As a captain in the Army his transport ship had been captured by a French naval vessel; all the officers were lined up and had their names taken before being consigned as prisoners below. But to his great surprise, when he said that his name was Arthur Trollope he was at once asked if he was related to Captain Henry Trollope and on saying he was his brother, the French captain expressed his warmest friendship. The captain destroyed his uniform and asked him to dress as a merchant, and on arrival at Brest, Arthur Trollope was taken to Paris as his guest, where he was introduced both to Marat and Robespierre and after considerable 'intercession' leave was obtained for him to return to England.

The professional relationships and honour between opposing officers at that time are not always matched today – but the spirit can live on. When Sir Henry's great-nephew, Captain John Glossop, commanded HMAS *Sydney* when it sunk the German raider *Emden* in November 1914, he approached close to the battered ship now aground and sent a letter over in a small boat to Captain von Müller:

HMAS *Sydney*,
at sea
9th November 1914

To: The Captain,
HIGNS *Emden*

Sir,

I have the honour to request that in the name of humanity you surrender your ship to me. In order to show how much I appreciate your gallantry, I will recapitulate the position:

(1) You are ashore, 3 funnels and 1 mast down and most guns disabled.

(2) You cannot leave this island and my ship is intact.

In the event of your surrendering, in which I venture to remind you is no disgrace but rather your misfortune, I will endeavour to do all I can for your sick and wounded and take them to hospital.

I have the honour to be,
Sir,
Your obedient servant,

John C. T. Glossop

Captain R.N.

He received a reply and Jack Glossop boarded the *Emden*. On the very battered fo'c'sle Captain von Müller handed him his sword which Glossop reversed and handed back as a token of respect (whether this was the last naval occasion on which this was done, I do not know).

Captain Arthur Trollope, who died in 1799, had married Mary, daughter of Barnard Foord of Beverley in Yorkshire. His granddaughter, Eliza Maria

'Joh' Glossop, Lion River, Natal, in her studio about 1940.

Campbell and Mary Sanctuary with their family at Mangerton, 1923.
From left: General Max and Mary Brander (*seated*), Arthur and Evelyn Sanctuary,
Peter and Barbara Sanctuary, Harry and Eileen Sanctuary,
Tommy and Gemma Howard (*seated*).

Trollope, married the Reverend George Goodwin Pownall Glossop, Rector of West Dean in Sussex and later of Twickenham (who had previously married Mary, the sister of the collector Alfred Morrison of Fonthill, but had been left a widower with a daughter, Bertha). My grandmother was the eldest of his second family, marrying Campbell Sanctuary. One of her brothers was 'Uncle Jack', the Captain who sank the *Emden* and later as an Admiral commanded the Australian Navy; another was the Archdeacon of Nyasaland (who translated the bible into Chinyanja and caused the Cathedral to be built on Likoma Island) and one of their sisters was 'Joh' (Allerley Glossop) the well-known artist in South Africa.

It was a labour of love to trace one's ancestors from their thrones to the block, and from their castles to homesteads – but it provides a perspective and it allows you to feel that you know who you are, and that you have a responsibility to remember them.

An informal use for the newly installed top floor fire safety slings
at Bridport Industries offices.

CHAPTER 8

Net Profits and Losses

My interest in politics turned more to getting to know the West Dorset constituency and its many branches, spread thirty miles from Charmouth to Sherborne, than to the business of the political world itself. Under the guidance of Colonel Shirley, the West Dorset agent, there were speaking competitions among the Young Conservatives, of which I became the Divisional Chairman – this was useful practice for some, but not enjoyed by all. Both at political meetings and more social occasions like opening fêtes, I always felt that the audience was often as bored as the speaker by such rituals!

A few years later I had to open a fête at Bridport Industries, held on the lawns behind the tall offices. There had recently been installed new safety equipment in case of fire, including slings and fireproof cords which could automatically lower anyone from an upper window in imitation of abseiling. As the crowd waited for the fête to open, the company fire fighting team raced to the building with bells ringing and played water on a figure in pyjamas descending from an upper window towards a large full water tank placed below. Very wet, and holding an umbrella, I only had to say, 'Ladies and Gentlemen – I now declare this fête open' (the reporter for the weekly *Bridport News* nearly filled a page with photographs, which is more than could have been expected of any speech).

It was, I think, in 1956 that Bridport Industries bought the fine silk spinner and twine maker James Pearsall of Taunton, a company of their own ilk and of whom Richard Harris Barham wrote in the early 19th Century in the *Ingoldsby Legends*:

> ... and buy from Pearsalls in the City,
> Three skenes of silk –
> Colour no matter, so its pretty.

The silk trade had increasingly flourished in England since the importation of silk from China in the later 17th Century and the fibres, yarn and twine were far finer than the flax and hemp then growing in the Dorset valleys, which had been the staple raw material of Bridport and Crewkerne for a millennium. The advent of nylon and terylene in the 1950s had, however, confused the picture, for it seemed certain that it could be spun and manufactured, dyed and twisted exactly as silk (and, as production rose, at a far lower cost) and was almost indestructible – not requiring preservatives unless they were needed to protect against ultra violet light or, in Bridport's case, 'seal' the manufacture of knots so that they did not slip. It is difficult to over-emphasise the advertising potential of the nylon stocking which within a few years had swept away silk stockings into a Victorian grannybox. So it proved to be in many textile fields, including netmaking and cordage.

Bridport soon found, and I was frequently at the experimental forefront of this discovery, that a great many nylon nets were stronger, longer lasting, lighter and soon to be cheaper than the natural fibres. The purchase of James Pearsall was an immediate entrée into this market, and already they had silk machinery which could handle many types of synthetic fibres. One of Pearsall's specialist fields was silk surgical sutures for operations of many sorts including sewing eyes, which required twine so fine that it would take more than a week of continuous manufacture to fill a single small bobbin.

As a Bridport factory manager I was one of the first to visit Taunton and spent considerable time with the dynamic owner of Pearsalls, Colonel Reg Besley, who, with the Hextall family who had been shareholders for a hundred and fifty years, had rescued Pearsalls from certain dissolution as synthetic fibres took hold. We were soon using less expensive Pearsalls' twine in fine fishing nets for Canada, Iceland, Norway and elsewhere. It was not long before Reg Besley was the Managing Director of the combined Bridport Industries, spending three or four days each week in Bridport. There had previously been no managing director with group authority in Bridport.

Reg had a very open and practical mind and within a few months suggested to me that having had almost ten years of experience of factories and production that he would like me to be a sales manager reporting direct to the Sales Director, Leonard Parker, with particular responsibilities of export markets of every sort. I was surprised and pleased and readily accepted, for it altered my horizons.

The innate conservatism of much of British industry was typified to me about that time when I visited a manufacturer in Aston, Birmingham. Bridport had developed a new type of sheep netting which could not only be stretched across huge acres of sheep farming land, but which included a wire line which could be electrified so that the sheep would have no incentive to bite their way through.

A considerable sales operation was planned with Wolseley Engineering who had for some generations been the leading manufacturers of sheep shearing equipment. I visited Wolseleys in Aston and had lunch with two or three members of the board after a detailed tour of their factory. In the boardroom there was a picture of a very early car and a man standing beside it and I was curious. The company had had a very able young chief engineer who about 1905 had 'reinvented' sheep shearing by making many types of clippers much easier to handle and had, I think, even invented an engine to which the clippers could be linked so that there was a high degree of automation. This was particularly welcome in the large Australian market where hand clippers had made for generations of very hard work.

The engineer had also invented a car which was called a 'Wolseley' and suggested to the then board that they should move much of their manufacturing into car making – a new and emerging market. The board's reaction, I was told with a wry smile, was that there was a much safer future in sheep shearing machinery, particularly with large orders coming from Australia. In due course their engineer, Mr Morris, moved to Oxford and started making cars on his own, while Wolseley cars became one of Morris Motors' brands.

*　　*　　*

My first visit to export markets was to Norway and I greatly enjoyed flying to Oslo and catching a train to Bergen where our very energetic Norwegian agent, Trygve Mickelsen, lived. His charming wife had earlier been a governess to the Pauncefort-Duncombe family in England (it was a neat link that I had been at Stowe with Pauncefort-Duncombe). Bergen was a delightfully refreshing city, clearly built round the fishing trade, and although there were a number of fine period merchant houses along the harbour, it was filled with modern activity. I stayed with the Mickelsens in their house overlooking the city and took part in occasional daily tasks, like going down to the harbour to view the fish tanks and choose which fish we would like for supper. I later experienced a similar choice in other places, including Boston, but always felt a slight feeling of guilt as I chose the finest fish in the tank and it was at once netted and killed (an idea which has now spread worldwide). Bridport had supplied the Bergen fishing trade with an increasing quantity of netting for their purse and other seine nets, and Trygve was active in opening up other markets between Trondheim and Alesund. The principal supplier had, in the past, been Gundrys, but this was now changing.

While Bridport had traded with Norway for many years, the advent of much more complex machinery and synthetic fibres had made it easier to compete. Some of the local small networkers were anxious to co-operate with Bridport Industries, buying their bulk sheets of netting and shaping it into their own purse seines. So long as this included the bulk of supplies coming from Bridport, this was acceptable to us and in fact helped us compete successfully with the other major suppliers worldwide.

The Swedish market at that time was quite different, and if one flew along the coastline it was possible to observe, even from 10,000 feet, the long eel nets which stretched into the sea round the coast of southern Sweden. The migrating eels, which spent part of their year in the Sargasso Sea in the Atlantic, returned to their native coastline to spawn, and as they encountered the nets they turned to avoid them, but many found themselves in pockets which were regularly visited and emptied by the Swedish fishermen. I always enjoyed the Swedish food including many kinds of smoked and sweet-preserved eel, and it was an added satisfaction that one felt as if one was playing a real part in this food chain.

Occasional visits to the Danish market had a special meaning because not only did they fish along much more of their coast in a similar way, and in competition with the Swedes, but one of the by-products, inflatable buoys and floats, were being made by a company in which Trygve Mickelsen had a stake and consequently Bridport became the world-wide distributor of Polyform buoys.

But there was another reason why visiting Copenhagen on business was fun – I now had a brother and sister-in-law living there. In the early 1950s, Mary North had become the governess to the Danish princesses, indeed on more than one occasion they came to stay at Netherbury. While working there Mary had met a charming and successful Dane, Mogens Harttung, who was an occasional sailing partner of the Danish King, and the agent in Denmark for a number of aircraft and helicopter companies as well as owning the supply ships and having the contract for supplying Greenland with consumables – a responsibility of very long standing in Denmark.

When Mogens, whose first wife had died, proposed to Mary, the King and Queen offered to hold the wedding party in Fredericksborg Castle in Copenhagen and arranged everything themselves as if they were part of the family. A small family party flew from England and stayed with various well-connected families, most of them long-standing friends of the Harttungs. There were also one or two English guests, particularly John Henniker-Major (later Lord Henniker), the British ambassador, who was a friend of Mogens (and a Stoic).

On the day of the wedding we assembled at the church and the King and Queen insisted on sitting in the fourth row on the bride's side. When the first hymn started most of the English members of the congregation rose to their feet, as did Dudley and Eilean, but a firm hand pressed downwards on my

The wedding of Mary North and Mogens Harttung at Fredericksborg Castle.
The bridesmaids – the three Danish Princesses and Mogens' two daughters
by his first marriage.

shoulder and an even firmer voice said quite loudly, 'You do not stand in Danish hymns.' It was King Frederick. The three princesses were all Mary's bridesmaids.

After reaching the castle, the King and Queen with Dudley and Eilean received all the guests as would be done at an English wedding, and we were the guests at a fine reception in a great room with delicious food and faultless service. Looking out through the great windows into the courtyard I soon noticed that one or two were covered in signatures done with diamond points. The King came over to explain that it was a tradition of the castle when great leaders were entertained, and I saw the signatures of the Romanovs and those of German families, mixed with royalty from Britain and one I recognised at once, that of Winston Churchill, who had visited Copenhagen shortly after the liberation of Denmark from the Germans.

Mary and Mogens enjoyed the usual send-off with kisses and confetti, and we lingered a little to thank the King and Queen for their wonderful hospitality. It was a truly extraordinary affair, although slightly tarnished two days later when the Norths returned to Netherbury to find that some front page tabloid publicity had led to a major burglary and almost all their family silver had been stolen – a few pieces only being recovered because of the identification of their coat of arms.

From then onwards we visited Mogens and Mary quite frequently and they often came to England. Indeed, not long after this Mogens was created an honorary KBE for his role as chairman of the Anglo-Danish Trade Federation. One of Mogens' friends was Oscar Husum, a banker who married the daughter of the Danish Ambassador in London, and still a great friend today.

Mogens had a lease on a country estate south of Copenhagen and a house in the city. When we were there we would hurry round in an unaccustomed social whirl. I remember later an interesting afternoon with Isak Dinesen who wrote the best-selling book *Out of Africa*, and with whom it was easy to converse as I had, by then, travelled much in Africa. In the later 1960s he purchased an estate on Jutland, Barritskov – now the home of his son, Thomas, whose younger brother Mogens ('Nono') is my godson. There he entertained his shooting friends widely (while Barritskov today is the largest organic farm in Demark). Sadly both Mary and Mogens died of cancer in the 1970s, but I remember them with the greatest affection. (To my great surprise, some years ago in London at the wedding of the daughter of Oscar Husum, I found myself talking to Princess Benedikte and was amazed when she said at once, 'You were Mary's brother-in-law, I think.')

*   *   *

It was pleasant and commercially worthwhile travelling in Scandinavia, but there was an added feeling of excitement visiting Iceland. When I first visited I believe the population was scarcely more than 200,000 and flying into Reykjavik from Scotland, via the Faroe Islands, one felt that one was visiting a new and private world. The islands had first been inhabited by the Vikings who sailed past Scotland and Ireland and almost certainly reached Newfoundland (I was later shown what was considered to be a Viking settlement on Newfoundland). As colonisers as well as raiders, they captured largely Scottish and Irish girls and took them westwards into the mists – from this grew a distinct race. In the Middle Ages extreme weather conditions almost wiped out the Icelanders, but I was shown on their barren icy shore the place where their early parliament had met, and there is no doubt that they could claim to be one of the earliest democracies.

Originally a dependency of Denmark, they became independent after the war, and there was a fierce national pride in the population. I was to experience this almost at once, for the Icelanders were most protective of their fishing grounds which included much of the best cod spawning ground in the North Atlantic. British trawlermen resented their stance and the Icelandic interference with trawlers which sailed too close to their shores, and the British government's reaction was to send armed fishery protection and naval vessels in what became known in the 1960s as the 'Cod War'.

On my second visit I was having dinner with Icelandic friends in a well-known Reykjavik fish restaurant when two burly Icelandic trawlermen came to the table and asked me to leave. Had it not been for my Icelandic friends I might well have been forced to go and could have experienced a confrontation outside. From then onwards Gier Jonson would always walk back the short way to my hotel or drive me there.

More interesting visits were to friends in the country at weekends. At one home chess was played almost incessantly. I can well understand that on the edge of the Arctic Circle, when in mid-winter there was no light for about twenty hours, chess by candlelight was an absorbing occupation to Icelanders in the days before radio and television (and echoes the game played in the Scottish Hebrides in the early Middle Ages).

On more than one occasion I drove with Christiaan Gudmundsson to the northern city of Akureyri. Christiaan was a hardened man who in 1940 had sailed solo in a small boat in winter from Norway to Iceland to escape the Germans. Yet he explained to me that in Iceland it was not safe to drive alone on the only north/south road, even in his Mercedes, although the road was straight and well made. He insisted always on leaving *before* the daily bus because if one broke down there would always be another vehicle following you that day. It was not unknown for travellers to be found frozen to death at night on the one hundred and fifty mile road along which there were virtually no houses or villages.

He told me, too, of when he was a boy and wished to visit his grandmother in Reykjavik before the building of the road. At the age of fifteen he would set off alone and stay the night in one of the stone huts which spanned the country at ten to fifteen mile intervals. Each night he would let himself into a hut and eat a tinned meal from the provisions he found there, cooking on an oil stove. Before leaving in the morning he would leave one meal from his own sled, so that that hut would *always* have food for the next traveller. In such conditions at that time it was essential to live by these traditional rules, for failure on the part of any traveller to do so could result in the death of another guest, weeks or months later. It would be nice to think that people today in other situations could behave with such responsibility and consideration.

Akureyri was a practical fishing port lying exactly on the Arctic Circle. The trawler owners had their own net lofts and riggers but lacked the supplies of bulk netting. (It would almost certainly have been impractical for a factory to start in such a place without skilled operatives and engineers – far better to encourage competition from suppliers, the principal ones now being a Japanese company, the Gundry company in Bridport, a Scottish netmaker and ourselves. We had not, until the link with Pearsalls, been strong in their market.)

The question of price was of paramount importance and two or three of the leading ship owners would meet at one of their superheated houses, and after dinner and bottles of wine, finishing about 11 o'clock, the wives went to bed and the men settled down to negotiate contracts over brandy and whisky and endless black coffee. Such sessions might end at 4 am or after dawn, and I would return to Christiaan's house exhausted and sleep until lunchtime. Christiaan was much respected and carried great weight in his community, while my own manufacturing experience came in useful at 3.30 am when everything turned on whether we could deliver two extra tons of fine netting and give a final extra discount of 5% (and not charge extra for dying it blue grey!). I'm glad to say that over about four years we added very materially to Bridport Industries' share of the large Icelandic market, and I regarded Christiaan, who would come to stay at West Milton, as among our warmest friends. He had a charming German wife whom he seemed to have 'smuggled' out of Hamburg after the war.

Gier Jonson, too, in Reykjavik, also provided numerous orders and I was very glad to take some 'off' days in Iceland to see some of the more spectacular sights and enjoy the country at different times of year. In the north the great lake Mivatten (Midge-lake) was beautiful and restful, and Christiaan had his own motor-cruiser there. Further south the areas of molten lava produced hot springs and other surprises. We stayed two nights in a delightful hotel where in the attendant greenhouses were grown two crops of bananas per year, and if one went to swim in the outdoor swimming pool in winter, one could choose the heat – from the temperature of a hot bath to much cooler areas which one could enter by rolling over a dividing stone ledge as the snow fell.

About 1961 a huge new modern hotel was built in Reykjavik for 'the tourist trade'. It was, I think, called 'The Saga'. A friend of Gier Jonson was the manager, and we had what we were told was the first guest lunch in the dining room, fashionably laid out on the top floor. Alas, I haven't been there since. Another thing which always intrigued me was the telephone books. Iceland retained many ancient Norse customs, and Icelandic names ended in 'son', or 'dottir' for a lady. The telephone book was arranged alphabetically but by Christian names, with the family name next and a single trade name (i.e., 'fisherman', 'storeman', 'butcher' etc.). This was enough for all local readers but was sometimes hard for outsiders. I don't know if it is still the same today.

*   *   *

It was inevitable when already half-way across the Atlantic, that we should look even further west, and thus I found myself flying on a number of occasions from Reykjavik to the airport at St Johns in Newfoundland. The flights were by Icelandic Air, who at that time still held the rights to most flights to and from Iceland, although British Airways also stopped in Iceland on transatlantic flights. St Johns, Newfoundland, felt like Cornwall and the population was British to the core. On my first visit I went to the signal hill above the harbour where Marconi's first message had reached after crossing the Atlantic – sent from the hut next to our house at Tresawle on The Lizard. The Boyd Butler family, who ran a general fishermen's supply warehouse, were very welcoming, and after the first visit I stayed with them in their comfortable St Johns house (and they with us when in Dorset).

When looking at the telephone book I was amazed, for almost half the names were the same as those in Dorset directories: Mr G., the Lloyd's agent at St Johns even had the same Christian name as Mr G., the Lloyd's agent at the tiny harbour at Bridport. In the 18th and 19th centuries many merchant ships plied their trade between Lyme Bay and St Johns, taking cargoes of cordage and netting for fishing the Newfoundland banks and bringing back

An international fishing exhibition, 1961.

The new Marketing Director.

salt cod which had dried in the air on the racks still ranged along Newfoundland's Atlantic coasts from St Johns to Carboneer and northwards. It was, in fact, a trade which had originated in the 17th Century when the routes often included four legs: 1. from Bridport with cordage and netting to Newfoundland; 2. from St Johns with salt cod for West Africa; 3. from Lagos with slaves and spices to the West Indies; 4. from there back to Britain with molasses and rum.

Bridport had supplied Newfoundland with cordage for at least two hundred and fifty years and most of the cod lines used on the Newfoundland banks had come from West Dorset. The Newfoundland cod nets were quite similar to those used in Vancouver, even the length of mesh and rigging were similar. Very considerable supplies had formerly been sent in the earlier 20th Century in bulk from Bridport to Montreal and then *back* to St Johns, but with improved transport, particularly by air to St Johns, this was changed to direct supply and both the Boyd Butlers and ourselves benefited.

A considerable part of Bridport's fishing net and cordage production had, in fact, gone to Canada for more than a century. Gundrys had been the leading supplier, but with a link between Bridport Industries and the Gourock Ropework Company at Gourock on the Clyde, a company called Bridport-Gourock had been formed in the early 1950s and was increasingly successful under its Scottish director, Bill Bone, who lived in Montreal. (Bill was a delightful man who was always anxious to demonstrate his co-operation with French Canadians, and thus addressed *everyone* he met 'Bonjour monsieur' or 'Bonjour madame'. It seemed to work and he was widely met everywhere with a smile – although they were almost the only words of French he knew.)

Bridport had also long been the supplier of the salmon nets which were used extensively in British Vancouver in the Vancouver and Fraser rivers. These nets had to be very accurately made, for the Canadian fishery inspectors would decide annually on the minimum mesh allowed in an effort to protect smaller fish. It was, for instance, laid down that the minimum mesh would be $5^{1}/_{4}$ inches or $5^{3}/_{4}$ inches in one river and $5^{1}/_{2}$ inches in another. Any fisherman found using too small a mesh had his catch taken and was forbidden to fish until next season, and such a sentence could of course mean ruin.

On the other hand if the mesh was too large, an increasingly high percentage of the catch could escape through the net, thus reducing catches. It was therefore of the utmost importance that meshes were correct and the twine not elastic (when after a little use too many fish could swim through). I had struggled with this problem in Bridport in the factories and it was not too difficult when the twine was flax (linen thread) which has very low elasticity. It was much more difficult with nylon which had at least three times the elasticity. Our co-operation with Pearsalls proved most rewarding as a result of their managing to 'pre-stretch' the twine so that it behaved like linen. Our sales of salmon netting improved greatly in the late 1950s and '60s.

It was always a long day flying to Vancouver from Montreal. A hasty breakfast before touchdown at Toronto and then the long haul across the dramatic Rockies, via Moosejaw and Medicine Hat, and the beautiful landing at Vancouver where, after what seemed all day in the plane, it was only just after lunch. Bill Bone and I would stay at the Hilton but always dined with fishing boat owners, usually along the China 'strip' where there were numerous excellent Chinese restaurants serving very tasty fish, and charming (though completely proper) waitresses who bent low as we sat cross-legged round the low tables.

It was then a long non-stop flight back across the Pole to London, the first half of which would usually be occupied with writing a long report, and then some sleep before landing, a hurried trip to Paddington and thence to Bridport by train. If the train stopped at Powerstock at a reasonable time of day Elizabeth could meet me there.

*   *   *

Life was not all work, however. The 5th July 1960 was the 275th anniversary of the Battle of Sedgemoor after which many West Country men who had supported the Duke of Monmouth in his rebellion against the Catholic King James II were 'on the run' after their defeat. Judge Jeffreys, in his infamous Bloody Assize, sent many who were caught to the gallows, while others were sent to the West Indies as slaves (a few of whom eventually prospered greatly there).

Beaminster decided to commemorate this anniversary in which a number of local men took part, and I was able to persuade a friend at Coldstream headquarters to send a Company (at Beaminster's expense) to 'guard' the town against the return of twenty known local men who were 'on the run' and had been photographed as fugitives. (I was one of these.) Many plots were hatched to get back into the town but by mid afternoon, after some had been caught by local scouts in the surrounding countryside and one had tried to charge into the square on horseback but was dismounted, no-one had made it, and the 'Judge', Jim Spicer, a personal friend, began to think that no-one would succeed by the deadline of 6 o'clock. But late in the afternoon a party of Bridport ropeworkers with an old rope machine came to give a display in the square and, after each had been carefully scrutinised against the photographs, were let through to play their part. One tall but clean-shaven cripple with a stick, and ponderous nose and puffy cheeks, walked up to Jim and said, 'I've done it.' He turned in surprise and said, 'Who are you?' 'David,' I replied, as he looked at the stranger in disbelief. It is surprising what you can achieve by way of disguise if you shave off your moustache, colour your hair, put cotton wool up your nostrils and have a pronounced limp and a stick as you wear unfamiliar tattered clothes.

It was not long before Philippa was eight, Sophie was six and Jo just three. Pear Tree House had been enlarged and was very comfortable with bedrooms for the children and a large guest bedroom. The garden had matured and was securely surrounded by hedges and a wall, but I remember one day when Jo was sitting in the autumn sun in her long red stockings. I was gardening in a different corner when I heard a commotion and found three of our neighbour's dairy herd had pushed through the hedge and stood looking up at Jo who was seated in a reclining chair. When I reached her she had one leg in its long red sock and was putting on the other and said, 'It's all right Daddy, I looked underneath and knew it was all right to put my socks on again – they're only cows.' She was completely calm, but I never discovered who told her of red rags and a bull.

Eilean lived alone now at a cottage in Netherbury, for Dudley had died the previous year and had been buried at sea off Portland from a destroyer – an impressive moment as his coffin slipped away, covered in flowers, and was slowly taken by the waves.

Life was a whirl, and although I managed to attend regular meetings of the West Dorset Conservative Party as a Vice Chairman, I didn't have the time for as many functions as in the past. I had been pleased at the beginning of 1962 to become the Sales Director of Bridport Industries and it was particularly satisfying to note that our company sales were, in fact, increasing in almost every area from sports nets, agricultural netting and, particularly, a wide range of fishing netting and cordage, while new markets grew in air cargo nets and in other fields. I remember one failure, which had promised to be exciting, and that was shark nets to protect Australian bathing beaches. These, like sheep netting, were to be reinforced by electric impulses, but although we made a number, they just didn't work! But overall I felt both secure and successful – especially in gaining an increasingly good share of the market from our old rivals Gundry.

With a growing family (and growing income to match: I was now paid the amazing sum of £4,000 per year with more promised – *and* travelled everywhere first class!) our circle of friends continued to broaden. We frequently saw friends from the past, usually from Stowe or the Coldstream, who stayed with us, perhaps on their way to holidays in the west. Among these were Colin Wallis-King, who had left Stowe just before I arrived although we served together in Palestine; John and sometimes Charmian Bourdon-Smith, whose silver business prospered; and Martin and Margaret Arnold. Martin was the chairman of the largest educational suppliers in England – E.J. Arnold – while Margaret had been at school with Elizabeth and Mary at Downe House, where we were considering sending Philippa. Elizabeth's friends who stayed frequently included Deborah Spranger (also Downe House) who was an actress and whose parents' Italian home outside Florence made an excellent place to spend a holiday. We also increasingly saw other friends in Dorset, including Rosemary and Colin Kennard; he had in the last three years left the Brigade of Guards and joined Gundrys and had just been appointed director in charge of sales. He was a cousin of Sir Philip Colfox, the former MP for West Dorset.

One evening in August 1962 we had a quiet dinner planned at Pear Tree House. There were, I think, Rosemary and Colin, and Winfie and Jim Spicer (my Conservative friend and later to become the next MP for Dorset when Simon Digby retired). After dinner Colin cornered me as we were leaving the dining room and said, 'I'm a bit embarrassed, but I do hope you understand what has taken place and I so much hope we can work together.' I told him that I did not understand what he meant at all.

We returned to the dining room with our cups of coffee and sat down. He was amazed and shocked to discover that, as a director, I had not been told that Bridport Industries Limited had just amalgamated with Gundrys (in effect bought Gundrys for an agreed share), and that as there were fewer directors of Gundrys and it was important to maintain a balance of power on the board, he had been appointed the Sales Director of the new Bridport-Gundry Limited. Colin, whom I had always liked, was horrified that I didn't know – presumably because no-one wanted to tell me – and said he did hope that I would be able to help him with his new responsibilities, many of which were entirely new to him, as he had only a limited background knowledge of the business as yet.

When our guests had gone I told Elizabeth, and on arrival at work next day telephoned Reg Besley in Taunton, but he was not coming to Bridport until the end of the week. When we did meet, he was very apologetic and clearly upset at the turn of events. He seemed to think I already knew. By then I was articulate enough to say that I thought the concept was a great mistake and that if we had continued our sales growth of the last few years we would have been able to take over Gundry at far better terms, if indeed we wanted to at all as much of their production mirrored ours and neither was fully used.

I learned that Ted Gundry, a keen hunting man, was to become joint Managing Director with Reg, and as he was considerably the younger of the two, I foresaw a situation when he would be in charge, and it might be many years before I had any chance of promotion. At the end of August I wrote to the Chairman, Campbell Edwards, resigning from the company at the year end.

In such situations it is difficult to know if one is right; however, it was not done in anger but in the conviction that I, who had only the most token shareholding, would never now feel easy in an environment of promotion which had demonstrated how much revolved round family shareholding. Inside, I felt I would lose my self-esteem and integrity if I acquiesced. I had no other job, nor any idea how I could keep my family, but there were no long-term fixed expenses and with Elizabeth's support we felt we would survive because we had many business friends who had expressed great surprise and support, although a new job would almost certainly not be in Dorset.

Before leaving Bridport I was invited to attend, as an assistant director, a meeting of the new board. There were three Gundrys: Joseph, the Gundry Chairman; Gerald, fully dressed in 'pink' as joint Master of the Beaufort Hunt, who had to be gone by noon so as to be at a meet near Bath at 2 pm; and Ted Gundry, who resigned as joint Managing Director within a year but stayed on the board. Six months after I left I had a friendly letter from Reg Besley asking if I would reconsider my position, but I declined the kind offer. In the 1980s and 1990s Bridport-Gundry Limited increasingly found international competition very fierce in a changing world and, after disposing of some specialist departments as small independent companies, was sadly wound up in 1999 by its Chairman and five other directors (none of whom was in the company, or had any connection with netting or Bridport, in 1963). This was just thirty-six years later.

For me it was a wrench to leave a company environment in which I had been happy and felt strong roots after sixteen years of work and some success. But I was to learn that one takes experience with one and can often turn this to good use in a new life. It was to be of lasting benefit that I had seen much of what had made family-owned manufacturing businesses prosper over the centuries, but was to learn that increasingly 'acquisition' over 'organic growth' was to set a new fast-track pattern for industry in the future – a pattern which was usually at odds with my instinct and better judgement unless planned very selectively.

CHAPTER 9

Leeds and the Caribbean

Although I stayed in Bridport for the remainder of 1962 and did my best to hand over our agencies and agents in an orderly manner, I had to devote some time to planning for the future. One possibility was to train as an industrial consultant, and I had had a friendly relationship with one who had advised Bridport on various matters. However, in September I had a telephone call from Martin Arnold who told me that he had heard I was leaving and that E. J. Arnold were seeking to expand their educational markets world-wide and wondered if a new post there, initially Export Manager, would interest me. I travelled to their headquarters in Butterley Street, Leeds, and stayed two days with Martin and Margaret while I saw their extensive factories and considered the existing sales and what might develop.

After discussing things with Elizabeth, I agreed. Although it would at first entail a considerable fall in salary, the opportunities in the world of education in the early 1960s seemed limitless working for the largest school supplier in the country.

Martin's brother, Olaf, who had also been at Stowe, was in charge of all production, and other directors were in charge of school contract business – by far the greatest part of Arnold's sales – and products and development of school equipment. There was also a flourishing publishing business in the primary field. The senior and oldest director was Mr Wood, who had been in the business all his life and whose father had been the founder's first manager when the business was started in Barnstaple in Devon at the time of the first Education Acts in the 1870s; as education prospered, the company did so too, and moved to Leeds.

Finding somewhere for our family to live produced interesting choices, for Margaret's brother, Nicholas Horton-Fawkes, had a comfortable flat on the Farnley estate which was offered to us and which enjoyed marvellous views, while the house itself contained the finest collection of Turner watercolours in private hands, for Nicholas' ancestor had been a friend of Turner who often stayed in the late 1820s and did a series of paintings of local scenery – more than twenty-four – which still hung, carefully screened against the light, in the dining room. Although isolated it would have been fun. But Philip Colfox (Colin Kennard's cousin) had an old friend in the village of Aberford near Leeds, Sir Alvery Gascoigne, who owned a beautiful dower house to the

Hicklam House, Aberford, in the 1960s.

Jo, Sophie and Philippa with their friends
at Hicklam, 1964.

Lotherton estate, the lease of which had just become available because the estate agent was retiring and much of the rest of the Lotherton estate was shortly to be given to the City of Leeds. I wrote to Sir Alvery asking if we could become tenants (he had for some years been the British ambassador in Moscow and had himself served in the Coldstream in the First War; his only son, sadly, being killed after the Normandy landings in 1944 with the Regiment).

Sir Alvery kindly gave us the lease of Hicklam House, and we were able to move there in the spring of 1963. (I had left Bridport in January and lodged for a number of weeks at the Gascoigne Arms in Aberford.) Hicklam was a beautiful and ample Queen Anne red brick house on the Old Great North Road just south of Aberford. It stood opposite one of the finest alms houses in Victorian gothic style which had been built by the Gascoigne family in the mid 19th Century for retired employees on their estates.

We found ourselves with three acres of garden and a five acre field between us and the new motorway north, and it was a happy move – the children all having large bedrooms, while our own looked over an ancient rose garden. I was to spend many hundreds of hours in the garden.

The drive from Butterley Street, Leeds, to Aberford took little more than twenty-five minutes through the ancient village 'kingdom' of Sherburn-in-Elmet. (The Elmet Kingdom had survived for centuries at the limit of the Viking invasions into Yorkshire in the 8th Century.)

With the family safely at Hicklam in greater style than they had previously known, we were able to find excellent schools and plan that Philippa should soon go to the Mount School in York as a weekly boarder: a school of outstanding quality and Quaker persuasion, although the majority of girls were not Quakers.

With the help of the Arnold family we were soon involved in a social life where small private dinner parties and bridge evenings made life pleasant. The children were able to find numerous friends, while work in Leeds was interesting and I found myself with as much work as I was prepared to take on and an efficient secretary.

*   *   *

The school supply business of which Arnold was the largest (and still private) company focused on council contracts from all over England and Scotland that were awarded annually for the supply of *all* their educational supplies. Thus, Arnold not only manufactured a great number of stationery and other basic items, but held huge stocks of pencils, rulers and every type of science equipment, and had, perhaps, the largest book wholesale warehouse in England. In all, more than two thousand employees worked in various warehouses and manufacturing units and a fine new printing works had been opened in Elland Road where a wide range of primary books was printed, written by a number of authors for Arnolds since before the war. I arrived at the time when computers were first being installed, but in the first year or two all the very large number of school invoices were still created manually and there was an office of totallers – more than a dozen in number – who did nothing other than add up invoices by hand. (It was impressive to watch the men who had worked for Arnolds for up to fifty years adding columns of figures: the pounds, shillings and pence at the same time; and producing answers as accurately and quickly as 'totalling machines'.) The volume, too, was impressive and at certain times of year more than two thousand consignments a day would leave Butterley Street, while the correspondence department which just received and answered sales letters numbered about fifty.

The quotations for contracts were complex and employed a department under Mr Metson, but I was given a free hand to find and develop similar contracts throughout the world, for at the time of my arrival no export trade was pursued, although I found records of vast numbers of schools, from as far away as Papua, New Guinea, who had received Arnold catalogues for years but who very seldom replied. One file of schools in Africa numbered many hundreds, but the addresses were all in 'The Orange River Colony' (which ceased to exist as a separate state after the Boer War).

I visited a number of government departments, particularly the 'Crown Agents' who frequently purchased on behalf of some of the smaller colonies. All were concerned with export trade, and I was not long in finding that while we were looking for export markets, the rapidly declining colonial infrastructure in Africa and elsewhere was looking for competitive suppliers. Soon I found myself engaged in wide-ranging correspondence with education departments in the Caribbean, West Africa, East Africa, India and the Far East – although this was necessarily confined to the English-speaking world, for Arnold equipment was all based on the English language and British methods of teaching.

*   *   *

I am fortunate in still having most of my detailed reports to the Arnold board of my visits all over the world from 1964 to 1968 and although there are some hundreds of foolscap pages of information, largely dictated on a hand dictaphone, often on flights or in hotel rooms, I have tried to select over the coming pages some information (sometimes laced with local gossip) about these markets. It can only be a fraction of what was written, but gives an idea of the world of education supply before most of the countries became fully independent. The market estimates will seem very small today, but gained from government sources. If Arnold's new export manager could quickly build a market of more than £1 million, this would be a first step forward and develop relationships which would continue to grow rapidly in the future.

As our experience grew it became clear that while the traditional method of appointing local agents might still be appropriate in some countries, it could work in a more dynamic way in the emerging markets if our 'agents' were in fact co-owners. Many were energetic and ambitious men with local capital, and Arnold soon found that it worked well to have joint companies, nearly always with us retaining 51%, and using these to obtain as much of the local market as they could while negotiating special prices with Arnold for overall ranges of equipment. This eventually led to more than a dozen such companies, most of which had the local man acting as Chairman, but with myself as Director reporting to Leeds after each meeting (usually not less than two per year, with additional visits to England). The system had to be based on mutual trust and friendship, and thus I frequently stayed in the homes of our partners (the local 'Managing Directors'), and when they came to Leeds they stayed at Hicklam.

*   *   *

In mid 1964 I heard that the agent of the leading supplier in the Caribbean had become seriously upset by delivery failures (not unknown at times in Arnold, although we actually manufactured a far greater share of our own catalogue products than others). Armed with backing from the Arnolds and promises from our product and publishing directors (Bill Wilday and David Bell) I wrote to Jamaica to say I wanted to meet Mr Speyer and had a favourable reply. It was to be the first export market we tackled. Official government records in London showed:

> The potential Caribbean School Publications and Equipment Market is in the neighbourhood of £310,000 (Government) plus £125,000 (Private) – and is likely to rise by about 10% each year in the foreseeable future.

while in my first report of November 1964 I added:

> Arnold's share in their year ending October 31st, 1965 should be not less than £50,000; in 1966 approx. £100,000; in 1967 approx. £150,000. It is never likely to be more than two thirds of the total market.

I was met at Kingston airport by Mr and Mrs Speyer who had arranged a comfortable hotel near their luxurious home. He was a cousin of Sir Edgar Speyer whose family had come to England from Frankfurt in the 19th Century and was in 1906 created a baronet, although the title was extinct by 1932. We sat long into the night on his verandah (until it was realised that the time was 6.30 am in England) discussing how many equipment catalogues would be needed to reach every school in the West Indies. Every year Arnold published thick catalogues, brimming with educational aids and ideas, and sent out well over 100,000 of these at home – they were the envy of our competition.

Clearly the Speyers wanted to introduce me to their friends, for two nights later there was a dinner party at which were the local directors of Peat Marwick, Colgate Palmolive, Cunard (whose ships were increasingly visiting Kingston on cruises) and, to my amusement, the nets and cordage division of William Kenyon with whom I was able to have an interesting gossip, and had even briefly considered joining two years earlier. Days were spent visiting education departments and schools (and signing the visitors' book at Government House, so that, I was told, I could be invited to a reception if one coincided with a future visit).

I learned that text books in Jamaican schools were in very short supply (less than two per child to cover all subjects) and I was later to see on another poorer island in the Caribbean that exercise (writing) books usually ran out after one term each year and most written subjects were carried out on the borders of old newspapers brought to school by the pupils.

Mr Speyer employed a number of 'local' representatives who travelled to schools and took what orders they could from catalogues. He said he would arrange that wherever possible they would meet me and help me on my Caribbean tour. Science equipment was in particularly short supply, but the head science master at the leading technical college in Jamaica was enjoying a bonanza because he had returned his order as instructed in triplicate to the Kingston education authority and they had, in error, processed each copy, with the result that he had received three times his required supply. (So much for the department's 'new supply system'.)

Mr Speyer had many contacts throughout the Caribbean, and we discussed those which were appropriate for my first tour. A week later I flew to British Guyana with a visit to Trinidad on the way. Arriving at the airport in late evening, I was lucky to find a friendly taxi man to take me to my hotel, the Normandie. It was before the days of a main road from the airport and we drove fast along country roads with lorries parked without lights in the darkness along the way. I was alarmed by the number of near-misses that we had, but was nevertheless delivered safely to my hotel where the driver asked if he could act for me for the rest of my stay. I took his card and telephone number – his name was Angel Gabriel.

I had to be up at 4.45 next day to catch the 6.30 light plane to Georgetown. Atkinson airport was a wooden shed in the jungle, twenty-eight miles south of Georgetown and at ninety feet above the sea was the highest point for a hundred miles. As soon as I arrived I telephoned the Chief Education Officer and we spent the afternoon discussing what might be possible. By the evening it seemed that rather than set up a central educational store, Arnold would supply export catalogues to all schools and full sets to the Ministry as required, together with a wide range of samples. It was clear that both the Educational Department and the Finance Department thought it far preferable that headmasters had freedom to choose their supplies, within budget, rather than have to accept what was bought into a central store, with possible disagreement as to what should be chosen centrally.

That evening I had talks with the British Trade Commissioner in Guyana, Mr Payne, and he left me near my hotel. The local evening newspaper had a front page banner headline 'Bullets in her Brassière' telling the story of a local girl, 'Gloria White', brought before the magistrates for being found walking in the street with pistol bullets concealed in her brassière 'contrary to the emergency regulations'. There was shortly to be an election.

The next day I met the Permanent Secretary of Education and a number of headmasters, and in particular the head of the teacher training college, all of whom were anxious to receive various samples and were amazed at the equipment that could be shipped direct to schools, a delivery system on which Arnolds had been built.

The election violence was growing during my stay, and I was amused by the parting remark of one headmaster, 'I wish you all were on the British Commission Inquiry into elections. I'm sure you all would be the right man for that job.' I was very glad I wasn't!

My last day in Guyana on this occasion was a cocktail of experiences. The Education Officer for East Demerara took me to an all-age mixed school called 'Vryheid's Lust Government School'. On arrival I was asked to give a fifteen minute lecture on schools supplies. This over, I visited a primary class which illustrated the wide diversity of race in Guyana – Amerindian, European, African, Portuguese, Chinese, East Indian and Guyanese – and was presented with a photograph of the class which I still have. We drove back along the coast and made a brief visit to Georgetown Museum where, to my amazement, a Chinese armorial mug of a service I had never seen sat on a shelf, the gift of a long-dead British resident, which I was able to photograph. We also called at a record shop to buy a local record called *Itanami*, which I can still hear throbbing, for it had a marvellous rhythm. [It is an incredible coincidence that as I write this paragraph thirty-nine years later, the telephone rings and my daughter, Jo, says, 'Daddy, we were with someone last night who travels widely and they had a tape of that song *Itanami* which you brought back from Guyana. Do you remember, it starts *Captain, Captain, put me ashore, I don't want to go any more...*?' I had not heard it for more than three decades, and Jo had been only four and a half years old at the time.]

Atkinson airport was still wretched and the plane four hours late – while the jungle swarmed with mosquitoes. But I loved Guyana.

*   *   *

It was good to be able to enjoy another night or two at the Normandie hotel in Trinidad and tour part of the island in Mr Gabriel's taxi. It was, of course, just over twenty years since I had first been there in the spring of 1944, but then we had just sat in the bay.

My first call was on the Permanent Secretary for Education, a Trinidadian, and he listened to the idea of catalogue distribution and large numbers of samples, appearing to be enthusiastic. Visits followed to the university and training colleges and towards the end of the day the Catholic college, St Mary's, where I was able to see the principal, Father Valdez, and discuss the library budget – the largest I had so far come across in the Caribbean of £6,250 per year, which he spent with a London bookshop. Our offer of delivering books free of carriage charges seemed to interest him greatly.

The last paragraph of my report on Trinidad reads, 'I board the *Federal Maple* at 8.30 pm. She is 1,900 tons dead weight, and there are some 160 passengers on board, rather more than half of which are deck passengers for the next island – Grenada.'

*   *   *

The *Federal Maple* was built in 1961 and was the gift of the Canadian Government to the West Indian Federation, as was her sister ship, the *Federal*

Palm. Both ships sailed alternately about every ten days from Trinidad, up the islands of the Antilles and, after St Kitts and Nevis, across to Jamaica when they refuelled and took on cargo for the return journey. Each usually sailed about 10 pm as dinner was over, and docked at the next island about 7 am.

This mode of transport was ideal for the commercial traveller who wished to visit every important island without the long delays of air travel, and also for tourists who wished to sample the flavour of the Caribbean in a two-week holiday. Cargo was carried to and from the islands and it was also convenient for local workmen and their families, who wished to travel cheaply on deck.

Our first call was Grenada and I disembarked sometime after 7 am and met Mr Phillip, headmaster of the Wesley Hall School, at the dock gates who drove me to see the Chief Education Officer – proud to be called Mr La Grenada. We next visited Grenada Boys Secondary School and I see in my report:

> Mr Baptiste confessed himself a little alarmed at any questions on the Education Authority purchasing, because this might disguise a Catholic plot to force Methodist Schools to use Catholic textbooks. A detailed discussion lasting about an hour on Communism, Church Unity and Catholic Plots did something to reassure him that E. J. Arnold & Son would not be party to any such Machiavellian scheme.

After visiting other schools, Mr Phillip and I had lunch in an 'air conditioned' (not working) snack bar, and he delivered me back to the *Federal Maple* about 4 pm after a visit to his own school; it might have been a Wesleyan Hall in Cornwall a century earlier.

The *Federal Maple* sailed soon after dark and we arrived at St Vincent before dawn. It was Sunday, and I thought I had an arrangement to meet the Education Officer after church, but my hopes were dashed. I visited the tourist bureau and they helpfully rang him at home but he'd gone to the beach for the day. Having hired a taxi it was possible to visit every part of the island (which I did for six hours – cost £2) and eventually reached the Education Officer's home where I had tea and discussed education supply for nearly two hours. As a lay preacher he was particularly interested in religious books and he stressed the great importance of being incorruptible on St Vincent (particularly as the Prime Minister's wife was awaiting trial for embezzlement of government funds).

Arriving next day at Barbados I discovered Mr Speyer had an office there, shared with a textile firm, and met his new educational representative. We set off to the Education Department where I had what might be almost a 'Royal Flush' – meeting the Minister, Permanent Secretary and Chief Education Officer within an hour. All were happy to chat about supplies. Present suppliers all quoted 'F.O.B.' (Free on Board, i.e. plus carriage), and I felt that the suggestion that we quote the same 'C.I.F.' (inclusive Carriage, Insurance and Freight) would be enough to win much of the market; but our catalogues, as always, were the main draw.

I spent some time with the principal tutor of the science college who had developed his own science equipment after a visit to Canada and was teaching trainees to make it. Apart from the inevitable jam jars with metal lids fitted with a wick so that they could be used as burners, he had a range of flasks made from light bulbs from which the elements had been removed and replaced by a cork into which fitted a glass tube. His enthusiasm was heart-warming and I longed for him to have proper science equipment, which shortly he would.

It was sad that the *Federal Maple* called at St Lucia and Dominica on the same day, but I started early on the beautiful St Lucia and first visited St Joseph's Convent School where we were received by Sister Anna. The previous week they had been visited by the Duke of Edinburgh who had asked the tutor of the senior class who were making cakes, 'How do you judge for success in a bakery lesson? Is it by the size and health of the husband?' This remark had been an enormous success on the island.

I noted: 'An interesting feature of the architecture was that there were no windows but all the walls were built with hollow blocks laid alternately sideways and upright so that between 10% and 20% of every wall was open, and this provided ample light and kept the classrooms beautifully cool.'

At another school I met a teacher who had visited us in Leeds earlier that year as part of a teacher training course, but my guide (and Speyer's agent) had to break the speed limit on the way to the quay, and I ran up the gang plank as the ship's siren sounded and the plank was pulled aboard.

Dominica, more than five hours away, was delightful and we anchored off Roseau as the sun fell. I went ashore in a tender and met the Education Officer in his home off the main street for an hour, but there was no time to see a school.

Walking down the rough main street in the dark – lit only from lights in houses – I fell down a manhole (the workman had forgotten to put back the cover). Luckily I managed to catch the edge and was not washed down the drain. I limped down to the jetty where there was a new hotel which had opened four days earlier; the management was delighted to see me, so I sat down to dinner. Nursing my bruises, I had an excellent meal and was rowed out to the *Federal Maple* before it set sail at midnight with the heavy rhythm of an unofficial West Indian band and dancers on the deck.

Montserrat, with a population of barely 15,000, glistened in the morning sunlight, and as we landed at Plymouth, the tiny capital, I could see the beaches of black volcanic sand. I met the Education Officer and his inspector of schools who took me to see the Mother Superior of St Augustine's Primary School. This school provided primary education for 10% of the children on the island and their annual budget for equipment was eighty West Indian dollars – or £17 per year for 260 pupils. They were overjoyed at receiving a visitor and I received an immediate order for £13 of supplies, with profuse apologies for having already spent £4 elsewhere that year. I promised that we would send from England a free consignment of damaged books but, as she pointed out, while this was most welcome, illiteracy was not the only problem, for only five children in her class were born in wedlock and only three still lived with parents. One was at once humbled by the disadvantages of these children and determined to see if something could be done. The island's whole budget for education equipment was £3,000 per year in 1964.

I was told that during the year only fifteen children had taken 'O' levels (among 4,000 at school) and eleven 'A' levels, with just one reaching university. That evening I spoke to the Administrator and his financial secretaries for education and agriculture at a cocktail party on board the *Federal Maple*. Clearly they felt it much more important to promote agricultural training than to spend on schools, for this was where most of the job opportunities lay. I nevertheless felt uncomfortable that the cost of the gin and tonic in my hand would provide equipment for more than one child for a year in Montserrat.

*   *   *

There could hardly be a greater contrast in wealth arriving in Antigua next day – the holiday home of many wealthy Americans. Taxis waited at the jetty, and jets landed from Europe and North and South America.

After lunch with Mr Hankinson, the Education Department Librarian, at which we discussed how the book supplies could be increased, but more importantly how books could arrive quickly rather than taking more than half a year from time of order via the Crown Agents to arrival, he drove me to English Harbour, which encompasses Nelson's Dockyard (Nelson's wife was born on Antigua). The harbour was then filled with a considerable number of fine yachts proclaiming home ports in America, England, Denmark and numerous other countries.

The teacher training college was the most advanced I had seen in the Caribbean, and Princess Margaret's School was obviously a government showpiece, endowed by more than one American millionaire. (During the afternoon I watched boys being coached in football by a former Arsenal player.) While at least twenty children went to university annually (in contrast to one from Montserrat) I was told of the problem with training teachers. Although there was a thriving carpentry school, none of the children took up careers in carpentry, while agriculture was still by far the largest employer on the island – but there were no courses in this at all!

My next day was the last one on the *Federal Maple* and I was sorry to disembark before she sailed the last two days to Jamaica. But I greatly enjoyed visiting St Kitts, and my short stay at the Blakeney Hotel in Basseterre was a pleasure, where the staff had been warned to expect a guest for breakfast at 6.30 am and were waiting (the waitress asking me to add up the bill for her because she wasn't very good at figures).

As I emerged from the front door, a very old car drew up beside me and a voice asked if I was Mr Howard. He was the Education Officer. After coffee at his home I spent the morning at the Education Office, and after lunch visited the SPCK Bookshop (Society for the Promoting of Christian Knowledge). After a call on the headmaster of the island grammar school, Mr More, he insisted on touring the island with me. We had tea with the Administrator, Colonel Henry Howard, a retired Coldstreamer and *very* distant relative.

(Quite the most impressive Fort in the West Indies must be that of Brimstone Hill – a massive rock about 1,000 feet high and four acres in area at the top, on which the French built a fort taking 40 years. Months before it was completed the English climbed the rock one night and took it without a shot being fired. Much of the fort is still in excellent condition and overlooks half the island.)

Flying into St Thomas on the first flight of the morning was like leaving the 19th for the 20th Century. Originally French, it was then Danish until 1917 when it was bought by America. The main street was all duty free shops where Swiss watches vied with Crown Derby porcelain and Japanese cameras. This was not a market for Arnolds, but I spent a day visiting the Department of Education and discussing the rapidly increasing interest in the Montessori educational system. I enjoyed my day, but didn't have time to visit the British Virgin Islands.

At the airport the customs man did not really believe that I had no liquor on leaving St Thomas and searched everything carefully. When I got out at St Kitts for five minutes I found the golfers of Basseterre just driving off from the first tee beside the runway for their annual Open Tournament (eight players) and I talked to two whom I knew. Suddenly I saw the aircraft – door closed – starting to move up the runway, but luckily the pilot noticed me running back and stopped to let me board. I changed at Antigua and was back in Jamaica by 3.30 on the Sunday afternoon.

The morning papers were full of a speech made on Sunday afternoon by the Minister of Education to the Jamaican Labour Party. Heavily laced with political innuendo, he nevertheless said the island faced a crisis:

> It has now been proved that children cannot start schooling at 7 and be ready for secondary school by 11. … In spite of school places being 12,000 last year and planned for 15,000 next year, only 3,341 children sat GCE and only 139 received a certificate. … If we are not careful higher education will become the exclusive reserve of those that can pay.

The stark figures behind his speech were listed in the paper:

> Only 60% of children go to school. The average attendance of those that do is 70%. The GCE pass rate is only 0.4% of children in Jamaica.

In this environment Mr Speyer and I discussed the opportunities and action that should be taken both in Jamaica and the whole Caribbean well into the evening, and I then rushed to catch BOAC's night flight to Nassau and London, leaving the plane in Nassau and catching the morning flight to Freeport, Bahamas, which then had its own separate educational system.

At Freeport, Mr Lord (until three years earlier a grammar school master in Lincoln) met me at the airport and took me to my hotel, the Caravel Club. The receptionist apologised for having to carry my own bags and told me there were no keys to the rooms, 'but we haven't ever had any trouble,' he assured me, 'just don't shut your door from outside.' Having told me I had Room 1, he added, 'I'm not quite sure where it is, but if you go along that path you should find it.'

In Freeport itself nothing was unplanned or left to chance, for the island had been leased to a private consortium. Mr Groves, the genius who ran the island as a personal fiefdom, and his associates were thought to have spent $100 million on this venture, and few in Nassau doubted that under the presiding control of Sir Jack Hayward, the senior shareholder (whose name I remembered on the houseroom board at Stowe), it would be an excellent investment.

One of the first institutions needed was a school, and this had opened two years earlier in two classrooms with 28 children. There were by then 350 and the numbers increased by between 8 and 15 every week. They expected to have 700 by the following September and 1,000 in two schools by September 1966. The school was heavily subsidised, although the parents paid fees, but Mr Groves was determined that no executive whom he would like to have in Freeport would be kept away by lack of adequate schooling. The buildings were all single storey and spread over an acre. They were equipped to a very high standard, and every feature, from lighting to marbled floor, told of the attention to detail.

I had dinner with Mr and Mrs Lord at an excellent Chinese restaurant. I woke, more by luck than judgement for the room telephone was not working, and caught the morning plane to Nassau. The morning papers quoted a speech by the Prime Minister, the theme of which was 'The Bahamas are better organised because the Government is a government of businessmen.'

I spent nearly three days in Nassau and had long discussions with the Permanent Secretary and the Director of Education, Mr Greig, and his assistant, Mr Bain. The annual expenditure per child was £42 – far outstripping the islands I had visited in the Antilles. The Minister of Finance and Development was Sir Stafford Sands (whom I met at a small dinner party given by his nephew Norman Solomon and remembered from my years in Nassau) and he had recently said that the education budget was one and a half million pounds for 35,000 children. Even in Nassau, however, absenteeism was almost 15%.

I had many full and detailed discussions with Mr Greig about supplies, and once more a promise of large numbers of catalogues and direct shipments was welcomed. The immediate potential for Arnolds was about £40,000, rising quickly in succeeding years if things went well, although the much more sophisticated retail trade established in Nassau was anxious to ensure that they could take a 'commission'. Visiting three of the four main schools and the technical training college, I discovered that the headmasters were very anxious to order supplies direct and *not* through a local bookshop. All this was a sensitive matter politically, but I was even given some small orders and promised supplies for an equipment showroom.

It was raining heavily as I boarded my BOAC flight to Bermuda and as the aircraft was parked on what seemed like the opposite side of the airfield, we were all given large golf umbrellas to splash across the runway. On arrival I found that my hotel near the harbour was comfortable; that a large notice in the foyer forbade ladies from wearing shorts; and that no family could have more than one car (166 inches long), speed limit 20 mph. 'D.J.' Williams, the

Director of Education, was helpful and friendly (a double Oxford Blue in rugby and athletics in 1938 who played cricket for the West Indies after the war). It was fortunate that we had both played rugby with Noel McGrath (Oxford and Ireland – later Dorchester!) and this provided a useful link.

I had lunch with him at the Bermuda Hotel School, which taught hotel management, and he came to 'have a drink' at my hotel but stayed for dinner and got home at half past midnight, getting something of a rocket from 'Mrs DJ'.

The next day I met the Chief Supply Officer (again rugby, formerly Cardiff and Welsh Trial), the only such appointment I met in the Caribbean. Much of the day I spent at seven secondary schools; at one, The Salters Grammar School, the headmaster was called Mr Hallet. I asked if he had come from Bridport, where there are a number of Hallet families, and indeed his grandfather had left there in 1890. I called at the Educational Department on my way back to the hotel and DJ kindly dropped me there in time to pack and get to the airport.

Midnight in Bermuda is 4 am in England, and the Boeing 707, leaving on time, touched down in perfect conditions six hours later. I was in Leeds by 4.55, somewhat tired as it had proved to be a 42 hour day. Apart from the 21 reports, 72 letters which had been written confirming discussions, and a great many samples sent, I had travelled over 12,000 miles in the 31 day tour, costing in all about £800.

Against this the prospects for Arnold were considerable, with a potential of over £250,000 of which it was planned that more than half should be Arnold turnover within the next three years in this expanding market.

CHAPTER 10

West Africa

It is now no longer possible to track the rapid growth in export trade which developed in the various English-speaking markets for educational equipment from Arnold, but the preliminary results of the Caribbean tour were sufficiently promising to lead as quickly as possible to a similar tour in West Africa – a very different market which might have to be approached in a different way. But first it was necessary to explore.

Flying via Lisbon I reached Las Palmas in the evening of a very sunny day in April 1965, but unfortunately had to be up at five next morning to catch the plane to Bathurst in The Gambia where I reached my hotel on the beach by midday.

The British Trade Correspondent picked me up at two. Mr Val-Phatty was a Cambridge-educated African and was very anxious to help. It was soon clear that while occasional visits were paid by other publishers, this was a small but enthusiastic country dealing with a vast education problem. The Gambia at that time had no newspapers, only an occasional broadsheet, and this was matched by figures I was quoted by Mr Scraggs, the acting British High Commissioner, of 10% adult literacy, 10% of children going to primary school and 1% to secondary school. The Gambia's Education Department spent about £10,000 on equipment each year, and the Mission schools about twice that – but the only bookshop in the country opened three afternoons per week, and Arnolds help in developing direct book supply and sending catalogues would be much welcomed.

Unusually, I lost my voice about teatime, but at dinner with the local correspondent of *Newsweek* he gave me some excellent tablets which seemed to do the trick. The other dinner guest was the Supervisor of the Peace Corps in West Africa, Mr Bable. It was clear that they were still learning about West Africa and wanted to introduce new teaching ideas.

At the Catholic college, the Bishop of Bathurst left a lecture to spend some time with me – an overwhelming civility but typical of the very strong feeling I gained of a desire to move forward. The principal, Father Clearey, spent an hour and a half discussing education and had received a catalogue sent from Leeds and marked many pages for discussion. Indeed, after lunch the principal drove me to the Ministry and I was given an actual order on condition that it could be delivered by the summer; supplies often took up to eighteen months to come (I was hearing stories well learned in the Caribbean). Letters posted in Bathurst were on their way to Leeds before I left, and my visit gave me a positive feeling.

Although up at 5 am to catch the early flight to Dakar and Freetown, I had to wait five hours at the airport. Lungi Airport at Freetown is on the other side of the bay and the Sierra Leone River and, with a long ferry ride, the bus took more than an hour to reach the capital.

I was in the hands of Professor Stanley Hockey of Fourah Bay College, who had lived there for seven years and was a well-known eccentric given to driving on the wrong side of the road in his car which had no first gear, but he had just learned that as part of the Africanisation of education he was one of the 90% of all Europeans who would have to leave within a year, in his case returning to Newcastle University.

He insisted that I stayed at his house at Fourah Bay College, which was 1,000 feet up overlooking the bay, but in return I insisted on taking him out to dinner each night (especially as he usually only had bread and cheese) and we had drinks at the City Hotel – the place described graphically in the opening chapter of Graham Greene's novel *The Heart of the Matter* – and dinner at the Government Rest House, a smart canteen built by the Government because there was no respectable hotel before the Paramount was built later. One night we had dinner at the Cape Club (soft lights or none at all, and very poor service) and the next at Lucy's Bar-Restaurant where we had chicken and orange sauce ('because we could not find a duck') and 'pancakes flambé' (flames two feet high). Lucy herself knew that Professor Hockey liked classical music so we heard 'The Planet Suite' a number of times; the cook had a wireless on with a honky-tonk piano; the crickets made their everlasting noise, and next door was an African dance party celebrating the 4th Anniversary of Independence.

The recent history of Sierra Leone is bound to the slave trade, where many freed slaves settled after the 1830s. Most had European names and their villages were called Kent, Sussex, Regent, Wellington and so on. They were collectively known as 'the Creoles', and there appeared a gulf between them and the original African population, both politically and socially. In a population of about two and a half million there were some 250,000 children enrolled in schools, of which about half were at denominational schools. The economy of the country was already dominated by the diamond trade which was then officially worth the enormous sum for Africa of £20 million per year.

In all I had made six appointments from England, Stanley Hockey making others, and among these was the Chief Education Officer and the principals of the two largest training colleges. On Sunday I spent the day at Fourah Bay

College and after an early lunch we drove south along the coast to villages like York (one of the original settlements of the freed slaves) where the coastline was idyllic and the beaches beautiful. We stopped at the home of the principal of the Sir Milton Margai College and sat on his verandah overlooking the coast discussing educational catalogues until it was dark, repairing to a Government Rest House for an adequate but unexciting dinner.

Monday morning I spent with Mr Knox-Macaulay, the local advisor on rural education; he had already prepared an order for Leeds, his friend having visited Arnolds the previous year. After an introductory visit to the Freetown Education Office I took a taxi and asked for the 'Methodist Headquarters' (I had to say it three times). The journey was a few miles and we eventually turned into a large garage – the 'Mercedes Headquarters'. The taxi driver thought it a huge joke but with helpful directions from the garage we were soon at our correct destination. (The Mercedes was rapidly becoming the favourite car in Freetown as the German company had been 'kind enough' to give all fifteen ministers one – it was a telling marketing move!)

The rest of my time was spent visiting the UCC (United Christian Council), the Catholic Education Secretary and (at last) the Methodists. It was clear that book supply played a major part in their thinking and their total expenditure was in excess of £100,000 annually. It was a welcome challenge for our book supply department, for 965 primary schools were certainly well within our reach.

*   *   *

The journey from Lungi Airport to Accra in Ghana was uneventful and I settled into the Ambassador Hotel which was huge and comfortable (although when the guest in the next room turned on the tap, the water ran in my bathroom as well!). The principal problem for traders was not getting orders, but getting paid. The well laid-out city of Accra had dual carriageways leading in all directions, but the contractors had not yet been paid. Doing business depended on an import licence and thus gaining an order was only the first step. Remarkable progress had been made since independence – the best known project being the Volta River Hydro-Electric dam – and on education very large sums had been spent already on new schools and equipment, and the authorities were now waiting for further licences.

President Nkrumah publicly blamed 'Imperialist Plots' for their financial woes and a moratorium on debts (said to total £500 million) was freely discussed. Prices were high: a Kodak film costing 36 shillings in England was 50 shillings in Accra. But this was potentially a large market and our new agents, Caffrey Saunders & Co., were confident there was business to be done, suggesting a minimum of £10,000 in the first year.

There were in all some 10,000 schools of all kinds, and Arnolds was already supplying 650 with catalogues. This could be increased dramatically and Mr Sam Brabe, the formidable managing director of Ghana Book Supplies, was to discuss this with Mr Saunders; it was largely a question of which British supplier could offer the best terms. After spending the morning with the Catholic and Presbyterian book depots, I called on the Chief Education Officer for secondary schools, Mr Boateng, who was helpful but cautious.

Hiring a car from the Tarzan Travel Agency I set off next day to drive myself to Cape Coast, stopping on the way to visit the Education Department's audio visual department near the seashore. At lunch I invited the manager to have a meal with me, but the nearest café was eighteen miles down the road so I drove on past two large 'slaver' castles to Cape Coast and had lunch in a very warm 'Catering Rest Home'.

After visiting the new University College of Cape Coast, on a hill overlooking the Atlantic with great breakers pounding the beaches, I went to Elmira as a tourist to photograph the most impressive castle on a promontory, which was then the principal police training college for 'illiterate police' (illiterate police wore red caps and literate police wore blue caps). Two fine looking trainees were very anxious that I photograph them and send back prints from Leeds. This I promised, although they had to find a 'blue cap' who could give me their names and address.

Next day Mr Saunders' manager drove me round the old part of town, still known as the Danish part of Accra, and we spent the day together visiting his house where he showed me a photograph of his grandparents: one, he said, had been on the staff of the Danish Embassy (I was given his name and some years later discovered in Copenhagen that there had indeed been a senior official of that name in Accra). I had tried to take a photograph of Kristianborg Castle but as I stood in the street a police official shouted at me and stood in the way. It was apparently illegal to photograph the castle because it was one of the President's residences.

*   *   *

It was a local flight in an old DC3 to Lagos in Nigeria, and most of the time we flew low enough to see people moving on the ground. Landing at Lomé, the capital of Togoland, and then Cotonou, the capital of Dahomey (a name I had often seen stamped on the bales of nets and cordage Bridport sent to West

Africa), we arrived at Lagos at dusk. A chaotic taxi drive took me to the Federal Palace Hotel and considerable luxury.

In the morning I telephoned the senior British Trade Commissioner whom I had met at the Leeds Chamber of Commerce the previous summer, and he soon arranged meetings with a number of senior education officials for three weeks hence when I would be returning to Lagos after visiting various Nigerian regions. I did, however, have time to see the advisor of technical education and later Chief Awokoya, the Permanent Secretary to the Minister for Education, a large and genial man who occupied an office which would have done credit to the Chairman of ICI. It was again an early supper for I had to be up at 5.30 to catch the local plane to Ibadan at 8 o'clock. It had been a busy day in Lagos but very useful in arranging visits in the four regions, which each had different education policies.

*   *   *

Ibadan was at that time perhaps the largest African city, with a population of over half a million. I was met by a friendly Mr Webb, the Assistant British Trade Commissioner, with a formidable list of appointments, and we set off at once to the Ransome-Kuti College of Education. In the hall a notice on the board said that 'Mr Howard of E. J. Arnold will address the staff at 11 o'clock.' No-one was about and I waited till midday when Mr Webb came to take me to my next appointment, telling me that this 'often happens'.

But I was welcomed at other colleges and treated to an excellent lunch which I could hardly eat because I had been suffering from a bout of 'African tummy' for nearly two days (locally known as 'palava'). Fortunately my host was Dr Davies of the University Faculty of Art and he gave me a large bottle of Dr Collis Browne 'chlorodyne' which cured everything from colds and neuralgia to my own complaint. It was most efficacious and became a regular companion on my journeys in Africa.

The Dean of the Faculty of Art at the University told me proudly that he had accepted a post in September from the University of Leeds, and I was also introduced to the Chief Inspector of Schools who believed strongly that supplies should go direct from abroad to the schools and not through the local retail market – where much could be 'lost'.

The Assistant Chief Inspector whom I met next day minced no words and said it was his job to see that the huge expenditure on education should be properly used. He said that orders for £1,000 of equipment would usually result in £750 of supplies arriving, the remainder going to the local trade or a 'colleague' of the headmaster. Such practices, he said vehemently, had to stop (although he admitted there were local political pressures to prevent the type of direct supply which Arnold could provide).

With the help of my taxi driver, Wabi (who, in spite of my protestations at which he laughed, reached 90 mph on the wrong side of the road and twice scattered crowds alighting from buses), I visited the principals of a number of other colleges that afternoon and more the following day before catching a small plane to Benin City the next day. We were delayed while ten wooden crates were piled beside the plane and a policeman sat on top with a rifle. He told me that they each contained £100,000 in small notes and he had to watch them until the plane took off. We arrived at Benin about 10 am where a friendly policeman helped me into a comfortable taxi.

I first met Mr Skinner, the British Trade Commissioner, who told me that my stay might be a difficult one because the Sardauna of Sokoto (Sir Ahmadu Bello, first Premier of Northern Nigeria after Independence) was arriving in the morning with a large retinue and all local hotel rooms had been requisitioned (notwithstanding mine had been booked two months before). But I got a night at the Mid West Development Corporation Rest House, only to be told that that too had just been requisitioned from the following morning. The manager kindly suggested that I drive to Enugu, 150 miles by road and ferry (the latter often not operating) and stay there!

When my helpful taxi driver, Mr Iyamu, arrived at eight next morning he said he had found me a hotel and had 'booked me at the Mogambo Palace' for fear that soon there would be no rooms left in town. I met the manager and said I'd be happy to stay so long as there was some air conditioning and no bad smells (open drains ran down from some bathrooms into the stream).

At the third room these conditions were met and I moved in. The walls were red and black and there was some old lino on the floor. The single bulb was fifteen watts. But there was a window and a comfortable enough bed. At lunch I met an Australian, who had been moved in two days earlier, and he suggested that as there were no locks or bolts on the doors at night I put a few empty beer bottles behind the door and round my bed, and if anyone came in they'd kick them over and wake me up. Much reassured, I knew everything would be all right and that the worst I would experience would be the very loud Arabic music which played continuously from a juke box down the corridor. But what can you expect when the Sardauna comes to town?

It was a busy day and I met the recently-appointed British Council representative, Mr Barton, who was most helpful, and the regional Visual Arts Officer. Then, armed with various school addresses, I visited the Catholic college and the Benin secondary school. One or two suggested it would greatly help if we had a local bank account, so I met Mr Scott, the Benin manager of Barclays, who told me it would only cost 1% to make a monthly payment to England.

Mr Iyamu realised we hadn't had lunch and bought me a bunch of bananas for 2 pence. On the way to our next school we stopped at a large and pleasant house to meet his brother, who turned out to be the District Superintendent of Police for Benin (perhaps that was why the taxi had been given preference at the airport) and whose wife came from Nevis in the Caribbean. After more school calls I returned to the Mogambo Palace for a rest and a shower (in the communal shower, when they unlocked the door).

Mr Iyamu arranged for me to have drinks with his brother: cold Guinness and very spiced meat (more help from Dr Collis Browne needed). I gathered that there was more than one Iyamu in the police force, and that my friend's father had had sixty-four children ('Not all the same wife,' said Mrs Iyamu reassuringly).

At dinner afterwards at the Rest House I sat with a very pleasant man, Mr Diyan, who turned out to be the Chairman of the Federal Board of Customs – there because of the Prime Minister's visit. He was horrified to hear I'd been turned out of my room and wanted me to have his, which, of course, I refused. There was a mini-pantomime of 'No, I insist,' but I told him we would have a drink in London some time, as we were both leaving Lagos the following week on the same flight.

After a visit to the Chief Inspector of Schools, who had a painted board over his door reading 'Slow and Steady', Mr Iyamu drove me to Port Koko on the Sapele River to watch the Sardauna launch a boat. To my surprise I was approached by a huge police officer who gave me a black and gold invitation card to the Sardauna's reception (courtesy of Mr Diyan) and, much cheered, I mingled with the colourful throng. There was every type of head-dress from boaters with feathers to straw trilbys – one with 'Chief' embroidered on it – brown bowlers, turbans and mohair peaked caps and marvellous robes, the most notable being in crimson with playing cards scattered across it. The wives of each chief (a dozen in the same dress as one chief) clearly enjoyed the excellent reception which followed – the principal drink was cold Guinness.

Unfortunately it was dance night at the Mogambo Palace, in the main concrete yard (ten feet from my door), but no-one danced into my room and I soon fell asleep with an early rise next morning to get to the airport (and a fond farewell from Mr Iymau). If goodwill counted for anything, I felt we should get some good business from Benin.

I had arrived early at the airport to have breakfast when there was a fanfare of trumpets supplied by the Oba of Benin for the departing Sardauna. The

Sardauna boarded his green private plane while the Oba drove home to his mud and corrugated palace (in which the Sardauna had not stayed).

*   *   *

My flight to Enugu took an hour, largely over the Niger delta. Enugu was a mining town: coal mines and cement works. The Presidential Hotel was reassuringly comfortable.

As usual my visits started at the British High Commissioner's office who were always helpful with lists of possible appointments and places to visit. Within the day I had met the head of the UNESCO mission (a former school inspector from New Zealand) and a number of senior inspectors of schools. The eastern region of Nigeria had almost 1.5 million children in primary schools and over 50,000 at secondary ones. Two hours at the Ministry of Education gave me a good idea of competitors' prices and I still had various officers to see there the next day.

As usual the offer of large numbers of catalogues directed to schools was warmly endorsed. My taxi driver was enthusiastic and, realising that I must be connected with education, offered to be our agent. I had to turn this offer down, at which he was disappointed but cheered up when I gave him three shillings to buy some beer because of the heat.

The CMS (Church Missionary Society) Supervisor of Schools was most friendly and told me of his visit to England in 1953/4 and how he had bought a ticket to a stand to watch the coronation. He and two friends had later visited Stratford-on-Avon to learn about Shakespeare and, he added, 'On Monday and Tuesday we travelled into the bush to see some villages around.' The next day was Wednesday and my taxi was taking me eighty miles to Onitsha – and no doubt seeing some villages in the bush on the way. Indeed the journey was particularly interesting, for my driver, Mr Egbo-Sinba, was a native of one of these villages, and as we drove through a number of others off the main road he explained how each had a village god – a bat, a green snake, or in his village a tortoise – which led to large concentrations of these creatures, for they enjoyed complete immunity and were venerated in their own village.

My educational visits followed their usual pattern: I learned of problems and offered opportunities, and as nearly always the discussions were very positive, leading to correspondence, discounts and usually orders in the future. On the way to the airport and a flight to Ibadan, my driver insisted on calling on his cousin where we sat on chairs beside a sandy road and drank a glass of beer. They presented me with two Kola nuts, one to take back to my wife in England, as a token of goodwill.

In Ibadan the same routine was followed, and one Chief Inspector of Schools was so anxious that supplies were sent direct to schools and not through the local bookshops that he asked that we write to schools telling them that when they had a catalogue they could only buy direct. I agreed to do this but said we had to see whether it was a success or not. After meeting a Chief Education Officer who had taught in Leeds for six years until 1961, I had lunch with the professors from the university (all from Jamaica – Professor Robinson's uncle having been Minster of Education on that island).

*   *   *

My next flight saw me in Kaduna, the administrative capital of Nigeria, where the way of life, as well as education, did not match all the changes taking place in other regions. The Premier, the Sardauna of Sokoto, and the Federal Prime Minister, Sir Abubakar Tafawa Balewa, both most able men, seemed determined that the north should follow the traditional life of Muslim Africa.

I learned that with about 50% of the population, the north only had about 25% of the schools in Nigeria, and while only a third of the children in primary schools were girls, this figure dropped to one girl to five boys at secondary level. Education so disproportionate to the sexes was accepted by many of the Education Officers I met in the largely Muslim north as balanced, and I could not see that any real change was likely in the near future.

I had arranged a meeting with the Permanent Secretary of Education, Mr Mackellar, one of the rapidly declining number of senior colonial civil servants still in Nigeria, then doubling with work for the Ministry of the Interior. I only knew he was on the third floor and as I wandered along a verandah with entrances to large offices but no names I heard a voice shout, 'Well tell the Airforce to move the bloody Dorniers.' This was clearly my man. (The Chief of Police had just telephoned to say that he couldn't draw up the Guard of Honour for the visit of the Prime Minister of The Gambia because the airforce had parked their Dorniers on the parade ground!)

The Hamdala Hotel was the centre of European life in Kaduna, comfortable and international, where one was as likely to hear German or Japanese spoken as an African language. I had dinner with Ken Guiseman, the managing director of Paterson Zochonis in Nigeria, and a friend, formerly a senior ICI executive, who was advising on the maintenance of, and training in, scientific equipment. We touched on many subjects, including the situation caused by a new generation of administrators who had undergone top level training in England and were prepared to be 'in charge' – but didn't feel that this meant that they had to work.

It was surprising but pleasing to come down to breakfast on Sunday and see peacocks strutting round the swimming pool and hear strains of Bach, Mozart and Haydn, not on a loud speaker but directly from the Steinway in the main drawing room played by a visiting advisor, while the next table was occupied by an Austrian portrait painter, there to complete various commissions. Kaduna was then the Paris of northern Nigeria.

The well-tried routine of meetings and then visits to local training colleges and schools went into operation and I had a very friendly start with Mr Dyer, a Cornishman, who had spent ten years in Nigeria as a schoolmaster and was now the Finance and Planning Officer for the Ministry.

Much thought was being given to publishing text and reading books in Nigeria, for the subject matter of those currently being used was, at best, based on Indian stories and characters, but otherwise pre-war English. It was a thoroughly sound idea when carried out by knowledgeable local educationalists, but was later in some countries open to political and financial manipulation where relatives of officials in the Ministry were to receive 'royalties' for work in which they had not been involved. There were still a considerable number of British teachers working in northern Nigeria and the standards in Kaduna were obviously high. As Africanisation took place, it would be up to those who were to come to keep to this level.

My final visit of the last afternoon in Kaduna was to see the Purchasing Assistant of the Education Secretary, Mr J. O. Ojo, who proudly showed me some congratulatory letters for a scholarship he had received. Over tea he confided that he had never even sat the scholarship but was pleased, nonetheless, to have this accolade and felt it reflected well on his department. (A year or more later I was in a different part of Nigeria and had lunch with a Chief J. O. O. Ojo, the Principal of a teacher training college, who told me that he had won a scholarship in education, but rather sadly added, 'But they never sent me the certificates, so I can't show you.')

*   *   *

Among the more imaginative ideas being pursued in northern Nigeria was a project by the University of Wisconsin to improve teacher training, and I was able to spend an hour with Professor Mickelson before catching the morning flight to Kano where, in spite of the modern and comfortable Central Hotel, one felt that one had a glimpse of the Middle Ages, and the temperature was over a hundred degrees.

Kano was a spacious town surrounded by a vast sand and stone wall about sixteen miles long. There were highly cultivated areas inside the walls and my

A gateway into Kano, Northern Nigeria.

Sun-heated dye pits in the sand at Kano.

taxi-guide told me that it had not been necessary to defend the walls since the end of the tribal wars when the British came. (I was able to imagine easily how it looked when Sir Hesketh Bell was Administrator nearly sixty years earlier.)

Most of my visits had to be arranged in the morning for most work stopped at 1 o'clock, although many businesses opened again in the evening. But it gave me an opportunity to drive round with my guide, who told me that he could not afford a wife and that even the Emir had decided to have no more wives, so there were a lot of very good ones available; it was such a waste (and of course he could arrange for a very good choice if I'd like to take one back to England – it would not be expensive, he said).

The indigo dying pits allowed one a glimpse of the Africa which had remained little changed for centuries; the cotton cloth was lowered into the pits deep in the sand and the heat of the earth provided all the heat necessary for the transformation to a rich dark blue. As the bales of cloth dried it was beaten by hand with flat clubs and this gave it the rich silk-like finish much admired in Kano and throughout Nigeria. Nearby, the caravan trains of camels were loading and unloading as they prepared for their long desert trek to Sokoto and the very heart of Africa. I was able to see briefly the small museum which displayed two or three complete sets of chainmail and helmets. These had remained in Kano and had been used as ceremonial uniforms by the servants of the Emir, but they had been captured originally from crusaders whom the Muslim rulers had fought, far to the north, in the 13th Century.

*   *   *

I had to be up at 3 am to catch the international flight from London to Lagos which went via Kano, and joined the chaotic morning traffic back to the Federal Palace again. It had recently been announced that Nigerian roads would be changing from driving on the left to driving on the right. 'But,' as the Minister of Transport explained in a special broadcast, 'no-one need worry because the changeover will take place gradually.'

After another day in Lagos of meetings and making arrangements for the future I caught the VC10 back to London via Kano again. It was very nice to be home by the middle of May.

CHAPTER 11

Yorkshire and the Middle East

More than two of the past seven months had been spent travelling in a dozen recently independent countries and much of the follow up work and planning for future journeys was still to be done, but summer at Hicklam in 1965 was a happy time; the girls came home for the holidays and we drove to Cornwall to stay with my mother and father at Tresawle. It was a long drive from Hicklam, but if one started on a Friday evening the roads were usually quite clear.

My mother's old friend, Vera Paton-Smith, had bought the Old Smithy at The Lizard and turned it into a very comfortable cottage (I could remember when the smith worked there, shoeing farm horses, and Vera had been clever in her conversion, changing as little as possible). She was always a fascinating friend and had worked most of her life in MI5, both in the First and Second War, first in Egypt and later in a personal role liasing with the brave women agents who landed by parachute at night in Europe. She had known such heroines as Odette (indeed it was my good fortune in later years to know Odette's daughter, and I still have the card she sent me on the death of her mother, Mrs Hallowes). Such resolution as hers was a lasting inspiration.

Vera's early life, too, was tinged with memories for her father was the last British Consul General in St Petersburg in Tsarist days and she and her father travelled in the famous 'last train out of Russia', by permission across Germany to France, at the fall of the Imperial regime. Vera spent quite a lot of time at Tresawle.

My father had thrown himself with great energy into local Lizard life, and not only was he the Treasurer of the Lifeboat – putting in countless hours of work – but he was deeply involved in divisional politics, where the MPs were first Greville Howard (a very distant cousin of my mother's who became quite a friend) and then John Nott. (About twenty-five years later I was to meet Sir John again, after the Falklands conflict, and we had lunch together reminiscing on those days.)

The Lizard was also home to a number of interesting characters, and I remember our local fish supplier who for many years sold what he had caught the previous night. Mr Goddard was always helpful and, having come from 'away', had married a local fisherman's daughter. In the summer his brother used to stay at Housell Bay, and sit on a bench on the cliff path. I'm not sure how long it was before we realised that his brother was, in fact, Lord Justice Goddard, the Lord Chief Justice of England.

Philippa, now eleven, Sophie and Jo revelled in the daily climb down the cliff path to Housel Bay and the swimming there, whether there was a broad stretch of sand or whether it had been driven out by a storm and was largely rocks. Even today, nearly forty years later, they need little invitation to visit that happy beach again.

*   *   *

Moving from Bridport had in no way diminished my interest in armorial porcelain – indeed it was exciting to find occasional small pieces in Tadcaster and York (an 'expensive' coffee cup would be £5). Although I then seldom saw Cecil and Muriel Bullivant, we continued to stay in touch and this was more than made up by the friendship of Phil and Pat Cooke who lived barely seven miles south of Aberford near Pontefract. Phil had followed his father as a most successful maltster and was an influential director of ABM (Associated British Maltsters) who supplied most of the large brewers with this essential ingredient.

His father had started collecting porcelain in the 1920s from Sir Algernon Tudor-Craig, and by the 1960s Phil's collection was, almost certainly, second only to Cecil Bullivant's in size and quality; in fact many pieces had been bought from Cecil during his time as a dealer. Unlike Cecil, however, Phil and his father had collected largely on the basis of quality and beauty, and now that he bought many of his pieces from London, usually from Helen Glatz, he did not always know the background of some pieces in his collection. In this I was only too willing to help. As a very well travelled businessman, he was able to find pieces in a wide range of places from Cornwall to Edinburgh, and his collection included a great many pieces which had never been known to Cecil Bullivant.

It was first necessary to photograph all the examples I didn't know and then identify them. This was made easy because of Phil's enthusiasm and he greatly enjoyed learning details of new pieces he had bought from various sources. He also had a number of friends with other pieces or collections, and these I visited at weekends when the gardening at Hicklam was up to date.

Hicklam was a very well-placed home almost exactly half way from London to Edinburgh and within sight of the A1 (or the old Great North Road, built by the Romans in the 1st Century AD). Various old friends like John Bourdon-Smith would stay the night and occasionally unknown 'friends' – as when the pilot of a glider crashed in the field opposite after dark, and when an obvious businessman broke down on the verge outside the house and came for help about 11 pm. He made fine marble-topped small tables for Harrods, two of which he showed us. We gave him a bed for the night, and ten days later a beautiful table arrived (we still have tea on it in the drawing room). I'm not sure one would be wise to do the same today – nor would one need to, because this was long before the days of mobile telephones.

It was, however, annoying when cars parked in the outer end of one's drive on the road and the children knew my irritation. One Sunday, about five in the evening, a husband and wife knocked at the door and asked if they could have tea. There was no sign of such a service being provided, but to my surprise they gave me a piece of paper which they had found tucked beneath the windscreen wiper on their car. It read:

> You have parked in our drive.
> You must pay a fine of one million pounds – or come to tea.

Sophie and Jo were delighted. Their plan had worked and the very pleasant schoolmaster and his wife had tea with us as we shared the joke.

*   *   *

But all too fast the summer waned, and my work at Arnold required a new and different journey. The children were back at school and, using a network of known agents and export advisors, I set off to the Middle East in November 1965 to very different countries from those newly emerging states and islands I had been to before. Nevertheless, my technique was the same and it was the personal contact which was designed to pave the way for orders in the future.

The Lebanon offered widely differing opportunities and we had appointed an agent in Beirut, Mr Nassa Bahous, who had previously been in the Iraq Petroleum Company but now had a stationery store in central Beirut. He met me at the airport at 8 pm but I didn't leave his house until after midnight, so keen was he to explain the market to me.

Probably the largest potential single orders would come from the United Nations Relief and Works Agency who were responsible for 200,000 children at school and had an ample budget. I later spent a long afternoon at UNRWA and learned some of the niceties of quoting in the Lebanon. No product which had a Jewish name should even be mentioned in an order for fear the whole consignment would be rejected!

I travelled to Jordan with an UNRWA primary agent, Mr Maroum, and we had dinner in my hotel. I learned that Mr Bahous controlled a considerable part of their book purchasing and as the agent, too, of Longmans he had been instrumental in ensuring that 80% of the approved textbooks were from that publisher. If the right terms could be quoted, there was an opening for rival publishers.

Along the side of hills above the city were a number of large establishments and in the centre, the Brumana High School. This had an English headmaster, Mr Grosvenor, and pupils from all over the Middle East – so that the sons of Arab sheikhs were in the same class and were friends with Jewish boys from Israel. Under the strict and fair supervision of the staff this worked well. Mr Grosvenor told us that in all the school had pupils from twenty-nine countries and although it was very well supplied, we learned of a number of things that were required.

The Ministry of Education's textbook department was under the control of a remarkable woman whose father was Leader of the Lebanese Senate. She had the reputation of being incorruptible – an unusual reputation in that market. In all we spent two and a half hours in her department, meeting various assistants.

I was welcomed later by the principal of the Islamic Education College, where strong black coffee was poured continuously into small cups. It was then possible to meet the headmasters of various Christian denominational schools and until late in the evening we discussed library books and training equipment at the Istiklal library, leaving just in time to have a late dinner at the 'Ali Baba' restaurant where I recall two items in particular on the menu: 'Parsley Salad' and 'Foul'.

I spent thirty-six hours in Jordan but was at the airport at 6 am for a flight back to Beirut where Mr Bahous had a number of appointments for me, then flew on from Beirut to Kuwait.

*   *   *

Although the comet of Kuwait Airways taxied to the end of the runway twice, we didn't take off until four hours later at 1 am. The plane contained a large group of oil men returning after leave and Kuwait was perhaps not at its best at 2.30 in the morning. The Customs made a random search and opened anything that looked like liquor. One threw a carry-cot on to a pile of suitcases – not realising there was a baby inside, but no harm was done.

Arriving at our hotel after 3 am, we were told that our hotel rooms had now been given away and I slept in a lounge on a huge sofa with lots of cushions. Two oil engineers who arrived with me were very angry about these arrangements and made this most clear to the clerk on duty. (When I checked out two days later I found the two engineers still enraged with the same clerk, this time by the size of their bill. I was pleasantly surprised, however, at my own, and when I mentioned this to the clerk he replied, 'Sir, I put half your bill on their account because you no trouble when you arrive.')

There is today universal education in Kuwait and there could hardly be any others in the world to match those schools I saw – all secondary schools with theatres, laboratories, swimming pools and gymnasia, and all to the highest standard. The same could be said of the roads and many of the new buildings which had altered greatly in the last fifteen years, as the ruler had spent his vast wealth in improving the lot of ordinary Kuwaitis. That he was held in very high esteem was not in doubt, and as I stood looking at his portrait in the window of a smart shop in a main street, there was a shout behind me and an angry policeman pulled my hand from my pocket; it would seem that such lax behaviour in his presence could insult his memory.

Our recently appointed agent I found to be an aged Mr Abdulaziz Al-Rashid who employed sixty-five people in palatial offices and included such companies as ICI Explosives and Marley Tiles amongst his large range of principals. His assistant, Mohammed Ahmed, was briefed to look after me while in his area of influence, and I enjoyed my journeys with this very intelligent Pakistani.

Here the schools included Indo-Pakistani schools as well as the religious schools I had become accustomed to, and as we had already sent some supplies to Kuwait, it was of interest to get a complimentary feedback. I also spent time at the Ministry of Education and had discussions with the Chief Inspector of English, and it was clear here also that Longmans had a very large share of the reading market, in some cases with books adapted so that while the storyline was the same, the dress illustrated was for the Arab world.

After a busy morning, Mr Ahmed and I had an ample lunch at an Indian restaurant and then spent time with the assistant Chief Purchasing Officer of the Kuwait Oil Company who had responsibility for a number of schools and who preferred to purchase by discount from catalogues. I did not delay a late dinner with Mr Ahmed for we had to meet at five in the morning to fly to Bahrain, and, in my case, on to Riyadh in Saudi Arabia.

*   *   *

We had had a friendly correspondence from Leeds with Mr Hallows in Bahrain and I had considered appointing the company for whom he worked as an agent until I discovered that they already represented a competitor. But Mr Hallows kindly drove us round Bahrain for a morning, including the oil refinery, and left me at the airport at three after a magnificent lunch prepared by Mrs Hallows, a charming Anglo-Indian, at their palatial bungalow.

Almost at once things started going wrong. First, Saudi Arabia had just introduced a new anti-cholera injection requirement, and I had to take this at the airport, getting a rather sore arm. It was irritating, too, that Gulf Airways suddenly asked all passengers for a £5 'take off fee'. On arrival at Dahran on the mainland after a very short flight, I was greeted with the news that Arab Airlines had changed their schedules and there was now no flight till the afternoon of the next day; this would throw my own schedule much out of line. The only alternative seemed to be a taxi to Riyadh, five hundred kilometres inland. The fare quoted seemed a reasonable £14, so we set off into the gathering darkness with a promise that I'd be there for breakfast.

Although more used to local runs, my driver seemed confident that at a hundred kilometres per hour Riyadh would only be five hours away. Parts of the road were lit by the light from oil gas fires in the desert and the road itself was good but narrow, with occasional huge pot holes, while we normally swerved into the sand if we met an occasional oncoming vehicle.

But optimism was short-lived and after about a hundred kilometres an ominous rattle caused my driver to swerve down a side road and drive for thirty kilometres until we reached a desert town called Hassa. No effort was made to repair the damage, but my driver had long discussions with others who were clearly friends and finally reached agreement that one of them would take me the last four hundred kilometres for a share of the fee!

There were snags, for I was told his only English words were 'Mister', 'good' and 'no good' and the deal also included taking a local soldier, with his rifle, three hundred kilometres down the road back to barracks. But the car was modern and fitted with a gramophone on to which he threw disks at regular intervals – all with very loud Arabic music. About midnight we pulled into a transport café near the main road and drank a huge pot of sweet tea and ate a cake (paid for by the soldier who was grateful for his ride) and then were away again at breakneck speed. By use of the phrase 'no good' several times I managed to convey that a hundred and fifty kilometres an hour was too fast, so we settled for a hundred and twenty. The soldier got out with a friendly wave about an hour from Riyadh, but shortly after we came to a halt with a shuddering jolt just after hitting part of a wrecked car beside the road. One tyre was ripped off, but this was soon dealt with as the driver took off the wheel, rolling it away into the sand, and put on the spare wheel from the boot.

To my great relief we reached Riyadh after driving five hundred kilometres in six and a half hours including all stops, only to find the hotel I had booked had let my room as there were no further flights from Dahran. Paying the taxi proved another problem as I had no Saudi cash and the hotel had none either, so we drove on to another where a friendly representative of the Minnesota Mining Company, who happened to be in the lobby, cashed a cheque for me and we arranged to have breakfast together at eight. He showed me a third hotel round the corner where they had a 'communal room' and I quickly fell asleep on one of the four couches in a dormitory with my suitcase rolled up in a rug beside me. Luckily no-one else appeared – perhaps my luck was turning!

It was. Next morning I had breakfast with Mr Faud Farah, the Kuwaiti representative of Minnesota Mining and he took me to his new and spacious offices. I had been trying without success to appoint an agent by negotiation from Leeds and after two hours, and learning that he would welcome a publishing and educational firm as a partner, I met his two new Arab partners and promised to send supplies of catalogues and prices, while they offered a large display area. I felt that if Mr Farah and his friends were good enough for Minnesota Mining, they were good enough for Arnold.

We wasted no time and after a frantic day and many cups of black coffee had planned a showroom; visited the Chief Inspector of Schools; spent time with the Inspector of English, who confided that he would be delighted if the present monopoly of English book supplies could be broken; and had dinner with two Italians, one of whom was the Middle Eastern representative of an Italian finance corporation. We all felt that it should be possible to achieve a turnover of £20,000 in the first year and much more thereafter. Such are the 'downs' and 'ups' of the life of a roving educational representative.

In 1965 the time of day posed difficulties in Riyadh, for 1 o'clock was one hour after sunrise and so on (and it was necessary to reset one's watch each morning). Confirming times of plane flights was equally confusing and often led to waits at airports. At the airport I met the Middle East military correspondent of *The Times*, who had had his recent despatches censored due to the Saudi dispute with Britain over the Buraimi Oasis; he wondered if I could post them on arrival in England. Perhaps foolishly I agreed and put them in my case. But it proved no problem; they eventually reached their destination safely, and I later read them in *The Times*.

The plane for Jeddah took off at 'one hour after dark'. I did not know when that was, but caught it and was soon in my hotel room.

*   *   *

Mr Said El-Ajan, Mr Farah's partner, was there to meet me and told me over breakfast how he had recently bought property for £48,000 and sold it three weeks later for £75,000 – such rapid gains were common in Jeddah. We called at the British Embassy and then drove to the most prestigious girls' school.

The principal of the Dar El Hannan School, maintained entirely by a huge subsidy from King Faisal's wife, was a Mrs Halabi and while we waited for her to finish a meeting with the architects, we toured the entirely new buildings for the seven hundred girls – most the daughters of the wealthiest in the land (but including fifty penniless orphans). Mrs Halabi herself was a ball of fire, knew the Arnold catalogues well and had just ordered a preparatory £3,000 worth of equipment. She was to visit us the following summer in Leeds.

Even Mr El-Ajan was impressed, and that evening we plotted well into the night how we could let her have everything she wanted. We dined together on the open terrace facing the Red Sea and as we did so the main hotel dining room filled with thirty glittering ladies who we watched as they arrived in enormous cars, dressed from top to toe in black. As they left their 'carriages' they turned and threw their black robes into the cars, appearing in gold and white from Dior in the dining rooms, with western hairstyles. Although their thirty cars were waiting at midnight, the receptionist told us the party ended at 4 am.

In the morning we visited Mr El-Ajan's shop and then the Al-Thaghr Model School – the brother school of the girls' school seen the previous day. They were established in equal style, and I learned that the annual equipment expenditure was about £230,000 for the 532 boys. The morning passed quickly and we returned to Mr El-Ajan's home for a delicious lunch. The afternoon was spent at an equally well-endowed kindergarten. It was difficult to stay awake, but after a short sleep and goodbyes I went to the airport to catch the evening flight to Khartoum. The Caravelle was only half full but it was not reassuring to be asked by the crew to 'sit in the front to balance the plane'.

It was after midnight when we reached Khartoum, but I was met by a smiling Mr Tadros with whom I had corresponded from Leeds. I soon felt that the Sudan could be our most interesting market yet. He took me to the Grand Hotel, standing on the banks of the Nile, and I was soon asleep in a large colonial-style bedroom with huge 'punkah' fans slowly turning in the ceiling.

Joseph Tadros had abundant charm and an English wife from Surrey; he was fourth generation Sudanese of Turkish extraction. He already had eleven agencies in Khartoum and had recently won a million pound building contract for a British company after it had been awarded to an American company (the American ambassador had intervened without success). He was convinced that there were large opportunities in education, and his interest centred on the

Re-stocking the Sudan Bookshop, Khartoum.

Joseph Tadros and his family at his home in Khartoum.

largest bookshop in the country: the very substantial premises of the Sudan Bookshop, which had once had a near monopoly of educational supplies and turnover of £150,000 but had fallen on hard times because of inefficiency and dubious practices. The trustees were acting for the Church, and they had determined to sell their 'tenure in perpetuity' for £5,000 before there was any scandal, while the rent was secured at £4,000 per year.

By the following day I had seen the trustees unofficially – Archdeacon Martin, acting for the Bishop of Sudan; nominees of Barclays Bank, and Gelatly Hankey & Co., the principal British merchants in Khartoum – and had a strong feeling that they would welcome Arnold's participation. Joseph Tadros made it clear he would welcome a half share of all costs and the way was open to a 50% owned Arnold company, a pattern which was later to be followed successfully in a dozen other countries. The main competition was the locally owned Greek bookshop – the Khartoum Bookshop – which had taken a major share of the rapidly growing school market since 1959.

With ideas spinning in my mind, Joseph Tadros took me to visit a number of schools both of Christian and Muslim teaching. At the principal girls' school, however, I experienced my first total rejection when the English headmistress refused to see us as we had no prior appointment (a reaction which Mr Tadros called 'a piece of bloody British Imperialism'). Nonetheless we had interesting discussions and I rapidly gained an opinion that the whole Sudan market could be open to us if we moved quickly and efficiently.

Because I was anxious to have a meeting with the Ministry of Education in Nigeria, I changed plans at the last moment and was able to arrange to return to England via Lagos. But at the weekend I was also able to arrange dinner with the Commercial Councillor at the British Embassy, Mr Munro, and we discussed a possible purchase of the bookshop until late. It was clear that Joseph Tadros' winning of the building contract had amazed the Embassy and I had both a warm endorsement of such a plan and promises of support were we to establish a major educational supply system.

Sunday was a day off, and I was driven round Khartoum and was taken to the point outside Khartoum where the White Nile moves slowly up from the south and joins the Blue Nile down from the hills (creating a huge backed-up ripple of shades of blue, giving the river its name). Joseph also drove me over to Omdurman and to his amazement I walked back across the almost mile-long bridge to my hotel (where, as usual, 'Foul Sudan' was a prominent item on the menu).

On Monday we had time to visit a number of other schools and spent time at the Ministry of Education. In the afternoon I caught the Abyssinian Airways flight to Lagos. As we took off, the pilot made an unexpected announcement:

'Mr Prime Minister, Your Excellency, Ladies and Gentlemen, this is the Captain speaking...'. Sir Abubakar Tafawa Balewa, the Prime Minister of Nigeria, was on board. I watched as he was met at midnight at Kano airport after our trans-African flight by Sir Ahmadu Bello and a number of northern ministers. Both were to be assassinated in the Nigerian coup later the following month.

Unfortunately riots in Lagos made it impossible to reach the city and have my meeting at the Ministry of Education, so I spent most of the rest of the day at the airport hotel with a Dr Ross, who was the principal of the leper colony of eastern Nigeria. The usual wait was filled with a fascinating two hours of discussion ranging from leprosy to bubonic plague. I have thought frequently of my conversation with this dedicated man (he was shortly to take charge of the leper colonies in Ethiopia).

London in the early morning and Leeds by teatime; it was the run up to Christmas 1965.

*   *   *

I was very anxious to see Elizabeth who hoped that our next child would arrive in March. Fortunately all was well, but the commercial situation in Khartoum was such that Martin Arnold had agreed to come with me in late January to see the lie of the land and make a final decision on our link with Joseph Tadros which had to be finalised by the end of that month if leases were not to be offered elsewhere.

Five in the morning is not the best time to go to bed, especially after a night stop in Rome and more than an hour filling in forms and passing customs at Khartoum airport. But if one decides to fly 5,000 miles for a weekend business meeting and then fly home, one must be content if one only has fifteen hours in a real bed in five days. On Saturday we met the Bishop of the Sudan and agreed to buy the indefinite lease of the Sudan Bookshop – Joseph Tadros was delighted. Saturday afternoon saw a rare chance to visit the President's Palace, and we stood on the steps made immortal by General Gordon some eighty years before. As we walked round with Joseph Tadros, who had arranged this special privilege, we found on the second floor all was chaos, as one might expect when King Faisal of Saudi Arabia was coming to stay the following week. Someone had decided that the electric wiring was not sufficient and an array of workmen were chiselling away plaster, putting in conduits, climbing ladders, moving furniture and carpets and hastily cementing – so much so that it was barely possible to get into the State Bedrooms, slept in by the Queen when she visited Khartoum, and the

The Palace in Khartoum.
With Martin Arnold and a guard before the steps where General Gordon fell.

furniture was covered by a heavy layer of dust and cement. Perhaps a lift should be installed? Was a week enough to do this? Perhaps it would be better if King Faisal used a ground floor house in the grounds instead? Were there enough workmen available to do the work?

We drove through the centre of Khartoum (all the central roads had been laid in the outline of a huge Union Jack) and then Sunday evening was reserved for a private dinner party at Joseph Tadros' house before we caught the plane to London. We were not as surprised as some of the other guests when our host entered with the President, His Excellency Ismael El-Azhari and the Minister of Education, Sayed Hassan Awadalla.

The President was a smiling, kind-faced man who for many years had been a schoolmaster, and for one period during the Military Dictatorship had spent a time under arrest in southern Sudan. He was widely respected and much loved and one could not help but be at ease with him. Indeed, in his own house any Sudanese was able to call on him, present petitions and ask for advice or help. So much of his time did this take up that one wondered how much time he had for governing, for the Sudanese system then had both Prime Minister and President, but the latter had a role which was becoming increasingly like that of an American President.

As he sat down to dinner, one of the Sudanese guests sat too heavily and his chair collapsed. This was the signal for great merriment, and the President and Minister rocked backwards and forwards in an alarming way. The Minister of Education, who had been driving through the desert most of the day after opening a new school and was clearly a good deal more tired than we were, remembered the time that this had happened to him in Addis Ababa at a meeting of the Cabinet there and how one of the Abyssinians had said that they hoped that the collapse of a member of a visiting Government was not a bad omen. The Abyssinian Government fell two days later – he had never been invited there again!

Later, when all the guests had gone, we telephoned the airport to find out if the VC10 was one hour or two hours late from Nairobi – it was, of course, two. But there were some empty seats so we were able to lie down. Breakfast over Mont Blanc and London airport on a raw February morning; after an unspeakable grind through Uxbridge and Rickmansworth, Martin tested the speed of his new car and we roared up the M1 to arrive by lunch.

The next morning newspapers reported that King Faisal was in Khartoum. Undoubtedly there was a state dinner, but I doubt if they enjoyed it as much as we did our private dinner with the President.

CHAPTER 12

East Africa

Thomas was born at Hicklam House on 1st March 1966. All the girls were thoroughly delighted to have a brother, and their mother and I were very happy. It was a pleasant spring and we all enjoyed the Easter holidays, my parents coming up from The Lizard to see their new Howard grandson, but I was not able to linger as the summer developed. The expectations of success in the Sudan had awakened ambitions further south, and in mid May I flew by Nairobi and Kitwe to Lusaka in Zambia, where we had learned that there might be opportunities similar to those in Khartoum.

It was possibly no accident that within six months two such opportunities should present themselves to purchase bookshops which had previously been run by the Church. Politics had not helped the Church in recently-independent Africa, for while they had, throughout colonial times, been the leaders in education through their missionary societies, the rapid moves towards what was now seen as broader social justice seemed to portray the Church as part of an older and more conservative regime. The involvement, too, of the Church in the business side of the new competitive educational supply system could lead to moments of commercial embarrassment, while many of those within the missionary system did not feel that this commercialism was their calling.

Zambia itself, because of its huge exports of tin, was both a far smaller but far richer country than the Sudan, and it had moved very rapidly towards expanding education under its deeply religious Prime Minister, Kenneth Kaunda. It was planned to increase the school places from 440,000 in 1966 to 680,000 in 1970, and the Ministry of Education, which had still largely British staff at a senior level, was dedicated to achieving this.

The principal bookshop and supply system was, however, in the hands of the USCL (United Society of Christian Literature) who had already told the Government that they intended to withdraw from educational supply because of the increasing volume of slow payers and occasionally bad debts among their new customers, but had been persuaded to remain by a £75,000 interest-free loan because it was realised that otherwise the whole supply system could collapse at a time when the Government was most anxious to move forward, but had no system set up themselves.

The USCL was, in fact, controlled by a large committee in London of whom the Chairman was Lord Luke and Vice Chairman his brother, the Hon.

162

Frederick Lawson (whose family had been connected with the Society for some generations). The actual business was carried out by the Lutterworth Press, a general and religious publisher. In Zambia, however, the Society was largely controlled by Albert Stepney and his educational manager in Lusaka, Don Clarke, while there was a branch in Kitwe with an able accountant. I was able to assess the size and profitability of the Society quickly with the help of Mr Stepney and apart from the interest-free loan, it seemed that a total profit of over £40,000 could be made on the current turnover of £160,000 (which itself was expanding rapidly).

I attended meetings at the Ministry of Education with Mr Foxell, the General Manager of Lutterworth Press in Africa, and it seemed that, subject to a welter of detail and agreement by the USCL committee in London, it would be possible for Arnold to take over the loan for two years, the bookshop and their stock, and become the principal educational supplier in Zambia for about £95,000 (reading through my ten-page detailed summary at the time this is a considerable simplification of detail – but accurate overall).

The only serious competition was an organisation started the previous year by an entirely new company called Zambian Educational Distributors, which was largely financed by an unusual man, Theodore Bull, the hugely wealthy nephew of Sir Alfred Beit, one of the 'founders' of modern South Africa. An old Harrovian, Theo Bull had created some surprise by marrying the daughter of the King of Barotseland, whom he had first met at university in England, and apart from being the owner of the only European newspaper in Rhodesia to defy Mr Smith (and having the money to continue publishing his daily newspaper with a blank front page when it was made to withdraw an article of political comment) he was most anxious to help create a democratic liberal ethos in East Africa. In months and years to come we would manage to turn ZED from a rival into a partner, and I would spend a fascinating day in a private plane flying with Theo to meet his father-in-law, the King, at his capital in Central Africa – but that was a year or two ahead.

Don Clarke was determined to show me Zambia by road, and we set off on Monday morning to drive east to Fort Jamieson and the border with Nyasaland (in due course to become Malawi). The Great East Road was one of the only two oil and petrol supply routes into the country and must have been one of the most dangerous roads in the world, as huge tankers and lorries with trailers roared westward in clouds of sandy dust which made it all but impossible to overtake except by driving blind for up to a mile, making the vehicles themselves all but invisible. This was testified to by wrecked cars in the ditch and the nine burned out and overturned tankers we saw in two hundred miles.

Great East Road, Zambia. Quarter-mile dust clouds follow each vehicle.

A faster route in the bush – if there is a landing place. With Don Clarke in Zambia.

Four hours from Lusaka a road sign read 'Sharp bends for 47 miles'. On this stretch from 2 pm to midnight lorries travelling east had right of way, and from 2 am to midday lorries travelling west had the right (no-one explained what happened from 12 to 2!). As we had misjudged our start slightly, we travelled east between 12 and 3 and for the last fifteen miles had to swerve if a dust storm came hurtling towards us in the middle of the road, but at last we reached our goal, Crystal Springs – the only, tiny, hotel at Fort Jamieson (formerly the home of a ruined tobacco farmer) with six bedrooms.

We visited the excellent boys' secondary school at Fort Jamieson and had dinner with the headmaster, the next day turning to retrace our route to Lusaka. The four hundred mile stretch had only one small restaurant on the way where one could get a cold beer and a sandwich. We stopped at Kachinola and walked up the steps, but the counter and fridge were locked, and the African caretaker said, 'The Donna she in bed – she lock up all tea leaves.' In vain did we plead, but continued and breathed a sigh of relief as we negotiated the last bend in the 47 mile stretch. We had earlier stopped to see the headmaster of a mission school on the road and been told that three days ago his assistant priest had been killed on the Great North Road. As we reached the last bridge, thirty miles from Lusaka, we were halted as we watched a new stretch of tarmac being laid. There were thirty workmen spreading gravel on the new tarmac but only three had shovels, the rest carried armfuls gathered from the gravel lorry and dropped them on the road – apparently many had 'sold' their shovels and so were made to work without.

Next day I met the Commercial Secretary at the British High Commission and it was clear that Arnold would have their support in running the bookshop if all went well. It was clear also that it would be important to secure the continuing loyalty of the USCL staff, particularly Don Clarke who lived there with his wife, Pam, and their two daughters, but also the various bookshop managers. (Albert Stepney was due to retire in the next year or two.) Much depended on the distribution of a wide range of books through these bookshops and a number of publishers were concerned because Macmillans were anxious to obtain joint publishing arrangements directly with African governments in order to get a small range of their own text books recognised solely by the developing educational departments. Such a plan would not meet with approval by most independent headmasters who feared lack of choice and spiralling costs.

Filled with thoughts of these opportunities, I caught the plane home to what promised to be a happy summer, for it was now June. I was also told that, as my responsibilities had increased, my title was now to be the Export Director of E. J. Arnold although this would not give me a seat on the family board.

While we were able to spend another holiday in August at Tresawle and introduce Thomas to Cornwall, it was also necessary for me to have meetings in London with Lord Luke and his brother, and it was soon confirmed that Arnold should take over the USCL bookshops in Zambia. This, in turn, led to consideration of other East African markets and as soon as school was starting, I was on my way to Nairobi to meet a possible new collaborator – Book Distributors Limited.

I was met at the airport by Mr Shah and was soon introduced to his senior partner, Mr Rughani. They had successfully set up an enterprise aimed at the educational market which combined an agency representing six English publishers, a chain of six small bookshops and a 'Textbook Centre' which they hoped to develop into an educational equipment warehouse. Clearly they viewed Arnold as a possible partner in such an enterprise. Their vision did not stop there, for they hoped to be able to expand into Uganda where it was clear that the Uganda Bookshop, controlled by the Church, had a similar problem to that which we had encountered in the Sudan and Zambia, and was looking for a business partner who could provide the necessary skills of management, stock control and accountancy in the emerging situation of locally controlled education departments. Mr Rughani and Mr Shah were particular friends of the Patel family in Uganda, of which Mr Narendra Patel was the Speaker of the Ugandan Parliament.

In spite of their obvious connections Mr Rughani and Mr Shah were anxious to have an English partner of reputation, with a capital base which would allow them to offer suitable credit to education departments and schools that would attract a major share of the market. Arnold much appealed to them as such a partner.

We visited the Ministry of Education together and they later drove me through Uganda to Kampala so that I should see and appreciate the situation there. On the way we called at the Patel Press and the Uganda Bookshop and I stayed one night in Kampala before taking a taxi next day to Entebbe to catch a flight to Khartoum. I felt sure, however, that in Mr Rughani and Mr Shah, Arnold could have suitable partners for an enterprise similar to that in the Sudan and Zambia.

Entebbe is almost on the equator, near Lake Victoria, and most days a local Sudan Airways flight flew a Fokker Friendship northwards to Khartoum and returned the following day. I had been told that I would be the only passenger but at the last moment I was joined by an Indian family. The plane flew at about eight to ten thousand feet so one was well able to see much of the Kingdom of Buganda, passing near Kampala and crossing the Murchison Falls where the river runs northwards into the swamps of southern Sudan. Our only stop was at Juba, where the airport building, a single dilapidated edifice standing at the end of the only runway, stood in the intense shimmering heat.

We disembarked for a while and a group of turbaned tribesmen and two very tanned Europeans invited me to join them for a pint of fresh lemon drink. The only conversation was about the King of Buganda, Sir Frederick Mutesa, who had recently disappeared (and later fled into exile in Britain). After an hour we were joined by four more passengers, and after take-off were served with ham and cheese sandwiches as we followed the ever-widening Nile northwards. The river divided and subdivided creating huge mud flats, and for hundreds of miles there was largely barren swampy ground with small green cultivated areas and occasional clusters of thatched huts.

About three hours after leaving Juba there were signs of organised cultivation and suddenly a town with corrugated roofs could be seen. As we flew lower and it was possible to see the huge river from both sides of the aircraft, it was apparent that we were slowly approaching Khartoum. Joseph Tadros met me at the airport with a hug and a kiss and we drove to his house for supper. Two hours later the immigration department rang to ask why I had entered the country illegally. (What they meant was that they had forgotten to stamp my passport.) We had to return to the airport where I was asked why I hadn't *asked* to have it stamped – but the passport officer then looked up and smiled and completed marking off all the names on the passenger list.

I only had a day in Khartoum before I caught the next night's VC10 to London, but every minute was occupied in deciding what stock should be dispatched to the Sudan Bookshop and how the catalogues should reach the schools. The bookshop manager was a pleasant Sudanese called Mr Fahmi who also ran a fleet of taxis. At 9 pm each night (the shop closed from 1 to 5) each taxi driver would come into the bookshop in turn and hand over his day's takings. If these appeared to Fahmi to be adequate he was returned his share and all was well; if not, a discussion ensued, the ultimate threat being that his taxi would be given to someone else! A bargain was soon reached and Fahmi handled everything professionally and quickly. We hoped and expected that he would be as canny with local headmasters as they came to spend their money. But his first task was to return the bookshop to profitability and a turnover of about £200,000. Having seen how Joseph worked I had no doubt that this would soon happen. It was a pleasure to work in such an energetic atmosphere.

*   *   *

Although another visit to East Africa, and particularly Kenya and Zambia, was planned for December, I looked forward to an autumn at home. It was decided that I would not join my mother for her 70th birthday on 11th October, for she and my father planned to spend a weekend at Torquay, joined by the Branders who lived nearby.

That Friday evening Elizabeth and I were in Leeds at the theatre and I was surprised to get a telephone call after our return. It was my aunt to say that my mother was very ill in a Torquay nursing home having caught a chill on Dartmoor. Although it was 11.30 pm, I got into the car and drove through the night, reaching Torquay at 10 am after a short sleep in a lay-by south of Bath about dawn.

My father was also exhausted, having been up much of the night, but we drove to the nursing home to find my mother in good spirits but in an oxygen tent because of her breathing (she had had pneumonia thirty years earlier and still smoked, which would not have helped). Sitting most of the day by her bed and talking made her quite cheerful, and my father and I returned to the Branders to sleep at about 10 pm – leaving her calm and smiling. At midnight the telephone rang and the nursing home told us that she had just died. We drove back to see her peaceful face and I tried to comfort my father.

My mother had always wished to be cremated, and I drove my father back to Tresawle three days later with her ashes from the Exeter crematorium. He was desperately upset but Vera Paton-Smith agreed to stay with him as long as was needed and eventually I drove back to Leeds. Her ashes were later sprinkled along the cliff path at The Lizard which she had loved for more than twenty years. Throughout my life I had never known her to be anything other than 'firm but fair'. She would always insist on the right of everyone to speak their mind but be considerate of others, and she would say 'Never be rude to anyone – especially not to servants' (for they did not have the privilege of answering back). In the thirty-eight years I knew her I believe I was never angry with her, nor ever knew her to be wrong in her judgement.

*   *   *

In late November I flew out to Lusaka again to learn more about the market in Zambia and get to know Don Clarke better. This was to be followed by a journey up through East Africa which was to include a visit to Ethiopia to see if that hard-pressed country would have opportunities similar to the others which had opened up in East Africa. Don Clarke was anxious that after my introduction to Zambia by road I should understand the size of the country (and market) and visit some of the further flung corners of that deceptively large country. It sounded rather luxurious to visit provinces by private plane – quicker yes, luxurious no.

We arrived at Kitwe airport at 7 am, complete with a large picnic basket containing an array of puff pastries filled with every known kind of liver pâté, prepared by Mrs Macartney, our Zambian chief accountant, who had been born in Warsaw. Don, Brian Barrett (our Kitwe manager) and I took off in our rather small plane, and as we did so our Rhodesian pilot said to Don, 'Do you mind moving your knees so that I can reach that lever?' As we roared down the runway and banked to the right there was a nasty rattle as I leaned sideways and my door flew open, so in a splutter of radio 'Charlie Able Fox 7 why are you returning, over' we touched down, slammed the door hard and took off again.

In Africa's mid summer, at 8,000 feet, it is very warm and bumpy at midday. We flew over the 'Congo Pedical' (that long tail of the Congo which reaches south into Zambia) and after two hours at 170 mph we saw the narrow landing strip at Kasama. We were met by the Provincial Education Officer's landrover and had a constructive hour with him discussing local supply, and then drove back to the airstrip where Don and Brian guzzled paté pies under the wing of the plane while I stretched my legs along the deserted airstrip. As we flew on to Fort Rosebery, with the merciless sun beating on our tiny 'cabin oven', Don's face turned a distinct shade of green (Polish liver pâté is best eaten in Poland I suspect). But we were met by the local Provincial Education Officer himself for another planning discussion. This over, we returned to Kitwe and were thankful to find ourselves on a road again after the 'luxury' of our plane.

Next morning before seven we took off again, this time bound south west for Mongu in Barotseland with a pleasant New Zealand pilot who was hoping to reach Europe and a better job one day. As he didn't know the way, I held the map and we navigated largely by following rivers until they were crossed by a road, and we then turned right or left.

Mongu is difficult to reach by land for much of the year for the roads become impassable with floods and the resulting mud. The Zambesi swells from under half a mile wide to many miles. The airfield runway was built of bricks, laid exactly as those in a house, only sideways on the ground. This enabled them to adjust to both heat and rain. Our meeting with the Education Officer over, we all retired to a white house with bow windows and thatched roof where we ate lunch – this time smoked salmon, anchovies and chicken.

Our afternoon flight took us to the airstrip at Solwezi where there was a thatched hut and two boys asleep (there is as much difference in 'airports' as there is between the M1 motorway and a footpath on Dartmoor). But in a country at places 1,000 miles across and 700 hundred miles from north to south, air transport had turned days of travel into hours.

Next night I flew from Kitwe, north to Nairobi to meet Mr Rughani, but I certainly understood better the problems of educational supply in Africa than I had before. I also felt that Don Clarke understood as well as anyone the particular problems in Zambia and was the right manager for us there.

It was now early December and I had been able to have a point by point discussion with Mr Rughani about our joint company which would encompass publishing, book supply and every kind of equipment supply to be owned fifty-fifty between his company and Arnold. On 8th December Mr Rughani had organised a party to which four hundred guests were invited at the Text Book Centre, including two ministers of the Kenya Government (one being Daniel Arap Moi). That night there was one and a half minutes coverage on Kenyan Television news, while a few days later the weekly interviews of Kenya Television's *Panorama* were with a director of IATA (the International Air Travel Association); the trainer of chimpanzees at the Kenya National Circus; members of the cast of *The Man who Came to Dinner*, then playing in Nairobi; and the Export Director of E. J. Arnold, supplying Kenya's educational system. (Rughani's only regret, as he realised the success of his party, was that he hadn't invited President Kenyatta – he wasn't to know that Mr Moi would in due course succeed him.)

Next day a frantic round of meetings included the bank (overdraft limit), the Assistant Secretary to the Treasury (permission to invest in Kenya), the Curriculum Development Centre (discuss new programmes for schools), Mr Bridge, Managing Director of African University Press (Arnold to be their agent wherever we had companies) and John Nottingham, Director of the newly-formed East African Press.

We finished late in the evening and sat down to dinner at 10.30 to discuss further details of our organisation, which went on to well after midnight. But it didn't hinder us from meeting again next morning at six and driving to Uganda, arriving at Kampala at 11 am where we had a long meeting with Mr Raman Patel, a friend of both Dr Zaki, the Education Minister, and Dr Milton Obote, the Prime Minister. There seemed to be agreement that in this market it would be unwise to mix publishing with distribution, and it was clear that it was hoped that a consortium could buy the Uganda Bookshop from the Church with 50% Arnold, 25% Rughani and 25% Patel interests.

Next day we visited the Uganda Bookshop and discussed details at length with the manager who let us understand that the Bookshop, with ten local branches, had a third of the Ugandan market, totalling about £350,000. Nothing could be decided at such short notice but there was clearly an opportunity to add Uganda to our growing group of family-owned companies in East Africa. The following day we visited and had lunch with Narendra

E. J. Arnold's partners in Kenya: Mr Rughani (*right*) and Mr Shah.

Mr Rughani introducing the author at his launch party to Daniel Arap Moi,
the Vice-President of Kenya.

Patel, the Ugandan Speaker, in his beautiful house overlooking Kampala. He was clearly very interested in the idea that Arnold and Rughani should try to improve and develop educational supply in Uganda and was delighted that his own family would be involved.

We left to drive back to Nairobi by way of the Patel factories at Mbala where we had a guided tour and a meeting, and set off for Nairobi almost 300 miles away. It was planned that Mr Rughani would return to Uganda in the next year to value the stock and get final details of the accounts of the Uganda Bookshop before a final agreement was reached. Little could we have guessed that long before 1967 was over there would be a new President in Uganda, called Idi Amin, and that our enthusiastic host, Narendra Patel, the Speaker, would disappear and be one of those found floating in the river below Kampala.

*   *   *

I had always wanted to visit Ethiopia and was encouraged to do so briefly before returning to London for Christmas via Khartoum. There was only time for a journey lasting a day, but I flew from Nairobi to Addis Ababa and went straight to the Commercial Attaché at the British Embassy and then, armed with introductions, to the Ministry of Education and a fine missionary school. The Ministry gave me outline details of a huge scheme to build a hundred new schools, and it was as yet undecided as to whether they should be put out to tender in England or confined to Ethiopian builders. Although there was obvious enthusiasm for educational expansion, it was difficult to feel confidence in the uncertain political situation with the Emperor confined to his palace on the hill.

Ordinary taxis in Addis Ababa took fares when they could, and I found that when I stopped one for a short journey it might already have one or more 'fares' going elsewhere (unless you were on the way). But eventually I was on my own and able to pay a special fee for the rest of the day which included a visit to the palace to see the Emperor's lions, which prowled freely about the forecourt of the palace (rather as an alsatian might in a factory yard).

After dinner at my hotel with the headmaster of a European school, which I hoped might be possible to supply directly, I caught a morning flight back to Nairobi and later in the day flew to Khartoum again to see our Sudan bookshop as it prepared for Christmas. Joseph Tadros was away on business connected with his individual agencies and mining, and I spent two days examining the Christmas stock, much of which had come from Arnold, although some was still at Port Sudan on the Red Sea where it was, I discovered, 'awaiting customs clearance' (i.e. payment of customs duties!).

The bookshop, as Christmas approached, stayed open until midnight (instead of 8 pm) but the staff received no overtime – because, I was told, there were 20,000 unemployed in Khartoum, any of whom would be delighted to have the job of someone leaving! We had sent £5,000 worth of Christmas cards, decorations, diaries and crackers, and all of these had gone. Festive lights were everywhere but I was assured that by January everything would be back to normal. It seemed that the turnover in our first year would exceed £150,000.

It was, however, clear that book stocks were not yet under control and I suggested to Leeds that either Frank Harrison (the director of our book distribution department) should come out for a few days from Leeds, or that Don Clarke should fly up from Zambia. But much progress had been made in East Africa and the Sudan since the previous December when I first met Joseph Tadros.

Leaving Khartoum at night on the 19th December I had cut it very fine for Christmas shopping. It had been a busy but happy year, in spite of one very sad moment, and all six of our family enjoyed our Christmas at Hicklam.

CHAPTER 13

India and the East

Philippa was now twelve, and Sophie and Jo shortly to be ten and seven, and they were delighted with their new brother who was the centre of attention at Hicklam. Each of the girls had their own guinea pig who was guarded closely – although the cat found his way into one cage and there was a sad burial ceremony in the garden.

By 1967 the growing volume of export sales had made a number of changes at Arnold necessary. A new distribution manager with experience of satisfying widely-flung customers who were not part of Arnold's normal structure of home educational contracts, John Cooper, joined the company. In the export department, too, it became apparent that there would have to be someone to deal with the rapidly growing correspondence stimulated by the export director's widening responsibility.

During the previous year it had also become clear that the broadening world sales would require an enlarged sales organisation. It was very opportune that I had recently received a letter from my father telling me of a senior manager (a former Colonel) who had taken over his company when he had retired in 1951, but was now looking for a sales post – was such a candidate likely to appeal to Arnolds? Paul Jordan was both energetic and flexible and I was delighted when the Arnold board decided to appoint him as the Sales General Manager, reporting to me. I felt he was the ideal back up for our growing export effort.

When term time had started again I took the opportunity of following up further smaller collections of armorial porcelain and was soon considering how the huge volume of notes, reference cards and photographs I had accumulated could be brought together in an order which could be published (the idea was novel and exciting and still seemed like a distant dream). What still presented problems was how it would be possible to include all the facts I had accumulated in a form which could be used by readers who had little knowledge of heraldry – and yet could access quickly the information they wanted to find without poring over hundreds of pages unnecessarily. But all this was still an uncertain aim which occupied late evenings and some weekends but had no known answer.

*   *   *

174

In late March, Martin Arnold and I flew again to Khartoum to assess the first year's accounts and consider orders which were now flowing from the Sudan bookshop (the latest just received being for £50,000 worth of equipment and books). For me, too, it was the first leg of my longest tour yet, visiting twelve countries, eastwards round the world during the next eight weeks.

In the Sudan, however, it was not just a question of supply but of finance, and we had discussions with our bankers at Khartoum to make sure that the money could soon reach Leeds. Our first full board meeting of the Sudan Bookshop lasted from 11 am to 8.30 at night, with the frequent aid of lemon drinks and sandwiches, but the figures looked encouraging and promised a profit.

Next morning I caught a plane to Cairo, leaving Martin in Khartoum to conclude discussions with Joseph Tadros before flying home. Such a 'local' flight was fascinating as we followed the Nile and flew over the newly finished Aswan High Dam and could see the giant lake gently forming behind it. After a taxi ride into Cairo from the airport I had meetings with a manager of Dar Al Maaref, who were the recently appointed agents of *Encyclopaedia Britannica* in Egypt and were engaged in government plans to provide audio-visual schemes for the much broader teaching of English as a second language throughout the country. The manager was planning to come to England at the end of the month and particularly wanted to visit Leeds, in part to learn how our newly-installed computer system was working, for they were having problems with theirs.

After dinner they took me to the airport and I enjoyed a comfortable flight to Bombay arriving at 4.50 am where, to my great surprise, I was presented with a large bouquet of flowers and met by both Mr and Mrs Narayan, of whom I had learned through government sources and who were anxious to further education in their country by working with us. By the time I had settled into a comfortable room at their home I had been on the go for about thirty-seven hours (with a few cat naps), but I met the Narayans again after a late breakfast and they insisted on touring the bazaar before lunch knowing my interest in antiquities. Lunch was at the 'Gymkhana Club' and we sat and watched a cricket match in progress, while after lunch Narayan (who also used his surname as his forename) asked if I would like to sail on his small yacht to Elephant Island (ten miles by sea but seventy miles by road) to see the 7th Century temple carved in the rock, which had been damaged by the Portuguese in the 17th Century but was otherwise massive and fascinating. The day ended with dinner with the Narayans and a preliminary discussion of what they felt were excellent opportunities in education.

Although my dealings were largely with Mr Narayan, who besides his interest in education was also the owner of a small oil company, it would be idle to ignore the fact that Mrs Narayan was also a driving force. The daughter of one of Gandhi's principal lieutenants, she was herself an activist and had been imprisoned by the British for some months before Independence. Her mother, Satyavati Devi, had served a number of terms in jail in the 1930s (including one nursing her tiny daughter) and died aged thirty-eight in 1945. She was famous for having stood alone before a company of British soldiers who had fired over the crowd in which she stood, when all but she had fled. It was the same square in which her grandfather had stood in 1919 when, in the words of Nehru himself, 'the great Shraddhanand stood tall and stately … facing the bayonets of the Gurkha soldiers with his bare chest.' Undoubtedly this fire still burned in Mrs Narayan. In spite of this they regarded the British as India's good friends and were very anxious that the new India should strive to reach the standards attained in the days of Empire.

There were over a quarter of a million schools recognised officially, and it was very apparent that India was by far the largest market that Arnold had yet encountered. Quantities were vast and a single order of 10,000 sets of simple science books and equipment was one of the first requirements.

But I was bombarded with interesting new acquaintances including Dr Tendulkar, an old friend of Nehru; Professor A.B. Shah, Head of the Indian Congress for Cultural Freedom; Shri S. Bhatkal, President of the Federation of Indian Publishers, and others, and while they all wished to bring British technology to India, one publisher was anxious that Arnold represented them in Africa.

The next day was spent at Tata Press in Bombay with the General Manager and other friends, and in the evening a 'small dinner party for twenty-five' introduced me to members of the British Council and a number of business and professional friends. Although the guests did not all depart until 2 am we were up again shortly after six with another round of meetings and introductions. Dinner that night was smaller and I sat next to Laxman, the principal cartoonist of *The Times of India*.

Before leaving Bombay, Narayan was determined that I should visit Ellora and the painted caves of Ajanta (which had been discovered by chance nearly a century earlier by a British shooting party who had followed a wounded tiger into one of the caves). We were up at 4 am, and by 5 were driving along the busy roads out of Bombay. On the way we picked up an old friend of his, Mr Aziz, the Director of Archaeology for Maharashtra State. He was also a poet and had been writing a poem about the Ajanta caves for twenty-four years and had just finished it the previous year. As we drove he recited in rapid

Mr Aziz reads from his poem, twenty years in the writing, as we drive from Bombay.

Visiting the Taj at Aurungabad – with all the beauty of its more famous namesake but much more peaceful. Narayan and our party in the foreground.

Urdu stanzas of his poetry and suddenly turned to me and asked, 'Are you a poet? I hope not because I don't like other poets – but do you know some English children's poetry?' As we sped along I could only blurt out a favourite poem of the children's:

> *Fuzzy Wuzzy was a bear,*
> *Fuzzy Wuzzy lost his hair,*
> *So Fuzzy Wuzzy wasn't fuzzy*
> *Was he?*

This was greeted with howls of laughter and for mile after mile he repeated this to himself as if it were a lost Shakespearean sonnet. This eventually proved too much for him and he mercifully fell silent with a headache in the heat, and we had to take him to the local doctor (the actor and mimic, Peter Sellers, in face and voice). The surgery had an array of pills in different cracked saucers while the 'maternity ward' was on the verandah overlooking a courtyard filled with chickens.

As Mr Aziz revived himself, we went into the doctor's house and he insisted I write down 'Fuzzy Wuzzy' for his children. 'And another,' he said. So I obliged with:

> *There was a man whose name was Algy*
> *Algy met a bear and the bear was bulgy*
> *and the bulge was Algy.*

We laughed so much that the poet was quite recovered when we left.

Our day at Ajanta passed all too quickly, but I was able to see the cave paintings. The local curator had rigged up an ingenious lighting system for those who wanted to see what they were photographing in the caves and we only had to turn a switch.

On Sunday we were up at five and set off for Bombay, 230 miles away. As we passed Poona on the long hill down to the plains, poetry was still in the air and a huge government bill board read:

> *The more the merrier*
> *That's not true —*
> *FAMILY PLANNING*
> *Is meant for you.*

It was only a small dinner party at the Narayans this time and we were up at 5 am to catch the plane to Delhi.

If it had been apparent that the Narayans were well connected in Bombay, it became starkly obvious when we visited Delhi. Narayan had been lent the car of a leading Hindu writer, Mr Chandra Gupta, for our stay, but as he kept borrowing it back we frequently resorted to taxis. Travelling in New Delhi had recently become more hazardous. The council, anxious to reduce accidents, had decided to leave *all* lights at red (in all directions) in the hope that this would slow the traffic. But within a day it had the opposite effect.

We naturally visited the British High Commission who were most helpful, and the Ministry of Education, but Narayan was an indefatigable telephone caller and as one meeting was ending, the next was arranged for half an hour hence. It was a disappointment that I didn't have time to see the Taj Mahal (it would have been easy but taken too long) but in the evening we visited the Red Fort, the great Mogul fortress in Old Delhi, before meeting Shamlal, the editor of *The Times of India*. He was a quiet penetrating man, his rooms lined from floor to ceiling with books, and we sat in his garden drinking cool drinks as it grew dark.

All next day we moved from one Ministry to another: Finance (a director was an old friend), to make sure that we would receive approval for anything required; Foreign Collaboration (another friend), to make sure that any importations would be allowed; and a veteran MP who wished us to stay with him for the rest of our visit. We later visited Parliament and watched a session in progress. At the University we were invited as guests the following day to be present at the ceremony making U Thant, the Secretary General of the United Nations, an Honorary Doctor of Law. U Thant spoke persuasively of the importance of education at the end of this ceremony. The Vice Chancellor of the University, a very old friend of Narayan's, was Dr Zakir Hussain, a Muslim and leading educationalist and once a school master. He had recently become the Vice President of India (and was soon to become, for all too short a time, the President) and he invited us to tea later in the day. Seeing him in the Chair in the Upper House of Parliament, and then at the University, was no substitute for the honour of visiting his official residence for tea.

When we arrived we were ushered into a large, low-ceilinged room with gilt screens and sat on long low sofas, with servants standing back along the walls but just the three of us seated. We talked for half an hour of the problems of education in India and he asked if there was anything we needed to help Arnold's development in the country. He made it clear that Narayan had only to ask. I had no doubt that I had met a great man, well capable of being President of a country of 500 million people.

Our last day in Delhi produced an unexpected twist, for while it was apparent that there were huge opportunities for educational books and goods working with Narayan's company, 'Childcraft and Educational Enterprises', I had not considered an Arnold role in marketing Indian publications through our growing overseas companies.

Narayan and I first spent two hours with one of India's leading characters, the cartoonist, Shankar, who had written numerous children's books and felt they had a market outside India. He particularly hoped that Arnold's book distribution company would open new markets for him. We then spent much of the rest of the day with the Government of India's publication department who, on a much larger scale, would welcome help in marketing their children's books around the world. I had to tell Narayan that I did not know the scale of this idea, or whether it could be combined with other projects, but he urged me to try because handling the export of Indian books would open the way for larger import licences being granted to Arnold.

In the course of a week such huge opportunities for the export of Arnold products had opened up that it was difficult to calculate the size or profitability of the market. It would undoubtedly be necessary to invite Narayan to Leeds soon to explore these details further and make sure that there was also close co-operation with Paul Jordan's sales department. Although I was not able to do so until June, I was to draw up a business plan for India for the five years until 1972 and hoped this would be acceptable to the Arnold board.

*　　*　　*

It was dark as I said a fond farewell to Narayan at Delhi airport and boarded a plane to Bangkok. Dinner was served about midnight but the air hostesses were very upset, with at least one in tears, because all the passengers who had had fish had been given bottles of red wine, and all those who had had meat had white wine! Nothing could have mattered less and before long I was having breakfast at my comfortable hotel in Bangkok.

My appointment with the principal educational supplier in Thailand was not until the afternoon, so I took the opportunity of spending the morning on a boat on the river which still carried a great deal of the local traffic in Bangkok – an Oriental Venice. It was a relaxing experience to sail along the narrow 'streets' lined with houses and children swimming outside their front doors while their mothers washed clothes, opened mussels or offered wares if the boats should stop. Butchers cut slabs of meat and handed them to passing boatwomen out shopping, while fruit and tinned foods were supplied from shelves above the river. Unprepared Europeans would no doubt probably die of a variety of tropical infections, but the natural immunity of the residents seemed to keep them happy and healthy.

My meeting with the manager of Thai Watana Panish, the local school supply company, was of interest because I felt that their large showrooms and piles of parcels addressed to schools reminded me of Arnolds in Leeds. But there was no real enthusiasm that we should contact schools or supply them with selections of equipment for that was what they themselves did, the emphasis being on American systems and supplies.

Small opportunities undoubtedly there were, but after India and Africa this was not to be a major Arnold market. On the second night at the hotel I was surprised to meet Owen Martin and his wife, who had a rapidly growing educational company in Sydney called 'Dominie' with whom we hoped to co-operate in Australia and whom I was meeting in Hong Kong in a few days time; he was on his way there but had thought it would be nice to enjoy the comforts of Bangkok for two days.

Malaysian Airways greeted passengers arriving at the airport with the news that the morning flight was cancelled that day, but there was to be one in the evening which would arrive in Kuala Lumpur early the next morning. There was no alternative so I took the opportunity of visiting one of Thailand's most famous temples in which sits the golden Buddha – all five and a half tons of solid gold. But I think I remember the laughing faces of the children best, swimming in the river, whom I watched from my river boat.

*   *   *

It was 2 am when we eventually landed at Kuala Lumpur from Singapore and a welcome bed at the Merlin Hotel. My only real contact in Malaysia was Mr Loong Sow Ching, the energetic Chinese owner of 'Educational and Technical Agencies' whose products included polythene bags and a printing works, which had slowly moved into the educational market. He explained his forward plan carefully and after lunch we visited the new Technical Teachers' College who were much interested in audio visual equipment.

Mr Loong had six travellers visiting schools and thought that Arnold products could fit well with locally produced goods, although I had no doubt that if quantities warranted it he would consider producing locally himself. Next day I flew to Singapore after an excellent dinner with Mr Loong at which my chopsticks became progressively more difficult to handle as brandy and ginger followed wine and aperitifs.

Vast housing schemes and school building programmes were sweeping away the largely Chinese city that was Singapore. Workers' flats were completed at the rate of two an hour night and day and the educational programme was geared to support the rapidly growing professional skills of the population. It was clear that Arnold would have to treat Singapore quite separately from the slower pace I had witnessed in Kuala Lumpur.

I first contacted the Kong Beng Bookshop which had recently ordered some books from Leeds. The shop was bursting at the seams with packing cases stretching down the pavements. With the owners we visited the Ministry of Education and it was soon clear that anything which was successful would be copied and supplied from local sources. I noted that Kong Beng was supplying schools with quantities of modelling material called 'Plasterlene' from China!

I spent an hour with Alan Hancock, an Englishman who was developing educational television for the government. He had previously worked for the BBC but there was nothing in England to rival his programmes in Singapore. After seeing other publisher's warehouses, I had dinner with Mr Ban Yam, who had recently set up his own business, Beacon Publications, having been a manager with a much larger distributor before that. As we talked it was apparent that even if we were able to achieve some satisfactory orders, he would still wish to print local editions and pay us only a small royalty.

Next morning I had breakfast with Owen Martin who was flying to Hong Kong next day and as he, too, was anxious to have some of his small publications distributed in Singapore, we discussed the relative merits of having a small local agent, or both working through Mr Rupert Li's much larger organisation in Hong Kong – I was to meet Rupert the following day. I was inclined to agree with Owen that Rupert Li's professionalism and experience were worth cultivating providing we were not treated as just another name on his writing paper, but perhaps this initiative should be limited to Hong Kong.

The afternoon plane landed in Hong Kong on time. Rupert Li met me at the airport. We crossed the harbour on the ferry to Victoria Island, and I settled into a most comfortable room at the Mandarin Hotel, then on the harbour's edge. Owen was staying at the Peninsula Hotel on the other side of the harbour.

Although Owen and I were to have meetings at the Ministry of Education, I found that the Director of Education was shortly to retire and his Chief Inspector and probable successor was Mr Deans Pegg, whom I had known in Nassau twenty-five years earlier! We then spent much of the day visiting Rupert Li's four large bookshops in Hong Kong; we also planned a weekend of visits to Macau together and a day touring Victoria Island.

The journey to Macau saw us catch the ferry early and was a day which I shall not forget. It was an emotional excitement to cross the mouth of the Pearl River and close ones eyes occasionally and imagine the 18th Century East

Owen and Peggy Martin with a friend on Victoria Island, Hong Kong.

Returning to Hong Kong from Macau.

Indiamen sailing up to Canton past the island of Lintin – or later down again loaded with tea and, on many ships, consignments of Chinese porcelain.

Macau itself occupied most of our day and we had lunch in a Portuguese restaurant and visited a number of landmarks that were well known to the merchants and East India Company officers in their day. I would have liked to have stayed in Macau, but we still had much to do in Hong Kong.

I walked up Hollywood Road, behind the Mandarin Hotel, and still have two pieces of 'antique' armorial porcelain (*c*.1960) which I bought in an antique shop – both later illustrated in *Chinese Armorial Porcelain.*

We enjoyed meeting Rupert's wife, Margaret, who ran the Hong Kong Book Centre. They had five daughters of whom the eldest was married to an American and the youngest was in the sixth form at Cheltenham College in England. We had a very pleasant dinner at their home and the next night were guests at Rupert's father's seventieth birthday party – an immense affair with 380 guests and fourteen courses. (We all received elaborate invitation cards in Chinese, with our names also in Chinese – 'How' being a Chinese word, mine translated as 'Lively How'.)

We met Rupert's partner and new managing director Ernest Yu, a graduate of Shanghai University, who had married the previous autumn Heather, an English girl who had come to Hong Kong as secretary to a film company. On the day before we left, we sat down to discuss a new company – 'Dominie-Arnold-Asia Limited' – with equal share holdings for Owen Martin, Rupert Li and Ernest together, and Arnold. Such an idea appealed to both Owen and me, for we did not wish to be 'just another' on the long list of publishers represented in Hong Kong by Rupert Li, but we liked the idea of a new and different entity focused solely on education and on equipment in particular, under Ernest Yu as managing director.

During our stay, Owen and Peggy Martin and I had dinner most nights on various sides of the harbour, and lunched on Sunday with Doda Knight, the fascinating Hungarian Jewish widow of an Englishman who had owned a ship chandler's business in Hong Kong. She was to be found on weekdays in white overalls in the engine rooms of cargo boats in the harbour arguing with chief engineers. We then left to visit a tiny Cheshire Home on Victoria Island, in former gun emplacements overlooking the China Sea.

Owen and Peggy booked a different flight to Sydney and were there when I arrived after a long stopover in Manila, where, because of overbooking, passengers were invited to travel free to some different destination instead. Apparently a small number accepted this offer!

I had booked a hotel on the far side of the Sydney bridge, but after a night or two the rest of my stay was largely with Owen and Peggy at their comfortable home in north Sydney. Indeed I only ate breakfast at the hotel, and when not at a meeting it was discussions round his swimming pool, a fifty-second birthday party, and on Sunday a day on his yacht, which he hoped to enter for the Sydney-Hobart race the following year.

Owen Martin's father, who was still alive, had been born in Plymouth and after serving in the Navy settled in Australia, marrying a Welsh girl. Owen himself had played scrum-half for a leading rugby club and later became a superintendent of lifesavers on Bondi Beach. None of this interfered with his career as a schoolmaster, becoming the headmaster of a large primary school. Having married the daughter of a prosperous sheep farmer, he started writing text books and later founded Dominie Pty Ltd, handling a large range of school supplies, and already had sales of about half a million pounds, including publishing and supply and the agencies of a number of English publications. Owen was anxious that Arnold had a jointly-owned company which also held (and financed) a substantial share of Dominie and his other companies, and it was agreed that his accountant would come to England in June to discuss this.

It was clear that Dominie was already a major player in the market, and my task on behalf of Arnold was to provide back-up and support. Arnold already had a publishing agent in Australia through which some fifty thousand books were being sold annually, but this would change and become part of our own Australian company and be handled by Owen. He was also anxious to have the rights to publish a number of our books at his own press, which would save the cost of transport and still be part of Arnold. All this seemed eminently sensible and practical.

The trouble with travelling alone is that one tends to get looked after too well, and in Australia I was only alone from about midnight to 9 am, when Owen collected me from my hotel, and that time had to cover sleep, breakfast and writing numerous reports and letters. But the pleasure of far-ranging business discussions in Owen's garden, and my own efforts at repaying their hospitality in expensive hotels (Owen had a particular penchant for Sydney Bay oysters and even persuaded me to try them), was a very pleasant way to do business and cement a relationship between our two companies. It was also a good way to meet the next generation, although Owen and Peggy's son, Ross, spent much of his time training for cross country skiing in the Australian winter, for he was a member of the Australian winter sports Olympic team. With a weekend sailing on Owen's yacht and an ever busy social whirl I was sad to leave and catch a plane to Auckland, New Zealand, but I had to be there by the end of the first week in May.

*   *   *

I had been looking forward to my visit to New Zealand. I had always felt that New Zealand was almost like a part of Britain on the opposite side of the world, and as I spent a few days in Auckland, it seemed I was right but had probably stepped back in time – to at least pre-war days, a quarter of a century earlier.

Unlike many developing countries, New Zealand was not rich in raw material sources but had to rely heavily on an uncertain sheep and wool market. As foreign currency was not plentiful, many manufactured items were made from imported components to save foreign currency, but this made the cost higher in many cases. We had been approached in Leeds by a New Zealand publisher, A.H. & A.W. Reid, who had achieved some success in Australia and were, in turn, the agents of Dominie in New Zealand. But while I found them enthusiastic about increasing their market in educational supplies, it was almost entirely by manufacturing on licence – with the obvious problems of cost, as the scale would be too small. But we would have to discuss this in Leeds when Mr Reid and Owen Martin would both be there later that summer.

Unlike Australia, I found myself getting introductions to senior inspectors of schools and the Auckland Board of Education. It was clear that with three quarters of a million children at school (of which about 480,000 were primary school children) officials would greatly welcome a flow of the latest equipment and books, but had to admit that there would not be import licences available for them.

I had recalled that Uncle Harry had been friendly with a company called Brittain Wynyard in Auckland, and I made a point of calling on them and was very kindly received. While they were used to the distribution of netting and cordage to the many fishing towns and villages, the thought of educational equipment to schools was not appealing! Very little happened in Auckland at weekends and hardly a café was open, but Mr Brittain kindly drove me round the city and the surrounding countryside and I had dinner with them. There was also time to sit in my hotel and catch up with some report writing and letters before flying to Fiji on the Monday morning. But I didn't think it would be realistic to place much reliance on trying to develop the New Zealand educational supply market without a strong local partner and access to more import licences than were likely to be available.

*   *   *

In 1967 Fiji was still a Crown Colony and it was possible to feel the tension between the native Fijians and the Indian population which outnumbered it.

The island had a total population of half a million and there were 666 schools. While the principal employment was agriculture, tourism was rapidly growing. My hotel was at the international airport at Nandi and in the morning it was necessary to take a local DC3 flight round the island followed by a very bumpy forty minute bus drive to reach the capital, Suva.

The Chief Supplies Officer at the Ministry of Education was an Englishman, Mr Moffatt, who had come out to Fiji in 1947 on a two-year contract, but had stayed for twenty. He spoke very warmly of Owen Martin who had told him I was coming, and I had no doubt that Dominie could meet most of his needs. I arranged to send supplies of Arnold catalogues and he seemed genuinely pleased that we were co-operating with Dominie.

I quickly visited a number of schools although my taxi driver couldn't understand why I wanted to visit such 'boring' places and repeatedly suggested detours 'so that you can get a good photograph'. I was obviously not like his average tourist fare.

The flight back to Nandi was equally interesting and gave one a chance to see the whole island in a day. But I had been feeling increasingly unwell and took two codis and a large glass of brandy and went to bed with a fever. Fortunately I felt rather better by early morning and at 3.40 am caught the Trans-Pacific flight which was going to give me a day in Tahiti. A pleasant Swedish 'businessman' was in the next seat and we discussed all sorts of world problems. He turned out to be Air Force General Carl Berg who had just retired as Air Force Commander of the United National neutral force in Korea. Landing at Tahiti just after dawn, we went to a comfortable hotel on the shore where we were all given day rooms. After breakfast, General Berg and I decided to drive round the island, and in particular to go to Gaugin's house and museum near the shore.

It was a delightful day and Tahiti was a place where one could comfortably have stayed a week. It was fascinating to spend more than an hour in the Gaugin museum reading his notes and seeing his palettes and brushes and browsing among his things that had been gathered in the house. Carl Berg and I enjoyed every moment, but we had to drive on and later spent about an hour in the principal town, Papete.

We had to re-board our plane at dusk and embarked on the long flight to Acapulco and Mexico City, where I disembarked. Carl Berg and I exchanged Christmas cards for some years afterwards, but in spite of his invitations, I was never able to meet him again in Sweden.

*   *   *

Sydney Harbour: facing the entrance the mast of HMAS *Sydney*
which sank the German raider *Emden* in 1914.

General Carl Berg looks out to sea near Gaugin's home on Tahiti.

I had planned to visit Jamaica, the Bahamas and Bermuda on the last leg of the journey and as the Speyers were not in Kingston, I spent much of the day with Mr Sangster of Sangsters Bookstore (a cousin of the recent Prime Minister). It was a long day after a long flight and by the afternoon I was feeling increasingly unwell again. However, it was possible to invite Mr Sangster to Leeds during his summer visit to England and, with excuses about other appointments, I was able to escape and spend a few hours in my hotel before the night flight to Nassau.

Norman Solomon had kindly invited me to stay, and we drove to his home from the airport. By the morning I was somewhat rested but, he said, 'looked yellow' and his doctor said I should stay in bed for most of the day as I almost certainly had jaundice! But I had to get home.

The real worry was that if British Overseas Airways were told, they might have refused me a flight home, and I should have to stay in mid summer in a tropical climate for some weeks, when only a day away from home. But Norman and Mr Maura (whom I had known in my Nassau days, and was now the principal travel agent there) arranged to secure me two first class seats right at the front, and my yellow tan was hardly noticeable on the night flight to London. I had planned to spend a day in Bermuda on the way, where things were going rather well since my last visit, but cancelled this and arriving after dawn, was driven by an Arnold friend straight to Hicklam.

In my round-the-world journey I had flown 35,000 miles on eighteen separate flights over 54 days – all but the last three in almost continuous negotiations in twelve countries. On reflection it was too long and too concentrated, but until the end it had been a fascinating journey and I had met so many interesting people – some of whom were to be friends for years – that it had been an opportunity not to be missed.

I was able to dwell on it over the next six weeks at home in bed – very well looked after in comfort, but only able to talk to the children from the distance of the bedroom door for the first few weeks as I lay reading and writing papers for Arnold.

CHAPTER 14

Overseas Companies and Authorship

By 1968 it had become possible to assess the overall situation better. I had recently been restyled the Marketing Director of Arnolds – a post they had not previously included in their structure. I had two general managers: Paul Jordan was in charge of the sales force, and John Cooper in charge of all warehouses; both newly conceived positions in line with the much more focused marketing on new clients adopted by a company which for more than ninety years had been able to grow largely by the efficient handling of Government, County Council and school contracts, and the development of new and forward-looking equipment for education. The new focus would make it necessary to increase the sales staff and infrastructure to support the new joint overseas companies which were eventually to number twelve.

It was necessary over the next two years to construct a control mechanism – called E. J. Arnold (International), with its own Managing Director, a post which I was offered and accepted – so that as part owners of a dozen companies we could monitor the capital employed, the purchases, turnover and profit of our associates. With the aid of a new cost accountant this developed into persuading our partners to answer a very simple questionnaire each month providing the key figures of purchases, sales and expenses, which we co-ordinated in Leeds. I was also able to find a new Export Manager, Jerry Phillips, who increasingly did my leg work, and later still an excellent personal assistant, Roy Davey, who had recently completed a business management course at Durham. It was to take more than a year and numerous visits to some of our partners to allow them to see the benefit of this 'bureaucracy' from their points of view, but once it was working, and after one or two special visits at short notice, the system provided adequate quarterly accounts, so that Leeds could feel comfortable with its new friends abroad and know where we all stood.

The friendly relationship with the joint owners, the fact that they benefited in the same way as Arnolds and were well looked after when visiting Leeds (the best hotels with no cost to them) ensured that for at least the next five years all moved smoothly in the right direction, and the export market became something which Arnold found rewarding. As for myself, I was able to enjoy frequent visits to a number of our more successful (and closer) markets – such as the Sudan and Zambia, and periodic ones further afield – and at the same

190

time spend more time at home, although I was probably still away for up to eight weeks in each year.

*   *   *

As I recuperated from my jaundice – not returning to work in Leeds for ten weeks – I found time to focus in some depth on the question of publishing my book on armorial porcelain. I felt I had now devised a system of categorising border designs on the plates so that it would be possible for someone quite unacquainted with heraldry (and even with little real knowledge of Chinese porcelain) to match the border style and then see if the service they wished to identify was in the book and what was known about it. I had never really intended to write the introductory chapters on porcelain in the book, expecting that Cecil Bullivant would do so, but after my visit to Minehead later in 1968 it was clear that even if he had once wished to do so, he would no longer be able to as he reached his mid-nineties.

My visit to Hong Kong had also inspired me to learn more of China, and a friend suggested that my next step should be to learn Chinese and strongly suggested that I enrol for the Chinese course at Leeds University run by Professor and Mrs MacDonald, his Chinese wife. So I found myself twice a week spending two hours in the evening at the University and learning the rudiments of the Chinese language as the first part of a three-year course (of which I was only to complete one year). Nevertheless, even such a slight and basic knowledge of the form of Chinese words was to increase my understanding of the whole picture and I enjoyed my two evenings a week in Leeds – the only experience I have ever had of university life.

Whether it was this broadening experience which later persuaded Elizabeth to start a course in writing at Leeds I do not know, but the ease with which it was possible to blend into this more intellectual life was a satisfying experience for both of us. In 1969 she decided to improve her already natural skills in writing and started a three-year course at the university as an undergraduate reading English Literature and Philosophy. Her tutor was Brian Thompson, whom I later got to know when he and his wife came to dinner at Hicklam.

It was, perhaps, inevitable that the politics of the university spilled over into everyday life, and Elizabeth found herself on protest marches. Her long-held views on her preference for state, over private, education were to find support, and she focused more strongly on this in the future – although all our children spent most of their education at private schools, except Jo who went to Harrogate Grammar School. All this was to see a blossoming of her career as a writer under the name of Elizabeth North, although all the eventual consequences were not yet clear.

*   *   *

Although our joint companies in Africa and Asia occupied much of my time, there were also journeys to Europe which offered new opportunities and a different vision. Visiting, and later exhibiting at, the Frankfurt Book Fair gave increased publicity to Arnold books, and a carefully planned journey to exhibit at an international education exhibition at Basel a year or two later provided a new perspective. The trip also provided an amusing incident, for three of us drove in a heavily laden Arnold van, and stopping in the late evening at a German petrol station near the Rhine we encountered first excessive delays, and then two German police cars. The petrol station owner had thought we looked suspicious on a Sunday evening, while European police were looking for three Englishmen who had been part of a gold bullion raid at Heathrow. We fitted the bill. Matters were handled in a polite low-key way, and with our exhibition documents, following an examination of the van which only revealed cardboard gold coins, we were sent on our way

But by late 1968 I was again visiting Lagos, Khartoum, and Lusaka particularly, on a regular basis. It was now to deal with specific problems resulting from our growing export trading and although I was abroad for no more than two months each year, there were frequent journeys to London to meet visiting agents and education officers. (The breakfast on the morning express from Leeds was excellent, and one could be in London shortly after 9 am for a meeting.)

We had never made any great headway in the huge Nigerian market, but had become aware of a long-established London company called J. L. Morrison Son & Jones who had strong links there as well as in East Africa and Singapore. Their Managing Director, Harry McHugh, was an active but father-like figure and I enjoyed his company, especially when I had lunch with him and his deputy, Peter Hoare, at their club, the Oriental Club. I was later to become a member (being proposed by them) after the sad demise of the Guards Club.

His company had a number of branches in Nigeria that included stationery in their agencies, and with the success of Arnold's joint companies further east it seemed appropriate to make a similar arrangement with them in Nigeria. The Nigerian war had tested loyalties and honesty to the full, and while some companies had lost their offices and their properties, others had managed to withdraw most of their assets safely. Harry McHugh's principal Nigerian

An education minister examines an inflatable globe watched by Martin Arnold,
the author and Bill Wilday, Basel 1970.

An E. J. Arnold exhibition stand about 1970.

director was Mr Omwoodi who, at the height of hostilities, had driven from Northern Nigeria to Lagos on a number of occasions, through armed road blocks manned by undisciplined and trigger-happy soldiers, and had managed to bring much of the cash from their offices in the north down to Lagos and deposit it there safely. Mr Omwoodi was noted for his turn of 'European' phrase and he would say, when a complicated and obscure discussion took place, 'Now don't let's perambulate about the forest on this matter'.

Later in 1969 I attended a meeting in Lagos with Harry McHugh, Peter Hoare and Mr Omwoodi at the offices of the prosperous Lebanese firm, Leventis. It was a formal affair and eight directors of our companies attended in the Leventis boardroom, each place being laid formally with writing pads, pens and glasses of water. As Mr Leventis, well known as a hard bargainer, took his seat as the Chairman of the meeting, Mr Omwoodi ostentatiously produced from his substantial briefcase an exceptionally large pair of Zeiss field glasses which he stood before him on the table. Mr Leventis at first appeared not to notice, but then his curiosity got the better of him and he asked, 'And why have you put those field glasses on the table, Mr Omwoodi?' There was a pause and Mr Omwoodi replied, 'So that I can keep a very close eye on *you*, Mr Leventis.' No-one dared to laugh, but Mr Leventis agreed better terms for co-operation than either Harry McHugh or I dared hope!

We now had a far wider distribution of Arnold catalogues throughout Nigeria and the manager of one small stationery shop in central Nigeria in particular had asked us to send a quantity of extra copies for schools. With a day to spare we visited the store and were greeted in the large mud and thatch building with a brilliant display of decorated wallpaper, created entirely from hundreds of coloured illustrated pages from Arnold catalogues. It was, he told us, impossible to get wallpaper and these glossy pages were also more waterproof! (Perhaps the occasional schoolmaster read what was on the wall when he came in to buy his exercise books.)

Over my time travelling in Nigeria, there were occasionally unexpected aspects of local travel which always made it interesting. In one of the comfortable Rest Houses where I stayed three nights I was surprised to be served roast beef and Yorkshire pudding each evening, but discovered that the cook had been told that this was the only thing that Englishmen would eat; while a variety of foreign pilots were employed on the local airline, still flying DC1s, and during one particular flight the Captain suddenly appeared and asked if anyone who knew the area could come into his cabin, for it was a new route to him and he wasn't sure of his location in the dark.

* * *

On the eastern side of Africa I made frequent visits to the Sudan, usually on my way south to Kenya or Zambia, and Joseph Tadros often visited England and followed his other agencies, including mining – in which I was able to help him after his discovery of a deposit of tin in the Nile valley. I introduced him to my old friend, Alan Dalton, now Managing Director of English China Clays, and they sent an exploratory team to Khartoum but found the deposit to be much shallower and smaller than was hoped and not worth international development. There was no doubt that the Sudan Bookshop had re-established itself as the leading bookshop in Khartoum (and thus in the country) while in Kenya Mr Rughani and Mr Shah were very successfully establishing their bookshop as the leading school supplier in Nairobi.

However, it was impossible, or at least unwise, to develop educational supply in Uganda under the control of General Idi Amin and most of the Indian friends of Mr Rughani and Mr Shah there had left – either to return to India, or in many cases to come to Britain. But it was in Zambia that the greatest progress was made and among the many changes Don and Pam Clarke eventually left Lusaka and returned to England. In his place John Cooper and his family moved to Lusaka. John bought a very comfortable house in the countryside where I stayed on more than one occasion. His additional management skills led to close co-operation with Theo Bull and Zambia Educational Distributors. It was intended that the links with Theo Bull would one day develop into a company in Rhodesia, but the political situation there grew less and less stable and any supplies that Arnold could provide went direct to ZED who dealt with it themselves.

There were often surprises, as when we obtained a substantial order for 'extra large yellow blackboard dusters', and it was later discovered that they were being sold in some of the more remote areas as loin cloths. More worrying were our efforts to supply educational cardboard facsimile coins so that schools could teach the new coinage of *kwachas* and *ngwee*, particularly in rural areas. It was not long before these long-established European-style cardboard aids were being used as real currency in several of the more remote villages because the supply of real coinage was very slow in reaching some rural areas.

While a new and more management-oriented attitude was fast developing among the local government officers in education (which on occasions led to requests for 'special discounts' to be included in quotations for supplies) there was still a broad acceptance of the standards of discipline and order established under the former colonial rule, less than a decade in the past. This could occasionally manifest itself in unexpected ways as when our main bookshop in Lusaka, which normally had long queues waiting to pay the cashier, saw one queue joined by two firemen in full kit who patiently waited their turn to reach the desk. When they did so one fireman asked the way to a small local street. On being given the information they both hurried out to join their fire engine and tell them the way to the fire! (The British habit of the orderly queue dies hard.)

*   *   *

It was, at this time, becoming more difficult to get to South Africa because of the political differences between black Africa and the apartheid regime. I was, however, determined to get there and discuss educational supplies with a local agent with whom Arnold had already had some correspondence. In any case it was much easier to fly to Cape Town, which was a hub of much world air travel, and I did so – staying in great comfort at the Mount Nelson Hotel, below the peak of Table Mountain and overlooking the bay.

We visited the Cape Town Educational Department and learned of the current supply problems, but our main concern was again to create a joint company through which we could share in any opportunities that were available and joint-publish books in South Africa. South African publishers and suppliers were already agents for most English companies in this field, and our task would depend very much on the ability of an agent to win as many school contracts as possible with Arnold backing. There was a huge discrepancy between the value of supplies allocated to white and black schools in the Cape, and although we felt that this was likely to change over the coming years, there was, at present, only an opportunity for selling any of the more sophisticated equipment in white schools.

We flew on to Johannesburg where we spent two days and I had the particular pleasure of having dinner at his home with John Stanford, who had previously lived in Dorset and played rugby for Dorchester (our dates of birth were one day apart). He was happy and prospered in the life insurance business – which is exactly what he had done in Dorchester – but he felt that he enjoyed a better standard of living in South Africa. The return to Cape Town was by the especially comfortable Johannesburg-Cape Town Express. I talked to a South African mother and her son and was impressed by the 'old-fashioned' courtesy of the boy who automatically rose and opened the compartment door if an adult wanted to leave or enter.

In my last two days in Cape Town I had time to drive round Table Mountain and see it from the land side, and spent a while in the Cape Town Art Gallery where there were a number of my great-aunt 'Joh' Glossop's paintings (and a portrait of her) on view. Because of the political difficulties between South Africa and her northern neighbours, the flight to London was via Ascension Island, where we landed and refuelled and spent some hours on the ground. The island was then an important staging post – particularly for military aircraft – and remained so until the days of the Falkland War.

*   *   *

Back at Hicklam it was necessary now to spend an increasing time in Leeds and London because of the infrastructure that was needed to back the growing export trade which had been triggered by the journeys over the last five years to a total of some forty countries and island states – from which flowed interest in various forms, and visitors from all over the world.

The son of a northern Nigerian Emir declared his intention of visiting Leeds and bringing his latest young wife (who had never previously travelled outside Nigeria) with him. I arranged with British Rail a special first-class compartment and the Station Master at Leeds agreed to have a red carpet rolled out on the platform and met the Emir's son and his wife, wearing his British Rail gold ornamented cap. The evening before, Harry McHugh, Peter Hoare and I had given them dinner in London at the Oriental Club – but I think Lord Derby's town house was no match for the Station Master at Leeds.

Touring the Arnold works – and it was a morning's work to visit all the various warehouses, manufacturing processes and printing press – impressed the Emir's son very much and we had discussions in the afternoon with Martin and other members of the board. In the evening he was taken to dinner at a very comfortable hotel-restaurant along the Great North Road, famous for having been where Lord Byron had stayed on the night after his marriage.

It was, of course, in this way that goodwill was spread, and the flow of visitors grew considerably over the next few years. I frequently found it necessary to drive to London so that I could meet and entertain visiting academics and partners and, as Marketing Director of Arnolds, become involved in a wide range of sales matters rather than export. But it was good to spend longer in Yorkshire, for both Philippa and Sophie were now at the Mount School in York, and there were an increasing number of occasions which Elizabeth and I attended. Jo was still at her primary school and Thomas was soon to start. We even employed a 'nanny' who it was possible to lodge on the top floor at Hicklam.

It was also increasingly necessary to spend more time finalising my work on what had turned into a substantial book on Chinese armorial porcelain. Over fifteen years, I calculated that I had already spent about fourteen thousand hours collecting information, photographing and writing on the subject, and had identified the arms on about 2,600 services of which so far more than 1,700 were photographed. During the last year I had concentrated particularly on the introductory chapters and more general aspects of the China Trade, and I found myself by early 1970 with a 'manuscript' composed of 1,800 large cards and about 250 pages or more of closely typed pages for chapters. But what was now to be done with this work and would anyone want to publish it?

Through our own editor in Leeds I was given the names of one or two possible publishers in London and in 1970 arranged to meet one of these at his offices in Fleet Street. I carried with me as much as I could in a large suitcase – comprising about a thousand cards and all the chapters with illustrations. Our meeting was at 12 o' clock and I had been invited to lunch by two directors, so the suitcase was left safely in the first floor reception office with the receptionist. After lunch we returned to look again at the manuscript but couldn't find the suitcase; the receptionist had been called away for fifteen minutes and as the case weighed almost 50 lbs had felt it would be quite safe behind her desk. It was not.

The sense of shock was almost overwhelming and having spoken to the local police they strongly advised that I give it the maximum publicity in the hope that someone would return it for a reward. My Fleet Street friends spoke at once to someone at *The Daily Telegraph*, and the next day a four-inch column on the front page was devoted to the 'theft of rare manuscript' in Fleet Street. I meanwhile returned to Leeds and calculated that I could rewrite everything within about seven years. Fortunately the transparencies for the photographs were safely at home.

Next day was a difficult one as I came to terms with what would now be needed, but it passed without incident and on the following morning I was at a board meeting when my secretary, Barbara Levitt, asked to see me and handed me a note which said, 'Manuscript returned to publisher's office'. A nondescript gentleman had in fact walked into the tobacconist next door and, after buying a few items, departed. It wasn't until five minutes later that the shopkeeper realised that he had left 'his' suitcase behind. It was no good combing Fleet Street for him at that stage, so the case was opened and a letter from me to the publisher next door was soon found. In my acknowledgements to the published book I thanked the thief in a special paragraph, ending: 'No East India Captain was more thankful than I that his armorial porcelain had come home safely.'

*　　*　　*

Perhaps all this acted as a spur to greater effort, and it was fortunate that I met Eileen Brooksbank, a Yorkshire lady from near Leeds, who was also a friend of a number of heralds at the College of Arms. Not only did I meet them through her (and was later delighted when Anthony Wagner, Garter King of Arms, agreed to write the foreword) but was introduced to Faber and Faber, the publishers in Russell Square, for she had recently been involved with a book for them called *Monumental Brasses*.

It was a great step forward to be introduced to Fabers and particularly Richard de la Mare, one of their directors, who was both the son of Walter de la Mare, the author, and the uncle of Julian Thompson, later to be Chairman of Sotheby's for a while and still a director. It was also about this time that Julian, Colin Mackay (then his assistant and later a director of Sotheby's) and Anne Pollen, who had always been very helpful with photographs of porcelain sold at Sotheby's, visited Hicklam and were, I think, surprised by the volume of research I could show them. The friendliness of Fabers and Richard de la Mare was very encouraging and it soon became clear that if I could complete the manuscript and give it to them in a form which could be edited, they were interested. This led to my next piece of great luck, for they chose Patricia Herrmann, whose father had once been Chief Executive of Selfridges and whose husband, Frank, was an author/publisher of some note and was later to be a senior director of Sotheby's. Both were to become life-long friends.

*   *   *

It is inevitable that any sort of autobiography will dwell on one's own adventures and misadventures, thoughts and aspirations, and I have, so far, made little pretence to balance the very busy world in which I was living with the thoughts and aspirations of those about me. It had seemed sufficient to do what I thought was right and to share the slowly growing prosperity of our life with Elizabeth and the children; Hicklam, and my increasingly interesting life at Arnold, along with armorial porcelain, being enough to keep them contented too.

When I first read Elizabeth's first novel, *The Least and Vilest Things*, published by Gollanz in 1971 and inspired by her time at Leeds University, I found it easy to read but unnecessarily bitter in content, about a Dorset farmer's wife and her unsuccessful farmer husband gradually running his farm into the red. We had lived in Dorset farming country for nine years and I recognised the inevitability of toil, but not the huge frustrations of the farmer's wife who wanted to break into a more successful and different world.

Looking again at the book today, I see episodes which at the time seemed amusing or trivial, as a desperate *cri de coeur*. At the time some of my friends and family could not understand all the analogies and were disturbed by the contents. On the back flap of the book the last paragraph reads:

> Elizabeth North writes, 'Women feel trapped by the complex home structures they've built around themselves. Is the emotion that made them build in the first place a symptom of a basic difference in the men/women equation? This set of questions can never be far from the centre of what I write. Maybe in the next generation men and women will be more like each other and like each other more.'

The excitement of having a book published in the family overrode the contents, and I tended to see it all as a product of Elizabeth's undergraduate life; her reading and later meeting with other writers such as Germaine Greer; and as a solution in itself to her angry thoughts. When we met our friends, as one did every week for dinner or bridge, I could see that they were bemused or amused at what some regarded as an introspective novel and others as an enviable achievement.

Realising that our family life revolved round success and comfort for us all, I wanted to push forward in my business life as well as in the field of armorial porcelain. The unsuccessful farmer of her book, who sometimes in the dialogue said things that I might have said (although I felt that some other comment was emotive and not within my ken, but all part of an imaginative novel) worried me a little in that it was clear that he saw no future of leisure, and had insufficient capital to 'come out on top' in the financial world. None of this was helped by the fact that every spare pound we earned was committed to school fees (which Elizabeth neither liked nor agreed, but went along with) and that although by my own standards I felt fairly employed, there was no definite goal in my life but more work. In this respect it was probably fair to say that I was reasonably contented in a selfish sort of way as to how things had progressed – with my posts as Marketing Director of E. J. Arnold, and Managing Director of their International Division, and my own book within sight in two or three year's time.

But one nagging thought did possess me as my contacts broadened and I realised how many of the people we knew now had a capital stake in what they did, over and above their salary. If I had reached where I was after seven years and was now forty-two – and remembering my experience in Bridport – would it not be equitable to be able to buy (with what, I did not then know but was told by a friend that this was not a problem) a stake of up to 5% in Arnold so that if we continued to have some success in marketing and the international field, I would be building up something for myself as well as those for whom I worked. I knew the Arnold financial base and that the two executive directors controlled about 40% of the company – all the other shares being in the hands of family or, in the case of Mr Wood, a colleague of two generations who held, I understood, 5%. The idea did not evolve like a flash, but slowly became more dominant during 1971 and 1972, spurred on, to a modest extent, by Elizabeth's book.

I did not put the question to Martin until early 1972 and, although understanding of my idea, received a cautious reply. But it was clearly up to the other family shareholders to express their opinions, and he would sound out the possibility at his next family board meeting. The Arnold reply was not long forthcoming and rejected any idea that the shareholding could be broadened in the foreseeable future. It was a reply I had half expected, although I was disappointed, and I put it away 'on a shelf' to be considered again at a later date.

*   *   *

While I made another short tour to the East in late 1971, and others to Africa in the following year, it was now clear that a very determined effort had to be made to finish *Chinese Armorial Porcelain*. I made about two journeys a month at weekends down to Essex to deliver further parts of the manuscript in typed form to Patricia Herrmann, and learned something of what was to be involved in editing, with a publishing date now pencilled in for the spring of 1974. The journeys sometimes started after work on Fridays and finished at tea time on Sunday, when I returned again to Hicklam to catch up with the coming week.

The frequent visits to the Herrmann's, and the long instructional path laid before me by Patricia as I learned more of the publishing world (particularly as Frank was an author and publisher in his own right) were both hugely enjoyable and instructive, and the weekends culminating with the journey back to Hicklam began to suggest a future which would not all be played on African and Far Eastern shores.

There were opportunities, too, to discuss progress with Faber and for a time a major gulf opened between my hopes and the realities of publishing. It had been decided that because of the size and reference type of the book it would be printed by Oxford University Press, but they were determined on two things: one, that it would not be possible because of cost to print my 1,900 illustrations of services in colour (although I had colour slides) and two, that the book should be re-edited so that all the illustrations would form a massive section at the end, as was the case in virtually all such reference books at the time, and that the text should be catalogued in the form of a dictionary at the front.

I found it necessary, though with great disappointment, to give way on the first of these two demands on grounds of cost and agreed to turn all my transparencies by means of an 'internegative' into black and white prints. It was a mammoth task undertaken by a London processing company, but was completed on time, although at my personal expense of about £6,000. On the second point I felt adamant that the then-standard arrangement of illustrations listed at the end (or even in a separate volume) would not provide the close identification with the explanations and heraldic description necessary if two sections of the book had to be cross-referenced and endlessly examined in turn.

After a number of discussions with Faber, but supported by my editor Patricia, and a Saturday with a production manager of OUP, they finally relented and the format of illustrations opposite copy, although requiring extra editing and arranging, was agreed. Looking back, I notice that this seems to have been a watershed in decorative art reference book design. From about that time onwards, if *Chinese Armorial Porcelain* could do it with almost 2,000 illustrations, then it was possible for others to do the same in other fields of art reference. (It was also to be the last book that OUP ever published in letterpress.)

Working to a final manuscript deadline of 1st August 1972, having for some months struggled to refine the exact order in which the considerable mass of information should be presented, Elizabeth took the children to her mother's for a few days as the school holidays began before driving to Tresawle, and I settled down to meet my deadline of delivering the manuscript the following Monday in London. After a week at Arnold's, I prepared a large pot of black coffee and the first of a number of rare steaks (to stay awake and provide 'raw' energy) and started working at 7 pm on Friday, finishing the book without a break at 1 am on Monday. After a night in bed I set off on Monday after 9 am to drive first to London to deliver the final manuscript to Faber, and then turned west for two relaxing weeks holiday in Cornwall.

*   *   *

It was the first occasion when we were not all together at Tresawle, for Philippa had decided, in line with her increasing teenage freedom, to arrange a holiday with her friends, and they had decided to go to north Devon. In fact this was only one of the ways in which she had recently asserted her independence.

A month or so earlier Elizabeth had had a most difficult telephone call from the headmistress of the Mount School to say that she had received, that morning, a telephone call from the headmistress of Leeds Girls High School. This concerned an application she had had from a Miss Philippa Howard to complete her second year in the school sixth form at Leeds Girls High School and not at the Mount School. She declared that she wished to leave York to be a weekly boarder at Leeds. Neither Elizabeth nor I knew anything of this! A hastily arranged meeting at the Mount took place, as a result of which her application was allowed to go forward for consideration by the headmistress in Leeds, although to the considerable embarrassment of her parents. Philippa was, however, accepted and she stayed at lodgings in Leeds with some of her friends in the autumn.

Spurred by this obvious success, and with the agreement of Elizabeth who saw this as a break from expensive fee-paying schools, Sophie also asked to leave the Mount and join the local comprehensive school. I believe it was something of a culture shock at first, and Sophie quickly learned that it was advantageous to speak with a Yorkshire accent at school and with a different accent at home – but it worked and she enjoyed her new role.

With Elizabeth still at Leeds University, and my own frequent journeys to Essex at the end of a busy week at Arnold, it was a very full autumn.

*   *   *

Among the ideas which floated before me at the time was the possibility of a lecture tour in America after the publication of *Chinese Armorial Porcelain*. Nearly two years earlier I had been asked by Robert Rowe, the Director of Temple Newsam House, to organise an exhibition of armorial porcelain at the home of Sir Alvary Gascoigne; over the years we had received a number of kindnesses from Sir Alvary and been to dinner there on several occasions. This exhibition was to display 155 pieces from local collectors including Sir Alvary's own service and pieces lent by Robert Copeland, Phil Cooke, Lord Harewood, Sir Richard Sykes and others. As an inevitable consequence I had not only had to write an illustrated catalogue, but give a lecture. It was the first time I had done so, but found it relatively easy and satisfying as I had a very large collection of transparencies and no shortage of things to say. But in early 1973 I was unprepared one evening for a telephone call from New York from a person called Mottahedeh, who told me that they had learned of my name from Clare Le Corbeiller, a curator at the Metropolitan Museum in New York, and Fabers, and wondered whether I would like to see their collection in New York and, when *Chinese Armorial Porcelain* was printed, would consider possibly writing a book about it. I learned that it was only in part armorial, but that there was a great deal of other material. I didn't know of the Mottahedehs, but within a year they were to be great friends. They sent me some preliminary work done by their daughter-in-law and I could tell that the subject opened up vast new fields.

I'm not sure of the exact date, but about the same time at a dinner party I was asked by a friend, in a matter of fact way, what my plans were if Elizabeth were to leave Hicklam! I learned for the first time over dinner by this slip of the tongue, but later in a straightforward discussion with her at home, that she was deeply emotionally involved with her tutor at Leeds University. I was amazed, but there was no shouting – just realistic talk.

Looking back after thirty years, I can see that my single-minded pursuit of the unforgiving minute – whether at Arnolds, or in the field of armorial porcelain – was reflected in *The Least and Vilest Things*, although I did not at the time recognise my own single-mindedness as selfish, but regarded it as part of a career which would, in the end, benefit all our family.

I thought long and deeply and consulted a number of friends, some of whom were in the publishing and art world. It was undoubtedly, too, a factor that I felt it would be impossible ever to own my own share of the Arnold company which I felt I was helping to transform. It was certainly an attractive and interesting notion that I could lecture widely in America if I had the freedom to travel there with the goodwill of people like the Mottahedehs and Clare Le Corbeiller, with whom I had corresponded on numerous matters. With the publication of *Chinese Armorial Porcelain* little more than a year away, it occurred to me ever more strongly that it would be possible to support one's family by creating a small new company which would offer Chinese armorial porcelain and other armorial objects to families who were interested, starting a new career independent of the tensions and problems of the larger companies I had known. It would be <u>mine</u> and, with the considerable exception of my children, there seemed little to keep me in Yorkshire, for such a plan could only work in London while the deep tensions of living with someone who seemed both emotionally and politically apart made a new horizon inviting.

After much heart-searching, an eventual decision was reached that I would leave Yorkshire. Of my personal friends, some felt I should stay and fight, and others that it would be better to make a fresh start. As the years have passed it is increasingly clear that children have most to lose in such a situation. In this case it was particularly Jo and Thomas, for Philippa and Sophie were very independently minded and almost in sight of their universities. But the impracticalities of Yorkshire and the lure of London plans made the choice almost inevitable, while financial arrangements, including education, were not an immediate major issue.

On journeys to London I was able to consult people about whether to start a small shop in the suburbs and move to the West End when opportunity occurred, or whether to start in central London and rely on a reputation as an author and move forward. I was strongly persuaded by Guy Welby, of D. & J. Welby, a long-established silver business at the corner of Dover Street and Hay Hill, that I should definitely start in the centre if I could. He had a large near-empty basement opposite in Hay Hill and should I want it he would be happy to let me have it until the end of his lease in nearly twenty years' time at a very nominal rent, for he was near retirement. Guy Welby had always had fine export porcelain and I had identified armorials for him for some years. It seemed too good an opportunity to miss. I gave Arnold six month's notice and while Martin tried for some time to change my mind, and I felt uncomfortable, I was able to point out the problems likely if I still lived in Yorkshire. Although uncertain as to whether I was making the right choice, I could not forget the circumstances which had brought about my departure from Bridport, and in the end I said I could no longer stay in the north.

(It was a considerable sadness that only a few years later the Arnold family decided to sell their business to the publisher and entrepreneur Robert Maxwell, whom I had visited in Oxford with Martin a year or two before I left. It was to have very sad consequences when the Maxwell empire collapsed after his suicide and disgrace, and many of those I had known and worked with for a decade lost their jobs or some of their pension. The Arnold company had existed for just over a century.)

But it was to be a new and very different life that I started at the age of 45, with no experience as an antique dealer, and no regular salary.

CHAPTER 15

Heirloom and *China for the West*

One of the great advantages of the basement premises at 1 Hay Hill was that there was a room which had once been a drawing room-cum-office, a kitchenette with sink, other amenities and three further rooms, one of which was now to become a gallery. There was a grand entrance within the building, but also an adequate fire exit at the rear and by a passage and open courtyard into Hay Hill itself (filled in by intermediate building in the 1990s). The whole building had once been the residence of the Samuel family. I agreed the lease with Guy Welby and it was to be mine for twenty years.

It was not easy telling my father or my children of this new course of events – although the girls were very understanding – and of all those who would be upset I felt that Thomas, now seven, who may not have understood the implications at the time, could be most hurt in the long run. Exciting visits to Daddy's 'new home' were arranged. A small load of essential furnishings were sent to London, and I drove down on 6th September 1973. It was, purely by chance, the twenty-first anniversary of our wedding.

*   *   *

During the spring of that year I had visited Cambridge for a weekend, to be present at the Varsity cross-country race in which Hazel's eldest son, Nick, was to gain his 'blue'. Having struck up this extra friendship with Nick, who was also my god-son, I felt emboldened to ask both Hazel and Nick whether he would be prepared to come for a week to Hay Hill and camp with me in the basement and help decorate the rooms, which had probably not been painted since long before the war. The lease of this basement stated that it was not residential, but because there was an excellent back door (although no lock) and free access to the street, I felt that it was possible to live there quietly (some rooms even had a window opening on to the courtyard) and so Nick and I met on Monday and started work, using the front hall for all access. The building had other tenants including Hays Management and a political office of the PLO. But Nick and I made quite sure that after our quiet snack breakfast in the basement we crept out into the courtyard, through the basement fire escape, and walked ostentatiously in at the impressive front hall looking as if we had just arrived from elsewhere and chatting with the ever-

206

Heirloom & Howard Limited, in the basement of 1 Hay Hill,
Berkeley Square, London.

helpful doorman. This was to be my routine for a year or more. No-one ever queried my entrance before 8 am, particularly if it was raining and I crept out of the back with raincoat and umbrella and a remark on the weather to the doorman on the way in again at the front.

Nick and I worked feverishly until late each day and made remarkable progress, but we were not prepared for one distraction which happened during the second or third night. Because of the very strong smell of paint in the main rooms we slept in the corridor and left the back, fire escape, door open. I woke at about five and heard heavy snoring from down the passage from a tramp who, with his friend in a coal shed, had used 1 Hay Hill as a home for some time. I explained that this was no longer possible and that the row of little coal and refuse cellars would be locked. Only occasionally thereafter was there ever any sign of tramps, and there was never any loss or damage.

With Nick's help the painting was complete in a week, and some boxes of armorial engravings which I had bought in Cornwall during the summer and had framed, my own collection of armorial porcelain which was to be the principal capital of the display, and a few armorial objects I had bought recently or had been taken from Hicklam, formed the stock in a large, well-lit, freshly-painted basement in the heart of Mayfair at a nominal rent.

The three shops above were Riché (a smart hairdresser), Rocha, and an agency for the Aga Khan who was selling holiday villas on the Costa Smeralda. Between them there was a large frame for a poster and they kindly agreed that I could put some photographs of the basement on permanent display showing the shop and using for the first time the name which had been selected after a great deal of thought – Heirloom & Howard Limited. I opened the gallery on the Monday before the beginning of October 1973, and waited.

With a very limited budget there was little I could do but sit and wait in the basement at Hay Hill with the door open on that Monday morning. Of course. many of my friends knew where I had gone to ground, including those at Fabers and Sotheby's, the Herrmanns and Bourdon-Smiths, and I had written to as many people as I could. The location and address of Heirloom & Howard at 1 Hay Hill, Mayfair, could not be better, but one had to admit that the site was completely *out* of sight.

Of course, there was still much to do and there were no idle moments, but it was a great thrill when shortly after 12.30 I heard footsteps on the stairs and Jim Kiddell, for so long a very special director of Sotheby's, appeared. I think he spent £35, but it seemed like a million and we were on our way.

I realised that it wasn't possible to be the only person in such a shop premises so had taken on an acquaintance, Christopher Stones, who had started at Sotheby's and knew his way round antique London. Christopher was quick and better than I with a typewriter so did the correspondence, and we settled down to a routine of identifying every armorial item we could find, particularly unusual objects which we sometimes found in Portobello Road and sometimes in Sotheby's, Christie's and Phillips. It was to work well for about three years until Christopher decided, having been taught heraldry, that he liked the idea of Heirloom & Howard and wanted to do the same; we had to part company.

Whilst managing to post up to ten letters a day with the aid of my library of Burke's Peerages and *Who's Who*, I also established a twice weekly advertisement in the personal column of *The Times*, which then appeared on the front or back pages. It was inexpensive and very visible: 'Perceval, have you mislaid an excellent firescreen made in Victorian times by your grandmother? Write: Heirloom & Howard etc.' or 'Johnstone, would any descendant of Sir William, 3rd Baronet, be interested in acquiring his Chinese dinner plate? Please write …' This light-hearted approach had an excellent response, and as Christmas neared I tried to include an entry on most days.

Although we continued with this and similar variations for more than two years, the idea sadly came to a halt when I tried, 'Harmorial Hantiques, Heirloom & Howard, 1 Hay Hill, recover your family's possessions etc.' A pedantic gentleman from *The Times* telephoned to say that he had consulted the Oxford Dictionary and the words 'Harmorial' and 'Hantiques' were not in the dictionary and therefore could not be used in any advertisement. We had had excellent results for two years; perhaps it was time to try something else.

My first lecture tour in America was to start in late October of 1973, but it will be easier to follow that in a later chapter. With Christopher Stones in the shop it was possible for me to spend an increasing amount of time travelling again and know that customers who came in would be looked after. This was particularly important when people to whom we had written asked to come and see objects in Hay Hill, for photography was both time-consuming and, at the time, expensive.

On one occasion in the early days we found a particularly nice coach panel with the arms of Lord Bath and wrote to him in Wiltshire to tell him of it. Two days later a tall, spare figure strode into the office saying, 'I'm Bath, Thynne by name and thin by nature.' Of course he wanted the panel but asked if I could attach the Heirloom & Howard label to the reverse so that it could go into the inventory with the right details. This I did quickly with a brush of 'cow gum' (a rubberised paper glue). Impressed with the ease with which this was done, he asked what this glue was and I gave him the name and address in Woking of the manufacturer. About two weeks later, to my surprise, he appeared again in Hay Hill and said, 'That glue you recommended is no good at all. We have a chair with a broken leg so I wrote to Woking asking for some and they kindly sent a box of tins as a present. But when I mended the chair leg and sat on it, it broke again.' In spite of this misunderstanding he remained interested in anything I could find, and he was one of many who became regular customers when we could show that the arms were of an ancestor.

Over about twenty years we built up a detailed list of some 10,000 armigerous families which were wanted by about 6,000 descendants, and this made it possible to write to the most likely buyer as soon as something was found. Occasionally this could be embarrassing if two cousins both asked to be told, and if <u>one</u> was supplied, he might show off his new purchase to his cousin – but one had to learn how to move with diplomacy as well as speed.

Often friendships developed as a result of reuniting a family with a family treasure which had been disposed of decades earlier by a previous generation. This was so with John Sclater, whose family's unique Chinese service, with many scenes drawn from an ancestor's sketchbook, I had first seen in part in the Mottahedeh Collection, and was later offered a group of pieces by a well known English dealer. This was restored to the family, and I was to enjoy hospitality at John's home on a number of occasions in the 1980s.

Occasional articles in newspapers were very good news, such as when *The Daily Telegraph* published an article in April 1974 with a large illustration and the title 'Sleuth among the Heirlooms' and started, 'Sadly many heirlooms are lost for ever ...', continuing three paragraphs later, 'In fact the only antiques that stood a good chance of returning to future generations are those with a coat of arms or crest ...'. 'Basically Mr Howard is reversing the process of antique dealing which distributes antiques far from their original environment.' The article ended with the mention of a 'dictionary and reference book which records 3,000 services of armorial porcelain ... which is to be published by Fabers next month.' For a few days the numbers visiting us more than doubled and we had a number of enquiries about porcelain collections where I was asked to assess their worth and make suggestions either for disposal or, in most cases, how they could be enhanced. It was, after all, possible for great houses with collections to make further acquisitions through estate purchases, provided these were displayed to the public.

One exciting enquiry was from Scotland where the Duke of Hamilton was rearranging his porcelain and wondered which services he should keep or augment, and whether there were any other services I knew of which he should look for. I agreed to visit Scotland and discuss this, and arrived near Haddington on the night sleeper from Euston. In spite of the early train he came to meet me, and we went at once to Lennoxlove. It was to be the first visit of many over thirty years, and slowly and carefully his collection of

Mr David Howard identifying a family heirloom by its coat of arms. Picture by PETER WILLIAMS

SLEUTH AMONG THE HEIRLOOMS

Useful publicity in a national newspaper.

211

Hamilton armorial porcelain increased. (It was typical, perhaps, of the low esteem that many Georgian 'chattels' attracted, that so much of the Hamilton estate had been sold in the Hamilton Palace sale in the late 19th Century when a senior line had died out, and a sad decision was made to sell. This saw portraits and the library and so much else dispersed throughout museums and collections world-wide.)

A few years later I was able to bid for and acquire in a New York auction a very nice armorial service, made for the 5th Duke about 1730, from the estate of Randolph Hearst, and on a subsequent occasion it was possible to negotiate with Douglas Dillon, the President of the Metropolitan Museum in New York, a group of fine pieces which he was happy to exchange for other Douglas-Hamilton objects so that there should be examples of as many different services as possible at Lennoxlove. Today there are examples of some twenty services in fine, rearranged cabinets – an excellent example of family memorabilia of historic interest available for viewing by the public in the wake of a sadly unnecessary sale nearly a century earlier.

But not all Heirloom's visitors were so forward-looking. One 'client' clearly thought he was Charles I and would come occasionally, wearing a short pointed beard and dressed in a cloak carrying a long cane, and sometimes lie down on the floor. Another, called Mr McAdam, normally slept rough but would hope for a cup of coffee on a cold day. It surprised me to learn that his direct ancestor had invented 'metalling' of roads with bitumen and whose name was forever linked to tarmac. Another visitor was Mr Alleyne, a West Indian who claimed descent from a family of wealthy sugar planting baronets. When our shop was later on the street, he would come in to look round and make enquiries about his family's past, even pausing outside the window on a hot day to add shirt, tie, coat and gloves from his Victoria Station trolley, so that he should be 'properly dressed'. On leaving he would reverse the procedure and wheel away his trolley in more 'relaxed' attire.

In fact, it was a piece of good fortune in early 1976 that the Aga Khan had sold all his villas on the Costa Smeralda through one of the shops above me, and no longer required the premises. I was able to negotiate a transfer of lease with the manager so that Heirloom & Howard had a place on the street in Hay Hill. Within about three years the company was making a modest profit, and the relative uniqueness of the business (the last person to have had a similar business in London being Sir Algernon Tudor-Craig, who sold his shop at 100 Knightsbridge in 1929) made it a port of call for those interested in heraldry or ancestry.

*   *   *

From the outset, Philippa and Sophie, Jo and Thomas would come down to London at weekends or in the holidays and stay in the double bunks in one of the rooms in my 'apartment'. I suspect the doorman never discovered that a quiet tenant was living in the basement, and as nothing untoward happened, he had no reason to. But in due course there were other reasons why it became almost irrelevant.

Shortly before leaving Arnolds, Paul Jordan had introduced me to a number of London educational contacts and among these was the Regent School of Languages in Oxford Street. Their Italian specialist was a particularly sparkling lady called Anna-Maria Bocci, who not only was a skilled linguist but had much wider interests in history, Italian architecture and culture. In spite of my visits to New York in October and November, by Christmas I was seeing her most evenings although she already had a wide circle of friends and a number of admirers. I knew little of Italy and had hardly heard of Perugia where her widowed mother and sister's family lived – her mother's family having a small country estate in the Umbrian hills. It was soon felt essential that I should meet them, and in spite of an escalating schedule of journeys in England, a series of visits to America in connection with the Mottahedehs, and the publication of *Chinese Armorial Porcelain*, we spent a few days in Perugia in the spring: the mediaeval town and narrow streets being exciting and steeped in history, with Assisi a few miles away across the valley. Anna's mother, sister and her two daughters, Priscilla and Sybilla, were charming, and I fell in love with it all.

Back in England Anna and I discussed how we should regularise our relationship, for my amicable divorce and financial arrangements were complete. With both Anna and I having had stable relationships in the past, we were not sure as to whether we should get married; but we decided to do so, and after a ceremony at a London registry office, had a small reception at a hotel just behind Marble Arch at which members of both our families, my children and sister and Aunt Bunny, were present. It was an unexpectedly happy solution to what had started as a bleak option. For a while Anna tried to see if it was possible to combine her work in language teaching with running a stall in Gray's Antique Market in Davies Street, but this was to prove too much with her other managerial responsibilities, especially when she joined the Banco di Roma and became assistant to the London director.

*   *   *

Within two months of Heirloom opening in 1973, I had flown to New York and met Rafi and Mildred Mottahedeh. It was to be one of the most important

Anna is introduced to a Danish nephew,
Thomas Harttung, by Eilean North
at Sophie's wedding in 1979.

Mildred Mottahedeh at 225 Fifth Avenue, New York, explains the difference
between 1730 Chinese and 1980 Mottahedeh porcelain – but which is which?

meetings of my life. Rafi had been born in Persia and was a Baha'i, being related to the founder of that religion, while Mildred had been brought up in a Jewish family in north New York City. They met at university and were later married. Their son, Roy, was a brilliant scholar and an expert on mediaeval and later Middle Eastern religions, and later was awarded the McArthur Prize for his advice given to Mr Kissinger and the American Government at the time of the Iranian hostage crisis – for before responding to demands from the Ayatollahs it was first necessary to understand the *meaning* behind the words of what they proposed. The successful resolution of the hostage crisis was certainly due in part to a clear analysis of the demands in the context of Muslim aspirations. (Many years later, my daughter Sophie was photographing Mrs Mottahedeh in the garden of Berkeley Square for a bronze bust of herself which she had commissioned. A figure strode through the Square on the way to the American Embassy accompanied by three heavily dressed 'minders' and Mildred called out, 'Henry!' It was with scarcely repressed awe that half an hour later Sophie dashed into Heirloom & Howard in Hay Hill and said, 'Guess who I've been talking to in Berkeley Square – Henry Kissinger!')

But this was all to come, and in November 1973 I met Rafi and Mildred in New York and plunged into their world. They introduced me to their careful plans, conceived over more than thirty years, of collecting export porcelain – latterly with the purpose of turning it into a reference book which would become a prime source of learning about the subject. It was, I was to find, a major tenet of the Baha'i faith that education should be a prime goal, so that everyone could understand and benefit from learning.

Already they had poured profits from their business into the establishment of colleges in India, Africa and Korea, and although their interest in export porcelain was never intended at first as a mainstream subject, they wanted it explained as clearly as possible, particularly as they saw it as part of the world history of trade. Mildred herself was a brilliant porcelain designer who, at that time, was responsible for many of the most innovative design initiatives in the ceramic field, a great many of which were adapted from Chinese porcelain.

In the 1930s their attention had turned from trading in Persian rugs to the realisation that as fine glass chandeliers had first become redundant in many of the greater houses in Europe (through the introduction of gas light and then electricity) they had increasingly been displayed and used in the palaces of the Middle East. In turn, gas and electricity had spread eastwards in the earlier 20th Century, and eventually the same chandeliers were increasingly redundant again (particularly after the collapse of the Ottoman Empire), at exactly the time when the status and decoration of the finest apartments in

New York and elsewhere in America were 'calling out' for such symbols of affluence.

With his contacts in the Middle East and New York it was not difficult for Rafi and Mildred to turn this situation to their advantage. By the later 1930s their success had opened up new fields: the principal of these started with making Worcester-style candlesticks and developed into the creation of an additional supply of porcelain, largely, although not exclusively, of Chinese export taste – so popular in America until the latter part of the 19th Century, long after Europe had concentrated on the wares of their own manufacturers. Dinner services of 18th Century 'export' style were readily saleable; birds and animals after Chinese 18th Century forms were required by decorators, and a wide range of vases and decorative pieces also found ready markets – the only anomaly being that as the Chinese considered such wares 'elitist' (in spite of numerous requests to manufacture) the Mottahedehs had to have their porcelain made first in Italy and then Portugal, where the hard paste porcelain and skilled labour could produce very accurate copies of the original designs. However, because of both their faith and business acumen, Rafi and Mildred were determined to make sure that their work should never be regarded as 'Samson copies' or even originals, and thus pieces were always adequately marked, particularly after they found one of their earliest 1930s wares being sold as a Worcester original in a Paris shop after the war.

As a result, their private collection grew rapidly, because of buying large numbers of samples to copy, and later through collecting for its own sake, particularly in Europe where they found large quantities of Chinese export pieces, little cared for and at prices which were exceptionally reasonable. By the 1960s interest in collecting this ware was rekindled – both by their own success, but more particularly because of Lloyd Hyde's book, followed by those of Beurdeley and Clare Le Corbeiller, and other authors in the 1970s. Now they found themselves very anxious to have a work written which would be both educational and as near-comprehensive as possible.

Discussing this project both at their apartment on an upper floor of the block called 'The United Nations Plaza', just north of the United Nations buildings themselves on the East River and with a marvellous view looking down the river on to those buildings, and at their Company offices at 225 Fifth Avenue, it was clear that they were determined to move as quickly as possible and were particularly encouraged by Nelson Rockefeller – himself a collector. He first asked the Mottahedehs to reproduce the 'Swan Service' which he owned, perhaps the most important and well-documented of all early Meissen services and ordered by Count Brühl in 1738, so that he could dine from virtually identical copies while the originals could remain safely in their cabinets. (This was, in fact, triggered by the breakage of a tray full of original pieces dropped after a dinner party!)

Spurred on by the excellent 'duplicate' service he received, he decided to ask the Mottahedehs to make a range of, largely armorial, pieces copying examples in his own collection which were to be sold in a shop in 57th Street. It was, he felt, only right that a wide circle of people should be able to appreciate the quality of decorative ware that wealthy collectors bought and that he already enjoyed – and thus he set about making it available. (It was not without amusement that I had to tell him, when he asked if I could sell such sets of armorial porcelain with the correct arms to Scottish families, that to offer for sale in Scotland any object with the arms of the Chief of a Scottish clan (as two of the services he had had made) would allow the Chief, under ancient laws, to seize any such ware without payment. It was decided not to set up any branch in Scotland!)

*　　*　　*

Although much of this was still to come, having examined the Mottahedeh Collection in detail for a day or two, I expressed the strongest interest in writing a book about it, but felt that, particularly with the time scale they had in mind, it was work for two, and so asked if I could canvas a friend. It was a very happy choice that John Ayers, the Keeper of the Far Eastern department at the Victoria and Albert Museum, agreed, and thirty years later we remain close friends. But before writing a book covering the greater part of all Chinese export porcelain, with two authors from two such different backgrounds, it was necessary to agree on a *modus operandi* if we were not to overlap and waste much effort.

John and I visited New York again shortly after and drew up an outline of how the book would be divided into sections. We then agreed who would write each section – John on the range of decorative styles and the figures and non-porcelain pieces, while I would write on porcelain evidently produced for trading, with historical context, religion, mythology and history, armorials, American history and everyday life. The introductory chapters would be long, but two only: before 1700 by John, and after 1700 by me.

When each had written a section or group of entries, these would be given to the other to read, comment on and even correct. But having delivered such comments, it was the absolute unchallenged right of each original author to make only those changes he wished. I can recall that we never had a single serious disagreement and believe that it would be almost impossible for a reader to know who wrote what. Great thought was given to an all-embracing title, but it was John who first suggested *China for the West* – to immediate agreement, including the Mottahedehs. Looking back, I have never had any wish to change a word.

We were fortunate that Sotheby Parke Bernet agreed to publish, for while they fulfilled their role well, including much of the marketing, they did not intrude any stylistic or format changes without our agreement and support; it was, in fact, a pleasant publishing experience (as had been my experience with Fabers) in spite of the size of the two-volume project.

*   *   *

I do not recall how many times John and I visited New York between 1974 and 1978 when the book was published, but it was on many and various occasions; there were even times when we stayed by ourselves in the exciting apartment at United Nations Plaza when the Mottahedehs were away, for they still travelled widely on business.

It was first necessary to select and agree on some eight hundred objects from their much larger collection. Having decided which would be included, John was able to offer the very considerable task of photographing everything to two senior photographers at the V & A, Peter MacDonald and Stanley Eost, who came to New York in their free-lance capacity. We had marked and catalogued every piece, for everything was to be illustrated with the text in the same way as *Chinese Armorial Porcelain*, although in a more relaxed form. Peter and Stanley stayed at the Gotham Hotel and after supper each evening retired to their rooms and turned their bathrooms into laboratories, developing film before going to bed, so that when we met again at the Mottahedehs' apartment the following morning they were able to confirm that every piece in the previous day's group had been developed and would make an excellent print. (They had perfected their efficient operation in many parts of the world, including the European homes of Baron von Thyssen, and more than one royal family.)

While John and I knew almost every nook and cranny of the apartment in New York, we also had the pleasure of spending a number of long weekends at the Mottahedehs' most comfortable home at Stamford, Connecticut, where Mildred and Rafi drove most weekends and where large parts of their extensive collection were displayed. Whether it was winter, when I might spend some hours clearing the drive with an efficient snow plough, or summer, when we dined in the garden or on the terrace, I grew to know this home so well. While John only came to New York for matters concerning the book, I was able to visit on many more occasions – when passing through on

Rafi Mottahedeh and Vice President Nelson Rockefeller at Mottahedeh Inc.,
Park Avenue, New York, in 1977.

lecture tours, and later when I was there so frequently attending to business with Stair and Company in New York. But there was always something to discuss with the Mottahedehs and always a welcome, and one was fortunate to meet a great many of their friends, often at friendly informal dinners at their apartment.

There were a number of months when I spent as much time in New York as in London, but Heirloom in Hay Hill greatly profited from an influx of the new friends I had met in America. The hours of writing were longer than ever, but the work on the new book was complete and all in the hands of the publisher by the autumn of 1977. Greatly daring, I wrote to Nelson Rockefeller who, in spite of being the Vice President, found time to write a foreword. We asked the binder to prepare four special leather copies so that the Mottahedehs, Nelson Rockefeller and the two authors could all exchange signatures after the book was published. Alas it was not to be, because before we received the copies both Rafi and Nelson Rockefeller were dead. It was a great sadness for Mildred, but Rafi had seen a pre-publication volume and was delighted, and Nelson bought a number of copies for friends.

My only regret about *China for the West* is that the illustrations were not all in colour. Within a decade this would have been standard, but at the time it would have created many technical problems and increased the price of the book greatly. The dispersal of the collection over the last twenty years (at prices undreamed of when the porcelain was purchased) has made it now impossible to reprint in colour and the book has long been out of print.

Sotheby's had given us a launch party, and shortly after publication Mildred gave a special dinner party to a number of friends who came from a wide area, including Jack Dorrance, Chairman of the Campbell Soup Company, who came up from Philadelphia in his helicopter (a heliport close to the United Nations buildings making this very convenient). He was later to invite me to lunch in the country. One guest, 'George', whose name I didn't hear as we were introduced, asked me to sign his copy of the book which already had an inscription '… from Nelson and Happy.' We talked for quite a while over dinner when he asked me particularly about my experiences in Africa. I was surprised at how much detail he knew of African governments, their problems and finances – it was some years since I had been able to talk of what was now a 'past life'. After dinner when the guests had departed, I asked Mildred his name again. 'Oh, he's George Woods, President of the World Bank.' I might have guessed – the Mottahedehs always had such interesting friends!

CHAPTER 16

Stair & Company and the Porcelain Tours

Following the departure of Christopher Stones and the move upstairs, Heirloom had to have some more assistance, particularly as I was away lecturing or researching for up to three months each year. First to come was Michael Walshe, who had had wide experience in a life spent in India. He worked with us for a year or two, but has remained a good friend ever since. For secretaries I was fortunate to find Ginna Mostyn, followed by her sister-in-law, Zinnia Davies-Cooke, and later Sally Wagstaff and Mary Angell, all of whom, over eight years to 1982, were a pleasure to work with and added their own presence to Heirloom when Howard was away. At no time did I feel concerned, even when I was away for up to two months at a time.

It had been in early 1974 that I first met Dewey Curtis and lectured for him at Pennsbury Manor, but it was to lead to far more than a day's lecture. For some years Dewey, with his friend Joseph Stanley (who owned an antique shop in Pennsylvania) had guided groups of Americans in England and elsewhere. In 1977 a September tour of English villages and towns was planned, and in March 1978 a tour of Egypt with a cruise on the Nile. But following the lecture I had given in London to an earlier group (and not without some suggestions on my part, for I had, in the early 1970s, written a chapter on oriental porcelain in a book called *Treasures of the National Trust*) Dewey and I conceived the idea of a Chinese Export seminar and tour from 17th to 30th October 1977 on which I would be the lecturer and guide. The tour would only visit houses in which one of the principal displays was Chinese porcelain. I already knew most of these and had included their armorial porcelain in my book, or their other Chinese porcelain in my chapter for the Trust.

All the 'Stanley Tours' were limited to a maximum of twenty-five participants as it was usually difficult for one guide to marshal and direct more than twenty absorbed followers. The first two days were in London; both John Ayers and I gave a lecture at their London hotel, and the group visited Christie's, the Victoria and Albert Museum, Hampton Court Palace and had a buffet supper at Heirloom. The following day we drove out of London and for the next twelve days we were to get to know each other well as we examined and toured houses, mostly of the National Trust, and lunched and dined together in a number of comfortable hotels.

Our first visit was to Clandon Park in Surrey, where Lord Onslow kindly took us round the house which had been in his family for almost three centuries. It was an excellent place to start, for much of the Gubbay Collection of porcelain, including an array of exotic Chinese birds, was on display there. In the afternoon we drove the short distance to Polesden Lacey, once the home of Mrs Greville (frequently visited by Edward VII) where Duveen had found a ready buyer for *famille verte* porcelain. Some pieces were the pair to examples in the Taft Museum in Cincinnati, while others rivalled Lord Lever's Collection at the Lady Lever Gallery in Liverpool, all supplied by Duveen and at prices which were not exceeded until the 1980s.

We stayed near Basingstoke and in the morning drove to Buscot Park where some 17th Century Japanese jars had the initials of their original owners. I was so excited by these that Lord Faringdon could not help remarking, 'You might also mention Rembrandt's *Portrait of a Man* which hangs above it!' We then went on to Blenheim where apart from the Chinese porcelain there were more than enough other objects of interest, spending the afternoon at the Ashmolean Museum where it was possible to compare the collection of Chinese porcelain and Rissik Marshall's collection of Worcester armorial porcelain. We stayed two nights in Oxford and marvelled at the two Rothschild collections at Ascot and Waddesdon Manor, where there was again much else to see as well as porcelain. Driving to Bristol for three nights, we had an interesting morning at Littlecote where the armour and history was more impressive than the porcelain, and the rest of the day in Bath, with its architecture and antique shops – for some on the tour were as acquisitive as they were inquisitive, and the spare seats in the bus filled with packages and a number of smaller pieces of furniture. The next day at Dyrham Park provided not only an excellent array of porcelain, but the National Trust laid on an excellent dinner.

Turning northwards we drove via the Dyson Perrins Museum at Worcester, and antique shops in Ludlow, to Shrewsbury where we had a private dinner, and next day to the Lady Lever Art Gallery at Liverpool, where we all found the porcelain fascinating but most were overawed by the paintings (Duveen again). On our way back to Shrewsbury we called at Erddig (once the home of Elihu Yale, the East India Governor who provided much of the original funds for Yale University) where Philip Yorke, the last remaining member of that branch of the family, lived out his eccentric life and relished any opportunity to show guests how he rode his penny-farthing bicycle.

Philip had inherited the house from his elder brother, who had no children either – but before this lived in a small cottage on the estate and was only invited to Erddig House for Christmas lunch! When his brother died and he found himself the owner of Erddig, the house was then in a poor state of repair and for three months Philip slept on a camp bed under the grand piano in the drawing room because it was the driest place in the house. When I first went there at his invitation, shortly after his inheritance, I saw the bed made up there. On the next occasion he was sleeping in the cook's quarters where we had lunch in a tiny staff kitchen, and while I was given the only pieces of silver with the Yorke crest in the kitchen, he used a knife and fork which he proudly told me had come free with a special Kelloggs offer.

After Erdigg we had tea with Colonel Edmund and Mrs FitzHugh and saw the only remaining piece of the original service of Fitzhugh porcelain which had, until recently, been used to catch drips under the kitchen sink, and next day, driving towards Yorkshire, we spent a morning at Shugborough where the Anson service and so many other objects which had belonged to Lord Anson, and to his descendant, Lord Lichfield, were on display. (I was later to be invited to take part in a BBC programme with Arthur Negus, then the leading antiques television personality, at Shugborough.)

The next day was pure armorial, for Phil and Pat Cooke had said we could visit their home near Pontefract to see one of the two finest collections of Chinese armorial porcelain in the world. To some it was a defining moment which would never be forgotten.

And so we drove south, calling to see the collection of the Fitzwilliam Museum at Cambridge and then the great Rotunda – the home of the Marquess of Bristol at Ickworth, where almost every object in the central house had a curved contour, including walls and doors, and there was part of the Hervey service and much other porcelain on display. That afternoon was spent at Long Melford Hall with Sir Richard and Lady Hyde Parker, where not only was the porcelain spectacular, but its history and provenance was decisive. Much of it had been taken as prize money by Admiral Hyde Parker when he captured a huge Spanish galleon, the *Santissima Trinidad*, in the Pacific about 1760, whose cargo of porcelain was said to be intended for the Spanish Court.

On the last day we visited both Woburn Abbey and the shops at Woburn, arriving back in London wiser, I think, than when we had set out – which was the purpose of the tour. Two or three participants, including Beverly DuBose (later to become my greatest friend in America), asked whether it was possible to organise other such journeys in the future with a similar focus. I had to say that I would discuss that with Dewey Curtis, for it was he who had asked me to join his tour in the first place as a guide. Somewhat to my surprise Dewey raised no objections, so long as future tours were built only round porcelain, and that if he needed me, I would give a lecture for him or accompany *his* tours if they, too, concerned porcelain. In the event this never occurred, and I felt free to consider another porcelain tour in England in the autumn of 1978.

*   *   *

Among the less expected results of Heirloom now having a window in Hay Hill was that what had previously been considered a 'consultancy business' was now seen as a West End antique shop. To my surprise I had an invitation for lunch from Alastair Stair, whose very successful furniture shop in Mount Street had one of the finest reputations in London. He asked if I would be prepared to co-operate with Stair in putting high quality armorial and other Chinese ware on display in Mount Street, and in particular in Stair's two very impressive stores in 57th Street, New York, where Stair and Company looked across the street at 'The Incurable Collector', which fulfilled a decorative role in the New York market to match their role as the most prestigious furniture shop in that city.

I was obviously flattered, and at first prepared a list of some twenty or thirty items which could be displayed. It was then suggested that their new manager in New York, Angus Perceval, would like to start a modest scheme for buying porcelain on commission from the company. It was clear that Stair had broader ideas, for they had also asked an English picture dealer, John Sainty, to display a range of his pictures – particularly 19th and 20th Century ones by Munnings and other artists – at The Incurable Collector. (It was a coincidence that the Sainty home had originally been at Hassocks, in the same valley as Belmont School, and that there were reasonable grounds for speculating that the names of Sainty and Sanctuary might have had a common origin in the 15th Century.)

The whole idea was exciting and I spent some time at Stair's on each occasion I visited New York and the Mottahedehs. I was encouraged to have an exhibition of Chinese armorial porcelain in 57th Street and Angus Perceval and Hope Hood, his most helpful assistant, were both to become good friends. I was not, however, prepared for the next step, for in early 1980 Alastair Stair sold his business to the enormously successful oil and industrial tycoon – David Murdock of Los Angeles, the owner of Pacific Holdings.

One afternoon in Hay Hill, David and his wife Gabrielle Murdock walked into Heirloom and after a discussion which revealed her to be an enthusiast of Chinese export porcelain, they invited me to dinner at the Connaught Hotel. It was a relaxed social occasion, but there was little doubt that David was sizing up the situation as to whether Stair should expand further into the porcelain field. Both *Chinese Armorial Porcelain* and *China for the West* had now been published, with which Gabrielle was clearly familiar.

The next time in New York I spent far longer at Stair's, and during 1979 and 1980 an ambitious plan of expanding into decorative Chinese export porcelain was drawn up – with purchasing extended over the two years to some hundreds of thousands of dollars. This was both exciting and did not clash with Heirloom's more modest path in the armorial field. I produced a series of full-page advertisements for *Antiques Magazine* and with the help of Angus and Hope each journey to New York became more interesting. My lecture tour in early 1979 (largely in Michigan and Ohio) gave me two visits to New York, and while I sometimes stayed with Mildred, my time was largely spent at 59 East 57th Street, and I was also the guest of Alastair Stair at the nearby Metropolitan Club.

The typical New York customer was certainly largely unknown to Heirloom in Hay Hill, and I recall one day Alastair Stair telling me that Mrs Imelda Marcos (wife of the then President of the Philippines) had been in the shop and had bought some very expensive furniture, including a large cabinet which contained many of the finest pieces of export ware I had recently bought in London. As she turned to go Alastair Stair said, in a gentle way, 'Don't you think it looks so much nicer with all the porcelain?' She stopped to consider and then said, 'Yes, I do – you'd better deliver that as well.' The total retail price of the porcelain was over $800,000. No, this was not Hay Hill!

The figures for 1980 must have looked good, for Stair decided to open a large Los Angeles showroom in December 1981. In March 1980 I travelled to California for a lecture tour and spoke first at the Los Altos Antiques Fair and then to the San Francisco Ceramics Circle. A day or two later I flew to Los Angeles and stayed in great comfort at the Country Club, where I was amused to find that there were then not only separate entrances for 'ladies' and 'gentlemen', but separate car parks for their cars. My first lecture was to the American Society of Designers, and that evening I had dinner with the Murdocks, who had recently bought the late Conrad Hilton's house at Bel Air. It was a very pleasant evening and I remember, particularly, some Picasso pottery in the room. The following evening I lectured to the Los Angeles County Museum of Art, of which Mrs Thomas Armistead was then the Chairman of their Decorative Arts Council. It followed a tour of the museum, and Tom and Cass Armistead are friends to this day. I made a number of other friends in Los Angeles, particularly a lawyer, Dennis Roach, who himself collected and has remained a personal friend for more than twenty years.

Two days later I flew to Denver where Philippa was now living and working as a secretary to the director of a hospital. It was fun to see her new home and meet some of her friends. From there I flew on to Dallas to stay for two nights with Bud and Betty Gertz and, amongst others, met Elton and Martha Hyder of Fort Worth. Bud and Betty lived an international life, for Bud's company, Guam Oil, which supplied much of the American Pacific Fleet, and their second home on Tenian Island (where in 1743 Anson had collected his breadfruit trees) provided endless opportunities for travel. Bud and Betty, who had a huge love of oriental export porcelain, were coming on Heirloom's next porcelain tour, now little more than a month away.

Elton Hyder, whose wife Martha's boundless energy was always to be marvelled at, had been a lawyer all his life and had been the Junior Council for the Prosecution in the War Criminal Trials in Tokyo after the war. On his desk stood an immense Victorian silver inkwell and stand which had belonged to the Japanese Prime Minister, Tojo. On the night before Tojo was executed, he had asked Elton to visit him in his cell and had given him this inkwell as a gift for 'being a successful adversary'. Elton was a 'larger than life' figure in many ways.

Staying with Bud and Betty was a treat – the first of a number – but all too soon I flew to Atlanta, where Beverly DuBose had arranged a speaking engagement at Emory University, and the next day we drove to Birmingham, Alabama, where I spoke, and then returned to Atlanta for another lecture at the Historical Society on the third day.

Travelling north on the following day I stopped first for a night with Rodney Frelinghuysen, who was then building a most impressive collection of blue and white porcelain, and then on to New York where, with the atmosphere of Los Angeles still in my veins, I needed to have further talks with Alastair Stair.

*   *   *

Returning to porcelain tours in England, which increasingly became part of Heirloom's activities in the later 1970s and early 1980s, I had agreed with Dewey Curtis that I would organise and guide the next tour myself. During the preceding months I had corresponded with the owners of many great houses (often agreeing donations to the 'Roofing Fund'), in many cases driving to see them first so that I could guide with adequate knowledge behind me.

On the tour, as well as Beverly and Duffie DuBose (this time accompanied by their son, Bo), were Harriet Tyne, Hugh and Marie Shackleford, Robert and Cary Doyle, John Shank and Joe Matthews, Reuben Getschow and his wife, Mark Alexander and other friends. This time we were to travel round southern England – as far west as St Austell and as far north as Oxford – with every moment focused on porcelain.

Our first day, as with Dewey Curtis, included visits to Clandon Park and Polesden Lacey, but we arrived at Winchester early and then drove to Royden Manor to have a private dinner party with Mr and Mrs Edward Morant. It was a perfect evening with infinitely helpful and kind hosts, whose family still owned the exceptional Morant Chinese dinner service, with many pieces copied from elaborate silver originals (one of only two services of this style, the other being for a friend of those days, Sir Nathaniel Curzon). In the 18th Century the family had made a fortune in Jamaica on their large estates at what is now called Morant's Bay.

The next day we drove to Stockbridge and had lunch with Lord and Lady Douglas Gordon as our guests, and spent the afternoon at his antique shop, leaving in time for a visit to The Vyne, a National Trust house and for centuries the home of the Chute family (whose porcelain was now largely dispersed). Visiting Breamore House the following day, the home of Sir Westrow Hulse, we enjoyed a full display of an ancestor's armorial service with many rare pieces on the dining room table. After a brief lunch in Salisbury we went on to Stourhead, the home for two centuries of the Hoare banking family, and then continued to Honiton in Devon where we stayed at the comfortable Combe House Hotel, then owned by John Boswell, a descendant of the diarist James Boswell, who still had much of his service on display in the hotel. We filled the dining room to capacity and I sat at a round table in one corner where we were waited on by two exceptionally charming waitresses. Serving someone in a corner is not always easy and as a waitress reached out to put the main dish before Mark Alexander she slipped and had to steady herself with a hand on his knee. Without a moment's hesitation Mark remarked in his Southern drawl, 'I'll give you just half an hour to remove that hand.' More than twenty-five years later I can still see her blush.

The following day found us in Exeter looking in antique shops, before an excellent lunch in The Close with Michael and Anne Pursey, both enthusiastic collectors; Michael then being a lecturer at Exeter University. We went on to Powderham Castle in Devon where the Courtenay family had lived since the 12th Century and where we had tea with Lord and Lady Devon, but had to hurry back to Honiton to be joined by my sister Hazel and her husband, Bob McKinnel, and Major and Mrs Noel Page-Turner, whose family had commissioned more than one fine armorial service from China in the early 18th Century – although there was then but one piece left (a situation now much improved!).

In the morning we drove to Plymouth and Saltram House, the home of the Parker family, Earls of Morley. After lunch in their ancient kitchen we spent much of the afternoon in the Museum, where there was the best collection of the earliest Plymouth porcelain, made by William Cookworthy from clay found at Boconnoc, in imitation of Chinese hard-paste porcelain. (This initiative had coincided with the importation into England of various Chinese clays in an attempt to produce a rival to Chinese porcelain – all of which much concerned Stoke-on-Trent, for they greatly feared that the popular demand for such porcelain, if made in the south west from local materials, could irreparably damage the Staffordshire potteries.)

At St Austell in Cornwall I had arranged with Alan Dalton, my old friend of rugby football days in Dorchester and now Sir Alan Dalton, the Managing Director of English China Clays, to visit the international clay pits of Cornwall which then employed about fifteen thousand people – the largest supplier of China clay for porcelain making and paper coatings in the world outside China. We visited a number of pits and had a working lunch with the technical director of the company who was able to answer many of the detailed questions which had interested collectors for years. On the way back to Plymouth we visited Lanhydrock House, once the home of the Robartes family, and then stopped to have a drink on Bodmin Moor at Jamaica Inn, made famous by Daphne du Maurier's novel.

From Plymouth we went to Bath, where the shops the next day were an ever-pleasant draw, with Dando's porcelain shop always a particular focus. But at four we reboarded our bus to drive to St Catherine's Court outside Bath, a large and unspoiled Tudor mansion then the home of Commander and Mrs Christopher (more recently the home of the actress Jane Seymour). Mrs Christopher was an expert on needlework, and after a memorable dinner she gave us a candlelit tour of the house before we settled into our four-poster beds.

In the morning we had a leisurely start, arriving at Berkeley Castle in Gloucestershire just after a picnic lunch provided by Mrs Christopher. It is always traumatic to see the well where King Edward II was held before his murder, but we concentrated on the Berkeley armorial service before going on to Frampton Court, the home of Major and Mrs Peter Clifford, the descendants of 'Fair Rosamund' Clifford, the mistress of Henry II in 1150.

Next day we reached Oxford, remaining the afternoon at the Ashmolean again, and from there on to Woodstock. The following morning was spent at Broughton Castle, the home of the Twistleton-Wykeham-Fiennes family since the 18th Century. Lady Saye and Sele's father had been a senior officer in the Coldstream when I was with the Regiment, and her husband had trained as an estate agent with my uncle, Peter Sanctuary, in Bridport, so we were assured of a friendly welcome. Most of the afternoon was occupied with wandering round Stowe by special permission of the Headmaster, where the scale of the home of the Dukes of Buckingham and Chandos and the landscaping of the garden was almost overawing to any not fortunate enough to have been to school there. The lack of porcelain was more than compensated for by the architecture, the portraits and the history.

After another night at Woodstock we turned again towards London, spending the morning at Gerrards Cross seeing as much as possible of the huge collection of Clive Rouse's armorial porcelain, and the afternoon at Aldermaston, staying three hours with Alan Caiger-Smith (then perhaps England's leading potter and with whom I had been at school both at Belmont and Stowe). Our group employed their new-found knowledge of China clay to ask some educated questions about his wares, while many took advantage of the opportunity to acquire some pieces before having tea in the garden.

Arriving back in London, ten days later, I felt that I had shared a worthwhile experience with the members of the tour, and I was asked at once when we could do another. It was not to be until the early summer of 1980.

It was in the mid 1970s that the IRA stepped up their aggressive terror bombing in London, and I was in a restaurant across the road when one bomb exploded in Albemarle Street. There had already been an attack near the west end of Curzon Street, and as I continued to use that street walking home each evening between seven and nine, I had become aware of two or three men in raincoats and hats who always seemed to be pacing to and fro. I was told by a friend who lived there that they were in the security services. But one evening I was halfway along the street when there was a flash and explosion which blew out part of the front of Scotts Restaurant opposite me and set alight a Mercedes parked outside. I did not hang about but hurried home, but this led to the Balcombe Street siege and the arrest of the terrorists.

*   *   *

The two lecture tours in America in the spring and autumn of 1979, taking in ten lectures while visiting eight states, had made it difficult to arrange another English porcelain tour that year, especially with the increased work involved with porcelain at Stair. But in late April 1980 we started on our most ambitious 'home' tour yet which had taken me some months to organise. It started at the Caransa Hotel in Amsterdam and included most of those who had travelled in 1978 but with Herbert McKay of Tampa, Margaret Shanks of Houston and the Morans of Atlanta added to the group. I particularly wanted to introduce a friend, Jack Kater, a Dutch collector and dealer who accompanied us on much of the tour, and whose experiences during the war must be mentioned here.

Being of Jewish origin Jack learned, soon after the Nazi occupation in 1940, that his name was on a list of those to be arrested and despatched to a 'camp' by the police. His Dutch wife continued to live in their home but told all their friends that Jack had gone away; however, at the top of the stairs a large clothes chest was altered to make a sliding panel and the wall behind also altered to give access by a ladder to a tiny roof space which provided just enough light and room to lie down. In this roof space, which I had seen, Jack lived for three years – through winter and summer – with only a daily exchange of food and other vessels through the clothes cupboard on the stairs. The care with which Mrs Kater had to disguise the use of extra food, and other details, can hardly be appreciated; but, unlike the story of Anne Frank, this ended happily when the Allies swept into Holland. Jack was normally reticent about his experience, particularly as it had ended more than twenty years earlier, but having stayed in his house it made a lasting impression on me.

On the 28th April we left early and our bus took us to Leeuwarden where we had coffee with Dr and Mrs Detmar, before going on to the Princessehof Museum, which houses one of the finest collections of export porcelain for the Dutch market, and lunch with the Director, Dr Barbara Harrison, a noted author, at her home. In the afternoon we drove on to Gronigen where Christiaan Jörg, who had just mounted a major exhibition of designs by Cornelius Pronk (on which he has since written one of his many books on the Dutch China Trade), was our guide.

Next morning we all spent our time in the antique shops of Spiegelstraat, but the bus was waiting at midday to drive to The Hague where we spent the afternoon in the Haags Gemeentemuseum before returning to Amsterdam for the night and an early start. It was a national holiday in Holland marking the accession of the Queen, so we drove via the bulb fields to Rotterdam where we had a cruise of the harbour before lunch. No museums were open but we all assembled later to drive to Europort where we boarded the *Nordstar* ferry for a comfortable night crossing to Hull.

We had already had breakfast on the ferry and were able to board our bus at eight in the morning to drive to Durham to visit the Gulbenkian Museum of Chinese Art at the School of Oriental Languages at the University. Our host was Mr Laszló Legeza, who had written a comprehensive book on the Malcolm MacDonald Collection of Chinese Ceramics at the university, embracing examples of 3,000 years of Chinese ceramics. In the afternoon we drove to Washington Old Hall for tea – the original home of the Washington family – and then on to Alnwick in Northumberland.

The small town of Alnwick is dominated by Alnwick Castle, the home of the Percy family who had flourished in England since the Norman Conquest

Presenting an 18th Century Chinese punch bowl with the arms of Home
to Lord Home at The Hirsel in 1980 during a porcelain tour.

Lord Perth at Stobhall with some Drummond porcelain.

and became Earls, and later Dukes, of Northumberland. But next morning we first visited the National Trust house at Wallington, for centuries the home of the Trevelyan family and where among many other treasures were two collections of Chinese porcelain: one brought into the family by an East India heiress, and another by a Trevelyan who had been a Governor of Bombay in the 19th Century. Later we had the kind permission of the Duke for a private tour of Alnwick Castle, guided by his agent, Bill Hugonin, who had been my almost-contemporary in the Coldstream, now over thirty years before. Bill was able to show us everything – including one of the finest Meissen dinner services made; for, perhaps surprisingly, there is no known Chinese armorial service of the Percy family. The Castle with its landscaped vistas, much of it, like Stowe, the work of Capability Brown, could not fail to excite (particularly myself as a descendant of the 1st Earl, 'Hotspur', who fell at Shrewsbury in 1403). That evening Bill Hugonin and his wife, and Sheila Pettit (the National Trust organiser for Northumberland) and her husband, had dinner with us.

Saturday, 3rd May, was an exciting day – for Lord Home, the former Prime Minister, had kindly agreed to show us round his home, The Hirsel, and we had coffee and morning refreshments in the drawing room. There had been a bowl with the arms of Home illustrated in *Chinese Armorial Porcelain*, and I had brought this as a tribute to Lord Home, sharing the cost with Beverly and the others. (I later had a charming thank-you letter.)

We did not want to be late arriving at Lennoxlove where the Duke and Duchess of Hamilton were to be our hosts for the next three nights (although six of us were to sleep at their 'home farm' at Archerfield). After tea and a wander round the castle, which I already knew from staying there previously, we had a very comfortable semi-formal dinner in the main dining room with an array of Hamilton silver displayed, although the services of armorial porcelain stayed safely in their cases upstairs!

After a leisurely breakfast we were able to wander round the garden before setting off again in our bus northwards to Perth where Lord and Lady Perth had invited us to a buffet lunch and a tour of Stobhall, which they had so lovingly restored. Every visit to Stobhall was a pleasure, but the guests were delighted to see one of the most carefully chosen collections of 18th Century export porcelain in the hands of someone who was himself a considerable expert in the field.

On the way back to Lennoxlove we stopped to have tea in the beautiful gardens of Kinross House, the home of Sir David Montgomery, and arrived back at Lennoxlove in time to go out to dinner at a nearby restaurant so that we could entertain the Duke and Duchess. However, at the last moment they had to go to Edinburgh on an official engagement which would keep him until at least midnight. After dinner we returned to Lennoxlove about 11 pm, to find the castle partly floodlit but completely bolted and barred on every side. All the staff had retired to their homes and we sat in the bus wondering what to do.

As I guessed that the Hamiltons might not return until at least 2 am, our thoughts turned to a 'break in', and noticing an open window three floors up in one of the towers we searched the maintenance sheds to find a long ladder. None was long enough, but with the help of the bus driver we parked close to the tower and lashed the ladder to the luggage racks on the roof – with every extension out it was just possible to reach the window. Although he had a twisted ankle in a splint, Bud Gertz insisted on scaling the ladder and we watched as he disappeared through the small window with his plaster cast and a large torch. There was then silence.

For nearly half an hour we waited, wondering what had happened to Bud, when suddenly the bolts on the main castle door were drawn and he stood triumphant in a dimly lit hall. On entering the tower he had only been able to find a spiral staircase down into the cellars where, after going through a number of doors, one had closed behind him and he was entombed in the subterranean vaults until he found a window which allowed him into a passage and eventually to the front hall. That Christmas all our tour received a Christmas card with a picture of the dramatic scene!

No-one was more amused than Angus Hamilton at breakfast, but it would be impossible to repeat the feat today due to the sophisticated alarm systems now in place. But we could not linger over our cornflakes, for we had an official tour of all the most interesting features in the house and then hurried into Edinburgh where my now-undergraduate daughter, Joanna, was to give us a guided tour of the city, ending, after lunch, at Holyrood House where the Duke has an official apartment, opposite that of the Queen, as 'Hereditary Keeper of Holyrood House'. After a glimpse behind the scenes we enjoyed our official cocktail party before driving back for dinner at Lennoxlove.

It was a wrench to leave Scotland in the morning and we drove south towards Harrogate where we were to stay the night at the Old Swan Hotel, stopping on the way for tea at Ripley Castle where Sir Thomas Ingleby, who had recently inherited the baronetcy from his father, gave us a most interesting tour. We dined at the Old Swan and afterwards, at the suggestion I think of Beverly, it was decided to telephone two antique dealers whom I knew, to ask if they would open from ten to midnight. Surprisingly they both agreed with alacrity and they were probably pleased with the result, for about 1 am we were wandering back to the Old Swan clasping a number of packages with Bo carrying a substantial chair on his shoulders, supported by Beverly. As we

A Christmas card, 1980, tells of a late night break-in at Lennoxlove.

reached the hotel two local residents weaving their way home stopped in front of us in amazement at the scene, one saying loudly, 'And you're the Chairman, I presume.'

Despite the late night, we were on our way early next morning to Sledmere, the home of Sir Tatton Sykes, the heir of the vastly successful land owning and Yorkshire merchant family of Sykes whose two armorial services and other porcelain and fine Chinese enamel ware were a small part of Sledmere's inheritance. (Sir Tatton's great-grandfather frequently entertained the future King Edward VII and Lillie Langtry, and it was with him as host that the greatest gambling scandal of the 19th Century, which included the Prince of Wales, took place.) After a buffet lunch at Sledmere, we drove once more to Phil and Pat Cooke's home to wonder anew at his vast collection of armorial porcelain while we had a kitchen tea. And so we returned to the Old Swan for dinner.

An early start saw us drive directly to Deene Park in Northamptonshire to have lunch with Edmund and Marion Brudenell. Edmund was the great-great-nephew of Lord Cardigan who led the charge of the Light Brigade, and Marion, a lady of great ability in her own right, was the daughter of Sir Reginald Manningham-Buller, the former Conservative Lord Chancellor who was created Lord Dilhorne. Perhaps the most emotive exhibit in the house was the head and shoulders of the horse that bore Lord Cardigan during the charge, perfectly preserved and looking as if alive in a glass case in the hall. Facing this was a group painted at Windsor Castle on the occasion that Lord Cardigan explained to the Queen and the Prince Consort how the charge had succeeded, the only exceptional feature being that there was a space near the middle of the group where Queen Victoria had been painted out (on her instructions when she was later told of Lord Cardigan's amorous adventures at Deene Park and elsewhere). We left Deene Park about four and were in London by six; tired but, I think, wiser.

*　　*　　*

Gabrielle Murdock told me that she had decided to decorate the dining room at Bel Air with a special wallpaper of 'tobacco leaf' pattern, with curtains made to match, and asked if I could find a porcelain service to match. The effect was quite sumptuous, but it was to be more than a year before I was able to complement this display with porcelain. Meanwhile Stair & Company had acquired excellent premises on the ground floor of 10900 Wilshire Boulevard, now renamed 'Murdock Plaza', which also housed Pacific Holdings.

The opening of Stair in Los Angeles was a glittering event in December 1981, and I still have two pages of *The Los Angeles Times* under the heading 'English Antiques find LA Home' which include a number of quotations from 'David Howard, an acknowledged expert on Chinese porcelains and an advisor to Stair.' Among other things quoted in some seven part-columns with two large illustrations are: 'It's a sign of maturity when people buy at home – it means the people and the city have confidence', and, 'Chinese porcelains were always meant to go with this kind of furniture. They add a touch of colour.' All of which sounded much like the words of a marketing man!

With Murdock Plaza open, it was not long before I was told that Pacific Holdings had bought the Hay Adams Hotel in Washington, and when Stair wanted me to investigate some antiques in that city I stayed in great luxury at the Hay Adams, in a suite looking across the square at the White House. I had dinner with the general manager of the hotel and amongst other matters the question of 'image' came up, which led me to comment that the rather feeble coronet looking like splash of milk which adorned their publicity could certainly be improved; he asked me if I could make suggestions.

Without, I fear, consulting the College of Arms, I researched both the families of Hay and Adams who had originally owned the site shortly after the Declaration of Independence – the Hay family being related to the noble Scottish house, and the Adams' of merchant stock in London. My design was simple in that it employed the two crests of these families side by side, while above was a unique coronet being formed alternately of three thistles and two swords (for London). This was an invention but they looked well together and with the crests below they represented the Hay Adams for some years on their menus, their matchboxes and their advertising matter (I still have some matchboxes, and even a crested soap dish). It was the only time I was likely to have a chance of designing a major hotel's 'image'!

*   *   *

On my return I hurried to Cornwall where my father had died suddenly at the age of ninety. He had had to have a leg amputated some years earlier because of circulation problems in his feet and although still remarkably active with his walking stick, had fallen out of bed and cracked his pelvis. The first I knew of it was when Hazel telephoned to say he was in hospital. That night he was given a sedative so that he could have his hip pinned the following day, but he died peacefully in his sleep with surprisingly little pain. He had been a man of strong purpose all his life to whom financial gain, even when in his grasp, had never been as important as honest work. He had built a business with more than fifty employees, and retired to The Lizard with my mother when sixty with modest means. He had later dedicated his life to good causes, particularly the Church and the Lizard Lifeboat, for which he received the Institute's gold medal. More than ten years later I was staying at the Housel Bay Hotel and talking to a local man who expressed surprise that a 'visitor' seemed to know so much about The Lizard. When I told him that my father had been Mr Howard at Tresawle he smiled, 'Ah – a right old character 'e were.' My father would have been pleased at this local comment, for he had loved his life at The Lizard for thirty years.

In early 1982 I had the good fortune to see that an elaborate and very varied service of Tobacco Leaf porcelain was to be sold at Christie's. It was a busy spring because once more Heirloom was faced with finding a new secretary, and I had seen replies from about twenty applicants and interviewed eight. The day of the sale coincided with the final choice of two candidates, between whom I found it almost impossible to judge and either would have been perfect.

I sat with James West at the auction and almost exceeded my top limit by bidding £80,000, and we later had a drink at his club in St James's, to steady down! In the evening, as I interviewed Angela Postlethwaite, I had a telephone call from Gabrielle Murdock who was delighted with the purchase, and I was able to give a quiet sigh of relief!

After some soul searching I chose Angela, whose business acumen (having lived in Florence and travelled regularly to London with fine embroidered work which she sold in Bond Street) impressed me, rather than Penelope, who later joined Martyn Gregory's successful China Trade picture gallery in St James's and is today Penelope Gregory.

It was during a visit to New York in early 1983 that David Murdock asked me to dinner. He was often in New York, travelling night and day in his private jet, and as we talked over dinner it seemed like a social affair, for he and Gabrielle had dined with Anna and me at our new home in Coleherne Court in London. The conversation later turned to one's aims in life and I was able to ask what he particularly saw as his goal. It was clear that he saw the making of more and more millions as his only real goal, for when I asked what he would do when he had fulfilled his wildest financial dreams, he replied, with some surprise at my question, that he would then try to make *more* money.

By contrast, having 'escaped' from the experience of broad managerial responsibilities within large family-controlled companies, I enjoyed my freedom as an independent 'expert' and while wishing to provide my family with comfort and security, my personal ambitions now lay in mastering the subject of the China Trade and translating it into written words so that one day

I should have the satisfaction of leaving something behind for the benefit of others. It was clear that there was little meeting of minds on this subject, but David then asked whether, if he was to set up and finance a major enterprise to cover many aspects of the antiques world when Alastair Stair retired that year, I would agree to be the overall manager – with a position on his personal staff, living variously in London, New York and Los Angeles, and a very adequate financial provision.

Dinner continued for another hour and we then walked up Madison Avenue to the Carlyle Hotel, where he kept a permanent suite, returning to the matter in question all the way. I had already made it clear that this generous offer was unlikely to be accepted, and as we stood looking at a window display I said to him, 'David, in spite of all you say, I'd rather be your poorest friend than your richest lieutenant.' It was a deciding moment, and he turned away, walking the last two blocks in silence, while I thanked him for a superb dinner in the foyer of the Carlyle.

Having enjoyed David and Gabrielle's hospitality at Bel Air on a number of occasions, I was very sorry to hear a year or so later of Gabrielle's early death, but I continued to work with Angus Perceval and Hope Hood successfully at Stair until one day in London I had a telephone call from David asking if I would now buy for Stair at half the commission previously agreed (effectively less than 3%). I explained that it was a task of considerable responsibility and that the costs and time involved would not make that economic, and he replied that Stair would then no longer need my help. By 1984 this was relatively much less important to Heirloom, and sorrow and irritation after what I felt had been some years of successful purchasing, were mingled with relief. I had heard that recently he had taken on an additional business advisor by the name of Haldeman – now almost freed from the tension of the Watergate affair. It was a great sadness that Angus was to die all too young, but I was able to visit him in hospital and hold his hand during his last week.

*   *   *

It wasn't until 1983 that I was able to arrange another porcelain tour in Britain. It was to be the last, for although numerous other ideas for tours had been suggested, the exciting and different events between 1984 and 1990 made them more difficult to plan and execute. I made a journey to Ireland and met some old and new friends which developed into a comfortable and interesting tour in late May. The participants for the tour were all from Georgia and Texas and included many of those from the previous tour, with four new ones – John Stembler, Gene Talmadge, Bill Curran and Sandy

Adamson – all from the Atlanta area. We met at the ever-comfortable Shelbourne Hotel in Dublin and on the first night had dinner with an old friend, Professor Frank Mitchell of Trinity College, and Frank Chambers, and after dinner repaired to Frank Chambers' Georgian flat to see his very fine collection of Irish furniture.

The following day we went to Dublin Castle as the guest of Gerard Slevin, the Chief Herald of Ireland, where one could appreciate some of the heraldic work which contributed so greatly to armorial porcelain, and after a quick lunch took our bus with Frank Mitchell first to 'The Casino', the fascinating Georgian classical building which had once been the home of the Earls of Charlemont, and then to Malahide Castle, the home of the Talbot family in Ireland – both of whom had armorial services. We then drove to Russborough, where the collection of paintings of Sir Alfred Beit were displayed (later to be the subject of a well-publicised burglary) and on to our hotel in County Wicklow.

In the morning we reached Cork and visited the Museum, guided by Dr Pettit who had long been a friend, and my host on an occasion when Heirloom had presented a tureen with the arms of the city to the Mayor, which was part of a service consigned to us by a film property company after it had been used in a James Bond film. We stayed the night at Ballymaloe House, where Myrtle Allen had created an enormous reputation for this Georgian hotel.

After visiting Fota, the ancient home of the eccentric Earls of Barrymore, we took a leisurely route to Glin Castle where we were staying with an old friend, Desmond FitzGerald, the Knight of Glin (a Stoic and one-time Deputy Keeper of Furniture at the V & A in London) and enjoyed an exceptional dinner at the castle arranged by his wife, Olda. Desmond, whose hereditary knighthood dates back to the 14th Century, had a very wide circle of friends and acquaintances in Ireland and amongst many appointments was President of the Irish Georgian Society and represented Christie's in Ireland. Next day was spent with George and Michelina Stacpoole, having lunch at their home and the afternoon at their antique shop in Adare, before returning to Glin where Desmond gave a lecture on Irish country houses in the castle gatehouse.

Next day we travelled on to Birr in County Offaly, where we had lunch and spent the afternoon with the Earl and Countess of Rosse. Brendan Rosse had been in the Irish Guards and his mother, Anne, was the sister of Oliver Messel and mother of the Earl of Snowdon, his half-brother. We spent a fascinating afternoon in the garden viewing the well-known Rosse telescope, created by an earlier Earl and for over a century the largest in the world. The following morning we went to Emo Court, the home of Cholmelely Harrison, who had been one of the first boys at Stowe on the day it opened in 1923. It was an amusing and eccentric house and we were entertained to madeira and cake before driving on to Abbey Leix, the home of the Viscountess de Vesci, the sister of Brendan Rosse, and eventually back to Birr where we had an exceptional dinner in a local restaurant.

Travelling north again, stopping at one or two small local museums on the way, we arrived at Crom Castle on a promontory in Lough Erne to stay with the Earl and Countess of Erne. Harry Erne and his Swedish wife Anna were very good hosts, and I remember with amusement that when I had stayed with them some months earlier while arranging the tour, I asked how many bedrooms were in the castle. He said that he really didn't know, but that he was fairly sure there were enough for our party. I had mentioned that Mark and Linda Alexander would be on their honeymoon and they were delighted to find flowers and a bottle of champagne in their room. Next day, after a walk round the estate, we visited Florence Court, the home of the Earls of Enniskillen, and in the afternoon, Castle Coole. The scale of these Irish houses, now administered by the National Trust, could not fail to impress, although the porcelain was not the principal focus of interest.

On the last full day of the tour we drove to Townley Hall which was now the home of Professor and Mrs Frank Mitchell. Frank, who had stayed with us in London, was an Irish writer of note and had bought Townley, complete with contents, from the university some years before. A few years before the tour he had decided to have the old safe in the kitchen basement opened by a locksmith and was amazed to find that the contents included the Blayney Balfour relics of the Stuart kings which had been exhibited in Scotland in the late 19th Century and which Balfour's uncle had acquired from an Italian, the Marquess Malatesta, who lived by the Spanish Steps in Rome and who had been a long-time friend of Cardinal York (the younger brother of 'Bonnie Prince Charlie').

Frank had asked me to visit Townley at the time, and I saw all these relics which he had 'inherited'. He also wondered how they could best be sold privately to those who had an historical interest in them: two miniatures of Prince Charles Edward and Cardinal York by Gavin Hamilton, the seal of Cardinal York, an amber flask and another small flask which had probably been made for Prince James Francis Edward (the son of James II and the 'Old Pretender') together with a letter from Blaney Balfour dated 1842 describing in detail how he had acquired these from the Marquess. I think this mission was completed satisfactorily and certainly Frank was pleased, as were those who acquired the Stuart relics.

Frank and his wife only occupied a corner of the whole house which was built round perhaps the finest circular staircase in Ireland. We had a buffet lunch and then all went down to Slane Castle, then lived in by Lord Mount Charles (who had once worked for Fabers and was now Sotheby's representative in Ireland), heir to the Marquess Conyngham, before driving back to Dublin where we stayed a last night at the Shelbourne Hotel.

It was a grey morning as we wandered round the shops in Dublin with Frank, and after lunch we had to gather our things together and say goodbye, for we had to catch the flight to Heathrow. Maybe we didn't see as much porcelain as on earlier tours, but it was a happy introduction to Ireland for the American members of the tour, and I enjoyed it greatly.

CHAPTER 17

America and Lecture Tours

While a steady routine of investigation and letter writing brought more people to Heirloom in Hay Hill, it was perhaps as important that the two lecture tours planned each year in America also made numerous friends across the Atlantic. Occasional articles in the press certainly helped, but there was no substitute for the personal introduction when, as a speaker, one was frequently the guest of a museum curator or director and as often as not private lunch or dinner parties were arranged by supporters of the museum to bring together enthusiasts in the subjects of heraldry or Chinese export porcelain, using the speaker's presence as a focus.

The fact that between 1973 and 1978 I was also in New York on numerous occasions to work on the Mottahedeh Collection made this easier; indeed my first tour, which was almost entirely at the suggestion of Clare Le Corbeiller and the Mottahedehs, took place between late October and the third week of November in 1973.

I have lectured on many more occasions in America than in England, and it is possible that Chinese export porcelain is a subject which has a greater following in America than in Europe, but I have often noticed a marked difference between the audiences in the two countries. Those in England were interested intellectually but didn't take things further, while in America the interest was more social, and over the following months a substantial number of those who heard me speak would either write or visit us in London. In London one was a dealer who also wrote and lectured – in America one was a lecturer and author who was also a dealer. As for myself, it was all a pleasure and excitement. The museums and collections one was able to see made the long hours well worthwhile, and many of the acquaintances I made have become and remained friends over the years.

I have no record of the content of any lecture, for I never wrote these down but relied on the slides and their sequence to prompt me. On setting out on a lecture tour, having agreed a subject title in each case, I would assess the history of any particular city or museum I was visiting, and select a few especially suitable slides (for Pittsburgh, perhaps the armorials of Pitt and Carnegie). Whatever the subject, I would ensure that every lecture included Chinese porcelain painted with amusing episodes: perhaps after political, historical, religious, mythological or scandalous European prints, and these could also be used to illustrate the dating of a border style as well as revealing some social history or a point of deeper historical interest. With up to 10,000 slides available which I had taken over thirty or forty years, the choice was wide. It was a question of thinking through the story in advance and having the right slides ready.

Before setting out, it was necessary to spend a day or two selecting the slides to cover all the lectures in the tour. It was possible on occasions to give the same lecture twice in different states on the same tour, but I would always spend my time en route adjusting slides to include others which were relevant to the place I was flying to. On occasions I would be speaking within two or three hours of landing and my priority on arrival had to be familiarising myself with the type of projector in the lecture hall and ensuring that the slides were in the right order for display. Wherever possible I would try to ensure two projectors, for this made for a smoother lecture and comparative material was much easier to present.

Everything depended on slides being in a suitable order so that the narrative would develop in a natural and consequential way, and never in thirty years was it necessary to read a lecture, for the slides themselves presented the visual story and acted as automatic reminders of what was to be said next. In this way lectures maintained a spontaneity which I always found was appreciated by an audience. Of course it was necessary to remember the details for every slide, or armorial, or scene, but in that I was fortunate in having a photographic memory.

*   *   *

My first tour started in 1973 with a visit to New Orleans as one of the lecturers for the Southern Antiques Seminar, which included Julia Raynesford of the Victoria and Albert Museum speaking on English furniture, Thierry Millerand on French furniture and Marilynn Bordes on the American Federal period. The atmosphere was exciting and the French restaurants we visited in the evenings delightful, while an introduction to Henry Stern, who then owned one of the most varied, historical and successful antique shops in America, was to lead to a long friendship fuelled by a common wish to recognise original ownership and provenance as a major interest.

Next morning I flew to New York and stayed for the first of many times with John Andrew, who had been a friend since 1960. He had recently become the incumbent of St Thomas's Church in 5th Avenue, New York, with charming and substantial 'rectory' at 550 Park Avenue. In the five days in New York we dined with the Mottahedehs, with Wendell Garrett (the editor of

Magazine Antiques), with Clare and Jean Le Corbeiller, with the directors of Sotheby Parke Bernet and, almost more interesting to me, with Sanders Holmes, who had followed a long quest of the origins of the Fitzhugh style of porcelain in which I was particularly interested. There was an added factor to its popularity, largely overlooked in England, that George Washington's youngest stepson, George Washington Parke Custis, who was brought up at Mount Vernon by the Washingtons, had married Mary Lee, daughter of William Fitzhugh, and thus the name was far more emotive on the American side of the Atlantic. In this social whirl – which was to characterise my American lecture tours for more than fifteen years – the actual lecture at the Grolier Club for the English Speaking Union was a focal point and to be the first of many I gave in New York over more than twenty-five years.

On the Friday I caught the train to Washington and was met by a car which took me to Colonial Williamsburg where the American Ceramic Circle was that year having their conference. The comfort of the Williamsburg Inn was legendary, and for the first time I was to find myself before an audience of ceramic experts rather than the more varied antique or heraldic audiences I had so far met. I was almost always safe on my heraldic platform, but it was more important than ever to link this at every stage to the Chinese export porcelain border styles. In 1973 *Chinese Armorial Porcelain* was yet to be published, and thus a large part of what I had to say was entirely new to those who listened, and in a few cases was not quite in tune with traditional thinking. A few days later I was to see this in practice when I visited a Philadelphia Museum and found a number of early and mid 18th Century armorial pieces displayed as being 'American' period (after 1776). When I enquired of the friendly curator as to why this was, she could only say 'but if they were dated earlier we couldn't display them because they wouldn't be American China trade' – such was 'knowledge' in its formative years.

On my return to London it was very reassuring to find a delightful letter from the Williamsburg Curator, John Austin, who wrote, 'You certainly ended my seminar on the highest possible note … The presentation was most enjoyable and the information was new to everyone there, which made for an exciting session.' John was one of many friends I met that day, for I was later to get to know, or stay with, John and Julia Curtis of Williamsburg (later to become a lecturer of note herself), George and Linda Kaufman (generous patrons of the arts whose company was 'Guest Quarters'), Arlene Palmer and Christina Nelson of Winterthur Museum, Crosby Forbes of the Museum of the China Trade at Milton, Massachusetts, and Jim and Celeste Whitehead from Washington & Lee University, as well as a number of other people whom I have met again at conferences over the years.

On Sunday afternoon I hurried back to Philadelphia and met Jean and Morgan Hebard with whom I stayed for two enjoyable days, meeting at dinner the Dolans and Diana Dripps (then a widow but later to become Mrs Jack Dorrance) and other friends of the Women's Committee of the Philadelphia Museum of Art. It was all too short a stay to see as much as I would have liked of Philadelphia, but Jean did her best to drive me round, and the lecture at the museum was in the grandest surroundings I had yet encountered. Before leaving for Rhode Island, I had a delightful tea with Matthew and Betty Sharpe (I can still hear her distinctive voice on the telephone!) who, with Elinor Gordon, were the leading dealers in Chinese porcelain outside New York. It was different again lecturing to the Rhode Island Ceramic Circle, and a major step on the way to my first visit to the Peabody Museum at Salem – undoubtedly the most deeply-rooted museum of the American China Trade.

Apart from the great interest of seeing the museum collections at Salem, much of which had been the gifts of early American captains sailing from New England to China who made a point of bringing home oriental objects as gifts for display, I had in store a particular treat in that I stayed with Dr Ernest Dodge and his wife; Ernest being a noted author of books on the 'Polar Ross family'. Their home looked out over the burial ground which preserved the remains of those involved in the Salem Witch Trials of the early 18th Century (more recently made famous in 1953 by Arthur Miller's play *The Crucible*). It was 'safe' in Salem to give almost the same lecture as I had given in Williamsburg, for I felt that it was unlikely that any of that audience would have been there. I was probably wrong, but it didn't seem to matter and as always one met so many new friends that any 'repeats' were lost in the goodwill.

On looking back over correspondence and press cuttings of that time, it is warming to read the comments (often before the event and therefore kind but hardly 'deserved') and this was to be a feature of lecturing in some thirty-four states over the next twenty-five years. Slowly this warmth and excitement would affect Heirloom also.

*   *   *

By January 1974 I was heavily engaged in correspondence with Dewey Lee Curtis who, as well as being the Director of Pennsbury Manor (the home in America of William Penn) was also an agent for lecture tours in both America and England. As mentioned in the previous chapter, this was to lead eventually to porcelain tours travelling in England over the next seven years, but at this time the invitation was for three lectures at a seminar at Pennsbury at the end of March 1974. The first was to be on the history of the China Trade, the second on the borders and decoration of export porcelain and the third on 'armorial decoration'. The whole fitted well with a further visit to the Mottahedehs in New York and was entirely in line with *Chinese Armorial Porcelain*, now actually at the printers at Oxford University Press.

I arrived in Philadelphia by train from New York and was driven some thirty miles across the Pennsylvanian countryside. Although Dewey seemed pleased with the outcome, my memories are more of Pennsbury and the very English atmosphere that surrounded Pennsbury Manor. An unexpected stroke of luck had placed the conference only a day before one at Winterthur and although not part of that programme, John Sweeney kindly invited me to take the role of a 'visiting scholar' and lecture to the staff on the porcelain at Winterthur at the end of the conference. It was a most interesting three days and I spent much of the time with Arlene Palmer, the curator, working through the Winterthur collection (both on display and in storage) so that I should have the broadest possible knowledge of what they had.

I also made another visit to Matt and Betty Sharpe and have only recently read again a letter I received on arriving back in England. It ended, 'Judging by the number of photographs you must have taken since your book went to press, we are looking forward to Volume II even before Volume I is off the press!' Alas, I was too slow for them to enjoy it, but Volume II (published in 2003) does have an occasional photograph of their porcelain at that time.

The months of June and July in London were exciting as *Chinese Armorial Porcelain* came out and a flood of letters and queries and ideas flowed in. I was surprised at how many letters were from those I had not met, as well as from those who had attended a lecture. There was little doubt that lecturing acted as an excellent stimulus for book sales, although that was all in the hands of Fabers who continued to be most supportive.

*   *   *

The next lecture tour coincided with the visit to New York of Peter MacDonald and Stanley Eost to photograph the Mottahedeh Collection and was also to contain a surprise. I had had a letter from Rita Reif of *The New York Times* who had had a review copy of *Chinese Armorial Porcelain* and she had both spoken to Mildred Mottahedeh and written to say that she thought this unusual subject would be a perfect episode for the then popular national television show *To Tell the Truth*. This might be built into my next journey which ran from 23rd October to 14th November 1974 – perhaps the most varied of my tours so far.

With George Hartness in Columbia, South Carolina, 1974.

With Bud Patten and Thomas before a lecture in Boston.

Jim Whitehead at the Reeves Center at Washington & Lee University had invited me to stay for two nights and examine the collection of porcelain they had been given by Mr and Mrs Reeves. It was to be the first of many visits to 'W & L' where it has been a pleasure to watch the collection grow over the years. It was, in fact, a remarkable achievement that Jim, who had little or no knowledge of export porcelain when the gift was made, should be able to add the duty of 'Curator Extraordinary' to that of Treasurer of the University and make such a success of the collection – both of porcelain and paintings.

But after little more than a day I flew to Columbia, South Carolina, where I had been invited to be one of the five speakers at a conference entitled 'Anglo-American Relationship in the Arts'. Two of the other speakers were Professors of History and one the President of the Historic Columbia Foundation. It was a particular pleasure that the other was Carl Dauterman who was Curator Emeritus of Decorative Arts at the Metropolitan Museum and a friend of Clare's. I stayed with George Hartness who went out of his way to help and drove me to Charleston for the day, for I was very anxious to see for the first time the homes of my Bull and Beale ancestors who had lived there in the 17th and 18th Centuries.

My next journey was to Savannah where I had been invited to speak at the Telfair Academy of Arts and Sciences at the suggestion, I believe, of Jim Williams, a well-known Savannah antique dealer whom I came to know well. I had also received a letter from Herbert McKay of Tampa, who had visited Hay Hill earlier in the year (being drawn downstairs by our display outside the hairdresser's window) and hoped to be able to come to Savannah at the same time.

After my lecture both Herbert and I had been invited to a 'period' dinner at Jim's house. The dinner (for ten, I think) was in an exquisitely furnished, late Georgian dining room. The period furniture was laid with late 18th Century silver and a set of Fitzhugh-style porcelain of the same date. Behind each chair was a liveried black footman in a white powdered wig, who anticipated every move. I felt that the Director of the Telfair Museum was as surprised as I was at the faultless display and the excellent meal with coffee served in the huge upstairs sitting room, where Jim himself played 18th Century chamber music on an elaborate organ in the corner. In many states over many years I did not again experience such a marvellous display.

But I had little time to linger and next day flew to Norfolk, Virginia, via the inevitable Atlanta, and was met about noon by John and Julia Curtis who were my hosts for the next three nights. Later that afternoon we drove into Norfolk to the home of Linda Kaufman's parents, the Hofheimers, whose collection of Worcester porcelain was one of the finest in America. Mr Hofheimer had already warned me that the audience at the Chrysler Museum was not particularly knowledgeable about export ware, but I was always able to adjust either my slides or my story so that the subject appeared more general/historical or more design/export porcelain orientated.

I spent the next day at Williamsburg with John Austin and Julia Curtis examining the export porcelain in a large range of houses. In a few cases the porcelain was original to the house, or due to the efforts of Ivor Noel Hume, the archaeologist of Williamsburg, had been purchased but matched exactly the shards which had been found in the waste pits of the same house. It was of particular interest that a broken plate had been found in the waste pit of the Governor's Mansion with the arms of Lord Dunmore, the last Colonial Governor who left in 1776 (and later gave his name to Dunmore Town on Harbour Island in the Bahamas where he had a cottage during his Governorship of the Islands).

Going on to Nashville, Tennessee, I stayed with the ever-helpful Harriet Tyne, a widow and considerable landowner in the city, who collected Chinese porcelain. It was a delightful two days, and I enjoyed my time at Cheekwood, the historic house which housed much of the best export porcelain in Tennessee, but it was only a short stay for I had then to fly to Boston where it was arranged that I speak at the Museum of Fine Art. I was met at the airport by Bud and Charlotte Patten and stayed with them in their apartment on Beacon Street. It was the first of a number of visits, and we remain friends today.

In New York a new experience was awaiting me, and arriving there on the evening of 30th November there was just time to prepare for the television programme *To Tell the Truth*, which was scheduled to take from 9 am to 2 pm to televise but in fact took considerably longer. The programme brought face to face before a panel of judges (one of whom was the well-known Kitty Carlisle) two characters. One was someone who had an unusual job; the other was someone who claimed to have such a job but did not. The job holder could only answer the panel truthfully; the claimant could lie as much as he wished. The panel had to decide who was telling the truth. The 'job', in my case, was investigating antique *objets d'art* with coats of arms – silver, porcelain or furniture – and trying to sell it back to the families who had once owned it. If you could fool the panel, which happened only rarely, that contestant won $500. The television company provided suitable 'claimants' for each contender.

I had been given the name and telephone number of my claimant, who turned out to be a pleasant Englishman teaching in a New York school. We spent the later afternoon together, and I had an opportunity of explaining exactly how Heirloom worked and gave him a list of heraldic words to impress the panel. The day came; we were at the studio at the Rockefeller Plaza at nine and were given a preliminary briefing by the producer. As they normally recorded four (or even six) quarter-hour episodes sequentially, we were allowed to watch while two other complete programmes were recorded. I remember particularly a New York lady who had applied to be a woman rabbi, and a Texan who bred cattle crossed with buffaloes to create larger and more juicy steaks called 'Beefalo steaks' (a live 'beefalo' came on stage accompanied by a very competent minder – with a shovel!).

Our fifteen-minute episode started with a string of questions about heraldry and the structure of coats of arms, and while I remained hesitant but correct, the claimant answered positively and well. He also gave an excellent description of how Heirloom worked, including mention of several noble families who had purchased there, while I was more restrained under questioning. A key series of questions concerned the heralds which he answered well, and after 'Garter King of Arms' had been explained as the senior herald who by tradition put garters below the knees of new knights, we were both asked what was the name of the Senior Herald of Ireland.

Quite truthfully I replied, after some thought, 'The Chief Herald of Ireland,' while my claimant said, 'St Patrick's Herald' (a name never used). The panel conferred privately for a minute or so and concluded that I was too hesitant and uncertain of the real meaning of heraldry, while the claimant undoubtedly knew the subject. We had won $500! Later, in talking over coffee with the panel, one said, 'Mr Howard, I really felt you had come straight from Central Casting!' I shared the welcome $500 with the claimant (although I fancy it would be a larger prize today).

It was more than a week later – most of which was taken up with photography but included a pleasant dinner with the Le Corbeillers – that I flew back to London.

*   *   *

Unusually, in 1975, I was invited to speak to the Officers' Wives' Committee of the large RAF Strike Command Headquarters at High Wycombe (through an introduction from the wife of Wing Commander John Horwood – of Nassau days) and this proved to be a friendly and enjoyable occasion. Later in the autumn it was another new experience to speak at Morley College in south London as one of a number of lecturers at a seminar on 'The Oriental Influence on British Ceramics'. Such conferences which link the China export trade, as well as earlier China influences on majolica and other ceramic wares provided excellent opportunities to demonstrate the crucial role of armorials in the dating of design patterns, while I found it particularly interesting at a time when *China for the West* was still in its formative stage.

An exceptional sale of armorial porcelain had taken place at Christie's during the spring which included almost exactly a hundred pieces of the extraordinary Okeover service (still acknowledged as a high point of design and armorial display with rare invoices linking it to consignments in 1739 and 1743). The prices exceeded the family vendor's dreams but for three decades those prices have paled into insignificance when compared with the prices of individual plates and dishes from this service in later sales, reaching a peak when a pair of dishes was sold in New York about 1990 for more than $100,000.

But in April another American tour was planned, and on this occasion Anna travelled with me. We started in New York and although we visited the Metropolitan Museum, there was no lecture on this occasion. The always-busy Mottahedeh visits were useful, for although I now had large numbers of photographs to work from in writing *China for the West*, it was always important to check the pieces 'in the hand' because it is all too easy to omit in a description an important decorative point if it does not actually show in the photograph to be published. This can come back to haunt you twenty-five years later when an object is sold at auction, but photographed from the other side! Before leaving by train for Washington, we had a delightful dinner party at John Andrew's Park Avenue apartment with the Mottahedehs and other guests.

Marguerite Clarke Boden (whose dish had formed the back illustration of the dust jacket of *Chinese Armorial Porcelain*) had organised an unusual lecture at the Sulgrave Club in Washington to 'The National Society of the Daughters of the Barons of Runnemede'. Not only were all the members descendants of the Barons who had met at Runnemede in the reign of King John and signed the Magna Charta on 15th June 1215 (almost exactly 760 years earlier), but it was very likely that they were descendants of more than one baron and King John himself – as indeed was the speaker. George Washington himself descended from the King and twenty-five barons. It was with some amazement, however, that I found that after the lecture most guests only wanted to talk about what it was like to be on the television programme *To Tell the Truth*. So much for history and ancestry!

We stayed for an enjoyable two days with John Shank, who showed us round Washington (I was later to stay at his farmhouse near Hagerstown and he joined some of the porcelain tours in England). By the weekend we were in Philadelphia again and another weekend with Morgan and Jean Hebard, and another lecture. On the Monday we were away to a happy visit to Charleston, where George Hartness kindly drove down from Columbia and introduced us to the owners of a number of historic houses. My lecture there at the Gibbes Gallery had been postponed to 1977, but we took a bus to Savannah and then a plane to Tampa, where we were welcomed by Herbert and Nancy McKay.

It was a most interesting two days, and I lectured at the University of Tampa. The McKays drove us round the Tampa Bay area, and it was particularly pleasant to spend an afternoon with Sheila Stewart – Elizabeth's aunt, who had always remained friendly – who was well known in the area because of a weekly radio programme she still hosted on topical news, a far cry from having been the first woman announcer on the BBC in the 1930s.

Our tour ended with an entirely more relaxed visit, for from Tampa we flew to Nassau and were able to stay with Norman Solomon, who was by now deeply involved in politics and about to be the leader of the main opposition party in the Bahamas. Nevertheless, it was great fun to drive round the island and enjoy the charms of Nassau before flying on to London two days later.

*　　*　　*

Our move from the basement at Hay Hill to the lower of the three shops on the street itself was both time-consuming and successful, and I was at once aware that many who had previously just hurried down the hill now stopped to have a look at the decorative display in the window – including Edward Heath and John Le Mesurier (both of whom saw something to interest them), John Profumo and later William Rees Mogg.

Not everyone, however, liked labels with information and prices, for one evening we were having dinner with a friend, Tony Yablon, when one of the guests, discovering that I had an antique shop, said, 'What I really hate are little labels in the windows of West End shops. There's a new shop in Hay Hill which has awful labels that are not only written all over but have prices!' I could only laugh as I saw his wife kicking him under the table, but on the whole people liked the information, indeed welcomed it.

It was fun to be asked if I would be the guest of honour at the dinner of the Keechong Society of the Museum of the American China Trade of Milton, Masachussetts on 10th November 1976 (I had never travelled five thousand miles for dinner before) and I accepted. The occasion was named 'A Call to Arms' and the dinner was to be held on board the S.S. *Peter Stuyvesant*, anchored at Anthony's Pier 4 in Boston Harbour. No sooner had I recovered from my surprise than I had another invitation to speak to the China Students Club in Boston on the afternoon of the previous day.

I was met at Logan Airport by Paul Molitor and stayed in comfort. The lecture to the China Students Club seemed to hit the right note and I was able to prepare for the following evening which was more formal, but did not include any lecture. The membership of the Keechong Society stretched wide in the Boston area and other guests included Horace and Elinor Gordon, and Rafi and Mildred Mottahedeh who had come up from New York. The dinner was excellent and I still have the menu, reading in part:

Consommé *Famille rose*
Salade *Celedon*
Veal *Fitzhugh*
Potatoes *Rouge de fer*
Beans *Famille verte*
Ice *Imari*

As dinner ended there was a speech of welcome by Mr Forbes Perkins to which I replied. I had brought with me, and presented, a framed set of two Chinese mother-of-pearl counters made for Queen Charlotte which were probably of exactly the same age as the American China Trade.

The closing speech, after a quite excellent evening and many liqueurs, was made by Murray Forbes, the Chairman of the Museum. After a few kind words he handed me with a flourish what he believed to be a special gift from the Museum – it was, in fact, the most amusing moment of the evening, for he had presented me with the gift I had just given the Museum; the end of his speech was drowned in laughter. But as it closed his cousin, Crosby, handed me a beautifully hand-bound leather edition of *Chinese Armorial Porcelain* with a special inscription. I use it every day still and treasure it.

*   *   *

I was soon to be off again but not before spending a happy Christmas in Perugia with Anna's family. We took a turkey with us with all the trappings and had a very English traditional Christmas day, which Anna's sister's children seemed to enjoy.

On 15th March we flew to Boston again and were the guests of Paul and 'Missy' Molitor in their home at the Robert Bennett Forbes Museum in Milton, Massachusetts. There was no lecture at Milton but an excellent opportunity to see and discuss the Museum's Collection, which was later to be amalgamated with the Peabody Museum at Salem. It was a particular pleasure to get to know Crosby Forbes much better, for besides being the leading world authority on Chinese Export silver, so often made in the image of British silver in the 19th Century, his family had been influential in Boston in the China Trade. On the morning of the 17th, however, Paul drove me into Boston and I gave a lecture in the Museum entitled 'China for the West' – perhaps the first time this title was used officially. It was an enjoyable occasion followed by an excellent lunch and a tour of the Museum. On the following day Paul kindly drove us to Historic Deerfield where we had an excellent lunch at the Deerfield Inn with Peter Sprang, followed by a tour of the Museum, and we then continued to Stamford by train where we met the Mottahedehs and then drove to New York.

After the weekend we took the Metroliner to Washington, staying once more with John Shank, and I lectured at the City Tavern Club. Following his visit to Hay Hill in 1976 I had started a correspondence with Tom Eagleton, the US Senator, who had a modest collection of Minton porcelain and wondered if we could find any with armorials. When I mentioned that Anna and I would be in Washington in March, he invited us to have lunch with him in the Senate dining room. This was the first of a number of meetings, and I later stayed on occasion at his and Barbara's home in Bethesda (and they kindly looked after Thomas when he travelled across America by Greyhound bus in 1983).

The following day we drove to Boonesboro where we spent the Saturday with John Shank and Joe Matthews, and on the Sunday stayed with John and Julia Curtis in Surrey, Virginia. I had been invited to speak at the Virginia Museum at Richmond on the Tuesday and John and Julia drove us there early so that we could spend much of the day learning of the Museum's large collection of Chinese porcelain, which included a number of armorial pieces. The lecture itself was entitled 'Chinese Armorial Porcelain' although, as I now had slides of many of the Mottahedehs' more interesting historical pieces, it was possible to elaborate on them as well, something which was probably appreciated by those less interested in heraldry!

Jim Whitehead had kindly provided a car so that we could be driven directly from Richmond to Lexington and the Reeves Center at Washington & Lee. It was another opportunity to see and discuss the Reeves Collection and Jim and Celeste hosted a very pleasant dinner party and saw us safely on the plane next day for Atlanta. The flight from Roanoke to Atlanta is just over an hour and it was nice to be met at the airport by Beverly duBose. Having travelled together on Dewey Curtis' English tour the previous year, it was a very happy experience staying with Beverly and Duffie in Atlanta. Beverly had had a varied business life but was now principally concerned with insurance, while Duffie was the niece of Robert Woodruff, who had controlled the Coca-Cola Company since early in the century after its re-financing.

But Beverly's principal focus was history, which had a public face as Chairman of a very active Atlanta Historical Society. Of all those I got to know over nearly thirty years of travelling in America, I felt closer and on a more similar wavelength to Beverly than I did with any of the many other friends I have met. My own experience of 'growing up' in industry, and allowing this to meld with history and research, seemed to mirror his own attitudes and experience.

While by 1977 he had included an interest in Chinese export porcelain in his 'portfolio', his original and deepest love was the history of the South, and in particular the suffering and successes of the South in the American Civil War. This was illustrated by his very broad collection of Civil War artefacts, many of which are today on display at the Atlanta Historical Society, and his feelings were encapsulated in the words which he wrote in 1964 and are now engraved on a plaque at the viewing point of the giant carving of figures at Georgia's Stone Mountain:

> *The vast majority of those who fought and died for the Southern Confederacy had little in worldly goods or comforts. Neither victory nor defeat would have greatly altered their lot. Yet, for four long years they waged one of the bloodiest wars in history. They fought for a principle … the right to live life in a chosen manner. This dedication to a cause drove them to achieve a moment of greatness which endures to this day.*

It was particularly interesting that one visit coincided with an annual private dinner of the board of the Coca Cola Company which, on this occasion, was given by Duffie and Beverly at their home. They had asked permission of the President of the company for me to be present; this was agreed, and I was seated next to the Chairman's wife and listened to some private conversations of considerable interest which I have never repeated. In spite of his achievements, his financial security and his influence, Beverly could always think like the common man and recognise what was right. This, and his love of a historical perspective, made him a very appealing friend in a world where such values are so often ignored.

I lectured on 'China for the West' in the Robert Woodruff Auditorium at 3 pm on 31st March and found the full audience as receptive as any previous lecture thus far. I can see from the elaborate full seminar invitation (entitled

'At the end of March England will be a little closer to Atlanta!') that, 'An English tea party will be held following the lecture'.

Unfortunately I had missed the lectures on the previous days: one given by Sir Peter Ramsbotham, the British Ambassador to the United States, on 'Britain and America – what we stand for', and the other by Professor J.H. Plumb, the historian, entitled 'New light on the tyrant George III', but Professor Plumb was still there for tea when I had finished.

We could well have stayed in Atlanta for longer, but I had arranged to fly again to Tampa and stay with the McKays at the weekend. It was an opportunity to study Herbert's fast-growing collection and spend a day sailing with his brother-in-law in Tampa Bay. On Wednesday we flew to New Orleans to spend an evening with the Melvin Rosenthals and on Thursday to Nashville, to stay two nights with Harriet Tyne. We arrived back in London after a day in New York and I was ready for Heirloom on Monday morning.

*   *   *

Fortunately January was usually a quiet month at Heirloom, because in early 1978 I was away again on another busy tour which promised to be as exciting as any so far. Between the 12th and 24th January, nine lectures to different societies had been arranged in five States. I flew in to New York, saw the Mottahedehs, and caught the morning train to Washington. For a whirlwind two nights I was to stay with Jim and Nancy Flather in Washington, with a particularly enjoyable dinner with Clem Conger, the Curator of the White House Collection.

My first lecture on 12th January, and its aftermath, were as interesting as any I had had, for I lectured to about three hundred people in a large open hall at the Washington Antiques Show. The audience included more than one well-known ambassador, and Nancy Flather's links with Washington society ensured a large and varied audience. As a pleasant lunch ended I was very surprised to be approached by the chairman, Mrs De Graff, who asked if I would guide Elizabeth Taylor round the show for two or three hours in the afternoon.

Elizabeth Taylor proved to be a very easy and understanding companion. We visited every stand, and she put up with rather more compliments than were necessary but showed a considerable interest in many of the objects and even bought two small items. At about 4.30 a breathless aide to her husband, Senator John Warner, asked her if she could join him in his helicopter which was waiting outside. She asked me how much more there was to see, and when I told her just two more rows of stands, she told him that she would be about twenty minutes. The aide hurried off but returned almost at once and said that 'the Senator says will you come at once.' There was a pause, and she turned to me and said in a loud voice, 'Men!', adding, 'We are going to see everyone.' She gave me a kiss as we parted twenty minutes later and thanked me for accompanying her. I would not have liked to have been in the helicopter when she boarded.

There was not much time to waste because I found myself invited to an informal dinner at the British Embassy as the guest of Peter Jay, the Ambassador. The other speaker at the show, Clem Conger, was also there. Peter and Margaret Jay were very undemanding hosts, and I had quite a long discussion with him, for he was Honorary Chairman of the Antiques Show that year and wanted to catch up on the 'gossip'.

The next morning I was lecturing at Mount Vernon at the invitation of Christine Meadows, the curator. It was an easy and informal affair, and with the help of a number of illustrations from the Mottahedeh Collection it was possible to focus firmly on the American period of the China Trade without entirely forgetting some armorial families who had contributed to the history of America in colonial days. That evening I also lectured to the Society of Maryland Antiquities at Towson, something which had been arranged by John Shank, who was now my host again.

Driving on to Hagerstown in Maryland, we stayed at the farmhouse where John Shank and Joe Matthews lived, and by now Anna had joined me for the rest of the tour. Two days later John had arranged that I speak to the Friends of the American Wing of the Baltimore Museum, and on the following night I was the speaker at the Washington County Historical Society at Hagerstown. John had fitted in these engagements very well, but there was still time to look at his ever-growing collection of Imari porcelain at their home.

It was, perhaps, as well that we had two nights with John and Julia Curtis at Williamsburg without a speaking engagement for, apart from the pressure of giving a somewhat different speech each day and rearranging my collection of some 250 slides so that appropriate examples were illustrated at each lecture, it was good to have two days off – albeit thinking and talking of porcelain most of the time! But on the 19th January we flew to Charleston for a lecture at the Gibbes Gallery. I hoped also to have an opportunity of seeing George Hartness, my host at Columbia two years earlier, who had suffered the terrible tragedy of having his eighteen-year-old daughter, Charlotte, senselessly murdered by a passing gunman as she sat in a car with her boyfriend in a lay-by on a busy road.

We arrived in Charleston and stayed for two nights as the guests of Mr and Mrs Robert Hollings, his brother being a Senator for South Carolina. It was a personal thrill to stay so close to the homes of my ancestors. The Gibbes Art Gallery had an interesting display of export porcelain including a number of pieces which were made for Charleston families or had been excavated in Charleston, and William Coleman, the Director, had arranged a pleasant evening and refreshments. The publicity, too, was the first to mention that the lecturer was an author of *China for the West,* although in fact the actual publication day had been put back until two months later. The friends introduced that evening, and others to whom I was introduced by the Hollings, made me almost feel like a resident of Charleston, and in recent years it has been a pleasure to get to know Katharine Danielson, William Coleman's daughter (who now has an antique shop in Charleston) and meet again her widowed mother.

But on that tour there was no time to spare and the following day we flew from Roanoke to Atlanta again to stay for the weekend with Beverly and Duffie. The invitation issued to members of the Atlanta Historical Society was decorated with leopards' heads from a Pulteney armorial dish and the lecture was entitled 'The Influence of Heraldry on Chinese Export Porcelain'. It was my 50th birthday, but there was little time to notice, although we enjoyed an excellent dinner afterwards. (Next morning I gave another, more technical, talk to 'docents and friends on the new collection of porcelain on loan to the Society'. This was, in fact, a collection of armorial porcelain loaned by an Englishman from Gloucestershire who had become a major collector at Heirloom over recent years.)

After the weekend we all drove down to Albany, Georgia, to stay with Hugh and Marie Shackelford who had a delightful home there, a nursery full of camellias, an antique shop, and had been with me on the most recent porcelain tour in England. The publicity material showed a huge floral bowl and the lecture was at the Banks Haley Gallery – but I remember best that there was local roast woodcock for breakfast, an unexpected delicacy!

Next day we returned to Atlanta, visiting some friends on the way and that evening flew to Nassau, where Norman was away but we were well cared for by Lena, and on the following day flew to Harbour Island for a week's rest in the delightful small cluster of cottages, known as Pink Sands. It was a surprise to find that Bob Huntley, the President of Washington & Lee University and his wife, were there at the same time. The contrast between Pink Sands and London in February could hardly have been greater, for we reached London on a frosty morning and I was immediately plunged into the business of Heirloom again.

*   *   *

In a tour in February and March in 1979 I had flown to Detroit, where Christina Nelson met me and organised a lecture at the Henry Ford Museum in Dearborn. The Henry Ford Museum itself is of great interest with its collection of vehicles and Christina and I spent a very agreeable day being driven round Grosse Point. It was also a pleasure to have lunch with Mrs Ford Ford.

Flying on to Cleveland, I stayed with David and Muriel Nachman, who have remained friends for twenty-five years, and the following day I was to speak at The Western Reserve Historical Society in Cleveland. It was, however, a close-run thing, for when I reached the baggage carousel at Cleveland airport, I was told that my suitcase had gone on to Chicago (and with it all my lecture slides). As we sat at dinner discussing what to do about this, David had an idea and hurried to the telephone. When I woke in the morning I was told the suitcase had arrived at 2 am in a special van. It was only later that I was told that one of the directors of the airline was coming to my lecture in the morning! But after that I always travelled with my lecture slides in my hand luggage. After the lecture I took a bus to Columbus, Ohio and stayed with a friend of David's for the night, continuing by bus in the morning to Cincinnati, where Anita Ellis, the Curator of Decorative Arts, looked after me all day and showed me round the Art Museum. We also spent a most interesting time in the Taft Museum, being the collection assembled by Charles Taft, brother of the President. In addition to a fine display of paintings, the *faience* and Chinese porcelain deserved great attention – particularly a very fine group of *famille verte* wares, many supplied by Duveen and some matching exactly the pieces in the Lady Lever Gallery in Liverpool, which probably once had been pairs.

I had to leave next day for a short visit to New York and then on to stay with Robert Calder, a Vice President of the Campbell Food Corporation who had kindly arranged a long visit to the Campbell Soup Tureen Museum in Camden, New Jersey. The following day we drove out to have lunch with Jack Dorrance whom I had met at dinner with the Mottahedehs, and entered another world as we turned off a main road to Philadelphia and were soon travelling through vineyards and a French village down towards a French chateau. Both chateau and village had been brought, stone by stone, from France and one would not know that we were not in the Loire Valley, but on the American side of the Atlantic.

After lunch I was treated to a fascinating tour of the chateau which included a number of very large, life-like white Meissen figures of animals and birds as well as, of course, some sumptuous tureens and other porcelain which seemed very much at home in their surroundings. In another room there were some piles of gaily wrapped parcels. For a moment Jack looked surprised and then said, 'Oh, these are just Christmas presents for next year.' After another evening with the Calders, it was a short journey to Philadelphia to stay as the guest of Winterthur, where I lectured at the weekend before catching a train for New York and a flight to London.

*   *   *

I had first met Wendell Garrett, the editor and publisher of the *Magazine Antiques* at Winterthur earlier in the 1970s, but Wendell also ran a series of lectures in New York for the Antique Collectors Club and the 1980/81 winter series included such diverse subjects as, 'French Gardens – The Italian Collection', by William Howard Adams; and 'Innovative Furniture in America', by David A. Hanks, a curator at the Smithsonian. In fact, in that season of eight monthly lectures, only 'China for the West' was not by an American. It took place at the Grolier Club and appeared to go well. Afterwards I had dinner with Wendell and Betsy Garrett and the Le Corbeillers. Such visits to New York were made easy by the fact that it was then necessary to see Stair frequently, and to be with them at the East Side Show in New York in January each year.

I had met on more than one occasion Betty and Charlie Wilds of Greenwich, and in 1982 they invited me to stay with them and speak to the Women's Club in Greenwich. It was a very pleasant occasion and lunch continued long into the afternoon, when I had to catch a plane to Bermuda. I had previously met Hugh Davidson at his antique shop, the Thistle Gallery, in Bermuda, but not his wife Brenda, and they are still good friends, although we now meet less frequently. Hugh was also the Chairman for some years of the Bermuda National Trust. Having met me at the airport we were able to visit a number of properties of the Trust and, in particular, see any porcelain, including a few pieces which had been found as part of the cargo of wrecks on the islands – although an article in the *Bermuda Royal Gazette* said that, 'Mr Howard does not know much about what Chinese porcelain has been found here and his lecture will not touch on Bermuda's history, but he is interested in the possible links between ships which have sunk off Bermuda's reefs, the porcelain cargoes they may have been carrying, and trade ... with the East India Company and China ...' (all this and a number of other paragraphs beneath a portrait of me carrying a copy of *China for the West*). I was to lecture on two later occasions in Bermuda and each time was impressed by the warmth and interest of the audiences.

There was no time to linger and immediately on my return we flew to

Monte Carlo for Sotheby's annual international sale, the outstanding lot being a part service with the Portuguese arms of de Castro which realised the then enormous sum for armorial porcelain of $350,000.

*   *   *

There were other occasions when I was between journeys for Stair, which gave me a glimpse of a different America from the East Coast sophistication. On one of these I spent two nights with Dr Michael Kelly and his wife, Lynn, in Oklahoma City, at what had been the edge of Indian territory until the 1889 Oklahoma Land Run, which redistributed much land to white settlers. I enjoyed addressing a group they had assembled, and later a fascinating journey to the town of Rogers, across Arkansas, at the invitation of a curator I had met from the Historical Museum.

The drive to Rogers passed through well kept lands notable for the number of Amish farmers who still drove horse-drawn vehicles and wore 19th Century dress in keeping with their religious beliefs. I found myself addressing an unexpectedly good audience at Rogers, on a subject possibly as unusual to them as my interesting visit to the town house museum next day was to me, which was filled with objects which would have been in everyday use a century earlier, but are now seldom seen.

Jim Whitehead at Washington & Lee University had long wished to display all the porcelain they had inherited from the Reeves Collection almost a decade earlier and introduce it, and the paintings of Louise Herreshoff (Mrs Reeves), to as wide an audience as possible, both at Lexington and nationally. On the weekend of 9th-12th September 1982 he arranged a decorative arts symposium entitled, 'The China Trade: Currents and Cross Currents of Taste', and it was, in part, held outdoors in very pleasant weather. The speakers were welcomed by Jim who was able to tell the full and amusing story of how he was introduced to the collection on crowded shelves and in piles on bedroom floors, and this was followed over three days by lectures from Crosby Forbes, Clare Le Corbeiller, Carl Crossman, Jennifer Goldsborough, Philip Curtis, Ross Taggart and David Howard, covering the widest range of China Trade subjects from paintings and lacquer and furniture, to 'A brief survey of 16th and 17th Century blue and white porcelain for export' by the last speaker.

With a candlelight reception and banquet, the symposium was, perhaps, the one I remember above all others in thirty years of lecturing in America. The importance of the Reeves Collection itself continued to grow under the subsequent guardianship of Tom Litzenburg in the 1990s, and now under Peter Grover and Holly Bailey, in a way which makes it ever more relevant to

Lecturers at Washington & Lee University, 1982.
James Whitehead (*left*) with Carl Crossman;
Clare Le Corbeiller (*centre*) and Carl Dauterman of the Metropolitan Museum,
with (*behind*) Jim and Nancy Flather, and Crosby Forbes (*right*) next to the author.

After a lecture: explaining a fine point on some fine Chinese porcelain.

the whole story of the China Trade, both in its history and its educational role in interpreting the decorative arts and their influence on western design.

*   *   *

Following the interest in two articles in *The Connoisseur* in April and May 1981 (the April article called *The Milanese Connection* – giving details of very well executed 20th Century additions to the painting of 18th Century Chinese export pieces enhanced in Italy and intended to deceive; and *From East to West*, being a brief summary of some early 17th Century Chinese porcelain painted in underglaze blue with recognisable stories) I was asked to write some short introductory essays for antique shows in America and gained considerable pleasure from one for the Ellis Memorial Show in Boston in 1982 called *Boston, Wilkes and Bartolozzi – Chinese Export Porcelain related to Boston*. John Wilkes, Lord Mayor of London and a controversial figure, having been elected MP while in prison, was an unlikely hero in Boston due to his resolute opposition to the establishment in London. There were occasional Chinese services copied after Bartolozzi (and others after Hogarth) but the extraordinary fact that an invitation to 'Dinner at the Mansion House, 17th April 1775, [for the installation of] The Right Hon. John Wilkes, Lord Mayor' was engraved by Bartolozzi after Cipriani *and* actually dated for the night before Paul Revere set off on his immortal ride, had not previously been noted.

The article for the Theta Antiques Show in Houston in 1982 was both fun to write and tied in well with a lecture tour which included seven lectures in nine states in just over two weeks. The article was entitled *Armorial Porcelain for America – A Tale of Two Earldoms*. Lord Stirling was the son of William Alexander, Surveyor General of New Jersey and New York, and Mary Sprott who had kept a provision store in New York. On the death of a very distant cousin in England he claimed the ancient Earldom of Stirling (a claim on which the House of Lords was divided), but he became one of Washington's generals and ordered an armorial porcelain service with his arms beneath an earl's coronet although, because of the war, he never received it. Extraordinary vases with the arms of another Earl (of Leven and Melville) were made with the supporters holding American flags. Was this because the son of the Scottish Earl fell at the Battle of Princeton, and was tended by Washington's doctor on the General's orders in an effort to save his life? The Theta Show was to be the second lecture in October 1982, and I hoped the article would introduce the subject of heraldry – which was not a usual one in Houston!

Having flown to Atlanta and again spent a weekend with Beverly and

Duffie, I caught a morning flight to Memphis and stayed for two nights with Tom Lee and his wife. Tom had been instrumental in arranging an exhibition of export porcelain in the Brooks Memorial Art Gallery, including numerous armorial pieces, largely from his own growing collection. The audience at Memphis was warm and seemed to enjoy the lecture.

I flew to Houston the next day and at once met a number of friends, for Bo and Eileen had come to view the Theta Show and we joined Stapleton Gooch, who had roots in Charleston, for lunch and then listened to Harold Sack, probably the leading expert on American furniture and President of his company in New York. Later the lecturers were to be picked up from our hotel by Wally and Margaret Shanks for a small reception in honour of 'English visitors' at the home of the British Consul, Malcolm McBain, followed by an excellent dinner for the three speakers – the other being Joe Butler, the Director of Collections at Sleepy Hollow, Tarrytown, New York whom I was to visit a year later.

My lecture next morning was entitled, 'Chinese Armorial Porcelain', which allowed me to range widely, mentioning as many American families as possible as well as Ima Hogg, who would have been a hundred that year and was remembered with affection by much of the audience. After lunch there was a most interesting visit to Bayou Bend with Michael Brown, a curator, and on the final day Joe Butler gave a fascinating talk on the Rockefeller family home at Tarrytown. That afternoon we visited the Harris Masterton Collection, ending the day with another dinner.

Among the guests in Houston were Upton and Trixie Beall, and it was a pleasure to drive to Tyler with them across Texas oil country and stay for a relaxing weekend with no lecture, but interesting company – we even speculated whether his Beall ancestors were related to Othniel Beale who had sailed out of Marblehead but settled in Charleston and was my direct ancestor. On Monday I flew to Denver and stayed with Philippa while lecturing at the museum on 'China for the West'. We had a relaxed evening with Ted and Anne Close and the following night Philippa and I had a delightful dinner as guests of Jay and Joan Crawford who had been in the oil industry in China.

The flight to Minneapolis on Wednesday gave me time to tour the most impressive Minneapolis Institute of Arts and learn something of its very broad compass from Bill Puig and Michael Conforti, who was particularly concerned with export porcelain. I lectured on armorial porcelain at 5 pm on the Thursday in a programme which included refreshments and a 'connoisseurship seminar' – basically a question and answer session. On the following day I was the guest of Mrs Leo Hodroff at their home. I had met Leo and Doris briefly before and Leo was, in fact, away, but I was not prepared for the truly exceptional collection I found in their Minneapolis home. There was little doubt that I should visit them again, although at that time there was no thought of any book about their collection. But I left saying that I very much hoped we would meet again in London in the spring.

Leaving Minneapolis on the Friday afternoon it was but a short flight to Columbus, Ohio where I was met by and stayed with Tom and Nancy Lurie. The lecture on 'China for the West' was scheduled for the unusual time of 1 pm on the Sunday at the Columbus Museum of Art, but the clash with Sunday lunch seemed to have little effect on the audience who were happy with brunch. Tom and Nancy looked after me well and we had a very pleasant dinner with some of their friends and long discussions on Tom's collections, of which export porcelain was but only one.

On Monday I flew to Chicago and stayed very comfortably at the Chicago Athletic Association for a night. Following dinner as the guest of Mrs Uihlein, I walked the block to the museum in the morning and after checking all my slides I was ready to lecture at 10.45 to the Antiquarian Society of the Art Institute of Chicago on blue and white porcelain for export. After the lecture and refreshments there was time for an all too brief tour of the museum with Lynn Roberts, who had organised all the details for me.

That afternoon I was collected by Arthur Liebman who, with his wife Ethel, had created an excellent collection of export porcelain which they had given to the Elvehjem Museum of Art at the University of Wisconsin. Arthur drove me to their home in Lake Forest where we had a delightful dinner with some friends and a deep discussion on the China Trade. Next day we drove to Madison where I was able to gain an idea of the scale of the collection now housed there – undoubtedly sufficient for a substantial catalogue or book (which Catherine Brawer achieved in 1992). In the afternoon I lectured again on 'China for the West' and later was sent an article from the *Milwaukee Journal* entitled, 'Chinese porcelains worth a few cracks', which started:

> Perhaps collectors have been taking Chinese export porcelain too seriously. That is the reaction more than one listener must have had as David S. Howard, a top British expert, gave an anecdotal history of this unique collectable at the Elvehjem Museum of Art … he peppered his illustrated talk with charming little tales about misperceptions of Europeans' instructions by well-meaning but uncomprehending Oriental porcelain painters … rival factions put the likenesses of their competing leaders on similar pots – stern portraits of Martin Luther and St Ignatius de Loyola, for instance, adorn otherwise identical vessels …

and three columns more. Next morning the airline took me to New York and on to London.

*　　*　　*

Reading again this brief record of so many lectures in America over more than a decade, one becomes aware of a common theme which scarcely hides itself among the many different days in new and interesting places. Undoubtedly the interest which Chinese Export porcelain could raise in more than thirty states was an indication of a deep-rooted need for information on, and understanding of, a past which was part of America's heritage as well as that of the European East India Companies. As a lecturer, it was something that was both inspiring and made it all very worthwhile.

CHAPTER 18

Everyday Life in Hay Hill

While lecture tours in America and occasional porcelain tours in Britain occupied a month or two each year (and took at least as long to plan as they did to execute) the everyday life in Hay Hill, the people whom I came to know, a few lectures in England and newspaper articles and television, all provided a patchwork of interest and variety.

Bevis Hillier had published in 1968 a book called *Pottery and Porcelain 1700-1914 – The Social History of the Decorative Arts* and it was fun to find myself included in an article by him in the *Sunday Telegraph* ten years later called, 'Bends, Chevrons, Piles and Fesses' which featured Sir Iain Moncreiffe (the father of the Earl of Errol, Hereditary High Constable of Scotland) and Lord Mowbray, the Premier Baron. It started with a number of paragraphs about Heirloom & Howard in which 'Mr Howard romantically speaks of his stock as "lost armorial things – objects which have unfortunately been separated from their families over the centuries" ... his stock shows the almost infinite uses of heraldry ... and in the first two years he was able to find homes for five hundred things within their families.' However, he continues in a later paragraph, 'Others regard heraldry today as an absurd anachronism and a foolish vanity.'

More light-hearted was an article two years later in *House and Garden*, called 'Is there blue blood in your family?' In two pages illustrating numerous pieces of stock, Amanda Harral wrote, after briefly describing a visit to the College of Arms and its role, 'You may, of course, be in the market for a whole range of decorative objects which carry your hopefully ancient arms. This will doubtless entail another visit, this time to Heirloom & Howard in Hay Hill in Mayfair. This specialist shop is stocked with a sufficiency of aristocratic wares to delight the eyes of anyone on his or her way back to a personal Brideshead ...'.

Neither of these articles, nor one or two others at the time, particularly mentioned porcelain, so it was a pleasure to read one from across the Atlantic by Bill Saks in the *Antique Trader Weekly* who wrote of 'a four hour interview ... with Mr Howard who is a dedicated research expert.' It was heart-warming stuff at the time, but I feel embarrassed now, although his eleven large photographs of the shop were largely of porcelain and coach panels with Howard in various poses, and he ended, some columns later, 'Thank you Mr

Howard … and now I think I'll walk about the London streets thinking about all you said.' (I hope it didn't turn to disappointment!)

An article called 'Finding Heirs for Heirlooms' mentions a decanter from Government House, St Helena, which is now back on the island, and this story perhaps merits retelling. About 1980 a lady brought me a decanter which she wanted to sell, saying that it had been given to an ancestor by Marshal St Honoré, 'one of Napoleon's marshals'. I was intrigued because I soon discovered that there was no such marshal and that the crest, which she described as 'a lion holding a handbag', with initials 'St H.' below, was in fact the crest of the Honourable East India Company (a lion holding a crown) who then owned the island of St Helena where Napoleon lived the last years of his life. Somehow the facts had been distorted over the years, for it seemed quite likely that he might have used the decanter on the island. I bought it and sold it to the Crown Agents who returned it to St Helena. A number of such examples were mentioned and the journalist ended the article, 'Not everyone is pleased … for when he recently identified the arms on a stolen piece of silver recovered by the police, and they returned it to the owner – he was most upset, "I was just about to get the insurance money," he grumbled.'

Richard Compton Miller, who wrote for the *Daily Express* and had a Saturday column (and was an occasional customer of Heirloom) had a page in May 1982 which was headed, 'Compton Miller meets an *eminence grise*, an armorial sleuth … and a very decorative lady', with portraits of us all. His paragraphs included, 'All the great heroes of British history parade through the studious Mayfair premises of David Howard – Admiral Nelson, Pitt the Elder, the Iron Duke, Lord Byron and Churchill live through their coats of arms …', and later, 'Howard's bookish "Mister Pastry" air works well in America where he lectures twice a year…'. (I've never quite understood who Mr Pastry was!)

But the most rewarding article was about two years later when Victoria Geibel wrote an article in *Town and Country* called, 'Mr Armorial Porcelain'. In a long and friendly four-page article, one paragraph read, 'With his sharp blue eyes, long, chiselled face … David Howard looks more like a nineteenth century scholar than a dealer as he pores over the reference books in his cluttered Dickensian shop … in fact with the exception of a small bust of Franklin D. Roosevelt made by his (sculptress) daughter Sophie, every item has a coat of arms.'

Unwittingly she added later, '… "No, there is no Mr Heirloom," Howard explained over tea and scones served at the shop each afternoon.' (I had not thought to tell her that a member of the Royal family had made an appointment to see us the day before but had been unable to keep the

Always something to identify.

appointment; we had bought the scones for tea to mark the occasion, but did not normally 'serve them each afternoon'!)

Perhaps the greatest pleasure and honour at the time was to be elected in 1979 a Fellow of the Society of Antiquaries of London (FSA) and have access to their friendly library at Burlington House, next to the Royal Academy. This was on account of my authorship of *Chinese Armorial Porcelain* and *China for the West*. One of my sponsors made it very clear to me that Fellows should never use the academic honour to further any trade ambition (indeed, some academic societies in the art field do not have dealers as members).

By the late 1970s Anna and I had moved to West London, to a ground floor flat at Coleherne Court in Old Brompton Road, a long Edwardian block of flats with attractive gardens behind. Few noticed a pretty girl move in three doors along, a year or two later. We never spoke to her, but she shopped at the local Indian corner shop on Earl's Court Road (often parking her small red car on the pavement corner). We were soon to discover that her name was Diana Spencer, and for a short while that part of Old Brompton Road was besieged by photographers.

We found Coleherne Court convenient and comfortable, and the large flat had space for drawing and dining rooms, four bedrooms and two bathrooms – enough room to display the furniture I had brought down from Yorkshire (which had been in store for some years) and with very adequate bookshelves for a growing library which increasingly concerned history and heraldry. We could also have guests to stay or for dinner in comfortable surroundings.

A real bonus was that my children could come to stay without the restrictions of Hay Hill, for although Philippa was now living in America, Sophie had recently completed her art degree at Winchester and Jo was at Edinburgh University studying philosophy and law. Thomas was now at Stowe, which seemed to keep him happy and certainly taxed my pocket!

*   *   *

A lasting legacy of Heirloom in the late 1970s and early 1980s was the number of clients who have since become very good friends, although as the years passed this number increased greatly. I should mention first, because sadly he died of a heart attack in Barbados in 1992, a special friend – Munson Campbell, who stayed regularly in London in furtherance of his business connections with the catering trade and a number of other international organisations. When in London he stayed at an hotel in St James's Place and he lived in Beekman Place in New York. He was a well-known member of the River Club in New York where he had a habit of introducing me to friends as

'Sir David Howard' – a habit he changed after I booked a room for him at the Stafford Hotel as 'Sir Munson Campbell'! Munson enjoyed journeys out of London, and on numerous weekends we would motor to places like Clandon and Polesden Lacey. We also met at Doncaster once at the invitation of Phil and Pat Cooke and he spent the day marvelling at the Cooke Collection, while in the mid 1980s he invited me to go with him on the Orient Express to Broadlands, the home of the late Lord Mountbatten. As time passed his collection grew. He had a particular fondness for the warm colours and earlier history of the *rouge de fer* and gold pieces, which later decorated many of his rooms when he moved to Minneapolis. After his untimely death his brother consulted me and made a decision that I think would have pleased Munson by giving much of his armorial porcelain to the Peabody Museum in Salem in his memory.

The sad death of Beverly DuBose in May 1986 left a void in Atlanta which could not easily be filled. But as the years passed, his son, Bo, greatly increased his knowledge in the fields which had delighted his father, and has displayed a remarkable singlemindedness in assimilating many aspects of both American and British history in a way which mirrored Beverly and would have pleased him. The custodial responsibility of his father's unique collection of Civil War memorabilia, much of which he has carefully passed to the Atlanta Historical Society, and his growing knowledge of the China Trade, have made him not only a friend, but a true connoisseur and collector with whom it has been very satisfying to share, discover and experience, and our very frequent conversations and meetings over the years, with his sparkling wife, Eileen, have been a source of great pleasure.

I think Chris Weld first wandered into Heirloom about 1978. A Boston lawyer, I felt that he was then more interested in shooting and fishing, sailing, and in collecting fine prints and paintings of sailing ships, than necessarily in the armorials we had to offer. He was one of a number who came once or twice each year to shoot, and on his second or third visit discussed his Weld ancestors and their arms, but we were never able to find any Weld antiques. However, I felt his interest later turn slowly towards the China Trade and export porcelain, which linked well with Boston's commercial past and his own interest in maritime trade and the conservation of the oceans, for he later sat as a member of a major international oceanic committee, as well as having close ties with the Peabody Museum. All this broadened slowly into a much greater friendship which saw him and his ever-kind wife, Susie, stay with us many times in Wiltshire in later years, and we with them in Essex, Massachusetts. I found that his broad vision, wide knowledge and legal balance, seasoned with an irreverent sense of humour, made him a particularly valued friend with whom it was fun to discuss anything without fear of prejudice, and in the certainty that his experience and broad understanding made him a wise councillor. Indeed, he has given some sound advice over the editing of this book.

I don't think that either Munson, Bo or Chris would have found it particularly easy to relate to Jim Williams of Savannah, for while I found him amusing and easy to be with, I think they would have had reservations about his style of life which did not immediately concern me. Jim would visit London at least twice a year and usually stayed at the Ritz, wandering round Mayfair in the morning, but by eight in the evening was ready for another visit to Crockfords or another place where the wheels spin continuously and unpredictably. If he had had a successful night when he came into Heirloom he was anxious to buy something exciting, and I would have lunch with him. If he had lost heavily the night before, I could tell at once, and he would have lunch with me, usually at the Mayfair Hotel Buttery.

He had faultless judgement in most artistic fields and a deep understanding of what was good taste. When I visited him in Savannah, staying on one or two occasions, this was abundantly clear, for he had chosen to furnish Mercer House so that it had the comfortable but opulent feeling of ownership established over generations. Jim was pleased that I saw this as his ability to appear as if he was 'old money' when in effect he had built up everything himself. I was amazed to find, years later, in the book *Midnight in the Garden of Good and Evil*, a mention of this in the first chapter (although some other details are incorrectly recorded). There is also a mention of the panel from Napoleon's coach, which was used on the day of the Emperor's wedding and which featured in the film of the book. I had found this in England some time earlier and Jim immediately thought it would look well in his drawing room. Other special purchases included two most unusual 'square shaped' Chinese porcelain garnitures both decorated *c*.1740 in the style of Cornelius Pronk, and a few months later I saw the garnitures illustrated again in a full page Estée Lauder advertisement, with their model standing before the sideboard in Jim's dining room with not one, but both the garnitures (occupying most of the illustration), for Jim was not averse to having photo sessions in his house.

Having met, and not warmed to, Jim's young friend who was later found dead in his library, I was greatly saddened by his trial for murder, his spell in jail and later appeal. We continued to correspond while he was in jail and later, after a visit to London, we had a discussion about whether it would be appropriate to use a Williams armorial to which he felt he had the right. In particular I persuaded Jim to focus on a suitable motto, and I received a letter with a particular suggestion one morning, only to hear next day that he had been found dead in Mercer House. Sadly I cannot find that letter in my files, or remember what his last idea was for a suitable motto. At a sale at Sotheby's of his property, Napoleon's coach panel reached an exorbitant price, but I was able to buy back a 16th Century blue and white punch bowl which he had had in the house, and it is a happy reminder of those interesting days.

There could hardly have been a greater contrast with such a collector of fine works of art than Arthur Gilbert, later knighted for his generous gifts to the nation. He had been an enormously successful entrepreneur in the property market immediately after the war in London and later in Los Angeles, and although he was never interested in Chinese porcelain, he found that Heirloom could identify the arms on some of the very fine silver he was buying in London. I became a consultant on that score and spent a fascinating two days at his 'private pinnacle' home in Los Angeles, driven there in his Rolls in which he kindly met me at the airport. I found the micro-mosaics which filled tables and decorated walls as interesting as the Paul Storr and de Lamerie silver which stood on Georgian sideboards between them.

Among those who asked for advice about their collections in the early '80s was George Overend, who had decided to collect export porcelain but was uncertain as to which style he should collect. It was an interesting question – ignoring the field of armorial – and I advised him, and his wife Carol, to spend an afternoon at the V & A to see which decorative period pleased them most. They were to return the following day with their minds made up that *famille verte* was most to their taste and they have, over the past quarter century, built a very fine collection in this style, including examples of almost all the *famille verte* armorial services, which displays beautifully in their Atlanta home, in which we have enjoyed staying over the years as friends.

It was a happy accident of fate which introduced me to François and Nicole Hervouët, and increasingly throughout the 1980s we met in London and later in Nantes. François had found the details in *China for the West* a useful starting point for his book on Chinese export porcelain, *La Porcelaine des Compagnies des Indes à décor occidental* (published in 1986) and although occasionally he found something at Heirloom which interested him, our meetings were usually over dinners in London when we were able to discuss some finer points of the China Trade. He and Nicole stayed frequently at a flat behind the Hilton in London, but it was a particular pleasure to meet them at home in Nantes, where they lived in a long top floor flat converted from one of the huge mercantile warehouses which had been an important part of the city when it was a principal port of France's 18th Century East India Trade.

Walking round the ample apartment there was little sign that it housed perhaps the most interesting collection of *porcelaine des Indes* in Europe. In the guest bathroom at one end of the long hall there was a large brass ring beside the basin for a towel. Taking hold of this and turning it opened a hidden doorway in the panelling and one could then walk down alleyways of cases set in the walls and filled with porcelain, telling the story which François was to illustrate so well in his book.

My occasional visits to Nantes and meetings in Monte Carlo at the time of Sotheby's annual sales were a very happy experience, and it was a sad reversal that François, with so much achieved in addition to his responsibilities as medical director of that region of France, should die at an early age.

It would require many extra pages to relate the kindnesses and understanding of other friends over those years such as Peter and Bea Frelinghuysen, and their son Rodney and his wife Ginny, who have managed to blend challenging political lives with other interests including works of art and Chinese porcelain in particular.

Nearer home, I had started a friendship in the early 1960s with John Andrew, to whom I was introduced by our mutual friend, John Foster, and whom I first knew as Chaplain to the Archbishop of Canterbury, and later was to become the Rector of St Thomas's, Fifth Avenue, New York. His clear vision, taste and generous disposition have made him a friend over forty years and he has kindly written a foreword to this book. Although it wasn't until much later that I got to know well Peter Gwynn-Jones, now Garter King of Arms, we undoubtedly share the same historical and heraldic perspective, as well as mutual friends from a Dorset past, and his visits to stay have always given great pleasure.

Other far-flung friends of up to sixty years ago included Norman (and later Kathy) Solomon, Alastair Tower, Oscar Husum, John Ayers, Frank and Patricia Herrmann, Alastair and Anne Aberdeen, Clifford Henderson, while many more who have added greatly to my own life, particularly over the last twenty years, are mentioned elsewhere in this book. In more recent years, Bill Sargent, who has successfully filled the gap which Crosby left when he retired from the Peabody, has stayed with us on a number of enjoyable occasions in West Yatton and has increasingly become a personal friend.

* * *

Today a common route to recognition in any field is by the television screen, particularly when the subject is more general and the audience wider. In the field of antiques and the arts in Britain, among those who have benefited considerably from this medium – indeed who have made it their main career on occasions – have been Arthur Negus, John Bly and David

Battie, all friends over the years and all of whom 'graduated' from an antique shop or as an auctioneer.

Although I was to take part in a small number of television appearances, I found that the time taken was, with one or two exceptions, out of proportion to the personal enjoyment derived from the occasion as a participant. Having taken part in one early *Antiques Roadshow* which involved more than twenty-four hours of time for less than three minutes useful discussion on air, I was asked if I would like to take part in a series, but decided to say 'no' – probably a mistake!

One of the more interesting occasions was an Anglia Television programme in 1980 which was actually called 'Heirlooms' and the principal co-ordination was in the capable hands of John Bly. However, the most interesting programmes were part of a series in the 1980s called *Arthur Negus Enjoys*, which followed Arthur (a retired country auctioneer of considerable reputation) to various great houses where he was able to employ his wide knowledge of furniture and historical background, and for half an hour to discuss this with different guests. In two houses in particular – Shugborough, the home of Lord Anson, and Wilton, the home of Lord Pembroke – I joined him, having spent, in each case, a pleasant evening beforehand having dinner at a local hotel and planning our discussions.

Shugborough had a very wide range of Chinese export art, including paintings and lacquer and a particularly fine porcelain service given to Lord Anson in 1743 by grateful Chinese merchants at the time his sailors helped to extinguish one of the disastrous fires which occasionally swept through Canton. The design was then unique on Chinese porcelain and has since been called 'The Valentine Pattern', probably created by Piercy Brett, the artist travelling with him in the Pacific. In the centre was a breadfruit tree, garlanded with flowers, which was no accident because for nearly three months before their arrival in Canton, Anson's expedition had been collecting breadfruit trees, largely on Tenian Island, so that they could be replanted in the West Indies to provide extra fruit for the slaves who were increasingly populating those islands. The design, which also included an 'altar of love', love birds on Cupid's arrows, and two faithful hounds, proved enormously popular in the West and was copied in one form or another on up to twenty Chinese armorial services made for other captains and merchants who were in Canton in the 1740s and '50s, and was also incorporated into European porcelain designs.

While Arthur allowed me to tell this story briefly, we spent more time round the dining room table where he was able to demonstrate that not all the chairs were from the original set. We then explored other rooms where a fascinating mixture of history and works of decorative art made it an excellent programme. It was at a time when he increasingly had arthritis and I recall that many of the close up shots when he pointed to details on the chairs and furniture were, in fact, my hands close up as he could no longer bend down and use his own.

At Wilton we explored the renowned 'double cube' and 'single cube' rooms, with their armorials near the ceiling revealing that the 1st Earl of Pembroke had married Anne Parr, the sister of Henry VIII's last wife, and examined the furniture and paintings which had remained in the same rooms for three hundred years, including the well-known portrait of Charles I and his family. Arthur had earlier enquired if there was a Pembroke table in Wilton House that we could look at, and learning, rather surprisingly, that there was not, we telephoned Lord Pembroke who lived little more than a mile away, to see if we could borrow one. A table was eventually produced so that Arthur could explain and illustrate on the programme a name which has found its way into the language of furniture. The porcelain vases and parts of two early armorial services gave me a chance to keep up with Arthur, and it was not only an interesting, but a very happy occasion.

*   *   *

But I did not only have the chance to visit interesting houses because of television. Sotheby's in the West Country arranged in September 1981 a most interesting antiques evening at Ugbrook House, the home of Lord Clifford, who had inherited part of two Chinese armorial services of the first part of the 18th Century and had been able to acquire more when a major part of a family service, which had been disposed of in the 19th Century, turned up at an auction house in Switzerland. I was invited to speak, and a most enjoyable evening ended with a buffet supper for the many who had travelled from all over Devon to be part of the occasion. Having stayed the night I was able to discuss the Clifford porcelain in detail the following day with Lord Clifford. It was not the first time I had spoken in the West Country, for two years earlier I had been invited to speak to the Asian Art Society of the South West at the Bristol Museum and Art Gallery. This had been very much the idea of Peter Hardie who was a curator at the museum and a considerable expert on earlier Chinese porcelain and glass.

Another evening in November 1981 proved a particularly happy one when I lectured at Symondsbury, near Bridport, to an antique forum organised by my god-daughter Amanda Streatfeild (*née* Edwards, of Denhay Farm and today, in a business run with her husband George, well known for Denhay organic cheeses and cured bacons – an industry which was just then starting). I stayed with her parents, Campbell and Pauline Edwards, at their home in Bridport, which I had not visited since I had left nearly twenty years earlier when Campbell had been Chairman of Bridport Industries.

Occasional evening lectures were usually easier in London: on one occasion at the British Museum on armorial porcelain, and on another to the Oriental Ceramics Society on 'European Influences on 17th and 18th Century Chinese Porcelain'. Looking at my correspondence at that time I see that the Society's Programme Secretary in 1981 was Jean Martin, who is still the Honorary Secretary in 2003. Later there were to be a number of lectures at the International Ceramics Fairs, so well organised by Brian and Anna Haughton from 1982 onwards, and at which Heirloom exhibited until the mid 1990s.

Once in a while more exotic tasks came my way, as when in 1983 the Swan Ball in Nashville arranged that one of their special prizes that evening should be 'A day spent as the guest of David Howard in London, visiting houses of the National Trust and learning of their history and particularly porcelain'. To my surprise it worked rather well, and we went to Clandon and Polesden Lacey and had an excellent dinner in London.

1983 was also an exciting year for Thomas, for in the spring he had won a travel prize at Stowe for the best essay suggesting an overseas tour. This had surprised me because he was only just seventeen at the time and his essay had focused on Central America. I wrote first to a director of Tate and Lyle, the sugar company, who was a client of Heirloom. He very kindly introduced me to their overseas director in Mexico and Thomas' first stay that April was there, giving him a chance to visit ancient temples and learn something of the country. He then visited Belize, which at the time was suffering political unrest, partly as a result of American policy in neighbouring Guatemala and Honduras. The British garrison included a company of Coldstreamers, and I had written to a friend who was there, and they kindly lodged Thomas for a day or two in a room adjoining the Sergeants' Mess.

Thomas spent longer in the city of Belize than was intended because he was the witness to a currency exchange mugging (on himself) and the police demanded that this seventeen-year-old schoolboy give evidence in court. This over, he made friends and stayed with a family of which the breadwinner was a local lorry driver and he travelled to the southern borders of the country in a way which would have provided thrills and risks for someone twice his age (and which luckily his father did not hear about until later!). Eventually travelling back across Mexico on local transport, Thomas crossed the border into the United States and took a Greyhound bus to Memphis where Tom Lee and his wife kindly took him in hand for a day and made him dress his leg, which he had injured the previous week. He then set off for Washington where he was met by Barbara Eagleton, and she and Tom kindly looked after him for two days before putting him on a plane to London. Tom was to tell me later that at a small dinner party at their home Thomas had argued fiercely with him and another Democratic senator against American policy in Central America – perhaps they did not often hear the robust views of a roadside café clientele in Belize! I still have a nice note from Barbara Eagleton reading, 'We so enjoyed having Thomas with us even though it was so brief. You will thoroughly enjoy his tales of Belize etc. Hope his foot is well soon – fondly, Barbara.' Needless to say it was a great pleasure to be able to take their son, Terry Eagleton, and his then girlfriend to visit some interesting houses in Kent when he was in England a little later.

At this time Heirloom had assumed an unusual role in permitting Burke's Peerage Limited, then short of London offices (and a few other things) to be 'sub-tenants' in its basement for a brief period. I'm sure this was not permitted in our lease but it passed without notice for a few months, and our visitors overlapped continuously while allowing Charles Teviot, perhaps the only old Etonian member of the House of Lords to drive bus tours for a living, to be also briefly a director of both Burke's Peerage and a subsidiary of Heirloom's all at the same time.

But in spite of all these diversions and some looming exciting times in New York and Amsterdam, Heirloom continued to prosper in the early 1980s with much of the everyday work in the hands of Angela, who was joined a few months later by Clifford Clewley as our accountant. (Earlier, on a number of occasions, we had been helped by Osmund Bullock, an actor by profession, who had a good brain and clear understanding of heraldry, and whose his grandfather had been Secretary to Sir Winston Churchill at one time.)

There were always some with whom I particularly enjoyed working and these included the ever-helpful and wickedly amusing Tish Roberts at Sotheby's in New York who was always ready to examine matters in (great) detail and send photographs when needed; while in London Donald Wilson's contacts with interesting clients were matched by his ability to find things of extraordinary historical interest (perhaps a ring worn by the best friend of the Black Prince, a Royal Crown no longer in the Tower, or a letter written by 'Bonnie Prince Charlie'). Indeed, this linked well with Heirloom, as did the growing interest of both Anthony and Philip Mould, the former specialising in old masters and the latter in pictures with known histories. Philip later founded his successful gallery called 'Historical Portraits', many of the figures painted mirroring the characters I knew so well at Heirloom through their armorials, and there was quite often an opportunity for co-operation.

One exceptional object came to us after a small auction in Somerset, framed under glass in a 1920s tea table. To my surprise I recognised the arms on the tapestry as being of Kings Charles XI and XII of Sweden before 1718, when Queen Ulrica succeeded. After mentioning this to the Cultural Attaché at the Swedish Embassy, I had an excited telephone call from the Director of the Royal Collection in Sweden who told me that the needlework was the original armorial from the tapestry still hanging in the Royal Palace in Stockholm, which had been cut out and replaced in 1718 when the arms changed. The piece is now reunited with its original, but how it came to be in an early 20th Century English tea table may never be known!

There were occasional moments of excitement, too, as when one Saturday lunchtime I saw a lady having her handbag snatched in Hay Hill and ran out on to the street to give chase, stopping for a moment to enlist the aid of the doorman at the Mayfair Casino at the foot of Hay Hill. Between us we cornered the bag-snatcher near Green Park tube station and handed him over to the police car which had been alerted. It was only half an hour later that I realised that the gallery had been left completely unattended with an unlocked door! I later discovered that the doorman was a rugby player, and had been until recently a sergeant in the paratroopers in the Falklands War.

Another less exciting but amusing moment was caused by Martha Hyder who had recently been staying at the American Embassy in Moscow and decided that the décor there was not as luxurious as she felt it should be, and needed alternative furnishings. She was on a comprehensive shopping tour in Mayfair (such tours often left her husband, Elton, up to three shops behind so he would settle down for a cup of coffee at Heirloom and wait for Martha to send a taxi for him). On this occasion the irrepressible Martha was on her own and I had a frantic phone call at 9 pm (why I was still in the shop I don't know) asking if I could help get her things packed, because her suite at Claridges had so much in it that she could not see the bed! I rang the ever-helpful Errol Nelson who handled our shipping, and by about ten we were at Claridges. Martha's room was indeed filled to overflowing, and Errol stayed until well after midnight packing rolls of wallpaper, rugs and chairs and a great deal else into cartons and cases and drove them away for onwards carriage. I hope the American Embassy in Moscow was pleased!

So many of these episodes made Heirloom fun, if hardly famous, although I was rather flattered one day when a well-dressed man with superior voice, whom I didn't know, came in and asked if his friend had left a message. I wasn't sure because I'd been out myself, but asked who his friend was. He told me, adding 'I arranged that we would either meet at my club or at Heirloom & Howard.'

CHAPTER 19

New York and the China Trade

January 1983 proved to have a very interesting start in New York. The East Side Show as usual was an inescapable draw, but *Antique Monthly* had prepared a wide-ranging conference at the Plaza Hotel at which, amongst others, John Bly was speaking on the first day on '19th Century English furniture', and after a fine reception that evening at Sotheby's the second morning was filled with unusual and interesting topics on, 'The Nuances of Insuring Antiques', 'How systematically to inventory your collection' and 'Problems in valuations for appraisers, collectors and donors'.

After an award luncheon, the speakers were Brand Ingles on, 'Unmarked Silver and Duty-dodgers' and (the last) David S. Howard on, 'The Rare, the Repetitive and the Repaired – how to choose your Chinese export porcelain'. (This is one of only three lectures of which I have a tape recording, although on occasions some others were recorded, I believe.) That evening we had a reception at *A La Vieille Russie* – another world.

But the great surprise of the January visit was still to come, for I had a very interesting dinner with James Bell, the recently-appointed Director of the New York Historical Society who, amongst other friends, knew John Andrew and Wendell Garrett well. He was anxious to breathe new life into one of the most prestigious and oldest organisations in the field of American history and the art world, and had secured a special budget, initially of over $150,000, for an exhibition to be called 'New York and the China Trade', to be open between late February and the end of August in 1984, and to which it was planned that there would be no fewer than 50,000 visitors.

A summary of the project had been prepared which read:

> The New York Historical Society plans to commemorate the bicentennial of the first sailing from New York to China with an exhibition entitled 'New York and the China Trade', which will open on February 22, 1984 and close on August 25, 1984.
>
> Between 1784 and the late 1840s, New York became the major American port involved in commerce with China. Emphasizing this period when New York rose to leadership in the China Trade, the exhibition will combine the display of porcelain, silver, silks,

and other luxury objects imported from China with a description of the trade itself. Maps, logbooks, merchants' records, diaries, newspaper advertisements and nautical memorabilia will provide background information on the history of the trade. The Society's museum holds paintings, silver and porcelain pertaining to the China Trade; in the library's manuscript department there are many collections relating to the China Trade, including the papers of the sloop *Experiment*, which sailed to Canton in 1785, only a year after the first voyage to China. In addition to the Society's own collections, the exhibition will include loans from individuals and other institutions.

In conjunction with this exhibition, the Society will present a series of four lectures on the China Trade as well as an audio-visual program which will be taken to schools, senior citizens' centers, etc. An illustrated catalog of 160 pages will also accompany the exhibition.

To my surprise and pleasure, Jim asked if I would be prepared to be the Guest Curator for the exhibition. Frankly, nothing could have appealed more and I agreed on an honorary basis – the only proviso being that the Society would meet any extra travelling and hotel costs. It was to be the start of more than two years working with the Historical Society, eventually covering two international exhibitions, and often monthly visits to New York; a very happy period of my working life which made sure that every minute was occupied!

The volume of correspondence to and from New York in 1983 was set to increase greatly, and the number of visits was to rise to seven during the year, some being of two or three weeks duration. I often stayed at the Mayflower Hotel on the south-western corner of Central Park and at other times, particularly if some work still concerned Stair, at the Metropolitan Club which was close to the south-eastern corner. In either case it was usually easy and pleasant to walk to the Historical Society along or through Central Park, using taxis only when there was snow or rain.

On reading again the correspondence of those days, it is clear that the original expectation of James Bell was that the majority of items to be on display would come from the voluminous store rooms of the Society, but in the final analysis I find that less than 15% of the 200 items or groups of items catalogued separately came from the New York Historical Society itself. Many of the catalogue entries were themselves multiples of up to eight items and the original perception of what constituted the New York China Trade grew monthly as more private lenders and museums became aware of the exhibition and agreed to help. It was, perhaps, inevitable that Chinese porcelain formed a major part of the exhibition, but it constituted a little less than 75% of the entries and certainly Chinese paintings, furniture and lacquer occupied far more space on display. By the time the exhibition was ready, the balance seemed right.

It would, of course, have been impossible to arrange in barely a year, from the other side of the Atlantic, the borrowing of 160 groups of objects from all over New York State and beyond, from the fifty-eight named lenders (and eight anonymous ones), without considerable teamwork – particularly when I personally had to see and consider the relevance and importance of the objects themselves, but Jim Bell had made available an excellent team from the Museum staff to handle the greater share of organisation once the decisions had been made. The team of six was led by Betsy Currie, who had previously been a graduate assistant at the Metropolitan, and curator and co-ordinator of exhibitions at the Historical Society for the previous two years. Of the rest of the team I recall particularly Mary Alice Kennedy and Charlotte Smith (whose parents I had met in Pittsburgh and was to meet again on many occasions). It was very encouraging working with such a team and Betsy in particular has remained in touch over the last twenty years. In addition, Jim Bell had made available Dr Conrad Wright, the Assistant Director for Development and staff historian at the Museum, who had a PhD in American History. He was to write an interesting essay on historical episodes in the period of the American China Trade which would form a substantial prologue to the 140-page catalogue.

The only weak link in the chain was the editorial control, which I should have insisted was mine from the outset, for while the publishers received regular copy and over 230 illustrations over ten months – many taken especially for the exhibition – they simply would not send proofs to the author of the copy, or page layouts, until they announced that it was too late to make any alterations in any case. It taught me a severe lesson that, as an author with almost total *responsibility* for an exhibition or book, it was essential that one must also have *control* over the editorial matters in so far as giving clear instructions to the technical design teams who cannot otherwise know exactly what is intended by the author or curator. Such questions of authority must be ironed out *at the outset* and I ensured that this was exactly what happened in four later exhibitions and books for which I was to be responsible.

*   *   *

Another visit to New York was planned for March and final decisions were already required on how such a major exhibition should be grouped. By now it was clear that there would be four main sections, but it wasn't until a month or two later that this crystalised into approximately:

A.	The Colonial Period to 1775	10%
B.	The first sailing and early American Trade to 1790	15%
C.	A century of American China Trade to 1875	65%
D.	The last century – to 1985	10%

Wherever possible the aim was not just to display pieces similar to those of the period under scrutiny, but to find objects which had *actually* played a living part in the history of New York, or were the property of those who were not 'unknown to history'. It was, for instance, of great historic interest to be able to borrow from the Sleepy Hollow Restorations at Tarrytown (with the enthusiastic help of Joe Butler) two damaged blue and white teabowls of *c.*1640 which had been retrieved from the Hudson River about 1945. They were found where the ancient quay of Philipse Manor was built, and from where ships in the 17th Century were unloaded from the time of Frederick Philipse, who had bought the then isolated manor from 'Gentleman' Van de Donk, from whose name derived the New York district of Yonkers. It was fun to be able to draw such interesting local history from a damaged cup. Later it was of interest to find that a Chinese tea service for a New Yorker made about 1785 was actually copied from a bookplate by an American engraver who didn't appear to know at the time what the American flag comprised and engraved it with stripes only. There were so many changes taking place at the time of the first American sailing to China – *The Empress of China* in 1784 – that one needs to understand the ordinary man's slow transition into the new order.

Because of the considerable number of new avenues that were already opening up, Jim Bell and I found that 'additional funding' was soon a problem. Successful approaches were to be made to major collectors of China Trade objects: David Rockefeller, Mildred Mottahedeh, Pamela Copeland, Jack Dorrance, Fred Johnston, Joy and Erving Wolf, and others whom I had met, in order to ease the path towards a fully comprehensive exhibition.

At our March meetings in New York we also drew up a list of museums, New York State institutions and societies who should be contacted. By the time of the exhibition twenty-five organisations had lent objects, in some cases a number with supporting material. Jim and I were by then aware that the New York Historical Society was not the only organisation aiming to celebrate the bicentenary of the American China Trade and that the Philadelphia Museum was planning a considerable display and a catalogue (which I still treasure) by Jean Gordon Lee on the Philadelphia Trade with China while the Museum of the City of New York, amongst others, was also planning displays. In most cases, however, items were drawn from their own collections only.

The question of advertising and newspaper support required more contact with the *Magazine Antiques*, Rita Reif at *The New York Times* and others, particularly to stimulate anyone with objects of interest to let us know. Tish Roberts at Sotheby's was most enthusiastic and scoured their auction records for the last twenty years to discover the names of any buyer of objects of the China Trade with particular reference to New York. Sotheby's had photographs back to the 1950s which could stimulate the search for moments of New York trade history. Clem Conger at the US State Department had a record of a number of objects in Washington which had New York connections including a large 19th Century dish painted with General Gates receiving the surrender of General Burgoyne at Saratoga, and a punch bowl with an unusual eagle holding a trumpet and an anchor and the motto 'In God we hope', made for John Jay of New York, the first Secretary of State from 1784-1790.

Nonnie Frelinghuysen at the Metropolitan Museum made available some exceptional bowls including their magnificent example of a bowl with the Order of Cincinnati made for Lieutenant Colonel Ebenezer Stevens, and another with two paintings of ships – perhaps the *Empress of China* and the *Grand Turk* – with the initials of John Lamb who on 23rd April 1775 urged his fellow New Yorkers to defend the 'injured rights and liberties of America'. Perhaps the most exciting was the huge bowl, 21½ inches across, with a remarkable copy of the best known engraving of New York harbour inside and American eagles outside, with inscriptions inside and out reading, 'Presented by General Jacob Morton to the Corporation of the City of New York, July 4th 1812' and, 'This bowl was made by Syng-Chong in Canton, Fungmanhe *Pinxit*'. Among interesting objects offered by the New York antique trade was a pistol-handled urn loaned by Bernard and Dean Levy which had the initials M.A.L.D. and crest of Mary Alexander Livingstone Duane, wife of the first post-revolutionary Mayor of New York.

The most interesting plans for me were various visits to up-state New York, particularly to Albany where I looked forward to meeting Norman Rice, whose great knowledge of early American silver, particularly that of New York State, had been published in his book *Albany Silver 1652-1825* as part of the Cogswell series. But Norman had a broader interest in New York history with which I could sympathise. On Sunday 1st May I took the train to Albany

A fine 16 inch Chinese punch bowl for Colonel Ebenezer Stevens,
member of the Order of the Cincinnati,
who after Independence owned a number of ships at Canton.

Another fine bowl for Colonel Richard Varick, Mayor of New York in 1789.

(the journey up the Hudson must be one of the most beautiful and interesting rail journeys there is) and Norman met me and took me to the Schuyler Mansion State Historic Site and later to Historic Cherry Hill. We found a number of interesting everyday objects: a Chinese chess set, a washstand set, a camphor wood desk and chest, painted wooden birds and a soapstone pagoda (all in its original packing case) which had been used by 19th Century members of the Van Rennselaer family, as well as their blue and white dinner and 'tea sett' that is recorded in the house inventory of 1852.

After a night at the Fort Orange Club (a long distant reminder of when the upper Hudson valley was the secure home of the Dutch) I spent the morning at the Albany Institute of History and Art, of which Norman was Director. The most interesting loan from the Institute concerned the journey of Captain Stewart Dean in the eighty-ton sloop *Experiment* which, with a crew of twelve, sailed down the Hudson River in 1785 and round Cape Horn to China in four months. He returned after eighteen months with a cargo of 'teas, nankins and costly silk damasks'. Among the 'Nankin porcelain' were thirteen tea services 'for such families as could afford and thought proper to indulge in such luxuries'. An unusual teabowl and saucer, with a design which is not elsewhere recorded, had a 19th Century label with the words, 'Brought by Captain Dean 1777' (intended for 1787). On the return of the *Experiment* in 1787 she is said to have been visited by two thirds of the entire population of Albany, few of whom ever expected to see the sloop or any of the crew again! Norman and I then had lunch with Arnold and Jessie Cogswell, who have become friends over the years, and later I was driven by Bruce Altschuler to Rhinebeck where we stayed at the very comfortable Beekman Arms.

Next day we spent the morning at the Livingstone family Historic House on the Hudson River (the Livingstones having been one of the thirteen families who ordered a tea service from Captain Dean) and then drove to Hyde Park, the Roosevelt home, and the nearby Vanderbilt mansion. After staying the night at Hudson House Inn, by the Hudson at Cold Springs, we spent much of the day at the Van Cortlandt Manor at Croton-on-Hudson and later at the Van Cortlandt Mansion and Park where we had lunch with Joe Butler, and he arranged for a very interesting selection of pieces with New York provenance to be added to the exhibition.

It was just possible to spend a day with Peter and Rodney Frelinghuysen in New Jersey before flying home, arriving in time to guide the porcelain tour to Ireland (already related in an earlier chapter) which took up most of the rest of May. But I was delighted to get a letter on my return from Jim Bell which said in part, '... following your whirlwind tour through up-state New York I am indeed delighted that you found your foray through the various historic houses and museums so productive; the excitement we are all feeling about *New York and the China Trade* continues to mount.'

By early June a new journey to New York was planned and this was largely to enhance and co-ordinate the display of early colonial porcelain, much of which was in the form of shards from up-state New York, but some which had been unearthed in lower Manhattan.

In London as much 'spare' time as possible was taken up in writing entries for the catalogue and this often entailed letters to the lenders – some of whom knew a great deal about what they had, some knowing very little, and in one or two instances there was doubt about provenance. The planned completion date for all entries was the end of September, at which time I hoped to be in New York to see the publisher and co-ordinate the illustrations and copy.

First there was another journey to New York and train to Albany. It was to be all too rushed, but in Albany I was met by Paul Huey, the archaeologist of the New York Parks Department in northern New York State. We drove to Peebles Island where I was able to see a very large array of Chinese and European porcelain shards from a wide range of sites including Johnson Hall near Saratoga, where a young William Johnson had come to the Mohawk Valley from Ireland at the age of twenty-two to manage the estates of his uncle, Admiral Sir Peter Warren, who had married Miss de Lancey of New York. Perhaps fortuitously Sir William Johnson, as he later became, died in 1774 while the estate thrived, for in 1779 it was confiscated by the new Government. Although most of the Johnson Hall porcelain was delftware and English, there were shards from a late Ming dish of *c.*1630, later 17th Century pieces, and fragments of a tea set of exactly the same pattern as had been found at Jamestown, Virginia. The latest ware was of about 1755. I have always regretted that I never had the opportunity to return to Peebles Island, for there was much to learn of early American history in beautiful surroundings.

Next day Jim Bell and I travelled to Washington and stayed at the Hay Adams Hotel again. In the morning we met Pie Friendly, the personal aide to Governor Averell Harriman. I was able to claim a slight link for Mrs Harriman had been Pamela Digby (before marrying Randolph Churchill). Her brother, Eddie Digby, had been in the Coldstream and we used to meet on occasions in Dorset. The Harrimans generously agreed to make four loans which we were able to confirm before catching the afternoon train back to New York. It was also decided to include in the exhibition both a painting and a punch bowl from Mount Vernon, although not directly concerning New York, as similar examples were sold widely in the New York markets about 1800.

I spent the next morning with Dr Nan Rothschild at Barnard College, New

Painting of Mount Vernon, the home of President Washington.
(*From the Director's office, Mount Vernon.*)

Painting of Mount Vernon on a Chinese punch bowl, *c.*1800,
from a similar engraving based on the scene above.

York, and saw the most interesting group of Chinese porcelain pieces which had been discovered at the site of a New York china shop in what was still Hanover Square. They, too, ranged from Ming blue and white from 1630, to a large number of late 17th and 18th Century pieces including some near-complete late 18th Century mugs which had almost certainly been part of the shop stock. The most recent pieces were about 1800 and all had been discovered in 1981 when the site was sold and the developers allowed a team of archaeologists to dig before it was redeveloped close to Wall Street. (In the next street, Pearl Street, New York's first newspaper had been founded in 1726, while the notorious pirate, Captain Kidd, had lived there in the 1690s before his execution near the Tower in London.)

That afternoon I spent at the Abigail Adams Smith Museum (the home of President John Adams' wife) in East 61st Street and after a dinner with Mildred Mottahedeh and a day at Stair with Hope Hood and Angus Perceval, I was back in London.

The next two months were largely taken up with writing the catalogue and it is very clear from the almost daily correspondence with Jim Bell and Betsy Currie that there were some growing tensions over the total failure of the publisher to send the author any proofs or layouts (one could only wait and hope!).

On another visit to New York in October, the question of how many galleries of the Historical Society's very impressive buildings could be made available for the exhibition raised doubts as to whether all the objects collected could be displayed. This, too, had implications for the catalogue production and did not improve an already difficult situation, although much of the administrative problems fell on Betsy Currie and her team.

There was also an opportunity to go to Milton, Massachusetts, to see again Crosby Forbes who had greatly helped with providing a number of pieces of China export silver with links to New York including a gold-topped malacca cane engraved, 'Warren Delano, October 28th 1849', for Warren Delano had spent many years as a merchant in China. His youngest daughter married James Roosevelt in 1880, and they became the parents of President Franklin Delano Roosevelt.

Arriving back in London before the end of October, the correspondence continued apace. By mid November I was delighted to receive galley proofs of the catalogue for the first time. It was reassuringly correct, but I still lacked any indication as to how the 180 to 200 illustrations would be sized, and the layout of the pages. After Christmas, and with a gathering sense of excitement, I flew to New York on 20th January having been told that the publishers would be able to show me the proposed layouts for the catalogue for the first time – but I was not prepared for what came next.

Having gone to sleep at the Metropolitan Club at 8 pm (1 am in London, which I had left after a long day), I was woken by the Club doorman to say that I had a visitor who insisted on seeing me. After dressing, this turned out to be the director of the publishing company who, although he had not made an appointment, said it was essential to get my approval for the page layouts at once because they had to be at the printers early the next morning! As the Metropolitan was not a business club, he said we would have to have the meeting in his car, which was parked outside on a very cold night and contained all the page layouts. As we sat down on the ample front seat with piles of pages stacked behind me he made it quite clear that there was no time to *alter* any layouts – only to comment and 'approve' them.

We sat for over an hour as I gazed at the pages by the light in the car – some adequate, but many containing glaring inconsistencies which could only have been created by someone with no knowledge of the subject: small illustrations of tureens the width of one column, next to custard cups occupying two columns, and pairs of large urns each being quarter the size of a single small teapoy, while the choice of colour plates was not at all representative.

At midnight in a car in the street in January, after many months of careful and precise planning, it was very distressing to have such poor work presented, but clearly all I could do was to acquiesce in the farce (and let Jim Bell know in the morning what I thought of it – which I did in no uncertain terms!).

Although it was a serious strategic mistake on my part not to insist on control of the catalogue at the outset (and this was a mistake I was determined should not be made again in the future) it was comforting to know later that the poor quality of the layout hardly affected the interest with which the catalogue was read. I had two or three sympathetic letters from curators in the museum world who regretted that the catalogue would have difficulty in selling well as a book in this format, and asking if it would ever be possible to republish in an acceptable layout because of the unique contents. In spite of the fact that I still have colour slides of the great majority of objects, this is unlikely to happen.

*   *   *

There was now gathering publicity about the exhibition and illustrated opposite is the invitation which was sent out very widely for the opening preview on 22nd February. But first I had promised to lecture again at Greenwich and enjoyed two nights staying there with Betty and Charlie Wilds.

NEW YORK AND THE CHINA TRADE

COMMITTEE OF HONOR

Chairman

The Honorable George Bush

Committee

Mrs Vincent Astor	The Hon. Arthur Hummel, Jr.	Robert Rauschenberg
The Hon. Bi Jilong	The Hon. Henry Kissinger	Mrs John D. Rockefeller III
John Brademas	Sherman E. Lee	Arthur M. Sackler
Jerome A. Cohen	Bette Bao Lord	M. G. R. Sandberg
C. Douglas Dillon	Mrs Rafi Y. Mottahedeh	Michael I. Sovern
John T. Dorrance	The Hon. Bess Myerson	Isaac Stern
John K. Fairbank	Arthur Miller	Chou Wen-chung
Wen Fong	Mrs Maurice T. Moore	Wan-go H. C. Weng
Peter H. B. Frelinghuysen	The Hon. Daniel Patrick Moynihan	His Excellency Zhang Wenjin
The Hon. Cao Guisheng	Robert B. Oxnam	Theodore H. White
The Hon. W. Averell Harriman		

In celebration of the 200th anniversary
of direct trade and cultural relations
between the United States and China

the Board of Trustees of The New-York Historical Society

and

the Board of Trustees of China Institute in America
request the pleasure of your company
at the opening preview of

NEW YORK AND THE CHINA TRADE

Wednesday, February 22, 1984
5.30 p.m. to 8.30 p.m.
The New-York Historical Society
170 Central Park West
between 76th and 77th Streets
New York City

R.S.V.P. by enclosed
card or by telephone
(acceptance only) to
Mary Moro at
(212) 874-4098

Chinese dress optional

Although there was time to fly home to London for two weeks in early February, I was back in New York by the middle of the month. As the galleries filled with the material for the exhibition on the ground floor there was considerable publicity, including columns in the 'Arts and Leisure' section of *The New York Times* and an excellent 'round up' piece by Rita Reif on the day of the preview, as well as articles in *USA Today*, *The Daily News* and a number of other papers and magazines, and an NBC-TV interview with visuals.

On 20th February, as the guest of Christie's, I was very pleased to give the first annual J. A. Lloyd Hyde Memorial Lecture, sponsored by The China Institute of America and The China Trade Museum at Milton, Massachusetts. It was on Wednesday 22nd February that the Preview opening of the exhibition took place. The feeling of satisfaction was overwhelming and, after more than a year of intense effort, it was a relief that in spite of all the problems the team had managed to draw together, display and catalogue perhaps the largest collection of China Trade wares with specific provenance so far exhibited in America, possibly in the world.

A series of concerts and lectures followed over the next month, with the first occasion, 'Songs and Yarns of the New York China Trade', brought together by the Kendall Whaling Museum and the Peabody Museum of Salem on Saturday 25th, and a lecture next day by the Guest Curator entitled, 'New York and the China Trade'. Later, lectures were given weekly by Clare Le Corbeiller, Arlene Palmer Schwind, Paul Henry, Crosby Forbes and others.

The previous day I had been entertained by the National Society of Colonial Dames in the State of New York to an excellent lunch in 71st Street and gave a lecture in the afternoon. 1984 echoed with memories of the China Trade, but New York was only the first of about twelve exhibitions to honour the bicentenary, of which the exhibition at Philadelphia had the best catalogue, but that in New York was drawn from the widest field.

It all seemed to me to be the close of an exhausting but exhilarating year's work – but one never knows what can be 'round the corner'.

CHAPTER 20

A Pageant of Heraldry in Britain and America

Having returned to London on 28th February 1984, there was just time to try to catch up and be off to Monte Carlo for the Sotheby sales on the 4th and 5th March. Anna and I enjoyed these, and we stayed very comfortably at the Hermitage, just round the corner from the rooms which Sotheby's took for their sales. It was, I think, the last time Heirloom bought for Stair. But there was no time to linger in the sun for Christie's spring sale was on 7th March in London, and I had a considerable number of commissions, for Gabrielle Murdock amongst others, while a major sale of underwater cargo was taking place in Amsterdam on the 14th March.

It was very heart-warming to receive a considerable number of letters from America about the exhibition in New York, and these were particularly welcome when they were from such as Joe Butler and Philip Chadwick Foster Smith, who had just published *The Empress of China*. Perhaps most appreciated were letters from more than one member of staff of the Historical Society itself who were very enthusiastic about the exhibition.

With so much to do in New York concerning the exhibition, I had almost forgotten that at the time I agreed with Jim Bell to be the curator of the China Trade exhibition in February 1983 he had mentioned that it would probably be followed by one on heraldry in late 1984. My only reaction at the time had been that if they would like some heraldic objects, I would be happy to lend them! Some time later in London I had dinner with Colin Cole, a Coldstreamer and recently appointed Garter King of Arms, who told me something of this exhibition which was to honour the 500th anniversary of the founding of the College in 1484. It was to be organised in part by the College of Arms Foundation in New York (of which John Andrew was an active member and later Chairman). Colin told me that the College was co-operating fully but that lines of communication were not always easy.

On Friday 24th February 1984 (the evening on which the China Trade exhibition opened to the public) I had a quiet dinner with Jim Bell and to my great surprise he raised again the question of the heraldry exhibition. It had, I understood, become difficult to co-ordinate between New York and London and there were fears that it would not open on time in October because of other commitments of the outside organisers in America. Jim Bell asked if I was prepared to become involved with part of the exhibition and work with the College in London. I think that my reactions were best expressed in a letter that I had typed by a friend over the weekend in New York and delivered on the Monday I left. In writing it I was determined that there were to be no loose ends or ambiguities, although I gathered it had already been decided that there would be no detailed catalogue, but wall plaques explaining all the exhibits. My letter read:

> Mayflower Hotel
> New York City
>
> February 27, 1984

Dear Jim,

I promised to let you know my feelings after our discussion on Friday evening about the possibility of my acting as guest curator for part of the exhibition which you open on October 17th 1984 in honor of the Quincentenary of the founding of the College of Arms in London. Frankly, it was not something I either expected or was looking for after spending the equivalent of some twenty weeks' work in the last year on 'New York and the China Trade'!

Having said that, I would not like you to think that I was other than a little flattered by the suggestion although a number of problems occurred to me and I would not undertake the task, if offered, without a clear understanding on the detailed points mentioned below. Perhaps you could consider these and when you yourself are clear, you could let me know.

a) It must be quite clear that either the present American organiser has resigned his position willingly or you have already terminated his arrangement. I am not prepared to push anyone out, nor have some kind of shared responsibility.

b) I would like you to undertake to let the Duke of Norfolk and Colin Cole read and understand this letter, for I would not wish to undertake a part in such an exhibition without their positive backing and complete understanding of the position.

c) It would be essential that my task was clearly delineated so that I could work directly with Betsy Currie, your Exhibition Co-Ordinator, and not through any third party. With the short time available, it would be essential to be able to get immediate decisions at any time of the day or night by telephone or courier without waiting for other opinions.

d) I think it very important to have an American section representative of what happened here before and after the Revolution. I have a clear picture of what I would like as the American section. After lecturing in thirty different states in the last decade on armorial objects, I feel I know what raises interest. It would be essential that the College agreed with my approach or something very close to it, for without that I would not feel able to produce the right effect. Key matters would be:

i) A range of silver, porcelain, seals, documents, etc. of colonial times – whether the arms are absolutely correct or containing some errors. This would include families who may have had Scottish ancestry in some cases.

ii) A similar range of objects made during the next century after the Revolution. I understand that the College is not happy, for instance, with the possible display of the Beekman Coach, but this seems to me to miss a great opportunity to make their point. The arms are either not recorded or completely bogus (indeed, quite different from other Beekman arms I have seen) and this highlights an historical fact, of which Americans are well aware, that they sometimes misused armorials in the 19th Century; to pretend otherwise is unrealistic. I would, for instance, balance the obviously bogus coach armorial with perhaps something like the grant of arms to Lord Astor (of New York origin), to show how things can and should be done.

e) Captions and explanatory notes would be of crucial importance throughout every section of the exhibition. It would have to be agreed at the outset that no alterations would be made by your staff to the captions for the American section. If any point was unclear or changes were wanted, this could only be done with your personal approval after a discussion with me.

f) The optimum size and floor space of the American section should be agreed at the outset as far as possible. Say: 20% of floor space; 40 to 60% items. I should then work within that.

g) My concern over getting the above details agreed at the outset is so that there shall be the minimum of time wasted later on. My normal schedule is an extremely busy one of up to 15 hours per day, six to seven days a week and there is no spare time for duplications or misunderstandings. I should be prepared to work on the same basis as the China Trade exhibit (no remuneration – all actual expenses refunded).

I would well understand, Jim, if you felt these terms to be too restrictive, but they would, I hope, lead to a clear, unambiguous approach to the American section which I hope would be in keeping with what the Historical Society would like, for I am sure that a strong American section would be very much appreciated by your visiting public as well as aid the publicity the exhibition would get.

Of course, it may be that the College would not agree to my suggestions and I would happily step down on that score, too. Their feelings and position is so much more important. In order to speed matters, I am sending copies of this letter to the Duke and Colin Cole in England on Wednesday the 29th. You may like to warn them by telephone before then?

With every best wish.

Sincerely,

cc: The Duke of Norfolk, K.G.
      Sir Colin Cole, Garter King of Arms

A few days later I was very surprised to have a telephone call from the Duke of Norfolk telling me that he had received my letter and was in full agreement. I was only able to add that if I were to find myself more or less in control of the exhibition as guest curator, I had to have power to make the final decisions after full discussion; this was, of course, subject entirely to his own authority to direct me on a different course if he wished. (As a former Major General in the Brigade of Guards, the Duke appreciated completely the importance of an absolute chain of command. Throughout the exhibition, and on some occasions over many years later, it was always a delight to work for the Earl Marshal.) Shortly after I had a very reassuring written reply:

Dear Mr Howard (or David if I may!)

Thank you very much indeed for sending me copies of your letters both to Garter and to Dr. James Bell of the New York Historical Society. I know that Garter has followed this matter up with Dr. Bell and I firmly endorse the points he made in his letter. I have also had a most helpful and reassuring letter from John Andrew, Chairman of the College of Arms Foundation.

I am very pleased to leave this whole matter in the capable hands of the Liaison Officers appointed by the College with the support of Garter to determine how best from our side this matter should be handled because my principal concern, as you will fully appreciate, is that the exhibition is of greatest possible benefit to the College and our friends in New York.

Yours ever,

Miles

The Duke followed this with a visit to Heirloom and a detailed discussion ending with an invitation to spend a day at Arundel Castle; it was to be one of a number of visits.

Although I was back for the first major sale of underwater cargo on 14th March in Amsterdam following the quick trip to Monte Carlo, it required a few days to organise the two hundred items for Heirloom stock which arrived very quickly from Holland. On 30th March I was able to have my first meeting at the College of Arms. Apart from Colin Cole I really knew no-one well at the College and it was very reassuring to be introduced to Peter Gwynn-Jones, then Lancaster Herald, and Graham Beck, the Bursar of the College, with whom I would work. They were happy choices for I found both

Peter and Graham quick and decisive, yet willing to listen to any concerns or ideas with which they were unfamiliar. They had already been involved in the organisation so far, but there were numerous matters which needed to be agreed quickly, for it was clear that there were various loose ends and some misunderstandings to tidy up.

I wrote to Betsy Currie on 2nd April (with copies to Peter and Graham):

> I had a good meeting on Friday (30th March) with Graham Beck and Peter Gwynn-Jones and also a talk with Colin Cole, who as Garter King of Arms is the Principal Officer of the College of Arms. I have also had a personal letter from the Duke of Norfolk in friendly and supportive vein and read James Bell's letter of March 16th which seems to agree the proposed working – in consequence you and I seem to be back in business!
>
> Time is now very short and Graham and Peter and I disposed of some outstanding problems quickly in the following way:
>
> 1. The Exhibition may be broadly divided into four main compartments:
>
> a)   The Origins of Heraldry
> b)   Heraldry in the 15th to 18th Centuries
> c)   Heralds and their work at the College – then and now
> d)   Heraldry in America.

and there followed four pages of detail covering a range of matters including the responsibility of all the team – that Peter and Graham should be primarily concerned with 'a' and 'c' and Betsy and I with 'b' and 'd'; how sections would be introduced on ceiling to floor boards; who should be responsible for getting such diverse objects as tents, an armoured knight and a coach with armorials; the time required to bring things from England (for the exhibition was to open on 20th October) and even the title of the exhibition, which was not yet agreed!

I had become accustomed to asking for the loan of Chinese vases, plates and cups and saucers; but coaches, tents, heraldic scrolls from England (but connected with America), collections of heraldic seals, orders of chivalry, helmets and banners, grants of arms – including that of Sir Walter Raleigh and his seal as Governor of Virginia – tabards, Churchill's crest and banner, silver, a fine collection of orders (lent by Commander James Risk), embroidered panels, and such everyday objects as fire buckets painted with arms and bookplates engraved for American families, was a new challenge and we entered it with relish!

Over the next few months it proved possible to find a very wide range of heraldic objects with American history including armorial documents, hatchments, seals or silver and porcelain belonging to Washington, Drake, Calvert (Lord Baltimore), Lord Berkeley of Virginia, Lord Stirling (who fought with Washington), President Adams, and of Perceval, Governor of Georgia. We also found the original painting of the arms of Pennsylvania (and a punch bowl which was once William Penn's), and items of the Goldsboroughs of Maryland and the Manigaults of Carolina, and a number of banners of the early States; the grant to Sir William Johnston; medals bestowed on Indian Chiefs; the pedigree of the Lee family, and numerous objects of silver and porcelain.

One of the more unusual but decorative objects was the sixteen-foot armorial scroll of the Lloyds of Stockton-in-Chirbury, who displayed 323 quarterings showing their family descents. (A reason for its display in New York was that the last Mr Lloyd disappeared about 1923 when he stepped into a New York taxi and was never seen again, although in the 1960s some of his possessions were discovered in a cupboard in America and it seemed as if he *may* have moved with a lady to the mid-west under another name, rather than being murdered as had been thought for forty years! The Lloyd scroll now lives permanently in America, whether or not the head of the family does, or even knows of its existence.)

Because of the widely-spread responsibilities for different aspects of the exhibition, it was necessary that a voluminous correspondence of agendas and minutes, notes and requests should be circulated on an almost daily basis (before the days of faxes and emails), and the responsibility of the new guest curator was, in retrospect, as much one of keeping a balance between the perception of the College of Arms who wanted to emphasise the 500 years of the history of heraldry, and the determination of the Historical Society that the American story was told to the full and that the exhibition itself was not seen to be a remote reflection of a past age of little real concern to New York – with that I was in full sympathy.

Matters gradually reached a common plane, and a four-page letter from Jim Bell with twenty-two queries on 10th April was met by the minutes of another meeting at the College of Arms on 17th April which contained most of the answers. (Meanwhile Heirloom was very busy dealing with a storm of interest in the porcelain from the Chinese wreck of *c.*1643 which kept me occupied in London and Amsterdam.)

A SMALL LOAN EXHIBITION

of

Seal impressions made in the 19th Century by an officer of the Heralds' College – probably Ambrose Lee – from a group of seals of great historical interest of the 12th to 18th Century. The present whereabouts of these seals is not known, but the impressions were sold in a small West Country sale many years ago and given to the present owner in 1974.

1. Walter (de Coutances), Marshall of England 1191-1193(?)
2. Robert, Archdeacon of Chester 1292
3. Patrick Dunbar, Earl of March 1292
4. King Robert Bruce – died 1295
5. John Cumin 1296
6. John Murray 1296
7. John, Lord Bardolph c.1300
8. Sir Robert de Hungerford of Farley
9. William Banaster, Escheater of Salop 1335
10. Gilbert Wace, Sheriff of Oxfordshire and Berkshire 1372
11. Edward, the Black Prince – died 1376
12. Margaret Stuart, Countess of Angus 1378
13. Henry of Lancaster, afterwards Henry IV – before 1399
14. Thomas, Prior of St. James's, Exeter 1428
15. George, Duke of Clarence, drowned in a butt of Malmsey 1478
16. King James IV of Scotland 1473-1513 – crowned 1488
17. King James IV and Margaret, daughter of Henry VII – married 1503
18. Sir Thomas More, Lord Chancellor 1478-1535
19. Mary, Queen of Scots 1542-1587
20. Betrothal ring of Mary, Queen of Scots, and Lord Darnley married 1565
21. Seal found at Stratford-on-Avon in 1810 and believed to have been Shakespeare's ring 1564-1616
22. Mrs Hall, Shakespeare's daughter
23. King James VI and I 1566-1625. King of England 1603
24. King Charles I 1600-1649
25. Queen Henrietta Maria after Charles I's execution
26. James Graham, Marquess of Montrose, executed by the Covenanters 1650
27. Also of James Graham, Marquess of Montrose
28. King Charles II 1630-1685 – when Prince of Wales
29. Frances Stuart, Duchess of Lennox, mistress of Charles II, and probably the original of Britannia on the coinage 1647-1702
30. Queen Mary II 1662-1694
31. King William III and Queen Mary – he died 1702
32. Prince Charles Edward, *soi-disant* King Charles III 1720-1788
33. Henry Stuart, Cardinal Duke of York, *soi-disant* King Henry IX, died in Rome 1807
34. Sir Henry Lee of Ditchley KG – died 1611
35. Ambrose Lee, the Heralds' College, who probably took these seal impressions – before 1896
36. The Heralds' College, London.

The next visit to New York was planned for 20th May and before that an important meeting was held in London dealing with numerous organisational matters from shipping and insurance, to the loan of a full-sized armed knight who would stand by the entrance to the exhibition before a tent specially made in mediaeval style. Unfortunately a fine collection of seals was no longer available because of disagreement between the joint owners, but by a great stroke of good fortune an exceptional group of seal impressions in fine condition was found to take their place (see list opposite). It still intrigues me as to where the actual collection of seals themselves, quite unknown to the College, is today, and how it was assembled in the first place, for the seals are those of many famous names in history.

Unlike the China Trade exhibition, the Heraldry exhibition was to be a considerable social occasion centred round the Earl Marshal of England who would attend a special dinner at Tiffany, make television appearances, and be much in evidence on and before 20th October. My visit to New York in May was to preview many of these arrangements and started with a formal dinner with John Andrew, now as Chairman of the College of Arms Foundation in America, who had invited senior members of the staff at the Historical Society, directors of Tiffany and others, to discuss a special dinner at Tiffany's itself at which the Earl Marshal would preside.

By May, too, the wheels of publicity were turning and it was no coincidence that the *Smithsonian Magazine* for that month contained an excellent nine-page article on heraldry entitled, 'Hail to Heraldry, a most intricate and revealing art.' Jim Bell was also largely responsible for giving details to all the New York newspapers and television studios so that they, too, could plan ahead. But after five days of meetings including important planning for the layout of the very varied exhibits in the galleries, I flew back to London to have final discussions with the College so that Graham Beck could ensure that everything was despatched on time, and also to receive the much discussed 'mediaeval' tents from friends at Bridport, who had been asked to manufacture them specially.

There were only a few days before Christie's second and largest sale so far of underwater cargo on 12th and 13th June, followed immediately by the Ceramics Fair in London. This time a total of more than five hundred pieces or groups of porcelain were to arrive and the next few weeks were much occupied by an Heirloom staff, now four including Clifford Clewley, our accountant, selling and distributing these. But looking back through correspondence, I find eighteen letters to or from the New York Historical Society in the first week of June and one on 12th June from the Queen's Secretary to Jim Bell reading:

Dear Mr Bell,

Thank you for your letter of 4th June 1984 about the Exhibition which the New York Historical Society, together with the College of Arms, are to hold in New York entitled 'A Pageant of Heraldry in Britain and America'. I have laid your letter before The Queen and I am writing to confirm that Her Majesty would be very pleased to loan King George III's Lesser George and King George IV's sovereign sash Badge of the Bath, together with a full set of Garter Regalia including the Mantle for the Exhibition. I am asking Major-General Desmond Rice, Secretary of the Central Chancery of the Orders of the Knighthood, to get in touch with you direct about the details.

I should add that The Queen was very interested to hear about the Exhibition which she thought was an excellent idea and Her Majesty hopes that it will be a great success.

Other particularly interesting loans included an 18th Century herald's tabard from a museum in Birmingham, Alabama; a painting with arms of General Lord Stirling from a family collection in Fort Wayne, Indiana; an armorial stained glass window from Albany; a mediaeval knight in armour from the Metropolitan Museum in New York and a silver spoon from Mount Vernon with the crest of George Washington.

Meanwhile the College of Arms arranged the packing of numerous helms with crests and the appropriate banners of Knights of the Garter, including those of Sir Winston Churchill, and perhaps most dramatic, the Westminster Tournament Roll of the early 16th Century which included a black trumpeter (called Mr White) and the Roll illustrating the funeral of Sir Philip Sydney — priceless treasures which had never before been seen in America. My role by August included the writing of a two-page press release which seemed to have some effect, for various facts were quoted widely in newspapers and magazines that normally would never think of mentioning heraldry.

On 1st October an exceptional and memorable dinner took place at the College of Arms in Queen Victoria Street in London, 'To Commemorate the Five Hundredth Anniversary of the Granting of their First Charter by King Richard III'. It was a splendid 'white tie' affair. I sat opposite Sir Hugh Wontner, then Chairman of the Savoy Group, and to my surprise found myself discussing Frank Goldsmith. On his left was Lord Lyon King of Arms. It was appropriate that the third course at dinner was 'Poor Knights of Windsor' (for

The entrance to the 1985 exhibition
A Pageant of Heraldry in Britain and America.

A gallery of heraldry, New York Historical Society;
Sir Winston Churchill's robes centre back.

this traditional and simple dessert, made of bread, milk and eggs, took its name from the impoverished group of pensioner knights lodged at Windsor in mediaeval times). Short addresses were made by the Bishop of London, Sir Colin Cole and the Earl Marshal. It was definitely an evening to remember.

By now the preliminary publicity was beginning to bear fruit, and the *New York-Pennsylvania Collector* printed a three-page article with a number of illustrations, and the Art Preview in *Newsday* (a magazine which highlighted exhibitions and television programmes) printed a three-column picture of a Georgian herald. Rita Reif in *The New York Times* wrote a long and detailed article entitled 'The Art of Heraldry Displayed', the opening paragraphs reading:

> A panel at the entrance to 'A Pageant of Heraldry in Britain and America', a splendid exhibition on view through Jan. 27 at the New York Historical Society, 170 Central Park West, tells us far faster than words can, why coats of arms came into being. Depicted are dozens of knights in suits of armor. And all the robot-like, steel-wrapped figures look alike.

> Obviously, in battle, with their helmets closed, it was impossible to tell friend from foe. The banners and emblems that were developed for combatants to carry or wear on battlefields and in tournaments, were not only highly decorative, but they were necessary identification, often spelling the difference between life and death. Out of this practical need to know who was who in battle, came one of the most enduring and appealing elements in the decorative arts of Western nations – the visual language of heraldry which was emblazoned on flags, surcoats worn over armor (from which derives the term 'coats of armor') and virtually every object a knight and his descendants might own.

> This lavish and literate presentation, the first major heraldic exhibition ever held in this country, offers a great deal more than a romantic trip to the past for anyone who ever read the tales of King Arthur and the Knights of the Roundtable. The show commemorates the quincentennial of the incorporation of Britain's College of Arms by King Richard III in 1484 and the quadricentennial of the first recorded English-American heraldic device – a seal struck by Sir Walter Raleigh, dated 1584, and bearing his arms as Governor of Virginia.

Above: Detail from the Great Tournament Roll of Westminster, 1511,
a 60 foot vellum roll illuminated in gold, silver and colours, made by heralds to
commemorate a tournament held to celebrate the birth of Prince Henry, the only son
of King Henry VIII and Catherine of Aragon. Exhibited for the first time outside
England, it is shown completely unrolled for only the second time in this century.
(*Courtesy: College of Arms*)
Below: A George III salver, made in New York by Lewis Fueter, c.1773,
with perhaps the finest engraving of the arms of the City of New York done in
colonial times. (*Collection of the New York Historical Society*)

Once the New York Historical Society and the College of Arms had agreed to do this show, and decided on the British material that should be in it, they left much of the organization of the rest to David Sanctuary Howard, guest curator, who is a British expert on genealogy, an author and a London dealer in Chinese Export porcelain. The exhibition combines sumptuous material, extensive history and some provocative insights into why people enjoy wearing and surrounding themselves with heraldic devices that reveal their roots. Collectors will find a feast of materials to admire in the displays of banners, books, porcelains, silver, textiles, and stacks of seals, most of which are duplicated in the marketplace where they can be purchased for anything from a pittance to a fortune.

Most of the material chosen has seldom been exhibited anywhere, especially in a heraldic context. The historical selections sent by the College of Arms – banners, pennants, tabards, vellum rolls, pedigree books, and a 1580s draft grant of arms to the city of Raleigh on what is now Roanoke Island, N.C. – are not on view to the public in London.

*   *   *

I flew to New York on 14th October and was not to return to London until 1st November, although part of the time was spent lecturing in Pittsburgh and Dallas (with a weekend in Nassau).

Among my responsibilities in the week of the opening was the organisation of transport for the Earl Marshal who, with the Duchess of Norfolk, had arrived at the same time and were staying in Park Avenue. A particularly smart piece of marketing was achieved by the Aquascutum company who invited the Duke and Duchess to an opening party of their new premises in 5th Avenue, and on the 15th we followed this with an excellent dinner at the Metropolitan Club at which Miles and Anne Norfolk were the principal guests.

The next day was, perhaps, the busiest, for Miles and Anne Norfolk hosted a lunch at the Westbury in honour of the supporters of the College of Arms Foundation, but then had to attend a ceremony at the Historical Society for photographs taken of heraldic objects by the Royal Mint of London. The evening was to see the most spectacular entertainment when over a hundred invited guests were to have dinner on the ground floor at Tiffany's. The store was to close early and the most elaborately decorated tables with fine silverware were to be set between the display cabinets on the ground floor. To my surprise the effect was successful, with arrays of candelabra set on the glass display cabinets so that every diner felt that he or she was specially seated.

While still at the Historical Society, Miles Norfolk remembered that he wanted to give the Director of Tiffany's a special message and asked if I would mind taking it by taxi but returning as soon as possible with an answer, as we had to dress formally by 5.30 for the reception at the Historical Society at which he was to speak. I arrived at Tiffany's at 3.30 and asked to see the Director as soon as possible. In spite of three further requests I was still waiting at 4.00 so asked if I could see his secretary on the top floor. On arrival there it still seemed to be a problem, and I explained once more that it was extremely important that the Duke had a quick answer. About 4.15 she said she would see if there was any chance of seeing the Director at once and returned to invite me into his office. To my surprise he was sitting talking to Mrs Jackie Kennedy, who rose and apologised most profusely for keeping me waiting. While the Director scribbled a reply, she chatted in a very friendly way, and I left feeling it had been well worth waiting!

Somehow we all reached the Historical Society on time for the reception and by 7.30 were on our way to Tiffany's, where the dinner surpassed expectations. Next day Miles Norfolk was surprised to find himself quoted in the press (and raising some eyebrows) as saying, 'It was a very glitzy affair.' Neither he (nor I) was aware that this was just not a New York term to describe 'glittering'. *The New York Times* started a column with the paragraph:

> Dinner at Tiffany's is better than breakfast, mostly because they bring out the diamonds. The Duke of Norfolk walked in and cased the joint and said, 'I've never seen so much kit lying about'. The Duke added that he hoped the Duchess was not in a shopping mood, but added, 'I've taken away her credit card in case'.

Next day Peter Gwynn-Jones and I met all the Society's docents in the galleries for the first of two intensive training sessions on how to answer questions about the exhibits. This was not difficult because everything was labelled, but required an overall grasp of the subject. Miles Norfolk, meanwhile, had been invited to make a television appearance, and when I met him before lunch and asked him how it went he exploded, 'They kept on trying to make me into a stuffy old Duke but I'm NOT a stuffy old Duke,' and after a pause and with a wink he added, 'Mind you, I know some who are.'

Lunch was a pleasant and relaxing affair with Miles Norfolk, Colin Cole and Rita Reif, whom I had invited to a 'behind the scenes' briefing. We soon covered the essential matters of heraldry and the informal conversation progressed into a range of topics as wide as bringing up children and contraception. Rita told me later that she found it amusing and reassuring that Earls Marshal were also everyday people. (I was relieved that her article made no reference to our discussion!)

That evening there was a dinner at the Colony Club at which Miles Norfolk took the chair and all the heralds and officials from the Society were present. By next morning, with the official opening to the public just two days away, Peter and I again spent much of the morning training docents and after an informal lunch with John Andrew we were ready for another (the last official) reception hosted by Mr and Mrs Danny Davidson on behalf of the principal sponsor, the United States Trust Company of New York, at which a hundred invited guests and some twenty members of the press were present.

The exhibition 'A Pageant of Heraldry in Britain and America' opened officially on 20th October 1984 and every visitor was given a small folded leaflet which included the full text of the four main display boards and other material, and commenced with a foreword by the Earl Marshal, which was our ample reward for months of intense work on the project:

> Today we hear more about our heritage than ever before. Perhaps the most important aspect of this subject is the human one of understanding our ancestors' and family history, and interest in this has increased greatly in recent years. Until now, little has been done to improve knowledge of their visible symbols – our heraldic heritage.

> 'A Pageant of Heraldry' provides a practical opportunity for Americans to get to know this fascinating part of their cultural heritage as it evolved in both Britain and America. It celebrates the quincentennial of the incorporation of the College of Arms – the ancestral home of British and American heraldry – as well as the quadricentennial of English heraldry in America through Sir Walter Raleigh in 1584.

> I offer my heartfelt congratulations and thanks to the Guest Curator – my kinsman David Howard – and to all those in the College of Arms Foundation, The New York Historical Society and the College of Arms, as well as to our many friends whose

objects, whose help and whose financial support have made this colourful exhibition possible. I am sure that you, the reader, will agree that it has been well worthwhile.

Norfolk
Earl Marshal

On the Sunday, I lectured to a full house on heraldic antiques to the same audience as Colin Cole, although we had ensured that we didn't cover the same ground. It seemed, from the excellent attendance on the opening day, that the exhibition would be a success. It needed a steady flow of visitors until February to fulfil initial forecasts. In the event they were met well in time. As always it was pleasing to receive letters of support and interest (although some asked related questions which were often difficult to answer!) and I was particularly delighted that Graham Beck wrote from the College thanking me for being a 'wonderful ally and workmate during our time in New York,' while I had very nice letters, too, from friends at the Historical Society. Under Jim Bell's light but efficient touch I had been able to work for much of the time over nearly two years with no tension in my dealings with the Historical Society and considerable pleasure and experience for me – experience which cannot but stand one in good stead for the future.

On Sunday evening I flew to Pittsburgh to give a long-promised lecture on armorial porcelain at the Carnegie Museum, returning for a night in New York before flying to Nassau for three days with Norman Solomon for a brief holiday after the work of the last month or two, where it was possible to get up late and sit in the sun in spite of it being late October. On the 28th I went on to Dallas to spend three days with Betty Gertz, who had been a major buyer at the sales of underwater cargo and was able to give a lecture there and conduct an amusing auction, of which hereafter.

On the last day of the month I caught the midday flight from Dallas to arrive next day on a frosty morning at 6.40 on the 1st November in London – back to everyday life.

CHAPTER 21

The Hatcher Cargoes in the '80s

Far from the whirl of New York, and many fathoms deep in the China Seas, another display was unfolding which yielded as many interesting exhibits as *New York and the China Trade*. These were to be the various sales of large quantities of Chinese porcelain ware sunk in the South China Seas in the 17th, 18th and later in the 19th Centuries, many of which were salvaged by Captain Michael Hatcher.

Mike Hatcher was born in England but brought up in Dr Barnardo's Homes and as a boy sent to a new life in Australia. He later lived in Singapore and engaged in maritime salvage. His first discovery of porcelain was made while searching the seas for Second World War wrecks which frequently yielded valuable scrap metals. In the first Christie's Amsterdam catalogue of this ware, sold in 587 lots in March 1984, Michael Hatcher wrote, 'I remember from a salvage operation some years earlier that I had sounded a wreck which could possibly have been an old sailing vessel. I sailed for a shallow in the international waters of the South China Sea. Forty metres below the surface I found, as I had hoped, a large wooden ship, whose hull had completely deteriorated. Although the hull had gone, crates containing her cargo stood beside the wreck, intact, it became clear that this was an ancient Asiatic merchant ship.'

Through the energy of Colin Sheaf, until recently the director in charge of the Chinese Ceramics Department at Christie's, a fully detailed catalogue with over 300 pieces illustrated was produced. The work involved in sorting and categorising this ware which was dated to about 1643 (corresponding to a cyclical mark on the reverse of one piece, and the well-known styles of some of the others) was immense, and, as someone concerned with the close dating and recording of armorial porcelain, I found the evidence of such a cargo not dissimilar and very interesting.

Although heavily committed with the new exhibition in New York, I flew to Amsterdam two days before the sale to examine the huge quantities laid out in a warehouse. To my surprise I found in London comparatively little interest in the antique trade in the cargo and was told by two or three leading dealers in the field of early Chinese porcelain that collectors would not be interested because of the damage and wear, and the fact that although a surprising number of pieces were structurally sound, almost all the glaze had a degree of rubbing which would not please collectors of this period.

I had written, amongst others, to Betty Gertz in Dallas (who was recovering from the tragic loss of her husband, Bud, when his aeroplane crashed) about the auction, but had not had a reply before the sale. All in all, while feeling excited about the cargo, I was uncertain as to how it would sell commercially. To my surprise and pleasure she was there on the day, having been in Europe on one of her well-known buying trips and thought the sale would be great fun to attend.

It was reassuring to know that Gabrielle Murdock had asked me to secure an interesting range of objects, and on the day before the auction Julia Curtis had flown over from London and she also asked me to buy a considerable number of the rarer and most interesting pieces. On the day of the auction itself there was a brief interval during the long sale, and we sat on the stairs in the saleroom in Amsterdam and had an up-market lunch from a hamper she had brought over from Claridges – excellent crab paté and wine from smart flasks with coronets!

Among the lots which I was able to buy on commission I found that in nearly every case the hammer price was well within the limit I had been given, although almost all the lots exceeded the top estimate in the catalogue, sometimes by between five and ten times, and it was clear that both Mike Hatcher and Christie's were delighted with the outcome in an uncertain market. Heirloom had spent about £60,000 – about 7% of the sale (which percentage was to remain the same for all the underwater cargo sales in the next decade). It was quite clear, too, that the publicity which attended the event awakened an interest more widely in this country, for every piece we bought had gone before the year end, the great majority within three months of the sale.

After the success of this preliminary venture, a further sale from the same wreck was held in Amsterdam in June, and this time the number of lots was over 1,300 (more than twice the March sale). In spite of tight schedules in New York, it was again necessary to spend two days in the Amsterdam warehouse viewing lots to assess which were in the best condition, as many collectors were particular about this, despite it having been some 340 years under the sea. This time, encouraged by the rapid success of the March sale, there was considerably more competition, but we bought as much again, and once more everything sold quickly. A major independent buyer was again Betty Gertz, who bought a very large number of vases and covers, at one moment in the sale turning to me and asking, 'David, when are they selling those shelves of vases?' I was able to reply, 'Betty, you bought all those about half an hour ago!'

The strain of Heirloom having many hundreds of pieces of porcelain selling so rapidly was considerable, particularly as I was spending so much time in New York. In fact I was soon to see Betty's vases again, for she had arranged a large exhibition and sale in Dallas shortly after the opening of the Heraldry Exhibition, to which I was invited to speak (and auction a quantity of porcelain for her).

A page in *The Dallas Morning News* with a large picture of 'David Howard with one of Betty Gertz's 17th Century Ming Vases' was entitled, 'Chinese junk proves to be the real Ming' above an article which started:

> Indiana Jones would be envious … Captain Michael Hatcher uncovered packing cases filled with blue and white porcelain. He wasn't sure what he had or whether it would bring much money but he spent half a million dollars over five months recovering 20,000 pieces of porcelain from shark-infested waters …
>
> Howard came to Dallas to conduct an auction … among the bidders was Stanley Marcus … Despite its historical significance, Hatcher's cargo was not an immediate success. He first tried selling it in Singapore but nobody was impressed … Betty Gertz now has the finest collection there is.

(Betty was a consummate saleswoman, and at one party a butler dropped a large tray of dishes – to the horror of the guests, who hastily bought what they could. They may not have known that it was a joke, for the tray had been laden with some broken blue and white porcelain!) It was a very successful and amusing evening, and Betty was to bring many more pieces to the Ceramics Fair in London in 1985 where her company, East and Orient, put on a great display with many of the best pieces standing on packing cases.

My short stay in Dallas was enlivened further by a lunch party given by Betty the next day. Among the guests invited was Greer Garson, who had been a personal heroine of mine since I had seen her famous wartime film, *Mrs Miniver*. Unfortunately she could not come at the last moment because of a chill, but we had an uproariously amusing lunch which went on throughout the afternoon, and I sat next to a Hollywood actress who had many stories, including one of when she rang late one New Year's Eve for a plumber to mend a lavatory; the agency sent a man who turned out to be Howard Hughes (who later owned an airline but at the time was out of work). It sounded as if the lavatory was soon forgotten.

It was a measure of Betty's kindness that when, more than a dozen years later, Greer Garson died, Betty bought from an executor her personal seal and two books from her library, and sent them to me as a surprise present because of my disappointment at not meeting her at lunch that day.

Back in London, later in the year, I was able to buy privately from Michael Hatcher some £48,000 worth of special pieces from the same cargo which he had kept back from the Christie's sale and all those, too, were to sell quickly. Although the staff at Heirloom was by now four, I was not sure if it was yet enough for the additional work, so was considering increasing it yet further.

*   *   *

Anna had left her post at the language school and was now an executive reporting to the director of the Banco di Roma in London. This entailed occasional visits by her to Italy while my own journeys to America had been more and more time-consuming. There is little doubt that these separate agendas led to a certain extent to separate lives. On one occasion, when she was away on holiday in Malaysia, I had the pleasure of Frank Mitchell staying with me at Coleherne Court, and in the evening we thought it would be far better to walk to a nearby Italian restaurant than run the risk of cooking at home.

It was in the days of 'strippergrams' (greetings and other messages delivered by pretty girls who, having revealed their greeting card, proceeded to reveal much more). Frank and I were enjoying coffee when a priest entered the restaurant and asked those at the table next to us if he could join them. No sooner had he sat down than he started to undress – cloak, dog collar, shirt and trousers – while to their amazement he was soon only wearing a fig leaf. Reaching down he produced a birthday greeting (from somewhere) which he read aloud to much giggling and then started to dress again, drank a cup of coffee and, leaving a speechless restaurant behind, departed – two Italian waiters saying, 'Good night Father!' as he walked out. It was to be Frank's last visit to Coleherne Court, but was certainly a memorable one.

One member of the Heirloom staff who did mostly secretarial work was a lively and intelligent girl who really wished to be a pop star, but although her boyfriend was in the music field she was only on the fringe. I knew that she had some financial problems but was surprised when one day she asked if she could borrow a considerable sum to pay an advance rental on the lease of a flat and later to have medical treatment which was not available on the National Health Service. Feeling sorry for her, on more than one occasion I gave her a personal cheque for rent or medical expenses (taken from a small legacy from my late aunt, but increasingly with little real expectation of repayment) and had letters, both from her sister, who lived outside London, and her godfather (a doctor in Australia) thanking me 'for my generous help'. Eventually, with increasing concern and after being warned by two male members of my staff that I was being hoodwinked, I telephoned a Harley Street doctor who told me he was giving her intensive private therapy for a serious drug problem – something of which I had been unaware. I later met her at her new London flat which she shared with her boyfriend to tell her that I could no longer maintain my financial support for her medical problems, and made it clear that she would have to leave Heirloom. After she left, I never saw nor heard from her again.

I had confided in Hazel over this worrying situation, but I never discovered whether it was over this or for another reason that Anna confronted me one evening in 1985 and suggested that we should separate, and that I should consider leaving Coleherne Court. With hindsight I can see that our very separate business lives over the previous three years, and particularly my long absences in America on tours and exhibitions in 1983 and '84, coupled with my unwise behaviour (if she knew of it), could have been construed as grounds for the amicable separation that followed, but that this could perhaps have been avoided had we lived closer lives earlier. Our later divorce raised no financial problems and in recent years we still meet occasionally in a friendly way at art functions, while Anna has enjoyed a successful commercial life and in her spare time sometimes lectures and conducts tours in the Victoria & Albert Museum and elsewhere. Soon afterwards, I found a flat in Pimlico and moved there on my own.

*   *   *

The lack of interest from most London dealers in the *c.*1643 cargo, and the fact that Heirloom had later been able to handle a considerable number of other pieces after the auction and sell them quickly (almost £100,000 by the end of 1986), together with, I suspect, some misgivings or bargaining on the part of Christie's, had encouraged Michael Hatcher to bring us details of his next venture in September 1985.

But first there was a diversion of great interest, for I received an official invitation from the American Ambassador and Mrs Charles Price to a reception at the American Embassy in London to honour the lenders (and authors) to what was to prove perhaps one of the most successful exhibitions of the later 20th Century – *The Treasure Houses of Britain* – which had been organised by Gervase Jackson-Stops. A short while later I flew to Washington and was met by a group from the Carnegie Museum of Pittsburgh for whom

I had agreed to act as guide. This was not without some preparation, for I had collected a copy of the impressive catalogue in England and although I had written some of the entries on Chinese Export porcelain, spent almost a week reading the rest of the substantial catalogue so that I should know as many answers as possible! I also took a morning to hurry round the exhibition to familiarise myself with the most impressive layout. After a very full day we had an enjoyable dinner before dispersing in our various directions.

Mine was then to Denver for Philippa's wedding, for she was to marry Bryan Poe, a doctor she had met while he was training at the main hospital there. Both Elizabeth, who had also flown out, and I were delighted. Brian's father and mother, Harold and Joleen Poe, came from Kansas, and Harold had spent much of his life in Dodge City, Kansas, where his forebears had lived for three generations, most of this time in the world of banking. I have always enjoyed Harold and Joleen's company, although I have never become involved in their passion for golf which has occupied much of their later life while travelling in a number of countries. There was an excellent dinner the night before the wedding in a Denver church and a happy reception after the ceremony. We all hoped this would be successful, for Philippa's life had not always run smoothly since she went to America not long after getting her degree, although her cool head had stood her in good stead. Soon after this I had to take a flight, via New York, home.

By January of 1986 we had had a number of detailed meetings with Michael Hatcher over the huge number of cups and saucers in a new cargo, which he was concerned would not sell well at auction because of the sheer quantity. He produced a very long schedule of marketing ideas, but although I was outwardly enthusiastic it was necessary to adopt a more cautious tone in writing, because the new cargo consisted of some 150,000 pieces and the date was rather later, from a then-unknown wreck of about 1750. Had Heirloom had the financial muscle it might have been possible to take the risk of selling these tea pieces direct, but there is no doubt that an auction attracts far more publicity than a private sale. Finance, and the question of a suitable warehouse for viewing when one was in central London, were problems which I felt I could not face with a total staff of five (all of whom had joined since 1982), even though our sales of the 1640 cargo had gone very well. It was also never clear at the time whether this would be the only marketing effort, for no agreements were finalised. However, by February, Christie's auction catalogue was publicised and I awaited the date of the sale. Our negotiations with Mike and his Singaporean partner, Ong Soo Hin, and the large number of photographs and samples we had seen, had given us a far greater insight into what would be available than anyone else. But no-one could have anticipated the whirlwind of publicity and interest which Christie's and the media managed to bring to bear by the sale which started on 28th April and took a week to complete.

Almost as light relief to what was fast becoming the most stressful time I had ever known at Heirloom, was an invitation from the Duke of Norfolk as Prime Warden of the Fishmongers' Company to dine as his guest at their Livery Dinner on 9th April 1986. It was the first occasion on which I had an invitation to dine with a livery company and one which I will always remember for its splendour. The Fishmongers' Company itself is one of the oldest and more prosperous livery companies, and in their great hall were seated about 140 diners at two very long tables, one in the form of an arch and the other up the centre. It was a pleasure to be seated among widely experienced men, from admirals to company chairmen (although I probably knew more of commercial fishing than any of them!). As the evening progressed, I learned too of the rituals of toasts and speeches, and gradually became immersed in the history of the Company.

At his invitation, I later spent a day at Arundel Castle with Miles Norfolk who walked round the castle and the chapel with me, explaining many family and official things displayed. I felt instinctively the aura of a man of natural authority blended with human inquisitiveness but understanding, which I had felt almost twenty years earlier when I had tea with Dr Zakir Hussain, the Vice President of India. We then had a very informal lunch in his office on an upper floor and later, sitting in the drawing room for two hours, discussed a wide range of personal, family and general matters quite outside the field of heraldry, although he said with a twinkle, 'You must have a coat of arms exactly like mine.' This was, of course, impossible, for I could not bear the Earl Marshal's arms, but the coat and crest granted had many similarities and I believe my grant in 1988 includes unique wording, '... and he being desirous of having Armorial Ensigns commemorative of his descent from the family of Howard Dukes of Norfolk, hath requested the favour of His Grace's Warrant *and with his encouragement for Our granting such Ensigns of the said family of Howard with such distinctions as We consider necessessary ...'*. It was as near as Garter could go!

Another enterprise, which arose in the month before the sale, was the offer of a series of lectures on a luxury cruise round England. A vacancy had arisen because an American lecturer could not attend and I would join as one of the three who would speak each day on a variety of topics (including export porcelain). The date was to be about two weeks after the sale in Amsterdam, and in spite of the timing it seemed too good a chance to miss.

In the spring I had made one of my visits to my sister Hazel in Devon where we discussed her third son, Jonathan, joining Heirloom. He had recently completed a course in London in another field and was then living in the Putney area where he later bought a flat. It seemed a happy arrangement, and Jonathan quickly fitted into Heirloom and became interested in export porcelain. Some months later he was joined by Miles Cato, who also wanted to learn the background of the antiques trade and today has a successful business of his own near Sloane Square specialising in Welsh art. I recall that they did not much like my insistence on their doing a typing course, but I was aware that the days of computers were fast approaching, and boys would have to use their own keyboards just like girls.

*　　*　　*

Christie's pre-sale publicity for the sale of the 1751 cargo was both extensive and very successful, with numerous articles in the press, continuous television tapes of Hatcher and his divers at work in their sales rooms, huge advertising with displays of porcelain in many places round the world, and a series of lectures and seminars in the City and elsewhere, with similar promotion nationwide and on the Continent.

The story of the actual wreck and the eventual survival of some of the crew was a particularly interesting one but did not 'break' until after the catalogue had been printed, for there is no mention of this in the introduction. The sale was promoted as 'The Nanking Cargo' (a name which had no direct link with the cargo itself but later became popular as porcelain made in the factories at Jingdezhen was brought down to Canton via Nankin). In fact, it was discovered at the last moment that the porcelain came from the wreck of the Dutch East Indiaman *Geldermalsen* which sank on 3rd January 1752 in the South China Seas.

Dr Christiaan Jörg in the preface to his book *The Geldermalsen – History and Porcelain*, published just in time for the sale, wrote, 'In December 1985 I received a telephone call from Christie's in Amsterdam. Michael Hatcher had found a new ship with over 150,000 pieces of porcelain. Most of it was already in Amsterdam for an auction in '86. Perhaps I could come and have a look?' He continues some paragraphs later, 'But if this find had really come from a Dutch ship, then which East Indiaman could it be? The most obvious candidate was the *Geldermalsen* which had sunk on her homeward voyage in 1752.' By the time he wrote the preface to the book in late February 1986 he had seen the ship's bell which was made in the year in which the *Geldermalsen* was built, and he examined details of the manifest in Dutch records which concurred with what was found, including 126 gold ingots.

The Nanking Cargo.
Thousands of teapots, spittoons and mugs in store at Christie's Amsterdam before the sale in 1986.

Six years later: examining The Vung Tau Cargo in Amsterdam in 1992.

The catalogue appeared in very good time, and while Christie's prepared for the sale, I was able to travel to Holland and spent three days examining the vast stock of porcelain laid out in a huge warehouse, with particular help from Hetti Jongsma who was in charge of Oriental ceramic sales in Holland. I had come to know her well after her help at the time of the sale of the 1640 cargo almost two years earlier. All this gave Heirloom time to write to all the clients who had bought pieces of that cargo from us, and by the time we travelled to the sale we had almost ninety clients wishing to bid up to the extraordinary total of almost £$^{1}/_{2}$ million. Heirloom had not encountered such figures before.

The sale was to last five days and there were 4,785 lots, the largest having a thousand cups and saucers in each lot. It was to start each day at 10.30 from Monday 28th April to Friday 2nd May. In the event bidding did not pause for lunch nor finish on some days until 8 pm. Everything was arranged with great precision, and because of the pre-sale publicity and the huge queues of people viewing the sale (one day almost half a mile long), television and press interest reached fever pitch. At the time of going to Amsterdam we were not to know that in the following week, before the sale ended, the BBC was to show an hour-long documentary on the cargo and its history.

The main room at the Hilton Hotel, where the sale was being held in Amsterdam, was packed, while another room was fitted with a television screen so that everyone in it could see and a subsidiary auctioneer could take bids and transmit them to the main auctioneer. Christie's also had a considerable problem with huge numbers of postal bids. It was just before the time of telephone bidding and commission bids were therefore 'stacked' in order of size and this had the effect in the room of meaning that the price of the first few lots of any pattern tended to be much higher until bidding in the room reached the same level as the lower of the commission bids. The reverse happened at the end of a long run of similar pieces when prices rose, as those who had withheld their hands moved in to bid before it was too late. This pattern of high-low-high continued throughout most of the longer runs of the sale. The art of the buyer lay in choosing the right moment to bid, as much as what to bid for.

The first ninety lots were stoneware bottles and European wine bottles, the contents of which would have been consumed by the officers on board. These sold modestly at about twice the top estimate. For the rest of the first morning blue and white dishes, plates and chamber pots sold for between two and five times the estimates. Prices varied widely throughout most of the afternoon because the mugs and dishes being sold had originally been enamelled, and the price depended on how much decoration remained, which varied from moderately light wear to very little design left. At 7.30 pm on the first evening the 126 eagerly-awaited gold bars were sold for hugely varying prices; we were able to buy three at a little over £6,000 each, while our other commissions fell short. Supper in a Dutch restaurant lasting until 11 pm or later with a rotation of staff from Heirloom, various friends, clients and dealers was a feature of each evening after the day's sale had ended, although planning for the following day also had to be carefully thought through. This could sometimes be a complex procedure as many clients had given us 'either/or' bids so that we could increase the bidding on a second day if we had not been successful for them on the first. This flexibility led to a high degree of overall success on behalf of our clients, but required careful control and constant review during the sale itself.

On Tuesday morning nearly 600 teapots, many in perfect condition, sold for between three and six times the top estimate, and the rest of the day saw tens of thousands of various bowls sold. Wednesday morning was the day of dinner services and sets of plates, salts and sauceboats. We were able to buy a magnificent service of 328 pieces in excellent condition, including tureens, salts and other shapes, for £183,000 for a private client, followed by a smaller one for Colonial Williamsburg for £56,000. Nor were those the most expensive, for a service of nearly 400 pieces sold for £233,000. We were subsequently able to buy a further service privately.

By Thursday the pace had not slackened. Butter tubs and covers were selling at over £1,300 each in some cases (almost ten times the estimate), and 18th Century rarities such as spittoons for £900 for the better examples, while some careful collectors preferred stoneware jars to which had become attached shells and even ferns, creating 'sculptures' in their own right, at comparatively modest prices of about £1,500. Friday was the day of the teabowls and saucers. Mike Hatcher need not have been concerned over these, for quantities unknown since the 18th Century itself sold for up to ten times the estimates – some in lots of 1,000 pieces which sold for about £35,000-£40,000. It would be possible to list many other lots of interest, and the electric atmosphere in the sale room survived the five days to the very end.

Paddle number 1100 (the card of Heirloom & Howard) had spent £784,000 by Friday, of which nearly a quarter was for stock and the rest bought on commission. This was just over 7% of the auction turnover that week. With such quantities one could only hope that the excitement in Amsterdam would be mirrored in London in the coming weeks! Although my bank manager had made friendly noises, he could not have anticipated our buying at this level, although much of the risk was in fact supported by the commissions.

*			*			*

Five day auction of The Nanking Cargo, Amsterdam, 28th April 1986.

Bidders in one room, with paddle No.1100 raised.

On the night the sale ended I had careful discussions with a Dutch carrier, and by offering a premium reached agreement that they would deliver to Hay Hill within 48 hours, for if we were to be successful we had to move fast. This was made possible in part by the fact that a great many lots were already pre-wrapped following the viewing a week earlier. Flying back from Amsterdam on Saturday, Angela and Victoria and the others spent a frantic weekend clearing space for the large number of cartons which would arrive. To my delight they did so on Sunday at about 7 pm in two lorries (when I tipped a driver £50 he turned out to be the firm's managing director – but still took the tip!). By working until long after midnight there was something of a display for Monday morning.

But even this foresight and the long hours could not prepare us for what was to follow, for the joint effect of the BBC programme and an article by Geraldine Norman (whom I had met in Amsterdam) in the newspaper saying, '… but if you wish to have a choice hurry down to Heirloom & Howard in Hay Hill…' had a startling effect.

When I arrived at Hay Hill about 7.30 am on Monday morning there was already a queue at the door. This grew to some dozens by the time we opened an hour later. (Such queues are seldom seen outside Mayfair antique shops!) So many people tried to crowd into the shop to choose a piece from the rows of samples displayed that we were fortunate that a tall friend, Jem Wilyman from Birmingham, who happened to be passing, was able to act as doorman for a while to control the flow. Nor did things slacken throughout the day, and as we gobbled a sandwich from a nearby café, or downed frequent cups of hot chocolate or coffee, the shop remained full until we reluctantly closed the doors at 9 pm. So persistent were the continuous telephone calls, which continued until well after midnight, that I finally took off the receiver. An irate telephone engineer appeared next day to complain that the exchange was being inundated with calls, and that it was illegal to do this!

There were many old friends among those who visited us that week and throughout the next month, but also a number we did not then know. Among these was Roger Bradbury who took a helicopter from Norfolk, and while this spent the day waiting for him near the Thames, he hired a taxi to Hay Hill. It was to sit for four hours outside the shop while he made an exhaustive choice, and then came back for more the next day. Another enthusiastic visitor on the Friday was an Irish entrepreneur who owned a market stall and felt his customers would like a chance to buy inexpensive pieces. He spent more than £3,000 and flew back to Belfast, but to our surprise was with us again the following Tuesday. An unusual visit was from two brothers, scientists at a Hertfordshire research station who had collected a lot of orders amongst their colleagues. They arrived about 7 pm, parking a large Bentley outside the shop, and brought their elderly mother inside where we plied her with occasional cups of coffee. In the end they left with a full load about 11.30 pm, returning several times in the next month. During this time numerous businessmen from Mayfair and the City called in to buy presents for their wives, while even a cab driver stopped and hurried in to ask what he could buy with his fares collected that day.

Meanwhile correspondence rose to an all-time (and almost unmanageable) high and every day brought further orders, including two blank cheques from clients who left it to us to choose. One letter, I recall, was from a house in a particular road in the suburbs. Having posted the cup and saucer, we immediately had orders from seven more customers in the same road! To our considerable surprise we were even approached by a number of London department stores. Harrods had sent a buyer to Amsterdam, but as all the prices had been above his instructions, he returned with almost nothing. We were able to let them have what they wanted at a modest mark-up and felt safe knowing that what we were selling in Hay Hill at a reasonable profit could be bought in Knightsbridge and elsewhere for rather more than twice as much.

*   *   *

It was only two weeks after the cargo arrived in London that I had to catch an early train to Southampton to join the cruise liner *Viking Princess*, and after reaching the quay was shown to a very comfortable cabin on the second deck. I had not been on a cruise before, although memories flooded back of transatlantic journeys of the 1940s. In fact the cruise was not as well attended as expected, because it was shortly after the *Achille Lauro* affair in the Mediterranean when an unfortunate American in a wheelchair was murdered and thrown overboard by terrorists. A number of Americans had cancelled.

The comfort and relaxation was welcoming, and I found that I had a dining table near the captain's with a number of very experienced cruising ladies and gentlemen who together had already crossed the Atlantic and Pacific in the last year, visited Japan, toured the Mediterranean and encircled Africa. They were not, perhaps, the dining partners I would have chosen for every night, but I was a supernumerary of the crew and had no choice.

I enjoyed particularly the company of the other two lecturers: Desmond Guinness (the younger brother of the present Lord Moyne) who was a charming and very experienced lecturer and author whom I had met on a number of previous occasions, and Jamie Crathorne, who had recently inherited his father's title and was a fine art consultant and shortly after assistant to the President of Sotheby Parke Bernet in New York.

The lecture hall on board was luxurious and excellently appointed as a theatre, and in the five days at sea I was only called on to give two lectures (although I had prepared three: on heraldry, the China Trade and on underwater cargoes – which could be combined with the China Trade). The lectures were either mid-morning or mid-afternoon depending on what views could be seen from the deck.

Having rounded The Lizard and the coast of Pembrokeshire, the cruise ship put into Dublin for a day ashore and I enjoyed accompanying Desmond to his father's home, Leixlip Castle, where we had lunch with his elder brother, Jonathan. It was, I felt, the best day of the cruise. Evenings on board were filled with cocktail parties, and after dinner cabarets and dancing in the ample ballroom, which gave me the chance to wander on deck instead, and catch up on sleep after three or four weeks of Nanking Cargo – although, in fact, I had an attack of vertigo which kept me in my cabin a full day.

The Scottish coast, and particularly the Western Isles, where we passed between the Isle of Lewis and Cape Wrath, was the most interesting spell on the cruise, and we then passed through the Pentland Firth and anchored in the Moray Firth off Inverness, where some passengers spent a day on Loch Ness hoping to sight its well-known resident.

Knowing only too well the work still being done at Heirloom, and hearing that I probably would not have to lecture again, as the cruise went first to Norway before returning to Edinburgh, I had arranged to disembark at Leith and caught the night sleeper to London, arriving just before opening time on Monday morning. I had some later correspondence with the cruise line who suggested I lecture on their Pacific cruises on underwater cargoes, but in spite of this exotic offer it was clear that it would be far too time-consuming to fit in with work in London and I felt that once had probably been enough.

*　　*　　*

The Heirloom team had worked very long hours for three weeks, until at least 8 pm, and usually I stayed until midnight. The results were excellent, for we paid Christie's account on time and had a positive cash flow within a month, by the start of the Ceramics Fair. This was not entirely without incident as one morning, at the end of May, Angela arrived at the office at 8.30 am to find two legs sticking out of the small kitchen door at the back of the shop. I had had another attack of vertigo and had to take two days off, going home in a taxi. By the end of a successful Ceramics Fair in early June, at which huge interest was paid to the cargo and buyers ranged from a number of curators, including one from the British Museum, to a great many who had never bought a piece of such standard porcelain before. We were able to buy extra stock ourselves within the next few months and, with a quantity of further pieces from Michael Hatcher, and another large dinner service from someone who had bought it in the excitement of Amsterdam but found it was not appreciated at home, our total purchases were almost exactly £1 million.

By the end of 1986 less than 2% of our purchases from the sale of the Nanking Cargo were still with us, but the memory lingered on, and I treasure the small enamel badge issued by Christie's to buyers at the sale, and still have our Christie's bidding card for the sale in Dutch and English. It was some weeks after the sale that someone we didn't know walked into Heirloom, saw me behind the desk and stopped in surprise. Having recovered his composure he said, '*You* were Number 1100,' and looking at the stock added, 'No wonder – this says it all.'

*　　*　　*

The sale of 'The Nanking Cargo' was seen by many as having been the most extraordinary of the 20th Century, with a wide popular appeal undreamed of, and an anxiety to have 'a piece of the action' in a sale which took place 234 years after it had originally been planned by the Dutch East India Company for the summer of 1752. There was, however, another view which particularly affected some historians and archaeologists. This is well expressed in *Historical Archaeology, Volume 26* by George L. Miller of The Center for Archaeological Research at the University of Delaware, who wrote a carefully-reasoned article which included the following paragraphs among many criticising the salvage:

> … Some archaeologists might argue that *Geldermalsen* would never have been excavated by professional archaeologists because of the logistics involved. However, any wreck that produced $16 million at an auction could have been funded for legitimate excavation.

> … The last comment on Hatcher is that he recorded almost nothing about the ship and provided almost no conservation for the artefacts. After removal from the wreck, the 'goodies' were packed into 1,400 large cartons and carried by a container ship to Amsterdam where it took six people a month to unpack and 'clean' the 150,000 Chinese porcelain vessels.

… Hatcher's strip-mining operation had nothing to do with archaeology other than it destroyed a significant site. He clearly understood the importance of this wreck. David S. Howard, an English expert on Chinese porcelain, gave a lecture on the *Geldermalsen* porcelain at the Colonial Williamsburg Antiques Forum in February 1987. There he explained Captain Hatcher's reasons why this wreck was so important and so well preserved. They were: (1) the wreck resulted from striking a reef, after which the ship drifted about 5 miles and sank; thus, it was not broken up on the reef; (2) this occurred in calm weather, thus the ship remained intact; (3) there was a soft bottom into which the wreck settled; (4) the tons of tea above the ceramics settled in around them and provided a protective cocoon for the porcelain thus keeping them in superb condition; and (5) this remarkably well preserved wreck is accompanied by excellent records from the 32 survivors as well as the ship's papers which have survived in Dutch Archives. According to Howard, Hatcher doubts that he would ever in a thousand years of searching be able to find a wreck meeting all these conditions.

… Hatcher's exploitation of shipwrecks for personal gain could not have been done without assistance. The second player, and perhaps the major force in the destruction of the *Geldermalsen* was Christie's of Amsterdam. Hatcher is only responding to opportunities that Christie's and other auction houses provide. The third player is those who purchase objects ripped from archaeological contexts. Without accomplices, he could not exist.

The article continued in like vein for two further pages and ended:

ACKNOWLEDGEMENTS

This review and commentary came about because of the purchase of some Chinese porcelain from the *Geldermalsen* by the Department of Collections of Colonial Williamsburg. I felt it was necessary to speak out concerning the destruction of an important archaeological site and to make an attempt at educating people concerning the ethical and legal questions related to such acquisitions.

I can well understand the disappointment of an archaeologist at the loss of the evidence that the *Geldermalsen* could have yielded, but Hatcher had no idea of the ship, the quantity of porcelain or other cargo, nor the value, when he risked his life and fortune in this enterprise in international waters (and I doubt that any institution would have underwritten research on what would have seemed a very wild estimate of $16 million gross at the outset).

There was also an unfortunate corollary to this view, for a few years after the sale I met an American graduate student who was writing a thesis on the design of 18th Century Chinese export porcelain, and asked my advice. When I pointed to the clear and unambiguous evidence of the many *Geldermalsen* patterns he told me that he was not allowed by his tutors to use that evidence because it was 'unethical'.

Might it not be argued that while it was particularly sad that on this wreck site which unexpectedly proved to be of considerable historical interest, that so much evidence was lost, that it was equally sad that the considerable and clear historical evidence that *was* yielded should be forbidden to be used in teaching – to the detriment of the very learning that historians and archaeologists seek to foster? Closing one's eyes does not make what is in front of one's face any different.

CHAPTER 22

From Hay Hill to Grafton Street

As a moment of academic calm, just as the excitement of the underwater cargoes was building to a commercial frenzy in 1986, I had a most interesting chance to be involved at a different level with an exhibition of great interest. *The China Trade 1600-1860* was the successful creation of Dr Patrick Conner at the Royal Pavilion Art Gallery and Museum in Brighton, and was held to recognise the way in which the Prince Regent had sought to furnish the Pavilion with objects ranging from Chinese tables and chairs and lacquer furniture, to wall hangings and porcelain, the Pavilion itself having been created in oriental style.

Patrick's catalogue remains an excellent record of a well-organised exhibition, and I was delighted to be asked to contribute a chapter on porcelain (and provide many of the seventy items exhibited in that section). Following my New York experience this was not at all stressful, for Patrick took all that load. It was, however, an exhibition which placed greater emphasis on the breadth of the whole China Trade and in that way was a forerunner for an exhibition of which I was to be curator in the '90s. The reception and dinner in the Music Room at the Royal Pavilion, given by the Mayor, was a most enjoyable occasion and was also attended by the Chinese Ambassador and his wife.

It was also a stroke of good fortune that shortly after the initial tidal wave of activity of the Nanking Cargo had passed, the lease of No. 1 Grafton Street, on the corner of Hay Hill and in our building, came on to the market as the very long established booksellers, Charles Sawyer, were moving. It had a prestige position, windows facing each street and mezzanine and basement floors, as well as providing twice the display area as our existing gallery. After a struggle we managed to secure the lease with the help of Peter Cranham, our property adviser, and were able to move quickly, for we only had to carry furniture, books and stock to the opposite corner of the building, while keeping our existing basement for storage. Our happy home of ten years shortly became a sandwich bar – and is so still. It was fun to have an official opening party on 6th November to which we invited numerous friends, with champagne and excellent refreshments provided by a well-known caterer of the time. The everyday life in Hay Hill for the last thirteen years had introduced us to a very wide range of enquirers and clients, some of whom

Heirloom & Howard Limited, 1 Grafton Street, Mayfair, 1989.

Outside 1 Grafton Street with my nearest American blood relative,
Mrs Sarah Clarkson of Columbia, South Carolina.

had become friends and are still today. Many started as chance acquaintances who came into Heirloom to enquire about an object, or ask if we could let them know if we found anything of their family.

James West, whom I soon found had inherited much of what remained of the service illustrated on the spine of *Chinese Armorial Porcelain*, became interested and when in London accompanied me to a number of sales. I enjoyed staying at Alscot Park several times, and James and Camilla kindly invited a group on a porcelain tour on one occasion. It was very sad that he died quite young, for he loved Alscot which his ancestor (also James) had bought in the early 18th Century and whose son had married a descendant of Sir Christopher Wren.

It was fun, too, to make a new friend in David McAlpine, who travelled widely on behalf of his family company, well known in the construction industry. By chance both he and his elder brother Alistair had been in Grafton House at Stowe (although he was born the year I left). But our common interest now was armorial porcelain, and this was to be tested to the full in 1988 when the Bullivant Collection was sold.

Another interesting friend was Sir Nicholas Fairbairn, whom I first met at Lennoxlove while staying with Angus Hamilton and who later made regular visits to Hay Hill. He was furnishing the ancient Scottish estate of Fordell Castle with taste and historical perspective, and invited me to stay, for he had chosen the medium of armorial antiques to enhance the interior, enjoying both their quality and stories. As a friend I found him very different from his public face as a minister and lawyer who had a knack of attracting the headlines.

Of the well-known banking family was Neil Ivory, who lived with his wife, Joan, in Canada, but was very frequently in London on business. Their modest charm and later serious interest in export porcelain made them natural friends, and when I later went to Montreal I was able to stay with Joan after Neil's sad and all too early death. As a collector he followed the salerooms closely and immediately after the last occasion that we bought a number of pieces for him he had to have an operation. It became a family joke that when he woke up afterwards his first words to Joan were, 'Don't forget to pay David Howard'! Some of his carefully chosen pieces are now in a Canadian museum as a tribute to Neil and his interest in a product which had fascinated other merchant bankers over three centuries.

Mildred Mottahedeh always spent time in Hay Hill when she was in London, and we often discussed the designs of export porcelain and her latest ideas over lunch or dinner at Browns Hotel in Dover Street, and on other occasions she brought friends. One such was Carol Price, the wife of the then American Ambassador to London – a visit which almost ended in disaster, for a copy of my weighty book fell on her foot and we feared that she might have broken a toe. On another occasion, late one Saturday evening, I was still in the shop when a quiet figure wandered in and asked if I had anything with the arms of Holden, which by a stroke of good fortune we did. Something about his familiar face 'reminded' me of Toulouse Lautrec, about whom I had recently seen a film. When I was given a cheque it was signed 'José Ferrer', and he told me he was on his way to stay with his fellow actor, Bill Holden, in Paris. We talked for a while and he mentioned the extreme discomforts of walking while filming with one leg tucked behind him. We also discussed the heraldry of Ferrer – we felt almost certainly horseshoes. 'Why not,' he said, 'I'm sure Verdi had a lot of green in his coat of arms.'

Larry Hagman, then very much in the public eye with his part in *Dallas*, and Linda Evans from *Dynasty*, both visited us on more than one occasion (and I had to use all my powers of persuasion to advise Linda Evans *not* to buy two nice armorial saucers for ashtrays). Cliff Robertson was very keen to find Robertson objects, and when I told him there were a number of Robertsons looking he was delighted to meet Duncan Robertson from West London, and we had lunch together at the Oriental Club – an interesting afternoon which didn't end till teatime.

There were also moments of amusement as when Sir Humphry Wakefield – much at home in his leather motor-cycling gear and helmet – tried to deliver a package to me late one evening in Grafton Street but had to leave it at a shop nearby, for we had left. When we were given it in the morning their secretary said, 'A courier left this for you last night – seemed to be a bit of a gent.' Humphry was enormously amused on being told! On another occasion a visitor came in and, seeing a copy of *Chinese Armorial Porcelain* lying on the desk, said, 'Glad to see you've got that, it's quite useful – the author's dead now of course you know.' Yet again there was almost a moment of drama when I explained to an American lady who had come into the shop the arms and date of a piece on display. 'I think you're wrong,' she said, 'Now if you look in Howard's book on the subject you'll find he says it's something else.' Luckily the telephone rang and I was able to disengage myself for a moment but had to return two minutes later to say, 'I think it's only fair to tell you I *am* David Howard.' (Her husband laughed so much that I thought he would choke!)

Harold and Joleen Poe had visited Heirloom on a number of occasions when in England, and as great golf enthusiasts had played on many of the finest courses in England and Scotland. I recall a telephone call one day from Harold arranging a visit and when I asked where he was he replied, 'I don't rightly know, David, but it's a very nice course half way up on the right hand side.' (I later discovered this was in Lincolnshire.) From time to time some of their friends would also visit Hay Hill, and on one occasion a tall military-looking man wearing a Stetson hat came into Heirloom and asked to see me. When Jonathan asked who he was he replied, 'I'm the Sheriff of Dodge City,' and turned a lapel to show his badge. Indeed he was, and a friend of Harold's who had been brought up and lived in Kansas when it still had memories of the pioneer west.

Two experiences, which I'm glad were not repeated, included on one occasion an earnest well-dressed man coming into the gallery who, after looking round, asked if he could examine more closely an armorial hung high on the wall. Miles and Jonathan fetched a ladder and with a bit of difficulty took it down so that he was able to have a closer look, but he decided not to buy. When I returned I asked where a rare teapot had been moved to; we never saw it again and Jonathan and Miles could only recall that their client had been wearing 'a long raincoat'! On another occasion, a seal with the arms of the East India Company, which had the word 'Chief Secretary' beneath the arms, disappeared. About a year later the ever-watchful Donald Wilson told us he had seen 'another' in the Silver Vaults in Chancery Lane, being told that it had just been bought in Canada. It was, of course, the same, but neither our insurance company nor we were anxious to trace its recent history. But it did illustrate the homing instincts of armorials.

*   *   *

There had, from time to time in the past, been opportunities which I would not have liked to slip by but didn't always have the cash flow at the time. However, a lifetime friend of my Danish brother-in-law, Oscar Husum, was often willing and able to step in and, for a fair commission, help us. One of these was the extraordinary chance to acquire almost six hundred small gilt metal stall plates of the Order of the Bath: KB (before 1815), GCB, KCB and CB, the great majority of which had been awarded towards the end of the Napoleonic Wars. For reasons of space they had never been installed on the walls of the Henry VII Chapel in Westminster Abbey, because there were so many that the Dean at the time was concerned that the plaster would be damaged. These armorial plates, finely enamelled on gilt brass with names and armorials, had been disposed of in the late 19th Century and had remained in the attic of a grandson of an official who had acquired them. Heirloom was able to buy them (each still wrapped in contemporary newspaper), and I set about finding the descendants of the Knights and Companions of those days, being successful in about half the cases – the others being sold, after every family avenue had been explored, to collectors. All left Heirloom in less than two years, to the considerable satisfaction of some families who were able to find such interesting historical objects associated with their ancestors. I was particularly pleased that the group included two of my own ancestors: the KCB plate of Admiral Sir Henry Trollope and the CB plate of Captain George Barne Trollope, his brother.

Another venture on a less grand scale occurred when we were able to acquire the seven thousand or more armorial family printing blocks used by Burke's *Peerage* and *Landed Gentry* over more than a century, and offer them also to the families named. These had been stored for more than a decade in old ammunition boxes and a great many had no labels, requiring considerable research in identifying the families. The fact that a few remaining ones are still here today speaks as much for families dying out as for lack of effort!

But these ventures were to pale into insignificance when shortly after the Nanking Cargo we were offered in the summer of 1986 the entire stock of portrait engravings of a very well-known print seller in Cecil Court (near Leicester Square) which had been in the Suckling family for more than a century, together with their portrait library and sales catalogues. Over a great many years some eighty thousand engravings had gradually become less accessible as they had been examined but not filed back in any order, and it took an American researcher, Yvonne Logan, the whole of the summer to 'alphabetise' them (the word alarmed me at first but it is now as familiar as 'categorise' – which the Oxford dictionary tells us has been in use since 1705). Almost all portrait engravings are taken from earlier portraits in oil, watercolour or drawings and never from real life. Many have additional heraldic identification, and in some cases the engraver is as well-known as the original artist. After many years of trying to restore these to families who have particular interest in their ancestors, I well understand how the Sucklings had built a business round them lasting three generations over a century. Among other aids for learning the history of the huge numbers of named sitters, I found that there was an excellent set of six volumes published by the British Museum from 1908 to 1925. Unfortunately Suckling had lost two volumes so I wrote to the Museum to ask, without much hope, if they had any remaining. To my surprise they did, which they supplied at the original published price – two guineas. When Yvonne left, the work was continued by Caroline Weeden who undertook the huge task of entering the details of more than thirty thousand different engravings on to our computer, which took more than a year and is still an indispensable record today.

As our clientele continued to grow, so too did the list of family names in which people were interested. Despite some eight thousand names it was difficult always to find the objects which they hoped would appear. Occasionally there were moments of good fortune as when we wrote to a well-known Cornish family about an elaborate embroidered armorial fire screen with their arms, only to receive an ecstatic telephone call – for they still owned the original drawing used by the embroideress, but the screen itself had passed out of the family a century earlier to the children of a second wife.

Increasingly, the large number of contacts we made among those interested in heraldic objects led people to ask our advice on identifying the arms on pieces in their own possession. This was sometimes for family research, but was often so that an object would realise its full potential in a sale. Occasionally dramatic differences in value could result from such discoveries, as when a spoon with 'two crests and a coronet' was found to belong to Lord Nelson and date to beween 1801 and '05, and when the arms on a unique but damaged Rockingham vase, bought cheaply by a dealer from a country house 'attic sale', showed itself to have been made for that house, was bought back by the present title-holder and is now in a museum. A fine armorial wooden bench was sold for £32,000 at Christie's in 1994 without attribution, but eight years later its pair, now identified as having belonged to William Beckford, sold for £240,000. There can be no doubt that provenance has a value, although this can be unreliable unless supported by armorials.

The work entailed in identification is frequently considerable and time-consuming, but is aided by an essential research library which has been built up over many years. It is also made much easier if good colour photographs are supplied, for many significant heraldic details are small and can often be overlooked by the amateur eye. The armorials also depend on colour, without which most can be interpreted in numerous ways and are often not otherwise identifiable except by motto, which itself may represent many families and is therefore not always reliable.

All this prompted us to try to create new armorial objects ourselves – heirlooms of the future – and one of the earliest efforts was in table mats which could be laminated so that they would withstand considerable use. Small 'library' paintings of armorials, something which had been particularly popular in the second half of the 18th and early 19th Centuries, could be ordered and almost everyone preferred their modern painting to be 'in 18th Century style'. Sets of engraved drinking glasses and decanters with armorials were also popular although it became more and more difficult to find craftsmen to fulfil these orders.

The great success of Honoria Marsh, a very talented artist and glass engraver who illustrated an anthology of Jane Austen novels with silhouettes of living characters dressed appropriately to the novels themselves, led us to consider miniatures, but although Honoria occasionally engraved a special glass for us, it was her personal company and lively anecdotes we enjoyed most, and we frequently had lunch together when she was in London. I recall her reliving an earlier and closely-fought court case in which she had to cross-question her accusers. She turned to the judge and said, 'Your Honour, may I call him a rat?' The judge replied, 'Certainly you may, Miss Marsh.'

Another and very long-lasting friendship was formed when I had approached, somewhat earlier, Anne Gordon, a most talented porcelain sculptor and painter, about the problem of creating modern armorial porcelain, and she produced numerous samples based on English porcelain. In the event it was not to be this which encouraged us to work together but her ability to model figures of any animal or bird and thus create white or painted models of crests. I particularly liked a pair of boar's head crests which I bought for myself and learned that they were one of only two such pairs made with the Gordon crest. Some years later I was in Chris Weld's library when I saw the other pair which he had bought in New York! But our contact over porcelain, and Anne's love of being a generous hostess, made it a pleasure to visit frequently Anne and Alastair Gordon – a talented artist in his own right who eventually, and surprisingly, inherited the Marquessate of Aberdeen (descended from the Victorian Prime Minister) even though his father's fourth son. Alastair's love of fun prompted him to write a book of amusing and risqué reminiscences which his many friends found endearing. (Some years later we were having lunch with Anne and Alastair's son, Alexander, in his Scottish estate when he announced that he had been clearing out an old gun cupboard the day before and found a gun case left behind by a former guest, Theodore Roosevelt, when he had been shooting there about 1910 after he ceased to be President. It wasn't to be the only, very brief 'acquaintanceship' I had with Theodore Roosevelt.)

Some time later I was to be introduced to a most creative and competent painter of porcelain called Michael Minoprio, who had a wide grasp of business and had founded a small company which specialised in supplying replacements for dinner services and, on occasions, whole dinner services themselves. With experience of the potteries in Staffordshire and Derbyshire, Michael's company 'Country Work' already had a wide clientele from his base at Locko Park, but we were able to introduce a number more, and in particular we co-operated over orders received from the London gunsmith Holland & Holland (for Michael was also a keen and regular shot). Eventually he employed a painter who had worked at Derby and set up his kiln at 'The Old Cowshed' near Mackworth (I recall that to visit, one was instructed to turn in 'opposite the green grain silos'). But there was nothing green about Michael's ability to provide a very accurate copy of any design, and one order in particular, later in the '90s, required the creation of a dinner service copying exactly a fine Yongzheng armorial service of about 1730 for a client who was descended from an East India Governor and still had part of the original service but did not wish to dine from it because it would destroy the delicate silver and gold decoration. All this echoed what the Mottahedehs had achieved in America in previous decades.

*   *   *

After a brief visit to New York in January 1987 for the auctions and the Winter Antiques Show, I travelled down to Colonial Williamsburg to speak at their Antiques Forum. Interest was still at a very high level over the Nanking Cargo, and Williamsburg had bought one of the smaller services from us. I spoke on the recent sales in Amsterdam and tried to place them in perspective as far as designs and dating were concerned – showing also comparative pieces with export subjects, including armorials, of the same dates. I also stressed the rarity of the Nanking Cargo as far as its condition was concerned because of the exceptional circumstances in which the *Geldermalsen* sank in calm seas after striking a submerged reef, for the cargoes of most wrecks are usually shattered by impact on the break-up of the vessel in a storm. Afterwards I flew to Washington for my flight home, and in a small plane from, I think, Charlottesville to the capital I sat beside an official-looking man whom I noticed had an impressive briefcase marked 'Top Secret' (clearly someone in the CIA). It wasn't until we disembarked in Washington that I saw that his case had on the underside 'Bottom Secret'.

But 1987 was to be clouded by more than one unhappy event, and it was very sad that after so much work and the publication of his excellent book, *La Porcelaine des Companies des Indes* in 1986, François Hervouët should have died, not living long enough to enjoy the real success it achieved. I missed his and Nicole's visits to London, and in the following June Sotheby's held the first of two intended sales of their collection in Monte Carlo. I was pleased that my sister Hazel could join me after her own bereavement, and we spent a busy long weekend in the sun. Heirloom made some modest purchases, but as always it was the delightful cafés, and dinners looking across the sea, that were most fun. (The auction of the second part of François Hervouët's sale in London in November was severely curtailed by the French Government who pre-empted the sale of numerous objects on the grounds that they were of national interest. In the event they were sold at a provincial sale in Brittany the following spring which Jonathan attended to represent Heirloom.)

François' departure was to be followed by that of another dear friend. After Cecil Bullivant's death in 1981, his wife Muriel had continued to live in their house in Minehead. I had been able to visit her on a number of occasions since then and in the period immediately after his death she had asked Heirloom to dispose of a number of objects which no longer fitted in the many cabinets of porcelain in the house. I still have all the correspondence of those days, for Muriel confided in me as far as porcelain was concerned. Three years later she asked that I approach Sotheby's to make an inventory, and following this wrote to say that when she died she would like me to finalise arrangements with them, which I promised to do at no cost. In late May 1987 Hazel and I, with Jonathan, spent a day in Minehead and we arranged to come again in July, while Muriel herself was in good spirits. On 11th June I had a letter from her which was clear about her plans for the future. But she died suddenly at the end of June and as I wrote to her cousin, Tom Gotobed, 'Muriel's passing marks the end of an era, I feel.'

Muriel kindly left me a small legacy, but I remember being very surprised that the executors did not ask my opinion over the collection as she had told me they would, and the sale of the porcelain unexpectedly went to Phillips who had a strong local agent, rather than Sotheby's (who had some objects already in their vaults). The will, of which I have a copy, also left rather more than 80% of the estate to a number of animal and other charities, to the considerable distress of some close relatives including her stepson, John. The will made it inevitable that the charities should sell the house, and all the other assets, and this is what happened.

In the years immediately after the second war, Cecil had been able to acquire a number of fine early services from families who no longer had heirs, or found the sale of heirlooms a convenient way of paying school fees, or renewing crumbling roofs. Prices in the post-war period were often very modest and because of Cecil's understanding of heraldry, an attribute surprisingly not shared by any other antique dealer at that time, he was able to sell pieces privately to other members of the family, or acquire for himself pieces of significant historical interest. (Occasionally he was rebuffed and I recall a label on the reverse of one item reading, 'On no account is this to be offered back to the family – they are a most unpleasant lot.' When I later bought the piece, I sold it to a family member I knew and gave him the label. He was most amused and said, 'My uncle *was* a very difficult man!')

In consequence of my own book, which at the time of the sale had been published for over a decade, and the fact that this included details of three times the number of services that Tudor-Craig had published in 1925, and illustrated a far greater number including all Cecil's collection, the subject was better understood by a range of dealers and collectors and the value, particularly of pieces of historical interest, had increased very substantially in the forty years since the war had ended.

Despite the unexpected change of venue, Phillips prepared an excellent catalogue for the armorial porcelain with a high proportion of the lots illustrated, and this included about 550 pieces in 380 lots. The sale in March 1988 encouraged considerable world-wide interest and among those whom we met were Peter and Barbara Miller from Canada, who had already started a collection and were increasingly to become friends. As a successful independent merchant banker Peter was always conscious of value and it was comforting that he regarded armorial porcelain as a safe investment. All too often collectors are carried away by their enthusiasm without particular regard to value.

The catalogue was produced well in advance, and Heirloom was besieged with bids totalling (after duplication had been eliminated) just over 400 pieces, which we had been asked to bid for at prices ranging from the top estimate to more than five times that figure. On the day of the sale the Heirloom 'contingent', including a number of American collectors, sat in three rows in the saleroom, and although the bids on every lot were agreed beforehand, I was not infrequently asked to bid higher as a limit was passed. That evening Heirloom received an invoice for £476,000 from Phillips (some 57% of the sale) and about thirty clients had been successful.

Cecil Bullivant had been the archetypal dealer-collector who had built his collection over sixty years, and armorial porcelain had indeed seen a very considerable rise in value over that period – probably by more than two hundred times – largely because of increased knowledge of its origins, a key factor in most collecting of antiques.

CHAPTER 23

And so to Bath

Whilst the interest generated by the sales of the Nanking Cargo in the summer of 1986 and of the Bullivant Collection in 1988, and the consolidation of Heirloom in their new and more prestigious site at the corner of Grafton Street and Hay Hill dominated the late 1980s, there were numerous activities which mirrored our trading in the 1970s and early 1980s which were to occupy the years up to 1989 when our relative size and capital base, and the fear of an approaching general economic downturn, led me to question whether a company of our size, although trading comfortably, could afford to support the very high overheads of central London, however convenient and prestigious. (By 1989 almost £50,000 per year was spent on rent and rates alone; by the early '90s it was to become more than twice that at the same premises.)

But the new premises to which we had moved in the late summer of 1986 suited us perfectly and were a delight to work in – particularly the considerable space now available to re-catalogue and display our huge stock of engravings, and the increased level of stock of all kinds which we could meaningfully display. For much of this time the total staff numbered between five and six, with Angela, now the manager, increasingly focusing on exploring how a computer could enhance our stock control and trading, and Jonathan and Miles fulfilling various roles and increasingly new initiatives. Clifford Clewley remained a solid and reliable accountant, and when Victoria Horton, who had been so essential at the time of the Nanking Cargo, and Yvonne Logan, who worked on the re-cataloguing and providing computer records for the engravings, both left, we were fortunate to have found Caroline Weeden, who gradually assumed most of the secretarial roles.

Meanwhile the pace of life continued in the educational and academic field which had occupied much of my time in the late 1970s and early 1980s when, on average, I was undertaking two major lecture tours in America and a porcelain tour in England each year.

A pleasant interlude in late September 1987 had been meeting an American tour party organised by Elizabeth Smith of the Carnegie Museum of Pittsburgh, with Robert and Pat Wilburn, the President of the Carnegie, and others including Henry and Lou Gailliot, and Talbot and Carolyn Hiteshew who were to become friends in the future. We met at Heathrow and the compact party travelled by bus to Hambledon Hall near Stamford. The following day was spent at Burghley House with Victoria and Simon Leatham, while John Bly joined us for lunch in the family dining room and later gave a lecture on the Burghley silver. That evening they were all our guests at dinner at Hambledon. I recall that cocktails started early, but we were the last to be seated at dinner!

On the Thursday we were the guests of Marian Brudenell at Deene Park, and on a perfect September afternoon drove to Rockingham Castle where we toured the castle and gardens (and enjoyed the commanding view) while Commander Michael Saunders Watson gave us a brief historical background. Next morning we left Oxford and drove to Broughton Castle where Nat and Mariette Saye and Sele gave us a tour of the house and coffee, before turning south to Winchester for a two-night stay. A morning in Winchester was followed by a visit to Broadlands where the party learned the story of Lord Mountbatten, while in the evening we visited Roydon, where Edward Morant and his wife gave us a splendid dinner and we were able to see much of perhaps one of the most interesting armorial services, with a Chinese tureen modelled after a silver original by Paul de Lamerie. The short tour ended next day with a visit to The Vyne in Hampshire, long the home of the Chute family descended from Chaloner Chute, Speaker of the House of Commons in the mid 17th Century, and we reached London in the evening having had an exhilarating week with rather more history and less porcelain than usual.

Among two or three lectures which had proved particularly interesting to me at that time was one to the Cambridge University Heraldic and Genealogical Society which I gave in Clare College, staying the night at the University as their guest, and another in the following spring to the Oxford Heraldry Society. It was at one of these that I illustrated a rare piece of porcelain painted in China with the inscription 'Dr G.B.H. Wright … presented by Fung Pak-liu'. As I read the inscription a semi-somnolent professor on a sofa near my lectern sat up suddenly and said 'What? What?' I had indeed called out his name!

In the spring of 1986 and 1987 I spoke to students at Christie's Fine Arts course and at Sotheby's Institute on several occasions, and it was encouraging to discover the considerable and increasing investment of both companies in education in the art field. As one who had experienced the link between fine objects and their provenance, I felt strongly that the more information that was available about something, the more sought-after it would become – and thus the more highly prized, not only in private collections but in the art market itself. My over-riding interest, however, was in the field of history, information and provenance.

It was a surprise and pleasure to be asked by Clifford Henderson to make a speech at his fiftieth birthday party which was held at Althorp with Earl Spencer and his wife, Raine, Countess Spencer, guests at the dinner. More than twenty-five years earlier I had visited Althorp at the invitation of the 7th Earl, who was then Chairman of the Advisory Committee of the Victoria & Albert Museum, so that I could examine and photograph the armorial porcelain. This later occasion was a most enjoyable evening and I particularly noted the great improvements of the last two decades. I had managed to obtain a copy of *The Times* for Clifford's actual date of birth in 1938 which provided some fascinating comparisons; while I realised, as I put on my dinner jacket (which had been my father's), that the date on the inside pocket was also 1938!

An invitation by the Swedish antique dealer, Björn Gremner of Antikwest, in Gothenburg, to speak there at a seminar devoted to the further excavation of the Swedish East Indiaman *Götheborg*, which sank entering Gothenburg harbour on 12th September 1745, had been accepted with alacrity. Although the subject of salvage operations at various times since, particularly immediately after the sinking, and again in the early 20th Century (when the work was curtailed because Swedish Customs claimed duty on the salvaged cargo!) the continuing work by Swedish enthusiasts was revealing more information all the time and our seminar was to continue in that vein, providing the opportunity to see the exact position of the sinking and to examine the great array of objects salvaged over the previous 243 years. According to her cargo manifest, the East Indiaman herself had on board some 6,000 ingots of silver, nearly 1.2 million pieces of porcelain, a thousand square metres of silk and 370 metric tons of tea. The ship was within half a nautical mile of the quay when it ran aground and sank, and a contemporary effort to salvage and dry the tea for use caused an outbreak of plague in Gothenburg because it contained a number of dead rats.

The success of the Hatcher salvage operations had provided a stimulus for such a conference, and all the leading Swedish academics in the field gathered in Gothenburg for the occasion. I was delighted to meet and dine with Professor Bo Gyllensvard and Jorgen Weibull and others from Finland, including Professor Sourander, as well as Anders Wästfelt, in charge of the continuing diving efforts. Jonathan came with me on this occasion and we stayed in a hotel overlooking the harbour, having considerable time to examine the collection in the Gothenburg Stadsmuseum and take part in such a gathering. It has not been possible to visit Gothenburg again since, but I have always enjoyed the feel of this city which was almost entirely built on the rise of the Swedish East India Company.

With the auction of the Bullivant Collection slowly fading into the past by late 1988 – although Cecil Bullivant's influence on the world of Chinese armorial porcelain will never fade entirely – it was possible to consider a further lecture tour in the United States and it was now much more convenient to combine such a tour with the Winter Antiques Show in New York in January, which always played a large part in focusing the attention of American collectors on their favourite subjects.

Arriving in New York on 23rd January 1989 I found myself in a continuous round of socialising, dining with Mildred Mottahedeh, Tom Holtz and Melinda Papp, and lunching with Herbert McKay and Hope Hood – a broad spectrum of experience and views which enabled me to catch up with what was happening. There was also considerable time spent viewing and bidding at Sotheby's and Christie's (although we were but small players on this occasion).

It was a particular pleasure to spend the weekend in Morristown with Peter and Rodney Frelinghuysen, for while it was always possible to focus on their marvellous porcelain, it was their breadth of experience and conversation which made it more interesting. But I had to catch an afternoon plane on Sunday from Newark to Pittsburgh where I was staying at the University Club before lecturing the following day. All the arrangements were in the very capable hands of Elizabeth McCance, and the lecture and lunch at the 20th Century Club was particularly enjoyable because most of those who had been on the tour starting at Hambledon Hall eighteen months earlier were there, and it was like a family party. As I left I told Elizabeth that she was 'like everyone's favourite aunt', and sure enough on my return to London there was a note from 'Aunt Betty'. The second night in Pittsburgh I stayed with Caroline and 'Tal' Hiteshew who had also been on the 1987 tour and spent a fascinating evening at their kitchen table learning about candlesticks, for they had a large and varied collection. After lunch at the airport next day I had to catch a flight to Boston where I was met by Charlotte Smith, Bob and Elizabeth's daughter, who had formerly worked at the New York Historical Society with Betsy Currie and was now Curator of the collection at Andover Historical Society in Massachusetts. There was barely time to arrange my slides before my lecture at 7 pm and afterwards we drove to Salem where I spent two comfortable nights at the Hawthorne Hotel and lectured again at the Peabody Museum, and particularly having dinner with Crosby Forbes at his home on the second evening.

By Friday I was on my way from Boston to Montreal, for Joan Ivory had kindly asked me to stay for a weekend. We visited friends (inevitably with porcelain collections) and had dinner at Rosemount or as guests of other friends at the Mount Royal Club. It was a blissfully peaceful weekend, and I only wished that Neil could still have been there. I was able to visit Robert Little, then a curator at the Montreal Museum, where much of Neil's collection is now displayed.

Lunch on the Monday was with Peter Miller, whom I had got to know at the time of the Bullivant sale when he had decided to take the plunge into collecting armorial porcelain, and he and Barbara had invited me to stay with them for the Monday night. It would be fair to say that while the weekend had been quiet and reflective, my day with Peter and Barbara was exciting and stimulating, and after dinner we discussed every angle of the export porcelain trade from its success in the 18th Century to its decorative and financial value in the 20th Century. I can't remember when we finally went to bed, but I was much impressed with his analytical approach to collecting which in some respects was akin to my own. The evening flight on Tuesday saw me safely at Heathrow at 7.15 and I joined the morning rush hour – finding myself sitting opposite Enoch Powell on the tube – arriving at Hay Hill in time for work.

*   *   *

My short tour to Pittsburgh and Salem was to be the last that I made on my own. Before Christmas I had asked Angela, whom I had now known for nearly seven years, whether she would marry me and to my delight she agreed.

I did not look forward to asking her parents, Robin and Pat Postlethwaite, whom I had met on frequent occasions in Hay Hill, but did not know well. I did know, however, that a twice-divorced man, more than twenty years older than their elder daughter, would not be the profile they would have hoped for – particularly as they were devout Catholics – but I was able to have a very sensible and friendly discussion with Robin, who is five years older than I (and had served in the War, landing at Arnhem and later in Palestine, leaving about the time I arrived). He had spent most of his career in shipping in Singapore with the Blue Funnel Line, becoming their Managing Director there, and later moved to the headquarters of their parent company at Bracknell in Berkshire before retiring to live south of Guildford. Over the years, as I got to know Pat and Robin well, I cannot overemphasise their kindness and understanding.

That Christmas I stayed with Hazel in Devon, who was delighted at the news. For me, having been married twice before but never having found it easy to share my interests with either Elizabeth or Anna – perhaps because of my own single-mindedness – it was an additional pleasure to be with someone who shared and understood them, and who seemed happy to bring them jointly to fulfilment.

On my return from Montreal in early February our attention was focused on our wedding which, it became clear, would ideally be on 1st April. Having worked so long in Hay Hill it seemed appropriate to have a wedding reception at Brown's Hotel, and it was easy and pleasant to arrange this with them for that day. (It was not until I had seen the reception rooms and had had a discussion with the manager that I learned that Theodore Roosevelt had held his own wedding reception there on 2nd December 1886 after his second marriage at St George's, Hanover Square – perhaps the nearest church to Brown's Hotel.) By good fortune Harold and Joleen Poe, Philippa's parents-in-law, were in London that week, and they and all my children and their husbands had dinner the night before with us in Chelsea at the Ebury Wine Bar, an old favourite.

Our wedding was at 11 am on the Saturday morning 1st April at the Westminster Registry Office, at which I also remember Hazel having long and animated discussions with Pat. We then repaired to Brown's for the reception and it was the happiest of gatherings, with all my own children, Hazel with hers, and Angela's family and cousins. I was particularly pleased that Basil and Sue Watts and Caroline and Miranda could come, for they had been at my first wedding nearly thirty-seven years earlier. Remembering the events of just over a century earlier in that very room, after Robin and I had made short speeches I gave each of the younger children a Teddy Bear (named after the former American President).

Leaving in a car for Heathrow, Angela and I just caught our planned flight to Dublin for our short honeymoon, and we were in time for a late dinner at the Shelbourne Hotel. After two nights in Dublin we drove southwest to Cork and stayed at Ballymaloe, still under the magic touch of Myrtle Allen, and from there we spent lazy days visiting the coast and wandering round the castle at Cashel and Bantry Bay House. On our return drive to Dublin we spent time at Kilkenny, but our journey was all over far too quickly as we flew back to London the following Sunday with a busy schedule ahead.

*　　*　　*

With what looked like a gathering economic crisis in 1989, and the high costs involved in trading from central London, it seemed necessary to consider the future. Heirloom's own circle of friends who visited and travelled in England widely, and our increasing turnover which now derived as much from orders by post (following photographs or bi-annual illustrated lists) as from actual visits to our shop, encouraged us to think in terms of leaving London and the introduction it had given us to the antique trade, and finding somewhere in the country where costs were lower and life could be more relaxed. Perhaps I even thought that moving to the country would provide time to start on a second volume of *Chinese Armorial Porcelain*. It was easy to underestimate how much else there would be to do.

In the preceding weeks we had made exploratory tours through the Cotswolds, south to Salisbury and as far as Bath, and although my mind was not made up, we had asked a Bath estate agent to let us know of a modest central trading property and a suitable flat or house. Bath had the advantage of excellent rail and road connections with London, for we foresaw the need to attend frequent sales there and equally to encourage American collectors to visit us. It also offered attractive period residential properties, although it was the re-siting of Heirloom that was most important.

It was, of course, essential that any opportunity outside London should be linked to a satisfactory sale of our remaining lease in Hay Hill, and we were delighted to be told by our agent, Peter Cranham, that our landlord was anxious to buy back the remainder of our lease which was due for renegotiation by 1996, and was prepared to pay a satisfactory premium if we would sign the contract before a change in VAT regulations came into force at the beginning of April, and leave within three months of that. We agreed, and immediately confirmed that we would buy a freehold property in Bath in a pedestrian area in the centre of the city near the Assembly Rooms. The only thing we didn't have was somewhere to live.

But first there was a last brief lecture tour in America before we left London, and just ten days after returning from our honeymoon, Angela and I flew to Atlanta to stay with Bo and Eileen for a few days. After a restful weekend we went on to Jackson, Mississippi, where I had agreed to lecture at the Museum of Art. Sadly, Jackson had lost almost all of its 'antebellum' houses in the last half century, but we lodged in the charming Millsaps Buie House in the main street with three other lecturers who were speaking at the antiques forum organised by Wendell Garrett on the China Trade. As always with symposia arranged by Wendell, it was an instructive and interesting two days, but we were anxious to catch an early afternoon plane on the Friday, for we were staying the weekend with Philippa and Brian in New Mexico and seeing their new home there for the first time.

Philippa, Brian and Gareth (then aged three, with Elizabeth within two months of arriving) met us at Albuquerque and we drove to Santa Fé where Harold and Joleen Poe were staying; we all had an enjoyable dinner together before setting off next day for a weekend in Aztec, near the 'Four Corners' in northwest New Mexico. Philippa and Brian lived just outside the town limit (with its sign announcing 'Winner All America City 1963 Aztec NM') and had just laid a croquet lawn on one side of the house, only made possible because of a sprinkler system laid beneath the turf. The house had a spectacular view over the southern end of the Rocky Mountains. The weekend was all too short, but we managed to see a good deal of Aztec; from Brian's surgery to the tiny local museum which wisely largely limited itself to objects within the living memory of the oldest inhabitants, including a 19th Century dentist's office with all the original equipment, for the town had but recently seen its centenary. Aztec itself had been given its name in error by the first settlers, for there had been no Aztec Indians within a thousand miles.

On the Monday we flew from Durango, via Denver, to Newark, spending two nights with Rodney and Ginny Frelinghuysen, before moving to New York for my lecture for Wendell Garrett at the Antique Collectors Club as part of their 1989 series under a new title 'Chinese Export Porcelain: Its Greatest Period and Discoveries from the Sea', for it seemed that everyone still wanted to know more about the cargoes, and a number had started small collections.

The night before we had had dinner with John Andrew at his Park Avenue flat and enjoyed meeting more of his friends. He was delighted we were going to Bath and was even considering settling there himself after his retirement, having bought a small flat as an investment, although this wasn't to be for a few years yet. The following night we had dinner with Mildred, when Angela was able to see for the first time her extraordinary collection, but also had time for breakfast with John and Hope Hood, and their daughter Emily, who we had seen the year before at the Bullivant sale, and lunch with Tom Holtz (sadly for the last time).

We flew home on 4th May and watched dawn as we landed at Heathrow. It was my last lecture tour from London, and as we returned to Hay Hill we knew that all our clients had received by now a letter telling them that we would be closing in Mayfair at the end of the month and reopening at Miles's Buildings in Bath later in June.

*   *   *

Although Angela and I had not yet been able to find a flat in Bath, we were fortunate that my old friend of thirty years, John Foster, the Rector of St Mary's Paddington, had recently purchased one in the expectation that he might retire there, and he kindly offered it to us while we continued to look round. (John was then nearing the end of his very successful encumbency of St Mary's Paddington, which he had been able to redecorate by a remarkarkable stroke of good fortune and sound stewardship. When the dual carriageway leading to the A40 was built close to the church, land had been sold to the Ministry of Transport by the Paddington Borough Council to make this possible. However, one of John's elderly parishioners recalled her father saying that the land had originally belonged to the church and had only been loaned to the Council. John investigated carefully and on finding this to be so, the payment was transferred to the church of St Mary, on the proviso that it was spent on architectural and decorative improvements.)

John's flat in Bath was barely three minutes' walk from Miles's Buildings and we gladly accepted his offer; it was to be our home for the next two months. We had for many years relied on the small shipping firm run by Errol Nelson for all our special packing and carriage needs, and during June he and his staff packed everything in Hay Hill and took it to Bath while our furniture was stored until we found a new home.

It was a sad day at the end of June when I finally said goodbye to Hay Hill and Grafton Street, which had been my home and place of work for sixteen years and seen Heirloom almost reach adulthood. It had proved to be the perfect place to have a business like Heirloom and allow people from all over the world to get to know us. We had made many friends in a way and in a space of time which it would have been difficult to achieve elsewhere, and both Heirloom and I had benefited greatly from the generations of highly reputed shops and companies which had flourished in the area, not least those of the antiques trade. My previous experience in business had been reinforced by the ideas I witnessed and was able to adopt in Mayfair, and because of that we hoped our reputation and our old and new friends would continue to support us in Bath.

Many years later, when Heirloom was in the country and existed in a more modest way than it had in Mayfair or Bath, an elderly collector, whom I did not recognise, came into our gallery and looked carefully at everything round him and as he was about to leave remarked, 'I've enjoyed looking round, this reminds me of a shop that used to be in Hay Hill, London, many years ago.' We were happy that he had remembered.

CHAPTER 24

Miles's Buildings and Sydney Place

It was a very different world in Bath and we were particularly pleased with our four-storey building with its spacious basement a few yards back from a major road and barely fifty yards from a restaurant, then very well known, 'The Hole in the Wall'. We were close to the main street but not exposed to its noise and fumes. A three-minute walk from our temporary flat was so much easier than a forty-minute drive and walk through London traffic. The antiques displayed well over two floors with offices above and we were, almost at once, too busy to regret London.

As well as the porcelain and other objects, our huge stock of engravings and thousands of Burke's armorial blocks gave us an opportunity to write to many existing clients and find new ones who matched the names and arms and were related. There was little difference to our workload from the first week of July onwards, but our staff was now only Jonathan, Angela and myself. For more than six months there was no lecture tour to distract me and we were able to get to know our new environment and make friends in a way that was much easier than in London.

Our attention, too, was now focused on our new flat, of which we had been able to buy all the 'remaining' nine hundred and fifty years of a thousand-year lease. In Bath this type of ownership was perhaps more usual than outright freehold, while conferring on its owners most of the same rights. We had been very fortunate to find an attractive flat in Sydney Place, just opposite Sydney Gardens and some ten minutes walk from our gallery, with a large courtyard and garden. The ground-floor flat (which usually conferred on the owner the sole rights to the garden) was once part of a fine mid-Georgian terrace that had belonged to Queen Charlotte, the wife of George III, who had occupied the whole terrace of houses in 1816 and stayed there when she wanted to take the waters or enjoy the social life (both of which Jane Austen so well describes in her novels) or when life became too difficult in London. It was possible to see in the extensive courtyard, which now has a small fountain at the far end, the outline of what had been huge kitchen chimneys and fireplaces behind the vine-covered foliage on the walls. There were stone steps up to a large and very old mulberry tree (said to have been planted by George III) which over-shadowed much of a small lawn and modest garden, and as this was on our southern side it enjoyed the sun for most of the day. It was also quiet, for the

Heirloom & Howard Limited, Miles's Buildings, Bath, 1990.

whole was set some twenty feet below the level of the road, and on two other sides further ample courtyards opened on to a row of arched cellars which must once have brimmed with supplies for the Royal household and were now dark caverns beneath the road, but provided useful secure storage.

Our builders, who delighted under the name of Plummer and Hockey, were able to transform this courtyard flat into a series of tall airy Georgian rooms. We moved in by September and found ourselves part of the community of Sydney Place, our front door being at the foot of a magnificent Georgian circular staircase illustrated in more than one guide to Bath. Angela and I were very happy in our new home.

For the first six months and through the winter into 1990 we had only four guests who stayed: Alastair Tower, who I had first known in the Coldstream but had got to know again well in Mayfair, and who also shared my interest in family history; Robin and Pat Postlethwaite, and my sister Hazel, who continued to live in Devon after the death of her husband, Bob, busy with local charities, being a school governor, and sitting on the bench as a magistrate. They all seemed to find Bath as relaxing as we did after the roar of London.

*   *   *

Although there was much to be done in our two buildings, we settled into our new home, walking down Pulteney Street each day and admiring its Georgian architecture. There was a reassuring flow of old friends to Heirloom, last seen in London but who now visited Bath, as well as some new faces. We greatly enjoyed meeting and having Bill McNaught to dinner (for the first of many times) as he had just been appointed the Director of the American Museum in Bath and we had many mutual friends. We also had a visit from Michael Conforti who was responsible for decorative arts at the Minneapolis Institute of Art and who we were sure we would see again in January, for we would be staying there as the guests of Leo Hodroff early the following year.

In Sydney Place we also got to know those in the flats above us, particularly Patrick and Vicki Shervington. Patrick was a Colonel in the Fusiliers at Warminster having served in India, the Middle East and Northern Ireland, and we were delighted to find that Vicki was looking for something to do and thought working at Heirloom might be fun. In fact it was exactly what suited us as well, for my next American journey was to start shortly after the new decade.

Mike Hatcher, stung perhaps by some of the archaeological criticism which had emanated from his previous salvage of cargoes, generously gave to Dr

Barnardo's Homes a number of pieces of 14th Century wares which he had raised, and these were sold by Christie's in an evening sale in mid December. This time we were buyers of only about twenty pieces, but it was one of numerous occasions on which we took a morning train to London to view and buy at auctions. After the local ease with which we had done so for many years, it was different but not too difficult, and we were soon used to carrying large packages back on the train to Bath. (I, too, was later subject to some gentle criticism when a visiting vermicologist noticed that I had cleaned some worm casts from an encrusted Ming dish, although had left the shells!)

On 23rd January 1990 Angela and I flew to New York and just had time to visit the East Side Show and go to the sale at Sotheby's before flying on to Minneapolis where we stayed at the Hyatt Regency Hotel as Leo's guests, and although we had an amusing afternoon with Munson Campbell, who now lived in Minneapolis, we spent most of our time with Leo, or at the Institute of Art.

Leo's collection, now of world importance, would undoubtedly make the subject of a book, and we discussed this at length. We spent some hours at the Institute and saw a gallery which it was hoped eventually would display export porcelain from his collection. On our final evening we had dinner with Leo and Doris, and Evan Maurer, the Director of the Museum, but had to leave next day for a weekend with Rodney and Ginny in Morristown.

We travelled on from there by rail and road to Sandy Hook in Connecticut, staying with John and Hope Hood who had recently bought and were renovating an old farmhouse, and on the Wednesday by train again to Boston, where we stayed for two nights at the Parker House. I spoke on Thursday morning at the Boston Museum of Fine Arts under the title, 'Inspirations of Chinese Export Porcelain', as part of a series called the Devens Lectures, and we spent much of the next morning at the Isabella Stewart Gardener Museum – a fascinating and unique institution which had preserved her vast and broad historical collection untouched and without the rearrangement of so much as a chair since she died many years earlier. We had time for a quick drive to Salem and a tour of the Peabody Museum there with Crosby and Bill before having dinner with old friends, Bud and Charlotte Patten. The following morning we were able to fit in a walk round Boston following the historic 'Freedom Trail' and also enjoyed the view from the top of the John Hancock Tower, where an auditorium includes an historical map of the city which illustrates with a series of light changes the development of the city from its colonial past to the present day.

Later that day we met Arlene Palmer Schwind and her husband, Bill, and drove up to their home in Yarmouth, Maine, where we spent a restful night.

With Crosby Forbes and Bill Sargent (*left*) at the Peabody Museum,
Salem, Massachusetts, in 1990.

My sister, Hazel, and Richard Barclay at Portsmouth in 1991,
after their engagement.

After a day in Yarmouth we travelled to their octagon house in the country, an unusual building which they had decorated entirely in keeping with its 1860s date, made all the more beautiful that weekend by a heavy snowfall, which only just allowed us to catch our flight to New York and take a car to Greenwich, Connecticut, next day.

Betty and Charlie Wilds had arranged a charming and comfortable two days and on one evening we had dinner as the guests of their friends Stephen Wilberding (a Managing Director of Merrill Lynch) and his wife Stevie. There was an exhibition of the China Trade at the Bruce Museum and I spoke at the Yacht Club on the Monday morning under the title, 'Chinese Export Porcelain for Merchants and Noblemen on both sides of the Atlantic' (the story of Washington's general, Lord Stirling, allowing me to illustrate the title of the lecture in full). Although we had time to spend a pleasant hour or so for tea with Mary Young, with whom we had often corresponded about porcelain, we had to catch the morning flight to Heathrow, reaching home in Sydney Place about midnight.

*　　*　　*

Our first spring in Bath saw us continuing to write to large numbers of descendants for whom we had appropriate engravings, and, with Vicki firmly in control of that project, we decided to make another journey to America in March where I had been asked to lecture at the Naples Antiques Fair. This was triggered by an invitation to Florida from Ken Main and his wife Nancy, who had for some years come into Heirloom in London when he was in Europe.

We flew to Miami on 8th March and were driven across Florida to Naples. Ken and Nancy had a beautiful home near the sea, overlooking one of the extensive channels and rivers which are a feature of the Gulf Coast of Florida. Naples was always busy in March with the Antiques Fair, and Michael Cohen from London was also staying with Ken and Nancy. We spent time walking round Naples and a delightful day in Ken's motor cruiser exploring the inland waterways. The lecture itself was in a lofty chapel, and part way through the lecture I had to stop and adjust the screen for sunlight was falling on it through a mullioned stained glass window. It was fortunate that Angela was there and knew when to change the slides, for otherwise I would have had to lecture from the back of the hall because of a faulty lead. But getting these minor problems under control was all in the spirit of the East India Company who so often had to work in uncharted territories, while the audience was very understanding.

Ken and Nancy's fine collection of export porcelain was well displayed in their Naples home and Ken was most knowledgeable about its history. Nevertheless, he was surprised when he pointed out on a high shelf what he called 'a fine 19th Century copy of a *famille verte* dish' and I turned to him saying, 'But that was made after 1974, Ken.' He replied in disbelief, 'How on earth can even you claim that, David, when you haven't even examined it yet?' However, he slowly smiled as I showed him three irregular but carefully drawn white shapes on the armorial shield, then showed him an illustration in colour I had taken for *Chinese Armorial Porcelain*, published in 1974, of a similar dish which had been part of a private collection since the 1920s and never previously photographed. The irregular shapes on his dish were identical to three patches of wear on the original piece and not part of the heraldry, and could only have been copied from the colour plate on page 117 of my first book. It was not the only example of this phenomenon I have come across since 1974.

After five happy days in Naples, we drove on across Florida again to Hobe Sound, another delightful and very well-appointed site on the Atlantic Coast where we stayed with Douglas and Eleanor Seaman, who had often visited us in London and whom I had visited in Wisconsin. Doug had a particularly fine collection of 'Palaceware', much of which he had bought at auction against Nelson Rockefeller (after whom this design is nowadays so often called 'Rockefeller-ware'). But even the late Vice President would have drawn breath if he could have seen the display facing Hobe Sound. I wish we could have stayed longer with Doug and Eleanor, for it was a beautiful and relaxing home in the Florida sun. We then drove to Palm Beach and spent two enjoyable days with Leo and Doris Hodroff, wandering round some of the main antique shops in the town.

But our comfortable journey was not to end for another long weekend, for we flew from Miami to stay with Norman and Kathy at their home a few miles east of Nassau itself. It was Angela's first visit to Nassau and Norman kindly lent me his car so that I could drive her to some of my favourite spots including 'Danger Go Slow', which was not too much changed over the fifty years I had known it, and across the harbour bridge to the old, then uninhabited, Hog Island, which is today unrecognisably bristling with skyscraper hotels and luxury houses and known as Paradise Island. It was almost a century since Sir Hesketh Bell had been Colonial Treasurer of the Bahamas and wild hogs still inhabited the island.

We spent two long and leisurely days enjoying the sun in company with Norman's six mastiffs (one called Winnie and another Clemmie) who had joined his household after two attempts on his life. In one of these he was particularly lucky, for when he switched on his car ignition he noticed a small palm branch on his windscreen, and as he got out to clear it the car exploded, leaving him in a bush but nothing worse. These were probably instigated by one of the drug cartels who did not like his very firm stand against their trade in his position as Leader of the Opposition for many years in the Bahamian Parliament. We planned to fly home via Miami because it was usually quicker than the flights from Jamaica via Nassau and Bermuda, but in the event had to wait for ten tedious hours at Miami airport where the outward flight had had to turn back in mid Atlantic because of an unexpected premature birth on board. But we were looked after well at the airport hotel and were able to sit by a roof-top pool (which would probably not have been the case today) arriving at Heathrow on Tuesday evening rather than morning.

*　　*　　*

Our first spring and summer in Bath continued to keep us busy with occasional visits from relatives: Kay and Aubrey Boutwood, Michael and Judith Shallow, Thomas, and in late June Philippa, Gareth and my newest grand-daughter, Elizabeth, just under a year old. Before that we had had an unpleasant surprise, perhaps more worthy of London, for the night before leaving by car to exhibit at the Ceramics Fair in London, our car was stolen from outside our flat and found by the police beside the road several days later. It was some thirty miles away near Shepton Mallet, with smashed windows, headlights and other damage, clearly done deliberately by the thieves who had run out of petrol three miles from the nearest pump and decided not to risk their luck further but vented their anger on the car! Most fortunately we had not left anything of value in it, but had to hire another at the last moment to take us with our porcelain to and from London.

During the summer we had our first weekend visit from Peter Gwynn-Jones, then Lancaster Herald, who had other friends near Bath who lived at Potterne; since then Peter has stayed at least twice a year with us in Wiltshire; a friendship I much value. I do not know Potterne near Devizes well, but it is embedded in my memory by the 14th Century rhyme concerning the Burgoigne family which I had read:

> *I, John of Gaunt,*
> *Do give and graunt*
> *To Sir John Burgoigne*
> *And the seeds of his loin*
> *Both Worton and Potterne*
> *Until the world's rotten.*

Other friends who stayed in the summer were Kathy (without Norman this time), Martin Arnold, and Harold and Joleen Poe, and it was pleasant to be able to sit in the courtyard and have a meal quietly and discuss both past and future.

It was in July that all of us who had been at Belmont in the Bahamas were invited by Gilly and Chris Willy to a delightful luncheon in the garden of their home in Wimbledon. It had been planned by Chris for some months and the 11th August 1990 was exactly fifty years after we had set sail in R.M.S. *Orduna* on our adventure and almost all of us were able to be there that day with our wives or husbands. Many of us had not seen each other for upwards of forty-five years, but those years dropped away and we found ourselves excitedly talking of events that had been almost forgotten. Of all of us who had sailed that day, one or two could not attend, but only Peter Allen could not be found. Chris had gone to great lengths to track down those with whom he had lost touch, even seeking the help of a radio show 'Where are they now?'

As a result of our gathering, a small committee was formed to try to help Bryan Archer visit Nassau again as he would much like to do. He had fairly advanced motor-neuron disease and was by then in a wheelchair, but was kept going by his devoted wife, Mavis, and they could not afford the fare and hotel. I wrote to all those who had been in Nassau at Belmont including Teddy and Jimmy Goldsmith (the latter sending a particularly generous sum) and Tom Sopwith, and we raised enough for them both to fly for two week's holiday to the Bahamas in early 1991.

Norman Solomon had arranged a comfortable hotel on the beach west of Nassau and the local paper, *The Tribune*, had a whole-page article on 15th February 1991 about motor-neuron disease with a large illustration of a smiling Bryan in his chair held by Mavis, and another of David Niven who had died of the same illness in 1983. Bryan's face was also on the front page below another of Prime Minister Pindling. On their return I had a letter from Bryan, typed by Mavis, thanking us for his holiday and referring to the great efforts of the 'M.N.D. Association' to find a cure or a treatment which would prolong his life. It was signed by Bryan – one of the last letters he was able to sign.

*　　*　　*

Among other friends who visited us in the summer was Alastair Tower, this time with his cousin, Christopher Tower, who had been the last British Ambassador to King Idris of Libya, and now lived in Greece. Christopher, who had also served in the Coldstream, had inherited Weald Hall in Essex when very young, his father having been killed in the First War months after his birth. However, he decided that the responsibility of a large country estate, when he was likely to be abroad much of his life, was more than he should assume, and Weald Hall was sold, with some of its contents going into a trust, although family members had to buy back what they wanted. In recent years, following the death of Christopher, the Tower Trust (not without considerable guidance and urging by his cousin Alastair) has managed to put on long-term loan the very fine collection of Tower portraits at Ashridge in Kent, and an excellent catalogue has been compiled by Alastair's son, Rupert, whose mother, Flavia, was the daughter of Daphne du Maurier.

Before Christmas John Ayers came to stay, the first of many visits, and immediately after Christmas Day we much enjoyed seeing Duffie and Eileen DuBose for several nights over the new year. They were on their way home from an extraordinary, and what turned out to be a very adventurous, tour of Thailand, where Duffie (then in her seventies) had stayed in native up-country Thai villages with few modern amenities, ridden elephants and had barely survived an unscheduled march on foot through the jungle ending in a near-fatal white-water journey with their suitcases on a raft. It was, perhaps, a reflection on modern life that they came to no real harm in the jungle, but were struck down by food-poisoning at the five star hotel they stayed at later. Sitting in the Georgian environment looking out on to our courtyard in Bath, it was almost difficult to imagine their exciting journey.

The previous autumn I had enjoyed a few days in Yorkshire again at the invitation of Phil Cooke. He was anxious that while a part of his collection of some thousand pieces should be given to the V & A, the rest should be divided equally and amicably among his four children. I was given a free hand as negotiator and arbitrator so that not only did each get most of the pieces they liked, but they shared equal values to within about 1%. One son decided to keep his share, two wanted to dispose of a few pieces over the years, and Mary decided to sell hers over a long period. Later, in 1995, I made a last visit to Pontefract and was honoured to address Phil's family funeral. Phil had been an ever-supportive friend over thirty years and while he paid great attention to his successful business as a maltster, he was also a well-known shot and fisherman in Yorkshire and Scotland. He had joined the Air Force at the age of 16 in the First War and when barely seventeen had been shot down in single combat over Germany, finding his way back across the German lines. On his 90th birthday the local RAF station had taken him up for a flight in their latest fighter which he had thoroughly enjoyed. But he had also lavished countless hours on what had beome the finest collection of Chinese armorial porcelain in England.

While Heirloom continued its business in the New Year, it was very largely still the continuing dispersal of engravings from what had once been Mr Suckling's collection. Our library and ability to research the descent of hundreds of families from the finely-engraved 18th and 19th Century prints kept us all busy, and while we sadly missed the opportunity of going to Monte Carlo for what had been routine sales at Sotheby's in the 1980s but were now discontinued, there were signs of continuing pressures on all financial markets, the antique trade included. The luxury of owning two virtual freehold properties in Bath with everyone experiencing bank interest rates of up to 15% and beyond was beginning to wear thin, and a letter from our bank, giving warning that overdrafts would shortly be slashed, made one question whether it was wise to have such a high proportion of one's capital in property when we lived almost entirely by trading in objects which required a buoyant cash-flow.

Nevertheless, as spring came, we very much enjoyed our broadening social life in Bath and Frank and Patricia Herrmann, and Anne and Alastair Aberdeen stayed in the early months of the year, followed by a very happy weekend in which Hazel came with her new fiancé, Richard Barclay, who had spent much of his working life with the bank which bore his name and was recently retired. Richard, who had four grown-up children, had been living near the Solent and we were delighted that they were to pool their resources and were planning to live in Devon. His interest in history and family genealogy was also appealing to me as a prospective brother-in-law.

While we were now actively trying to find somewhere in the country near Bath which would enable us to live comfortably but have an adjacent barn or building in which to put a slimmed-down Heirloom, I found myself spending increasing time on the academic and historical background of the China Trade. Although corresponding with Minneapolis Institute of Arts over a book on the 'Private Trade' with China, based on the collection of Leo Hodroff, I was also deeply engaged in a correspondence with Richard Kilburn, who had invested considerable time and energy into investigating the china shops and merchants in the first half of the 18th Century. This work had linked well with records of supercargoes in the East India Company who bought for the London china shops and were frequently related to those who had armorial porcelain. Richard stayed a weekend in late May, and we exchanged considerable material of mutual interest. I always hoped that he would publish a book on those trading links, but although I know he expended considerable time on the research, he died before it could come to fruition. However, he generously let me incorporate some of the information into my own book which was then to be called 'The Eye of the Private Trader' (perhaps because

I had recently read a book called *The Eye of Thomas Jefferson*) but was eventually published as *The Choice of the Private Trader* nearly three years later.

While continuing to live and trade and entertain in Bath, Angela and I stepped up our search in the countryside, particularly as Jonathan had told us that he would like to leave later in the year to resume the profession of being an estate agent, for which he had originally been trained. By good fortune we found a quiet byway near Chippenham in which a hamlet of some dozen houses lay, little changed in size since the 13th Century. The existing Manor Farm (of which one is recorded in about 1350) was built originally about 1450, but altered and brought 'up to date' in the 18th Century, when a stone was placed in the front wall saying, 'Repair'd 1748'. It had been sold by auction to a former oil company accountant about three years before, who had already converted three of its barns into houses and intended to adapt the farmhouse himself for his own family use. However, encouraged by his success so far, he had also invested in a number of other properties, and as the market fell in line with what were now severe economic conditions, it had become increasingly clear that he would have to improve his cash position to survive, and we were able to buy from him. The farm still included twelve acres, some stables and a wagon shed, although all needed considerable attention.

We, in turn, were fortunate, for John Andrew in New York, looking for a home in Bath on his retirement, stayed with us in June and fell in love with 'The Courtyard'. At the same time we managed to find a buyer for our gallery in Miles's Buildings, and this enabled us to sell two properties while buying only one, and in so doing to meet the stringencies of our bank who had made it clear that they could no longer authorise the overdraft facility for our Heirloom stock to which they had agreed earlier, even though we had not exceeded our limit.

In spite of these arrangements being complete by early July, there was much work to be done on the farmhouse and we remained in Bath for a further two months; Kathy from Nassau, Peter Gwynn-Jones from 'The College' and Martin and Margaret Arnold staying with us before we left. We also had an interesting short visit from Sir John Nott (for we had found a Nott armorial) who had known my father well from 1966 when he was MP for St Ives and my father was a Vice Chairman of that Division in Cornwall. John and his wife shared a sandwich lunch on the top floor of Miles's Buildings, where we sometimes had a meal when friends came.

As we were completing our plans to move from Bath, there was an interesting sale in Sussex in which a number of armorial plates and dishes were to be sold. I recognised at once that most had been in Clive Rouse's collection but did not comment, for I imagined that Clive, now in his nineties, had decided to sell some of the pieces which had languished in various chests of drawers. We drove to Sussex and had a successful day buying almost thirty pieces at Sotheby's, Billingshurst, although most had damage, as was usual with Clive's collection.

It was some months later, after we were settled in our new home, that I was talking to Colin Mackay at Sotheby's in Bond Street when he asked me if I had been told that Clive had had a burglary and had lost about fifty pieces – the exact number wasn't certain. He had recently been given a list and would send me a copy in case I saw any. Next day it arrived and I telephoned Colin and asked him to compare it with the Billingshurst sale of 3rd June 1991 – which he did, and immediately realised the significance. I was told later that the porcelain had come from a south coast trader and at the time there had been no particular reason to query the provenance. I said that most of what we had bought had already been sold, but that I would 'freeze' the remainder and, if called upon, would try to recover the other pieces now spread through five countries.

I later had a discussion with Clive's nephew and principal executor, who was a lawyer and who intimated that 'a financial settlement' had been reached. However, in spite of some clear evidence, it had been agreed that no case was to be brought before the courts because the vendor claimed that he had bought the pieces for cash from Clive. Although Clive had no recollection of this (and it was out of character), it would be unfair to allow a 92 year-old man to be cross-examined by an aggressive defence counsel in court. On balance, it was the right decision, and little of this touched Clive himself, whose remaining collection was eventually sold at Billingshurst in 1999 after his death.

By the time that Alastair Tower, both our first and our last guest at Sydney Place, stayed with us in Bath in early August, the builders were already at work on our new home. We drove out from Bath and wandered rounded the old farmhouse which, although sound in walls and roof, needed considerable attention. It was clear that much hard work was required before it would give us the comfort we had become used to in Bath.

CHAPTER 25

West Yatton, Bermuda and The Bahamas

The Manor Farm had always been an independent farm throughout its six hundred year history, for there had never been a manor house in the village itself. It must have been in a poor state of repair by the 1740s, because the restoration then undertaken was substantial and turned a traditional mediaeval farmhouse into one with more Georgian appearance and windows, although inside many of the ceilings were low. The large attic was created by using huge, iron-hard wooden beams which had clearly been used before, because a number had evidence of burning (unconnected with beams next to them) and most had slots cut in their gently curving shape which had no connection with their present use. I learned that this was not uncommon within a day's journey of the port of Bristol, for large numbers of early Georgian ships' timbers were sold by contractors for housing when ships were dismantled or repaired. Undoubtedly this accounted for the inappropriate slots and cuts and burn marks. The attic had no flooring, and between the ceiling beams were dozens of part-broken clay pipes of the 18th and 19th Centuries, probably left by farm workers or roofers when they had taken a break in poor weather. It was fascinating to find so many undisturbed!

There were many other features in the house that had survived over the centuries including much of a baking oven beside a large filled-in fireplace in the kitchen; two iron rings set just below floor level at the mediaeval open fireplace in the hall, used originally for supporting a spit; and internal walls which varied from straw-filled lath and plaster, to eighteen-inch elm planks dividing into two rooms what had once been a single large room occupying most of the ground floor – a division which probably took place in the mid 18th Century. We carefully preserved every feature that survived, and in one case 'unearthed' a 16th Century fireplace, while restoring two older ones of the 15th and 16th Centuries.

Every room needed redecorating and most rewiring, while a barn which was attached to the house needed a new floor (instead of earth) and ceiling. Other floors in the house, much worn over the centuries, needed repair or remaking with traditional materials. Although at the start this work was undertaken by a small building company, I did not employ an architect (for I had experience of such a home in Dorset nearly forty years before) and after a while found it easier to employ a stone mason or carpenter or electrician independently, rather than incur the management costs of a builder. Such independent craftsmen still survive and thrive in this type of rural environment away from cities.

We moved in officially in early September with the help of Errol Nelson who, with his two assistants, packed and transported everything from Miles's Building and Sydney Place to West Yatton, sleeping overnight in a downstairs room at the empty farm. The two burly South London removers later admitted to little sleep that night, having been so worried by 'strange sounds' (perhaps a fox scavenging) that they propped furniture against the door as a precaution, whereas the noise and bustle of their homes in London would not have disturbed them at all!

By the first week in September Angela and I were sleeping in the only habitable upstairs room, while each day carpenters and masons worked in neighbouring rooms (and we moved round with our suitcases as things were completed). In fact it all worked well because one could monitor progress closely, and the craftsmen of those days are still friends – although it seemed a long time before we could unpack properly. We had moved just as the fruit was beginning to drop from the old plum trees. Being unable to do anything with it, we told our carpenter to pick the fruit and take it home with him. We were very touched the next morning when he arrived with a pot of home-made plum jam for our breakfast. Even more surprising was the day when our plumber brought in a brace of pheasants, casually announcing that he had been shooting 'at Blenheim Palace over the weekend' (for he was a friend of the head keeper).

Perhaps one of the most important additions following shortly after the basic work was complete was the installation of a sophisticated alarm system with numerous separate areas. This has so far proved most efficacious, and we have only been disturbed by spiders and a bat who have occasionally set off the alarm at night. On one such occasion we had an impressive armed response when the off-duty guard normally employed to protect a former Northern Ireland Minister, who lives in a nearby village, turned up in three minutes and jumped out of their armoured range-rover with guns at the ready. Learning the nature of the intruder they had a cup of coffee and departed much amused; it was nevertheless reassuring.

Our first visitors were Chris and Susie Weld, who unexpectedly drove in on our first day, coming out from Bath to look for us and climbing over rubble to reach the front door. But with occasional inspections from the District Council's architects, for the farm and many of the outside walls and buildings are 'Grade II listed', great progress had been made by October. Our only overnight visitors ('camping' in rooms that were not quite ready yet) were

Manor Farm in winter.

Part of the garden at Manor Farm in summer.

Thomas, and Philippa and Brian with Gareth and a very young Elizabeth – all of whom were drafted in to work in the garden, which was now the focus of my attention.

The courtyard at the back of the farmhouse, in which cows had been milked for centuries, now witnessed long grass and tall nettles creeping in. Stone walls were everywhere in need of repair, and the remains of many bonfires and piles of rubbish needed clearing. It was only possible to work outwards from the house and design the new but informal garden as one progressed.

New walls, steps and eventually lawns took over from many years of agricultural use. Fresh gravel and some flowers transformed the courtyard into a place where one could entertain one's guests, and eventually a new herb garden and a croquet lawn emerged from where there had once been rubble and the remains of sheds where animals were once tethered. Vistas were created, and two small orchards planted where cows had once wandered from their milking stalls to the now sadly unkempt home field behind the farm, inhabited only by rabbits in the banks.

But all this was to take four years, as the wilderness turned into garden and walls were rebuilt and hedges and trees trimmed. I also enjoyed the help of Tony Shilabeare, who worked as a part-time gardener while working as a Ministry driver during the week, and was pleased that he talked of it as 'our garden'. In front of the house, repeated mowing and some hundreds of square feet of new turf turned what had been a muddy farm yard, where tractors drew their agricultural loads, into lawns bordering a driveway lined with daffodils in the spring and flowering shrubs in the summer and autumn. Slowly but surely this old farm became our home.

*   *   *

But before we had settled in we had the happiness of a day in Devon to see Hazel and Richard married. It was a quiet wedding at Bradninch Church with lunch afterwards at Banbury House, and for me an opportunity to see again some of Hazel's friends I hadn't seen for years and meet Richard's three sons, Charles, Michael and Angus, whose business lives took them from Europe to the Far East, and his daughter, Juliet, who lived in Cuba (and who was to write an excellent book on the architecture and museums of Havana).

Our overnight visitors in 1992 were largely from the family, although a few old friends came to stay, as did John Andrew from New York and Sydney Place. But our life was by no means one of gardening and entertaining, for Heirloom, in a new and slimmed-down form, was still very much part of our plan. I was now spending considerable time writing the book which was to be published as *The Choice of the Private Trader* and as the book took shape, it was necessary to fly back to Minneapolis taking with me Peter MacDonald and Stanley Eost who had photographed *China for the West*. It was reassuring that they had been asked do the photography, for we knew how to work together, and they soon found a local photographic store who would develop what they had completed each day, so that anything not quite as planned could be quickly retaken. They were able to complete the 350 photographs necessary in eight days – much time being saved because I already knew almost all the pieces required and it was possible to hand them, from adjacent rooms in the house, all the plates required, followed by upright pieces of similar shapes, so that there was the minimum time spent rearranging background and lighting. I felt that Leo and Doris were surprised by the speed with which the work was completed, and they were always very supportive.

*　　*　　*

In the spring of 1992 Christie's announced that there was a new and exciting salvaged cargo of about 1690 which was to be sold in Amsterdam. This was called the Vung Tau Cargo and was being sold on behalf of the Government of Vietnam, as the ship had sunk about 100 miles south of the Vung Tau Peninsula on the Vietnamese coast.

Among a number of factors which differed from the earlier Hatcher cargoes was that the United States did not trade with Vietnam, and thus direct purchase by American collectors and dealers was not permitted. It was clear from the outset that Christie's had negotiated the sale of the cargo after long discussions with the Vietnamese Government itself. What was not so clear before the sale was that considerable quantities of porcelain were already being traded openly in Vietnam, and that the Government would not be putting on the market all it owned.

Once again the pre-sale publicity was very successful in encouraging large numbers of buyers to come to Amsterdam. Heirloom had approached all those who had bought on previous occasions, and we were able to go to the sale with the knowledge that about 150 collectors had pledged over £250,000 as their purchasing budget (including the owner of a Japanese company who wanted to buy a considerable quantity, leaving the selections very much in our hands).

The cargo itself included a number of most interesting shapes, a few copied from European silver of the date, and a huge range of vases and garnitures, some unusually decorated with European buildings similar to those along canals in Holland. Among the rarest scenes was one after a 13th Century drawing of King Louis IX of France talking with his mother, Queen Blanche, who was explaining to the young King that it was not the kingdom of France, but the Kingdom of God that was the most important in the world – clearly intended for the French market (perhaps as an example for the profligate Louis XIV) although probably ordered by the Dutch. It was a treasure trove for the collector of blue and white porcelain of the late 17th Century. In the event Heirloom purchased for a total of about £320,000, and although some of the prices were high, we were well pleased.

But unlike our own strategy of having a substantial part of our cargo pre-sold when it arrived (even though the margins were relatively modest), one or two dealers, mesmerised by the reputation of the enormously successful Nanking Cargo, and perhaps unrealistically optimistic about their potential profits in a quite different financial environment to that of six years earlier, were disappointed by the poor sales that they achieved in London. Moreover, when another made an effort to sell in Singapore, he was taken aback to find that many Asian dealers had been able to buy similar pieces direct from the Vietnamese Government or other local sources at prices well below those achieved at the auction. It later became apparent that one buyer at the auction had reached an agreement before the sale with the Vietnamese Government and had been assured that they would be 'reimbursed' if they bought more than they could sell. The effect on the auction prices could only have been to raise the prices of some lots at the sale itself.

Although Heirloom was not affected to a dangerous extent, I was sufficiently disturbed by these revelations that, after discussions with some other dealers, I wrote to the Chairman of Christie's, Sir Anthony Tennant, who directed me to Christopher Davidge, then Managing Director. I was able to have two useful meetings with him, at which we had very frank discussions and at which Richard Aydon was present in a legal capacity, as a result of which (and after a discussion with my own legal advisor) I decided to take no further action in the matter, particularly as my advisor warned that any proceedings could involve costs in six figures, and since I was only a modest loser I would be unlikely to recover these.

On the second occasion that I saw Christopher Davidge, he took me to the lift afterwards and said with a smile, 'This will make an interesting chapter in my book about my life at Christie's.' Indeed, it was well known in 1993 that such a book was almost written. However, after Christie's later agreed to pay him £5 million in two instalments for 'loss of office' in the late 1990s (one only paid so far as is known), he chose to give tapes of confidential telephone calls with Sotheby's to the United States' legal authorities causing huge multi-million dollar fines to both companies, particularly Sotheby's, and the imprisonment of their Chairman for conspiring to fix commissions. But it has always intrigued me that in spite of his new-found leisure, the book has never been published. I would like to have read that 'interesting chapter'.

*   *   *

While the summer months in our first full year in Wiltshire saw numerous guests, and most weekends in June and July were happily filled with family visits, we were able to spend a weekend with Hazel and Richard at Bradninch. Hazel had, some years before, had treatment for cancer, and had just discovered that she needed more. She was a leading advocate in Devon of 'Cancer Call', which gave an opportunity to those who were alarmed at the onset or cause of their cancer to talk to someone with experience, so that they could regain confidence in themselves or their treatment. It was a charitable service that was very much appreciated by the growing number of victims who were unsure or confused about what to do. Hazel had always thrown herself into various charity work, as well as being a magistrate, and had a wide circle of friends in these fields.

In early January of 1993 Hazel's son, Nick, now the Rector of Hatherleigh in Devon, spent a night with us and told us that there was not long to go. On 2nd February we drove to Devon and I spent an hour at her bedside while she was still conscious, for she was in the hands of a most competent and kind Macmillan nurse most of the time. Sitting beside her bed and holding her hand it was only possible to think back over the sixty-three years we had known each other, in Cheshire, the Bahamas, and later in Devon, and realise that I could not think of a single occasion on which we had exchanged cross words in all that time. We had always shared views in total confidence and knew more about each other's lives than we could ever tell. I promised to help Richard and all her children, Nick and Simon, Charlotte, Jonathan and Toby, to ease any problems within my power in the family, before she closed her eyes and lapsed again into a drug-aided sleep. Hazel died next day, the 3rd of February. I felt particularly sad for Richard, for their new-found and obvious happiness had turned to sorrow so soon. Just over a week later there was a moving service at the church in Bradninch at which the Bishop of Exeter was present – less than two years after the happy occasion on which they had married.

*   *   *

We were lucky in the spring of 1993 to be able to acquire a part dinner service in London which had come from Fingask Castle and had been made for Sir Thomas Stepney, a descendant of the artist Sir Anthony Vandyke.

Some of this returned to Stepney descendants, while other pieces went to the National Museum of Wales, and Welsh collectors. But what was nicer was those who came to stay at West Yatton: the Herrmanns (when the idea of a party was born), John Ayers, Bill Sargent from the Peabody (who was never happier than when given a gardening task to do), Peter Gwynn-Jones, and George and Carol Overend who came over twice from Atlanta. The Reverend William Neely from Northern Ireland was both a collector of historical (and armorial) porcelain and had written on Irish church history and Co. Armagh in particular. Although we had met initially in Bath, it was the first of what have since become annual holiday visits. We were later to stay with William in his Rectory at Keady in southern Armagh, in the centre of what had been a very troubled area. Richard Barclay stayed with us three times that summer and all my children and their families at some time, while other welcome friends whom I had known for fifteen years were Henry and Dinah Moog, who not only ran an antique shop specialising in Export porcelain in Atlanta, but also spent much time in developing holiday properties in the Antilles.

While staying earlier in the summer, Frank Herrmann had very generously suggested hosting a dinner party in October 1993 at the Travellers Club to mark the 20th anniversary of Heirloom & Howard. Frank and Patricia had witnessed the events which led to the birth of Heirloom, and at that time I stayed very frequently at their house and felt very much at home, while two thousand cards and hundreds of typed sheets were turned by Patricia into an orderly *Chinese Armorial Porcelain*. Frank himself was always an interesting host – sometimes publisher or bookseller, sometimes a director of Sotheby's and author of a book on the history of that auction house (as well as writing children's books) and sometimes a book auctioneer himself. Life was always both stimulating and comfortable at West Bowers Hall, and this dinner party marked a particularly special moment in Heirloom's history with many old friends present.

We had, at last, been able to have both Norman Solomon and Kathy to stay in June and this led to planning a most enjoyable holiday in April of 1994, but it wasn't until after some early spring visits of Peter and Barbara Miller, the Herrmanns again, and Jem and Gill Wilyman, who besides doing much to help 'The Bookplate Society' also had a most interesting collection of armorial bookplates and other heraldic objects in Birmingham.

*　　*　　*

With so much travel over the last three decades I had hardly ever before taken an overseas holiday which was not part of a business journey, so that it was with great excitement that Angela and I set off for Bermuda on 7th April 1994 for almost three weeks in the sun in Bermuda, Atlanta and the Bahamas.

I had known Hugh Davidson and his wife Brenda for some years, and we stayed in their guest cottage, a few miles west of Hamilton, with a marvellous view across the ocean. We greatly enjoyed five nights in Somerset, spending a day in Hamilton visiting Hugh's antique gallery and wandering round the streets, and an afternoon on the Harbour Ferry, seeing all the local landing places and the old Royal Dockyards at the northern tip of the Island. Hugh spent another day with us at St George's at the eastern end of the Island, where his deep knowledge of the Island's history ensured that its story was not forgotten for its beauty. We were also able to visit a number of houses of the Bermuda National Trust, of which Hugh has been the Chairman. The beach and rocks of Horseshoe Bay on the southern side of the island were idyllic, and at night we dined with Hugh and Brenda at home or at some excellent local restaurant. It was very difficult to tear ourselves away by the end of the week, even though we were looking forward to flying to Atlanta.

Valley Road provides some exceptional houses, even for Atlanta, and George and Carol Overend's most comfortable home was no exception; their newly designed additions to the house and the landscaped garden complementing their excellent collection of *famille verte* porcelain. We visited the Swan House with George and Carol, it being twenty years since I first spoke there in Atlanta. I noticed particularly the brass plate on the wall reading 'Atlanta Historical Society: 1975: President Beverly M. DuBose Jr.' On this occasion Bo and Eileen were away in China so we did not see them, but spent an afternoon with Mark and Linda Alexander, who had been on the Irish porcelain tour, after having lunch with Henry and Dinah Moog.

Three days later we flew to Marsh Harbour, Abaco, in George's small plane, seeing the Bahamas from the air being a particularly good way of appreciating the huge number of small islands which make up this earliest western landfall of Columbus that had taken place to our south-west on San Salvador some 502 years earlier. Landing at Marsh Harbour, a small boat took us to Elbow Cay and we then drove the short distance to 'Pieces of Eight', George and Carol's octagonal house on a particularly beautiful stretch of coast, then closely linked by four matching cottages (now eight). The pool, sited by the terrace before the house, was cleverly designed so that looking out it appeared to be part of the ocean itself as the water fell away over the side. It was the Bahamas at its best: beautiful, comfortable, but not oppressed with the overbuilding of houses which has become a feature of Nassau and New Providence.

It was, perhaps, the most relaxing place we had known (or I had ever been to) and we were but a short distance from the small rural township of Hopetown on Elbow Cay, which included a modestly deep water harbour and picturesque lighthouse, making it a favourite anchorage for yachtsmen, some of whom had cottages along the shore. The white painted houses, with white garden walls covered by tumbling tropical flowers, created an unmistakably Bahamian scene as we wandered round.

On the third day Norman, now retired from his political post, and Kathy arrived by boat from Nassau. After two more days of leisure broken only by a visit to Chester Thompson's home on the highest part of the island and a day in George's boat sailing down the coast of Abaco to Man o'War Cay (a name rooted in the past, when the small harbours were host to pirate vessels waiting for the chance to attack rich unwary merchantmen), we tore ourselves away and returned with Norman and Kathy by air to Nassau. The following day we were up early and together with Herbie, Norman's long-term friend and right hand man on board, set sail for Harbour Island and Spanish Wells, and five days cruising down the Exuma Cays.

By late morning we reached Dunmore Town on Harbour Island, where I had first spent a holiday as a schoolboy fifty-one years earlier. Although there were some new buildings, many of the houses remained the same, with the pink and yellow window shutters pinned back against their white or shell pink walls. There were moments of nostalgia, too, when I gazed at the old rectory where we had stayed all those years ago, and when I was introduced to an aging shopkeeper in a small local store who remarked, 'I remember the Belmont boys,' and added, 'And how's Mavis?' (a pretty face in the school). Later beside the road Norman stopped at what appeared to be an unmanned stall – but a voice from within said, 'Who dat?' and Norman replied, 'Who dat say who dat?' to which, after a long pause, the voice replied, 'Who dat say who dat when I say who dat?' We might be there still had not a face appeared from behind the awning and exclaimed, 'Oh Mr Norman!', for he had been the MP for Harbour Island for much of his life and many people we passed turned to talk to him.

After lunch at a café over the water, before setting off for Spanish Wells for the evening, we had time to go over to the small Jacob's Island, just to the north of Harbour Island, which Norman had bought, planning to build a house for his retirement. So far there was a gardener's cottage and a path round the island.

Staying in an empty house belonging to one of Herbie's many cousins, we had a pleasant dinner with Herbie and his wife, and in the morning breakfast with an old friend of Norman's (who I remember was a great-grandfather at 52, not unusual in Spanish Wells where the very tight-knit community had less

With George and Carol Overend (*right*) and Kathy and Norman Solomon
at Marsh Harbour, Abaco.

Iguanas await sandwiches at Allan's Cay in the Exumas.

than twenty surnames common to most of the population, which had flourished there since the early 18th Century and had been founded by settlers after the Monmouth Rebellion in the 1680s, today existing largely on the profitable cray-fishing). In such a community where virtually all of the inhabitants were related, there was very little crime and houses were usually left unlocked.

The journey down the Exuma Cays, which stretch in shallow turquoise water and a ragged line for more than a third of the full length of the Bahamas chain, sheltered by Eleuthera, Cat Island, Long Island and San Salvador from the full depth of the Atlantic, was as beautiful as it was interesting. None is large enough to have attracted any major tourist development, and they remain a haven of peaceful and ecologically safe low-lying reefs. We spent some time at Allan's Cay, where in the uninhabited and empty bay some dozens of iguanas – only now known in a few places on earth – came down to the shore from a sandy grass and tree strewn ridge in curiosity or the hope that someone would throw a sandwich their way. As an endangered species, Norman's public outdoor zoo near Nassau had been given permission some five years earlier to take a pair for breeding. This was not achieved without some difficulty, and eventually four went to Nassau because of uncertainty about their gender.

We stayed the night at Highbourn Cay, where a single jetty and path led to a sheltered cottage above the beach, while standing on deck or the jetty one could see sharks and rays slowly circling in the hope of some titbit. Before going to sleep Norman and Herbie would lower some fish pots in well judged and known places in the hope that on our return later in the trip we could put some catches in the yacht's freezer.

The channel at Shroud Cay, which wound its way through very pale blue sea reflecting the white sand below and the pale clouds above, was completely deserted and almost eerie, but further south at Sampson Cay a dozen yachts were anchored, while a small island steamer, looking like a tiny replica of a Mississippi paddle boat but without paddles, nudged its way carefully from the jetty, although there seemed to be few on board at this time of year. There was, of course, an open table on the jetty so that anyone could gut the fish they had caught and throw the waste to the waiting sharks, which circled expectantly and made perfect subjects for any photographer who wished to photograph them against the pale duck-egg sand below.

At Mr Roberts Cay, on that day deserted, but where Norman knew the owner, we were greeted on the jetty by a number of wild chickens, who may have thought we had come to feed them but were disappointed and to our surprise flapped into the sea to swim to shore. One could understand how these aquarian fowl could, in earlier times, have slowly evolved into ocean birds, like some near-extinct varieties from Galapagos. Meanwhile Norman and Herbie sat under a shelter on the jetty preparing their latest catch of crayfish and snapper for the freezer, for we had turned northwards and were collecting the pots which we had laid down two days before.

It was a long sail home, direct to New Providence's eastern end across great stretches of shallow sea – Bahamian banks – where for much of the way, although out of sight of any land, one could see a jungle of ocean ferns stretching up to the surface. Indeed, a casual glance at a map of that part of the Atlantic cannot convey the huge land mass and coral reefs only a few fathoms beneath the surface, which, in turn, have protected the tiny unspoiled Exuma Cays since long before the days of Columbus.

Nassau was like a metropolis after the unspoiled solitude, and we were soon back in London and driving home.

*   *   *

It was not a moment too soon, for more than a dozen friends and relatives would be staying before July and there was a substantial sale at Sotheby's on 11th May at which we bought about thirty lots, some two-thirds being for clients. We had also arranged with Lady Jane Howard, who ran a company called Specialtours (and had brought museum groups before), for a lunch visit of about twenty members of the Seattle Museum with their curator, Julie Emerson, three days after our return.

But before that, it was very nice to have Hugh Davidson, our host in Bermuda, staying with us for a couple of days before travelling up to his croft in Caithness (the land of his ancestors) close to the Castle of Mey and John o'Groats. Other close friends continued to be regular visitors for a night or two over the summer, while I was particularly occupied from June to October with the final pre-publication touches to *The Choice of the Private Trader*, which was published on 1st October.

What had started with a much more modest plan to illustrate the 'masterpieces' of the Leo and Doris Hodroff Collection, had developed over the previous two years, with Leo's agreement, into a much more analytical approach, almost twice the size of the original concept, to reveal the whole role of the private trader in the China Trade, which had been largely overlooked or forgotten in the years since the East India Company itself disappeared. Fortunately the records of the Company in the India Office Library provided accurate evidence of this trade, and detailed accounts of the auctions in some years. As the literature about the book pointed out:

The Private Trade in Chinese Export porcelain, as distinct from East India Company Trade, has hitherto scarcely been recognised as a subject in its own right. And yet the officers and supercargoes of the Hon. East India Company took full advantage of their licence to trade on their own account; it is just this attractive and innovative ware, chosen by them at their own capital risk, that is most collected today. [This book] surveys more than two centuries of manufacture, and throws new light on how the trade was actually conducted. The Hodroff Collection, the largest and most comprehensive of its kind in the world, closely mirrors the tastes of the private traders and is the ideal source of illustration for this pioneering work.

It has been reassuring to find, in a field which has had a considerable number of books published in the last three decades, that this made a positive step forward in the understanding and motivation for much of the China Trade in the decorative arts. It also reinforced the argument that it is, more often than not, private initiatives – not governmental or large company moves – which so often set trends for the future. It was an understanding of this and their subtle involvement which enabled the East India Company to become the largest trading empire the world has ever known.

On a very different level the book kept us busy packing for the rest of the year!

*   *   *

1995 started with news of another and most interesting cargo sale in Amsterdam – on 6th and 7th March – and because it was very well documented, it aroused much more interest than might normally have been the case for Chinese porcelain of the relatively late date of 1817. It was fortunate, or perhaps symbolic, that the East Indiaman which sank shortly after leaving Malacca en route for Madras on 4th March that year was called *Diana*. The story of its wreck and salvage have been very well documented by Dorian Ball (an English diver who had formerly worked with Mike Hatcher) in his book *The Diana Adventure*, and in spite of some tension between the Malay authorities and the salvager, the operation itself appeared to have been a considerable success, although there was a later court case over financial matters.

While neither the quantity nor quality of the cargo matched some of the earlier Hatcher sales, the condition of the whole was excellent, and many of the dishes and plates of robust potting were of unusual and attractive designs. For those who were fascinated by pieces attached to coral and each other, or joined by rust to metal pieces where they had rested together for 180 years, there were numerous 'sculptures', while considerable interest was shown in 180 dishes with the arms of the Hon. East India Company bound for the residence of the Governor of Madras, although the design was well-preserved on only a small number, some of which we bought for leading museums in England and Scotland. As we had found with earlier cargoes, a separate mailing list to those particularly interested in the adventure and discovery of pieces from wrecks – 'sunken treasure' – had again gathered considerable support on this occasion from a much wider circle than porcelain collectors only. Among those who had planned to come to choose a piece or two after the sale, but had to delay her visit because her mother had just died, was a Mrs Lili Saunders. It was only when she was here later that we learned that her mother was Odette Hallowes, whose incredible bravery under torture during the war had earned her a George Cross and the admiration of a generation used to the sacrifices of war. It was a privilege to be able to give a small piece of *blanc de chine* porcelain in her memory, and I still treasure her funeral card portrait which I was given.

In all we bought almost £130,000 worth from the *Diana* and most had gone by the year end. There were a number of rare animals and birds in this cargo which will provide evidence of date in the future, and a number of unrecorded 'teapot funnels' which would have been inserted into teapots to protect their spouts becoming clogged with tea leaves. It was an initiative in the story of tea which can never have been a success, because they were somewhat clumsy objects which would have lain uncomfortably on an elegant Georgian silver tea tray, and they have never previously been recorded in ceramic records. Perhaps the idea was to be tried in India (where the tea leaves were larger) and it did not reach Europe until 1995 – where their final indignity was being sold upside down as candlesticks!

CHAPTER 26

A Tale of Three Cities

It was already a year since our holiday in the Bahamas, and in the spring of 1995, when the first rush of the *Diana* cargo had settled, we drove to Scotland for a very different holiday of discovery. It is an added bonus of membership of the Oriental Club in London that they have arrangements with a number of other clubs so that their members can stay elsewhere as guests. Fortunately the New Club in Edinburgh is on that list and we stayed there for three days, spending much of one at the Scottish National Museum where there is an interesting display of Export porcelain, while it was fun to explore the Grass Market (in which I discovered some armorial objects which had been Nicky Fairbairn's but were now dispersed after his death) and wander inquisitively down the Royal Mile.

Driving on to Skye from our base near Fort William, our journey nearly came to an abrupt end when a large tourist bus slowly backed into our car as we sat parked near the ferry. Fortunately we were able to get broken headlights and bent bonnet repaired temporarily at a local garage and drove on dented but undeterred. We could happily have spent much longer on Skye, but after visiting the MacDonald family history 'centre' near Ardvasar, we crossed by another ferry over the Sound of Sleat and were lost in historic reflections for an hour or two at Glenfinnan where Bonnie Prince Charlie set up his standard in 1745.

After leaving Loch Lochy two days later, and finding our road to the north of Loch Ness, it was but an hour's drive from Inverness to visit Culloden Field itself and try to imagine what had taken place there 249 years earlier. It was also our first visit to Brodie Castle and my first sight of pieces of some of the fine Brodie Chinese armorial services they acquired between 1775 and 1800. We stayed near Ballater and enjoyed during the following few days Drum Castle and Crathes (the homes of the Irvine and Burnett families) and a visit to Haddo House, the home of Lord Aberdeen – at all of which we discovered further armorial services.

Looking back, it was perhaps at this point, reinforced by our stay later in the holiday, that my mind started to concentrate on the huge task of writing a second volume of *Chinese Armorial Porcelain* – always a distant dream – for it was so clear as one travelled that there was much more material which was still unrecorded in my earlier volume and begged to be added to that record.

We felt, too, as we visited castles and other sites of the Scottish National Trust, that the unashamed display of family objects was more a part of the Trust's conscious policy in Scotland than was the case south of the border.

We drove south on a warm afternoon by the Pass of Killiecrankie, which had witnessed such heroism and slaughter in the earlier Jacobite Rising of 1689 in which 'Bonnie Dundee' fell as his forces triumphed over the army of King William (thus probably encouraging the Risings of twenty-six and fifty-six years later). But we could not linger too long, for we had arranged to meet David and Nancy Perth at Edinburgh Airport, who had kindly invited us to stay at Stobhall.

David Perth still lived a very busy life in spite of being just two years short of ninety, and his two private loves (after Nancy, whom he had married in 1934) were the Jacobite cause, for which his family had lost so much at Culloden, and the China Trade, in which he had worked in the 1920s and 1930s while his father was still Secretary General of the League of Nations. Our journey in the highlands made for an interesting conversation at dinner that night. It was some eighteen months since he had written the foreword to *The Choice of the Private Trader* (in spite of some opposition from the Minneapolis Institute, who felt that an eighty-year-old peer could not possibly reflect modern thinking on such a subject, but backed down eventually after I sent a letter from him accepting my invitation). It is impossible to read his first two paragraphs without understanding where his heart lay:

> When David Howard asked me to write a foreword to this book, there were three reasons why I couldn't refuse. The first was a friendship over forty years; the second was an opportunity to be involved in a book which I felt sure would add to the knowledge of all those who enjoy collecting Export porcelain; and the third reason was that my own ancestor, James Drummond, was one of those Private Traders of whom he writes. From 1801 to 1807 he was President of the Select Committee of the East India Company in Canton and his fine house and garden in Macao are today the City Museum. I am fortunate enough to have inherited some of the armorial porcelain, pictures and other objects that James Drummond, later restored to his Strathallan titles as 8th Viscount, brought home.
>
> As a child I accepted without questioning that there were in our house many Chinese things including a lot of 'Lowestoft' – such was my ignorance of Chinese armorial and other porcelain. Over

eighty years I have seen much and learnt much, making several visits to China, including a pilgrimage to Jingdezhen. It was during the time of Chairman Mao and we saw the factories still at work, but were much disappointed when our attempts at once again ordering some armorial porcelain failed. The Communist regime would have no truck with such privileged, degenerate and capitalist work! Now things are different – for in the end the Trader wins.

A day or two at Stobhall was always like a week of holiday, and besides seeing the latest alterations in what had once been an outlying turret of the castle, we spent much of one afternoon at nearby Scone Palace, the home of Lord Mansfield and a friend of David's. In a cabinet in the dining room was yet another service for a second volume, and David urged me to move towards such a book, while at dinner I urged him to consider getting a biographer to tell his own story, which would undoubtedly have been of the broadest interest – alas without result.

But all good things come to an end, and we sadly headed south after our holiday, stopping briefly to have tea with Kay and Angus Hamilton, with whom I had corresponded about Hamilton objects from time to time, but hadn't seen since we had left London six years earlier.

*   *   *

The early summer of 1995 was enlivened with an unusual sale in Dorchester of a large collection of armorial porcelain from an anonymous estate, which included a few more unrecorded pieces. Bidding in Dorchester revived old memories of my rugby football days more than thirty years earlier – although I was then more likely to come away with bruises rather than about sixty pieces of porcelain. More exciting in many ways was the discovery in South Africa of a small part dinner service made about 1725 for an East India Company captain called Haldane of Gleneagles, taken there by a descendant almost a century ago. It was painted with a unique design copied from a contemporary armorial bookplate – in every detail, including the edge of the bookplate – and we were able to return it to Martin Haldane who still lives near Gleneagles (which his ancestor had also sold and which had since become the international name it is today). It was also nice to find an unusual Brodie plate and return it to Brodie Castle, while a very fine private collection of eighteen coach panels, which we illustrated in a small brochure, included those of the Prince Regent, Queen Victoria and the Dukes of Wellington,

Buccleugh and Newcastle, and had all gone in a week.

That Christmas Bo and Eileen DuBose, and Michael and Anne Minoprio stayed, an amusing week which kept us very busy with many corks a'popping, while it was interesting to compare the carving techniques from different sides of the Atlantic – which almost proved there were too many cooks in the kitchen! Thomas joined us for the last three days of the year, but 1996 started with a very busy schedule.

Our first visitors of the New Year were Angus and Kay Hamilton who stayed for a night, quickly followed by John Ayers, William Neely and Colin Mackay – who invited us to a lunch at Sotheby's which was to have far-reaching effects for the rest of the year.

On Monday 12th March Angela and I had lunch in Sotheby's boardroom with Colin Mackay, Luke Rittner, then director of publicity, and Hugo Swire (now a Member of Parliament but then an assistant with a broad span of tasks and responsibilities). I was given an outline of a plan to hold a major exhibition on the China Trade in London, opening in early January 1997, which would coincide with Hong Kong becoming Chinese again after 100 years. It would also be accompanied by a substantial catalogue or book. It was clear that few matters had yet been considered in detail, and Sotheby's urgently needed a curator and author to guide this project – although it was realised that the timescale of little more than nine months would stretch the resources of the team, and the leader who took the task, to the limit – particularly as in my case I already had a full-time business to run and was busy enough with that! But it was an offer which I could not possibly refuse.

Sotheby's would provide a wide-ranging team to back the curator/author, and there would be a monthly (later fortnightly) meeting of all those concerned. The most important post of exhibition administrator, who would do everything possible to put into effect what was planned, would be held by Ruth Watson (Ruthie) who knew Sotheby's well and had once been Colin's assistant, later working in the administration and record-keeping of the Chinese Porcelain Department for some years with Anne Pollen. It could not have been a happier choice.

My own remit was very wide but particularly had to focus on ideas, which I could always run before Colin Mackay, the Director of the Chinese Department, with whom I had always enjoyed working. It would be tedious here to detail all the day to day problems which arose during the period to December, but by then there were to be ninety lenders, contributing more than 370 objects, all photographed, illustrated and described in a book of 270 pages. These would come together from three continents and ranged from small pieces of silver-mounted 17th Century porcelain brought back from

China, to ledgers of the Honourable East India Company never before displayed outside the India Office Library; and from the robes presented to General Gordon, to porcelain and pictures which had never left the families for which they were made. The accumulation of work which the team had to undertake was immense, and by July I was working full-time on the project and spending very long hours planning visits to lenders and collecting, often from them, information for what I hoped would be an original and really informative book which, like the exhibition itself, would have the full title (already chosen by Sotheby's) of *A Tale of Three Cities – Canton, Shanghai and Hong Kong* (to which was later added the sub-title *Three centuries of Sino-British Trade in the Decorative Arts*). Fortunately the planning of such an exhibition was familiar ground to me after the two exhibitions in New York, now more than ten years earlier.

In addition to the monthly meetings in London, I had numerous other discussions with Luke and Hugo, who were responsible for the overall cost, sponsorship and publicity of the exhibition (although others were drawn into this field as time progressed) and whenever I spent several hours at Sotheby's I found that I was occupying Mr Taubman's personal office which was comfortable and frequently available. The planning and layout in the five principal galleries on the first floor at Sotheby's Bond Street had to remain very much in one's head or on a drawing board until the last moment, for there would be sales in those galleries until a week before Christmas. Sotheby's gallery staff were familiar with creating new lighting and colour schemes over a weekend, but this too, although planned, would have to keep until the last moment.

As the huge range of objects was considered, chosen and viewed, and the owners notified in writing of the acceptance of their loans, plans were made for photography and delivery. With all the paperwork involved to cover insurance, it was necessary to keep various departments and carriers informed of what would have to be dealt with and when. But the very professional administrative staff at Sotheby's were more than able to deal with such problems as they arose because it was like a variant of their everyday arranging of auctions. Many things had to be agreed by September so that the photographs and layout of the book had time to adjust to what was planned for the exhibition, and it was as well that Angela and I had already arranged our holiday that year in April, for it would have been difficult or impossible later. We left our everyday affairs in the hands of Dorothy Smith at Heirloom, although we planned to speak to her each day from Italy.

*   *   *

We flew to Pisa early on Monday 13th April which gave us time to see the Leaning Tower and visit the nearby cathedral before catching a late afternoon train to Florence, where Angela's old friend Caroline Burke Vannuchi collected us and took us to her home. I hardly knew Florence, although Angela had lived there fifteen years before and knew it well, so we were able to enjoy visiting a number of the finest palaces and gardens and spent an afternoon at the Roman amphitheatre at Fiesole, which I particularly enjoyed after the bustle of the city. On the second day Caroline and Giovanni drove us to San Gimignano and I fell in love with this small hill town with its busy shops and restaurants. We lunched in the square and listened to a harpist under a loggia by a church. The views over the surrounding countryside, the tall towers and timeless architecture and relative quietness with little modern traffic noise made it somewhere where one yearned to stay longer. But staying in a quiet courtyard, beside their home in Florence, made it possible to wander out whenever we wanted and in five days we had seen a great deal, made another visit to San Gimignano and dined with Caroline and Giovanni in more than one local restaurant, before catching a train to Venice.

Venice was everything I had looked forward to, and we stayed in a small hotel close to the Grand Canal. Although Angela knew the city slightly, I had never been there and every moment was one of discovery. While journeys by canal filled the popular vision of Venice, it was fascinating to wander round the streets as yet uncrowded by summer visitors and observe the everyday life of the city. Of course we spent some time in St Mark's Square, but surprised ourselves by visiting the island of Murano, no more than half an hour by boat, where we spent a morning at a glass works and watched craftsmen blowing and decorating glass in the Venetian manner. Although clearly arranged for tourists, this was an interesting introduction to our visit. Inevitably we ended in their showroom where the pleasant and helpful manager to our surprise was called Weld – his grandfather having settled there nearly a century earlier. Back in Venice itself we were not drawn to the most famous palaces and squares, although the Doge's Palace was an exception, but enjoyed the atmosphere (and the cafés by the canals) while wandering by foot and by boat, which has rightly made the city a favourite destination for so long.

Travelling by train again via Verona we spent three peaceful nights on Lake Garda enjoying the comforts of the Grand Hotel at Gardone Riviera. With boats calling at the hotel pier every half hour it was easy to sail to the northern end to Riva and feel the influence of Austria, or enjoy the small towns from Malcesine and Limone in the north to Sirmione on the southern shore, with their castles and rugged streets and histories of tiny independent principalities in the days before Garibaldi. Lake Garda was also to become a happy destination in the future, but we had other things to contend with, and were soon back home with a very busy schedule ahead.

*   *   *

While Sotheby's exhibition was always uppermost in my mind, the summer months at West Yatton saw increasing visitors and in addition a manager from the Forestry Commission, for I planned to plant almost two acres of woodland at the lower end of our field. It had been much neglected for some years and had become the dumping ground of lorry loads of rubble and stone in anticipation of construction planned by our predecessor but for which he had not, thankfully, received planning consent. Two or three days in the spring with a bulldozer followed by two hundred tons of top soil sewn for grass had prepared the way, and we were given permission to plant in the autumn.

Almost every day we now had visitors. Ruthie increasingly came to work on the exhibition, while the many friends at weekends included Peter Gwynn-Jones who had recently been appointed Garter King of Arms, an appointment which seemed very sound, for he was both an historian and herald with a grasp of history and an organiser with a strong streak of the disciplinarian, something which is always necessary in a fraternity as diverse as the College of Arms. As the summer progressed the annual antiques fairs drew visitors from everywhere: George and Carol Overend and their daughter Catherine stayed a weekend, followed by Bo, Eileen and Duffie DuBose, so that we were well aware of what was happening in Atlanta, while I had two further visits from Richard Kilburn who kept a spare cell of my brain tuned to further research on armorial porcelain. But I was now in London about two days a week, either at official conferences at Sotheby's or at private meetings with Colin, Luke and Hugo, with legal or financial advisors, and with Pattie Wong who kept me in touch with publicity and promotion, although somehow Angela and I had time to drive for a long weekend in Scotland and stayed with Angus and Kay; a relaxation from everyday life.

By July, my time was increasingly occupied by correspondence and meetings with lenders for the exhibition, some of whom were friends or collectors, some well-known dealers and others large companies, museums or institutions. All proved helpful and enthusiastic to the project and welcomed visits over the months to early September when the lists were due to close, although Ruthie would be following up the considerable legal, insurance and transport matters with more than ninety lenders.

It would be invidious to mention most private names, but we were particularly delighted that the daughter of a very distinguished porcelain collector of the early 20th Century agreed to lend a fine group of *famille verte* pieces, and we much enjoyed a day at her country home choosing them. From a visit to Burghley House we were able to borrow a number of pieces, many of which had been in the Cecil family since the 17th Century, one in particular having been given to the great Lord Burghley by Queen Elizabeth from a group taken at sea by Sir Francis Drake and presented to his monarch. James Methuen Campbell at Corsham Court was generous with some exceptional objects ranging from an early 18th Century Chinese satin coverlet (which may never have been used, for the colours were still vibrant in the antique chest in which it was stored) to some unusual examples of *blanc de chine*, and from a Chinese tea service to a bidet. Among pieces lent by Lord Perth it was possible to gain a glimpse of everyday life for a merchant in Canton from the watercolour of the garden of James Drummond at Macau, while I was able to recall some exceptional pieces in private collections in America and in every case had an enthusiastic response – including some decorative objects from the Hodroff Collection, and a fine private collection of pewter figures which in the early 19th Century had made unusual candlesticks. A group of twenty-three watercolours was lent by a family who had owned them for generations, having been given the set after Earl Macartney's Embassy to China in 1792-4. It was a particularly fine group and told the story of tea planting, harvesting and eventual despatch to Europe, but it had not been certain whether twenty-three was the complete set, although they were to occupy the whole wall of a large gallery at Sotheby's. The group was complemented by an exceptional bowl, obtained from the Far East, showing five similar scenes of tea production. These were shown on a television show before the exhibition opened and the following morning a man came into Sotheby's with the twenty-fourth painting which had been in his family for at least two generations and was thought to have been bought in London in the 20th Century. They are now all together again.

Among the companies in the antiques field who were particularly helpful were Malletts, who contributed two fine pieces of furniture: a card table made in China and a superb lacquer bureau-bookcase (a feature of which being that every drawer had Chinese characters at the back to indicate where each fitted). Jonathan Harris, an old friend, also provided some excellent pieces of furniture and lacquer, while Michael Gillingham was able to lend some silver-mounted 17th and 18th Century porcelain. Khalil Rizk from New York was, as ever, generous with his help and among the pieces of porcelain he sent was a large tea caddy painted with European merchants discussing business with their Chinese counterparts in Canton – epitomising the spirit and reality of the China Trade. While Partridge loaned a number of birds and animals in porcelain and enamel, Peter Wain provided rare but interesting examples of 20th Century Chinese porcelain providing a less well-known insight into that century.

During the three months which saw frequent visits to London and elsewhere, I particularly enjoyed meetings with some of the great names of the late 18th, 19th and 20th Century China Trade: Matheson and Company, where Jeremy Brown was very supportive and we were able to borrow a number of paintings of ships and of life in Canton and Hong Kong; the Hong Kong Shanghai Bank where I was directed to Sarah Kinsey, their archivist, who was able to arrange the loan of a number of other paintings, and Swire & Company from whom we borrowed further objects including a six-foot model of the Hong Kong-Canton ferry *Fanshan* which plied the Pearl River after 1887.

But it was perhaps the specialist museums and institutions I enjoyed most: a visit to Lords cricket ground, where they agreed to loan the finest known Chinese punch bowl decorated with a cricket match painted after a 1748 engraving 'Cricket in the Mary-le-bone Fields'; Bristol Museum, where Peter Hardie agreed to loan some exceptional enamelled ware, and the Fan Museum at Greenwich where I was able to spend most of a day in September with Mrs Alexander who agreed to lend us eight Chinese scenic fans of the 18th and 19th Century.

The Fishmongers' Company were generous with pieces from their various Chinese dinner services, and at Freemasons' Hall Mr Hamill let me choose a number of pieces from their collection of punch bowls and tankards made in China. With the help of Simon Jervis and others at the National Trust it was possible to borrow a fine dinner service from Nostell Priory and a piece of Lord Anson's service from Shugborough, while from across the Atlantic Crosby Forbes and Bill Sargent of the Peabody Museum in Salem in Massachusetts arranged a very generous loan of Chinese silver and paktong after European forms as well as some 19th Century jewellery.

It was perhaps even more exciting from an historical point of view visiting the Royal Engineers' Mess in Kent, and with the very ready help of Colonel John Nowers borrowing from them, with the permission of the Gordon School, some robes and silk banners presented to General Gordon after his Chinese Campaign in the 1860s, together with some items of lacquer furniture and his Imperial Court Dress presented by the Emperor and an official seal of Command with Chinese characters, while another seal from a private collection had the Chinese characters 'Ge Deng' which translate as 'Advancing Spear' but would be pronounced 'Gor-Don'.

A final personal pleasure were the hours spent in the India Office Library where, with the help of Anthony Farrington, we were able to borrow a number of Hon. East India Company trading ledgers of the early part of the 18th Century. One particularly exciting entry, giving the daily loadings in Canton in 1727, recorded an armorial service for Lord King (recently made Lord Chancellor) loaded on the 20th December that year. Beside the ledger it was possible to display the teapot of the service itself. Such exhibitions give rise to the once-in-a-lifetime opportunity to bring together such records and objects and it was heart-warming that more than ninety lenders, the majority private, combined to make such an exhibition possible. In one case it was only as an afterthought that a lender mentioned that he also had an album of Chinese woodcut prints which had been given to his ancestor, a silk merchant in the 18th Century; it was found to have the original designs for a series of *famille verte* dishes on silk manufacture, two of which I was able to borrow from an American collection to display with the book.

As August turned to September and the number of objects loaned reached their limit (although the final number of 371 was not finalised until late October, and some of these included up to twenty component objects) the writing of the catalogue became the most pressing task. This was not made easier by what appeared to be a severe attack of stomach 'cramps' causing a number of completely sleepless nights which I spent in a comfortable chair with cushions and a rug and was able to write through the night as ever stronger pain-killers were prescribed and took effect. On the evening of 17th September, after my journey to Greenwich to make a final choice of fans at the Fan Museum, I saw my doctor again at 7 pm – as a result of which I was in the Bath Clinic by 9 pm. Three days of tests and scans showed that I had a fast-growing lymphoma of the stomach glands, and when I later asked if it would be possible to delay treatment until after the exhibition was ready, I was told that if I tried to do so, I would not see the exhibition at all.

I realised that I had to inform Sotheby's at once about the problem. I spoke to Colin Mackay on the telephone and explained the position. After recovering from the shock he asked if I felt that in spite of everything I could carry on. My reply was, 'Colin, with the team we have and all the plans so far advanced the answer is – yes.' He promised to telephone back after consulting the Chairman and did so later with the answer, 'If you are happy to try, we are happy to agree.' It was a decision of trust which I have since felt played a considerable part in my recovery, for with that much-disparaged gift of hindsight it provided an unanswerable reason for survival.

I was sent home until the results of further tests were known, but extreme pain took me back to the Clinic ten days later where I was given an even more powerful painkiller – this time heroin – following which I am informed that I told a risqué story to the senior surgeon before falling into a long sound sleep. Next morning I had an exploratory operation which confirmed the type of lymphoma and I was told that I should remain in the Clinic where chemotherapy would start as soon as possible (in fact ten days later) after recovering from what had been major surgery, with subsequent regular two-day sessions until February. Two weeks later I was home again.

During my time in the Bath Clinic (whose nurses I found to be always sympathetic and caring under the steady hand of Sister Lynn Melly) and the two-day visits there to the end of the year, it had been an essential task as well as a distraction to keep writing, and twice a day Angela came in, taking away anything I had written the previous day or night and turning it into entries for the book (while on some occasions bringing reference books to my room if they were needed). On more than one occasion I was able to 'attend' a committee meeting in London while sitting in my bed in Bath, for Sotheby's arranged a loud-speaker on the conference table so that I could hear what was happening and take part when necessary, while on two occasions national newspapers rang Heirloom's office for interviews and were told I would telephone back – which I did from the Bath Clinic, although they had no idea where the call was coming from.

I cannot overemphasise the vital role that Angela and Ruthie played at this time, but by November, and a series of visits to West Yatton by Ruthie, all the plans were laid and the book complete, including the page layouts which play such a vital role in this sort of publication and can only be planned by the author. By my early November chemotherapy (which was followed by another scan showing some initial improvement) I had completed the brief opening chapter and had discussions with the photographer, Ken Adlard, who was a vital link in the chain since every piece was to be illustrated and he had to travel widely about the country. Reading again the acknowledgements I see that I included the names of my three doctors – for they played a vital role in the production of the manuscript.

Sotheby's closed their five Bond Street galleries on 20th December after their last major sale of the year, and provided us with comfortable hotel rooms at the Westbury Hotel, little more than a hundred yards away. I was able to watch their very competent staff turn the galleries into the exhibition site I had envisaged with a map of where every one of the 371 objects was to be placed and what wall displays should be created, including greatly enlarged reproductions of Allom's 1840 engravings of Canton and the Pearl River. That evening I had a message from Colin that the first copy of the book had been delivered and we looked at it over dinner in a nearby restaurant with some relief and pleasure.

A Tale of Three Cities, Sotheby's London, January 1997.
The entrance room illustrating the journey to China and the risks,
with recovered sunken cargoes.

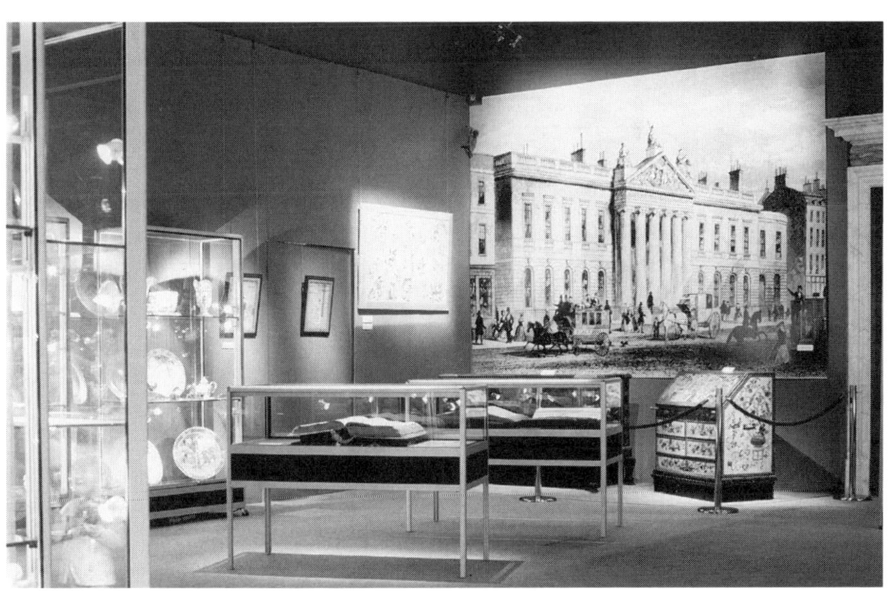

A Tale of Three Cities.
East India House, London, and some of the private cargo brought from China.

A Tale of Three Cities.
A wide variety of Chinese imports: furniture, carpets, silk, porcelain, lacquer.

The 19th Century and Hong Kong.

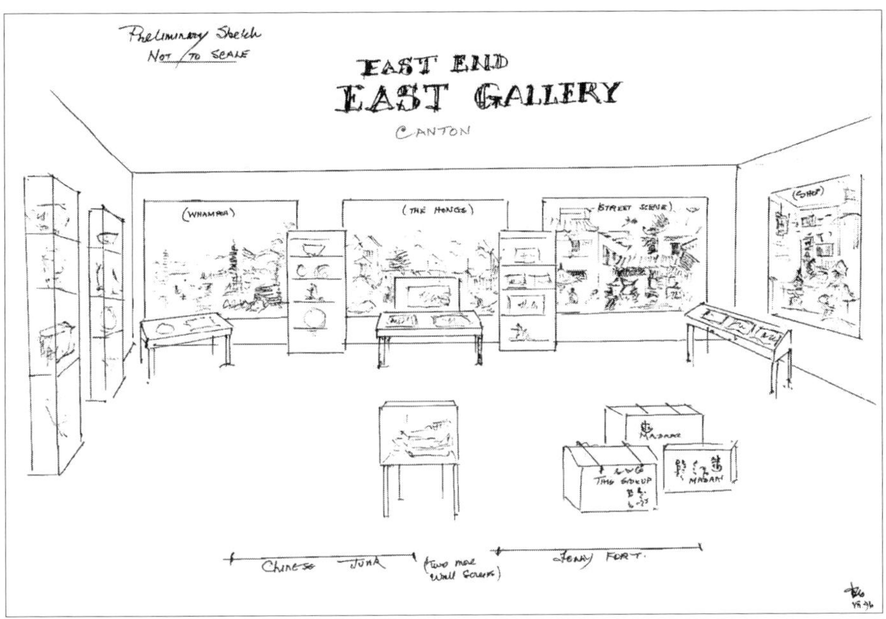

One of the many draft layout plans by the Curator.

The Curator on the day before opening, in the 19th Century gallery,
with porcelain, lacquer, ivory chess set and a Chinese export paint box.

We were probably not the only ones to be delighted to have two days off for Christmas, and on Boxing Day we had lunch with Jamie and Ferelith Drummond at their Somerset home, where his father, David Perth, was staying. But with no time to waste, on 27th December we caught an early train to London to be present at the unpacking of a stream of lorries and vans bringing exhibits, and by the weekend Philippa, who had flown in from New Mexico, and Thomas, had joined us at home. Philippa came back to London with us on Monday to help with the layout, which was to take more than a week. Although we took two days off for New Year's Eve and New Year's Day, we were back in London from the 2nd January sharing again the comforts of the Westbury.

The morning of 6th January was occupied by a press conference and considerable television coverage. (I was amused next day at lunch to be asked by the waiter at a nearby restaurant, 'Didn't I see you this morning on television?') After lunch the show was open and the first people I showed round were Chris and Susie Weld; it was a quite different experience to guide people round the exhibition as an independent observer. Two days later I was home for a chemotherapy session, and Chris and Susie spent the weekend with us.

Monday was a very important day, for Sotheby's had arranged a splendid reception and dinner for the lenders – in all more than 150 attending – and we dined in great style in the principal gallery by the light of Chinese lanterns and other oriental decorations. It was inevitable that there would be speeches and in due course the now almost bald curator rose to thank the Chairman of Sotheby's, concluding (from memory):

> But as one looks round this exhibition it is difficult not to recall
> the quotation:

> … But there's a fact you all should know,
> Whatever way the wind shall blow
> However rough the weather –
> That war and peace may come and go
> But *trade* goes on forever.

As I sat down Julian Thompson, who was sitting next to Angela, asked, 'Where *did* David find that marvellous quotation?' and was amused when she replied, 'He made it up in the bath this morning.' It was an evening one could not forget.

Next day we showed other friends round the exhibition, including George and Carol Overend who had attended the dinner the night before, and I was particularly pleased that my Bath oncologist, Ed Gilby, had come up to see the show; but we had to hurry back home to plan the photography for Heirloom's next catalogue – for Heirloom still had a vital role to play in our lives, although Sotheby's had kindly paid me an honorarium (the only exhibition for which I had accepted such an offer, for the pleasure of the final result always outweighs any other consideration).

There were still more days at the Westbury as Colin arranged a private dinner at Bucks Club following another reception which included Anne and Alastair Aberdeen who were in London, while I had agreed to show round a special group from Sotheby's Institute next day and we attended a dinner given by them. On the Saturday Arnaud and Veronique Maspetiol joined us for lunch in Bond Street after walking round the exhibition.

After another weekend at home, there was a dinner given by NatWest Markets, who had been the major sponsor of the show, and I was asked to provide a quiz of twelve questions about the exhibition which was completed before dinner and a prize given later to the winner (who I think got all correct!). But the most enjoyable occasion of the whole affair was a private lunch that Sotheby's gave, allowing me to invite personal friends and family at which Sophie made a short speech. It was my happiest moment after a difficult autumn.

On Friday 7th February we stayed for the last time at the Westbury and watched as everything was dismantled and disappeared in a queue of vans and lorries within two days. I can never enter Sotheby's auction galleries now without closing my eyes for a moment and seeing *A Tale of Three Cities* flash before me. (At the time of writing it is also a matter of some satisfaction that a well-known American university is now using the book *A Tale of Three Cities* as a text book for a small part of its decorative arts course.)

CHAPTER 27

The China Circle and Stockholm

There was nothing like the stark medical warning experienced in the previous year to concentrate the mind, and while 1997 witnessed a determined effort to ensure that Heirloom did not suffer from the distractions of 1996, it was now clear that the amount of information that had accumulated since *Chinese Armorial Porcelain* was assembled twenty-four years earlier was such that there was now room for a new volume.

When Sir Algernon Tudor-Craig completed his book in 1925, he had been able to name a thousand services for the British market. My own book published forty-nine years later illustrated nearly two thousand and listed about nine hundred more of which there was no available illustration. It now appeared that it would be possible to increase the illustrated services by more than 50%. I had taken so many photographs over the intervening twenty-four years and discovered so much more information, that it must now be worth the effort to pull it all together. But while there was a strong determination to achieve this, it was clear that it would not be realistic to expect a result in less than five years, and meanwhile there was much else to do.

One interesting and unforeseen episode in the closing months of 1996 had been a visit from the representative of *Colonial Homes* magazine in America, Kenneth Hunt, who wrote a balanced and generous article for their December issue entitled 'The World of Heirloom & Howard Ltd' of which the opening paragraph read:

> About two hours west of London, in the quiet town of Chippenham, Wiltshire, David and Angela Howard operate their 25-year-old business, Heirloom & Howard Limited, which specializes in armorial antiques. The objects they sell are emblazoned with the coats of arms that were first used to identify knights on the battlefield, and which eventually became distinguishing hallmarks of many landed and noble European families. Today, many people in Great Britain, and Americans of British descent, are interested in collecting these personalized antiques.

With Arnaud and Veronique Maspetiol in Paris, 1997.

With Francis Lesur at Hardelot, 1997.

It concluded with a suggestion that those who were interested should write for a catalogue which we were then producing annually. We were taken by surprise by some hundreds of letters which started to arrive before Christmas (and continued for several years!) asking for a catalogue. This gave some much needed encouragement to Heirloom which, of necessity, had had to take a back seat for the last six months.

Fortunately by March my visits to the clinic had relaxed into regular consultancies with my oncologist Dr Ed Gilby, and the regular blood tests and occasional scans that were required, but it was very re-assuring to renew a normal social life with visits from the newly appointed Garter, Hugh Davidson from Bermuda, James Dawnay, and a most interesting day with two senior museum curators from China – Hongxin Zhay and Yii Hwang – who were accompanied by their translator, a Nigerian girl who spoke perfect English. They had been sufficiently intrigued by *A Tale of Three Cities* to venture a whole day in the country to discover more about the export trade, but in fact I was able to learn much more from them, particularly about the designs on the earlier underwater cargoes of the end of the Ming Dynasty (before 1650).

We had also planned what, for us, was a new type of holiday, from mid April to early May in the Dordogne. After two nights on the way with Francis and Catherine Lesur at their home at Hardelot, and a day with Arnaud and Veronique Maspetiol in Paris, we travelled south to Le Manoir d'Hautegente, spending the days touring and visiting small towns and chateaux along the Dordogne River where the cliff-top villages as well as towns like Sarlat provided the perfect opportunity to relax. Before returning home via Paris, we took the train to Nice for three leisurely days with my old friend, Alistair Tower, who now lived in nearby Beaulieu-sur-mer.

The summer of 1997 was like earlier ones in West Yatton, with visits from Peter Frelinghuysen, Richard Kilburn, Tom and Lucy Lee from Memphis, Arlene Palmer Schwind, whose knowledge of table glass is unrivalled, Tom Litzenburg from Washington & Lee University, Pat Shea, the Welds and others. Henry Maertens de Noordhout had recently published a most useful book on Chinese services with armorials for the Belgian market, having been the director of the principal museum in Brussels, and it was interesting comparing notes on the subject over lunch here. For one who had turned to this field only after retirement, it was a remarkable achievement. We were also able to spend a really relaxing weekend in Norfolk with Colin and Annabel Mackay, and appreciate the dedicated work that Colin had put into his large garden, with new woodland and lake beyond, in a manner which I both admired and wished to emulate at West Yatton.

In early August we drove to Edinburgh to attend the opening of an exhibition at the National Museum of Scotland which covered much of the ground of *A Tale of Three Cities* but from a Scottish perspective. The exhibition was accompanied by a book by Susan Leiper called *Precious Cargo, Scots and the China Trade* and it was both stimulating and very worthwhile to see a completely different presentation of the same story. We stayed for two nights with Angus and Kay Hamilton, and the day after the reception drove to Stobhall with David Perth (who had, of course, been a lender to the Museum exhibition).

Nancy had died the previous year, and over the weekend we visited old haunts together in Perthshire where David was always able to tell us so much of the history, while we dined quietly at Stobhall and as often as not discussed the consequences of the Jacobite Risings of the '15 and the '45. It was particularly enjoyable to visit David Butter, who had been my company commander when I was in training at Pirbright almost exactly fifty years earlier. We had tea and he was able to find a photograph of the company in 1946. We left Stobhall on the Monday and stayed that night with James and Sarah Dawnay at Symington near Biggar, driving the following day to Carlisle and east through Brampton to Naworth Castle, the principal seat of the Howard family, Earls of Carlisle, until they built Castle Howard in the early 18th Century. As a descendant of the sister of the first Earl, I was particularly interested and had telephoned from Stobhall to see if we could call on a day when the house was not open to the public. Philip Howard, the brother of the present Earl, kindly welcomed us and we spent much of the morning in the castle with him – it being particularly interesting to see the bedroom in a tower where my ancestors were born. I could have stayed much longer but we had a long drive ahead and we tore ourselves away, having lunch by Lanercost Priory before setting off south for West Yatton which we reached about dark.

Bo and Eileen DuBose stayed for a happy week later in the month, and we also much enjoyed a visit from Anthony Hardy and Susan Chen from Hong Kong, whom we had met recently and who lunched with us. Meanwhile Angela had planned another Italian holiday, this time travelling with her parents to Umbria and Tuscany, while I would join them later for a long weekend on Lake Garda. They set off in the last week of September and we spoke each evening on the telephone, but I was quite unprepared for a call from Assisi, where they had particularly looked forward to staying.

She and her parents had arranged to stay four nights, but after visiting the Basilica on the first afternoon, they were woken by an earthquake sometime after midnight. Fortunately it appeared reasonably mild, although it was not easy to get to sleep afterwards and windows were still rattling at breakfast.

The following morning they visited the lower Basilica of Santa Maria dei Angeli at the foot of the hill, but while Angela was outside and her parents in the cloister bookshop another, and much more violent, earthquake struck and the spire swayed dangerously. People poured out of the church but not Robin and Pat. Angela ran back in to find them alone in the bookshop surrounded by books and toppled plaster saints strewn across the floor. She urged them to leave immediately but Robin replied that he had not yet paid for the book and postcards in his hand – although the girl at the cash till had fled! He left the money by the open till and they ran.

They had great difficulty in getting back to their hotel as, unknown to them, the Giotto ceiling in the main Basilica had collapsed with the second quake killing four people; but when they did, the manager told them it would not be safe to stay and eventually they decided to leave and drive to Florence. Their adventure was not quite over, for on reaching Florence late that evening they found nowhere to stay in an unexpectedly busy week, finally finding rooms in a convent in Fiesole, run by an Irish order who occupied a magnificent villa with views reaching far down into the city – in fact, it had been the location for the award-winning film *The English Patient*. (Sadly the convent was to close two years later when the city reclaimed the lease on the villa.) All this I heard on the telephone, but the rest of their journey was trouble-free and we met at the Grand Hotel, Gardone, at the weekend, enjoying five days' rest on Lake Garda.

October was to be a busy month with Alistair and Nicole Tower staying, and George and Amanda Streatfeild (my god-daughter), whose daughter was at school nearby. It was also interesting to get to know Count Peter Pininski who visited us to discuss some minor points for his book *The Stuarts' Last Secret* which traces the descents from Prince Charles Edward's three grandchildren after his defeat at Culloden, and finds new evidence for their descendants today, particularly through Peter's understanding of little-known records in Warsaw. It hardly merited an acknowledgement but he kindly gave me one in his most revealing book.

But October also saw an entirely new experience, for I had been asked by London University to be an external examiner for Christina Baird, who had written a doctrinal thesis on the 19th Century China Trade out of Liverpool. It was useful to have the information on the Liverpool China Trade, particularly as Christina had worked in the museum there; but as one who had not attended university, it was particularly pleasing to have been asked, and to have an opportunity of learning, even at this late stage, something of university life! It was an added pleasure that the other external examiner was Dr Crosby Forbes from Salem, and we had lunch at the university afterwards with Professor Roderick Whitfield, whom I had known for many years and whose father, Professor Humphreys Whitfield, had lived in Edgbaston and had been the Professor of Italian Language and Literature at Birmingham University from 1946 until his later retirement. He was a collector of armorial porcelain and *blanc-de-Chine*, and instead of a Christmas card each year he published a short 'birthday' monograph on a matter of literature or the arts, which I greatly enjoyed receiving (although did not always understand the sections written in Latin!).

The following week, at last, we planted the nearly two acres of trees which had been planned for the previous year; they seem to take to their new home, and six years later many of the three-foot saplings are between fifteen and eighteen feet (but Colin Mackay's woodland is still ahead!). This was a small preliminary for the last major event of the year.

I had agreed to lecture in November as part of a tour to Winterthur, Salem and St Louis. In the event Angela had to have an unexpected operation, and while I spent six quick days in America, I had, with great regret, to cancel a stay with Tom and Barbara Eagleton, and a day with Ben Edwards to see his exceptional collection in St Louis. But I had a comfortable stay in Wilmington, and lectured at Winterthur with Bill Sargent and others, under the somewhat cumbersome title 'European armorials and print sources as a means to understand the styles and dates of eighteenth-century export porcelain'. It was, as usual, a sophisticated and knowledgeable audience, which is always stimulating for the lecturer. On the closing day there were two 'workshop' sessions which enabled every participant to handle objects in the storerooms and ask questions of lecturers informally. These are rightly popular and very instructive. On the Saturday I flew to Boston and was delighted to stay with Chris and Susie Weld while I lectured at the Peabody on a similar subject, but within a week I was flying home to find Angela much improved. December was almost an anticlimax after the previous year, but we enjoyed seeing George Overend again and Dubby and Susan Wynne for lunch. However it was a relief to have a quiet Christmas at home with Pat and Robin, and Angela's sister Thérèse and her family in the run up to the New Year.

I have never bothered much about birthday parties, but was encouraged to make an exception in 1998 for my seventieth birthday. It was very good to be able to collect so many friends and relations for a comfortable lunch in a private room at the Bath Spa Hotel. I was particularly touched when Donald Wilson gave me a letter written from Paris by a Coldstream colonel just after Waterloo, describing the battle. Some old friends came from London, and Philippa was one of two from America, but most were relations, some of whom seldom saw each other. In the event I was delighted that we had the

With Peter Frelinghuysen in the courtyard at Manor Farm.

My 70th birthday – with Peter Gwynn-Jones (Garter) and
Canon John Andrew of New York.

Thomas and Jo,
Philippa and Sophie,
taken for my 70th birthday.

With Anne Aberdeen and John Ayers at my birthday lunch.

party, and it was the first time that we had gathered together all my children and all Hazel's children since our marriage in 1989. It was a prelude, too, to a busy spring, which included a long weekend in Paris, much of the time with Arnaud and Veronique Maspetiol, and having an interesting dinner with Pierre Debomy and his wife. I was later to write a short foreword to Pierre's comprehensive book on 'tobacco leaf' porcelain, and it was an education to see so much on display in his home.

As we continued to enjoy visits from friends, we planned a holiday in Ireland at the end of April, spending three days in Dublin and visiting many interesting places including the cathedral. Leaving Dublin we drove to Co. Armagh and stayed with William Neely (who was also a Prebendary of Dublin Cathedral and had come down for the day to show us round). It was to be a most interesting three days, with visits to Armagh Cathedral, long drives in the beautiful countryside of this much-troubled land and a day in Lisburn at the Linen Museum where Brian Mackey, the Director of the Museum and a friend of William's, spent the day with us and was, I think, a little surprised at what remained of my memories of the linen trade from my years in Bridport.

Leaving Keady, we drove on to Glaslough in Co. Monaghan to visit Castle Leslie, where we had arranged to meet Sir John Leslie, a retired British diplomat, who was interested in discussing some armorial objects about which we had written earlier. It was to be an amusing visit. The house had been in the family since 1660 when bought by Bishop John Leslie (known as 'The Fighting Bishop' for his defeat of Cromwell's forces at the Battle of Raphoe). Dean Swift also visited the house on a number of occasions and wrote:

> Here I am at Castle Leslie
> With rows of books upon the shelves
> Written by the Leslies
> All about themselves.

(This was one of the more complimentary verses he penned of the family.)

The house was run by Sir John's niece and her husband who took in paying guests, and Sir John, who was convalescing, met us in a comfortable bathrobe and pink slippers, and showed us round the castle, including various bedrooms with somewhat eccentric bathroom decoration. Over coffee we discussed a fob seal that a gardener had recently found buried in the grass verge to the drive. When we identified the arms after our return home, and gave him the name, it was found to have the arms of his father's late doctor, who, he felt, was last at the house in the 1920s.

That evening and for the next two we stayed with the O'Hara family at Coopers Hill near Sligo, who also ran a most comfortable guest establishment in the graceful Georgian house they had occupied for more than two centuries. We drove through Sligo and up the coast towards Westport and Clew Bay, and a day later headed southwest to our next destination near Clifden. From Connemara we set off south via Galway, spending a pleasant afternoon with George Stacpoole at Adare before arriving at Kanturk and the delightful Assolas House, the home of a branch of the Burke family, for the last five days of our Irish holiday. Days in Cork and Kinsale, on the Dingle peninsular and at Bantry House (with Valentia Island on the horizon, the original home of my Irish ancestors on the south-western tip of Ireland) occupied us until we had to drive to Cork, and home via the night ferry to Swansea.

*   *   *

There was a final twist to *A Tale of Three Cities*, for Sotheby's Institute had asked earlier if I would be involved in a major symposium on the China Trade in early November. It was a question of ideas and personalities, and I came up with the idea that the seminar should be called *The China Circle*, with a lecturer to represent every major western country that had taken part in the trade between the 16th and 19th Centuries. It was to be a stimulating task finding lecturers from eleven countries to speak on Chinese porcelain for fourteen different markets worldwide, but rewarding in that it would gather together many of the leading academics in the field. My main contact at Sotheby's Institute was Caroline Bloch, who was a pleasure to work with and handled all the administration. In the event there were lectures on the markets in Turkey and the Middle East, Japan, Portugal, Holland, Spain, Britain, France, Belgium, Denmark, Germany, Sweden, the Dutch Colonial Trade and America over three days. Together these presented a continuous picture of the China Trade from different perspectives, revealing the Chinese as adept in satisfying similar but competing demands from European and other merchants.

The summer, meanwhile, brought its usual share of visitors and we were particularly pleased to meet Kosei Kishimoto, with whom we had originally been in touch at the time of the Vung Tau Cargo in 1992 and who, with his delightful wife Junko, came to have lunch while staying the weekend in Castle Combe. He was the builder of the new Osaka Museum after the earthquake, which was to have a large display of underwater porcelain cargoes in a gallery under the sea. We also had a very pleasant three-day visit by my nephew Nick, who was anxious to try to wring from my copious manuscript notes and records an improved view of our family history, followed next day for the

With David Perth by the private chapel at Stobhall.

With Angus Hamilton in the newly created porcelain gallery at Lennoxlove.

weekend by Arnaud's two daughters, Virginie and Aurelie, who were travelling in England prior to Aurelie going to study international law at Cambridge University where she had won a place. Quite like old days we all gathered in Cornwall at Tresawle at the end of July for a week, even Philippa and her two children coming from America.

In August we drove to Scotland for a week and stayed again with David Perth, and Angus and Kay Hamilton, with an interesting and informal lunch at Holyrood where the other guest was Clarissa Dickson-Wright (then famous as one of the 'two fat ladies' whose television programme was much the rage) who was planning to open a restaurant at Lennoxlove. On our return there was a very special visit for lunch by Pamela Copeland, quite remarkably active in her nineties and as interested in discovering the quality of compost used on the garden as discussing her world-famous collection of Chinese porcelain birds and animals.

September passed with a fascinating Sotheby sale of a Welsh estate in Carmarthenshire, for which we stayed and spent a comfortable evening with Robert and Carol Pugh. Although we were unable to buy the other 'half' of the Stepney armorial service because of its very high price, we were later able to acquire a substantial number of pieces with various minor damage from the successful bidder, its history as well as its visual appeal making it an attractive investment for many collectors. A brief interlude in October was a visit from Martin and Margaret Arnold, and the years fell away as we discussed days in Dorset and Leeds forty years ago, and even Stowe, now more than fifty years behind us.

Surprisingly I had never lectured at a meeting of the Heraldry Society, but I enjoyed doing so at the annual meeting in Gloucester that autumn (and was delighted, some three years later, to be invited to become a Fellow of the Society). We hurried back to West Yatton the following day and several members of the Society came to tea on the Sunday on their way home. A week later it was a particular pleasure to be able to lecture for Bill McNaught at the American Museum in Bath, which was followed by one of his excellent dinners in his upper floor flat where the variety of guests, drawn from local dignitaries to American politicians and diplomats, always provided good conversation.

A long weekend in Bruges was a very comfortable diversion. We were able to admire both the architecture and the contents of a number of fine houses and museums, while journeys on the river boats undoubtedly make Bruges a 'Venice of the north'. It is a European experience not to be missed.

*　　*　　*

November was not to pass uneventfully, for months of planning and correspondence finally came to fruition and Sotheby's Institute seminar *The China Circle* was held over three full days at the Royal Commonwealth Institute. We stayed at the Oriental Club and dined with various friends from abroad each night. The Commonwealth Institute, just off Trafalgar Square, was also comfortable and well-equipped, so that we could have lunch and other meals there and attendance was such that a larger lecture room had to be found.

The lectures themselves were of a very high standard. There was a natural tendency for lecturers to present their own market in the most favourable light, although old hands like Professor John Carswell, who spoke on the early Middle East trade, Dr Christiaan Jörg, who covered both home and colonial Dutch trade, and Dr Oliver Impey, who spoke on the trade with Japan, kept a perfect balance. There is always an area of friendly disagreement when lecturers from Spain and Portugal discuss 16th Century porcelain, but Dr Maria Antonia Pinto de Matos and Antonio Diez de Rivera (an old friend and collector who was lecturing on porcelain for the first time in English) kept this to a minimum. Professor Liu Xinyuan from China spoke in Chinese but had a charming translator who made his lecture come to life, while Dr Friedrich Reichel from Dresden had no difficulty in enlarging our knowledge of porcelain in Meissen style.

Of the European countries with active East India Companies, Kristina Söderpalm represented the Swedish and Dr Kristian Jakobsen the Danish markets, while Monique Crick and Chantal Kozyreff provided different perspectives to the French and Belgian markets. Kee Il Choi chose to illustrate some unusual pieces for the American market while I represented, not for the first time, the Honourable East India Company. The audience of about eighty (the youngest being only sixteen), drawn from at least ten countries, was the most diverse I have encountered but included many old friends.

There was little chance to relax, however, for the following weekend Angela and I flew to Stockholm for a seminar organised by the Oriental Ceramics Society of Sweden and the Friends of the Museum of Far Eastern Antiquities, to complement an extensive and most interesting exhibition organised by Dr Jan Wirgin, shortly to retire as Director of the Östasiatiska Museum. Jan had written an excellent and wide-ranging book *Från Kina till Europa* which in many respects mirrored *A Tale of Three Cities*, although it contained greater background in chapters on the Swedish Company (and represented a much longer period of planning and assembly).

We had been invited to stay in a very comfortable hotel on the waterfront, and in addition to giving my lecture at the Seminar and visiting the exhibition with Jan Wirgin, we found time to spend a morning at the Riddarhuset (House of Nobles) which contains a fine collection of Chinese porcelain with Swedish arms. We also visited the fascinating and very well displayed wreck of the *Vasa*, then the largest ship in Sweden which capsized in 1628 on her maiden voyage after sailing barely one mile, but now displayed in her entirety in her own museum. While we had dinner at the homes of Margareta and Jan Wirgin, and Charlotte and Cleive Hornstrand (who I discovered had known well General Carl Berg, with whom I had spent a day in Tahiti some thirty years earlier), we also appreciated a fine evening given by the Friends of the Museum for the lecturers, who again included Christiaan Jörg and Kee Il Choi. It was an all-too-short visit to a city we would enjoy visiting again.

Although we had a number of other visitors in December and Angela's family for Christmas, we needed time to catch up, for we already had had prior warning of the largest sale of armorial porcelain since the collection of Cecil Bullivant in 1998. In the new year we were able to drive to Sotheby's at Billingshurst to see Clive Rouse's collection which was to be sold early in March in 150 lots, many containing a diversity of damaged but most interesting pieces collected by Clive over sixty years (and not a few illustrated in *Chinese Armorial Porcelain*). Although much of his life had been spent as one of the world's leading experts on the subject of mediaeval church wall paintings, armorial porcelain had been a special love.

But by now it was clear that every available hour of my time that was not required by Heirloom must be spent on Volume II of *Chinese Armorial Porcelain* if this was to be ready for a publisher by the end of 2002.

CHAPTER 28

The end of a Millennium

During more than twenty-five years since Heirloom was formed, I had photographed every piece of Chinese armorial porcelain which was either exceptional or of a service which was new to me. This had, to a great extent, been made possible by the steady flow of such porcelain through the salerooms which were the life blood of the antiques trade. As the years passed, it became possible to explore American and Continental salerooms to a much greater extent than was so in the 1960s and '70s, and all this had yielded examples of rather more than nine hundred services for the British market which were not illustrated in *Chinese Armorial Porcelain*, averaging about thirty-six each year for a quarter of a century.

More and more frequently, however, in the late 1990s, information made available on the internet and the willingness of overseas salerooms to send illustrations by the new digital technology had increased this to more than double that rate, and throughout the last four years of writing Volume II, the figure reached a hundred in a year. (At the time of writing, in mid 2004, pieces of no less than eight new services were discovered in one exceptional week at five locations in three countries.) All this led me to estimate that at one day in the future a total of about six thousand Chinese armorial services for the British market would be known – a figure greeted with a little scepticism in some quarters!

But for the purpose of the new volume I had now set a target of 1,300 new entries to be illustrated, identified and their brief histories told over the next three years, while at the same time updating and extending the information contained in about 150 pages of appendices and index from the first volume. (This was to be largely additional to the everyday business of Heirloom, although the two could work in tandem on occasions when pieces became available for sale and buyers were anxious to know their histories.) An essential part of the task was that as I wrote, Angela would be able to transcribe my writing on to a database which would enable a publisher one day to have the material printed without further transcription by an outside source. Had such technology been available twenty-five years earlier, it would have greatly eased the very high level of manual work that was then necessary for the first volume, although the satisfaction obtained from completing either made any such work worthwhile.

406

In practical terms, one of the most time-consuming tasks was to ensure every cross-reference was noted – for so many of the newly discovered services were found to be related by family, marriage, or by cargo of the same sailing to others already known. As it seems likely that on average throughout the 18th Century an armorial service was made in China every week for a century, the evidence this could provide for dating and understanding the wider trade was of considerable importance, particularly as there are virtually no Chinese records of their export trade to the 'foreign devils'. (In this respect porcelain copied from European prints also played an important role, but without such close evidence of dating.) But on this tiny proportion of the trade, aided in recent years by the discovery of datable 'underwater cargoes', the whole chronology of the styles of Chinese export porcelain, with or without armorials, and its dating largely rests.

As the first two months of 1999 passed I adjusted easily to the new regime of writing whenever possible, although Heirloom was busy with the January New York sales and its catalogue. In February I lectured in Herefordshire, and this gave us an unexpected opportunity to visit Ocle Court, with its church nearby, which Angela's great-great-great-grandfather had owned in the mid 19th Century. As we wandered round a large farmyard we met Matthew Oliver, the son of the present owner, whose grandfather had bought the estate from the Postlethwaites in the early 20th Century. He welcomed our unexpected visit and gave us the key to the church where we saw the window installed in 1859 by James Leech Harrison, Angela's ancestor, who died there and whose two daughters had married two Postlethwaite brothers. We were invited to tea with his mother and they showed us the house – an interesting visit which we much enjoyed.

In the last week of February we had a visit from Dr Jochem Kroes, who worked for the Dutch Bureau of Genealogy. He had been encouraged by Dr Christaan Jörg to write a book on Chinese armorial porcelain for the Dutch market – a project which I felt should be a success, for there was a surprising lack of published information about the Dutch families who must have ordered at least six hundred services and controlled the most important East India company in the 17th and early 18th Century, based on what were known for three centuries as the Dutch East Indies. Jochem spent two busy days here and was able to tell me much about a number of services with Dutch armorials of which my knowledge was insufficient. I also felt he was surprised by the considerable number of examples of Dutch services which I had photographed over forty years. In the week after his visit I was able to provide transparencies of over 160 of these which I look forward, one day, to seeing in his book. It was the start of a long correspondence over the next five years.

It has also been a pleasure to work with Antoine Lebel, a Paris dealer and fluent English speaker, who has collected a great deal of material on armorial porcelain for the French market. If all the known initiatives were published, this would cover the British and American, the Swedish, Dutch, Belgian, French and Portuguese markets (the latter catalogued by Nuno de Castro with his excellent book *Chinese Porcelain and the Heraldry of the Empire*) – some six thousand services ordered between 1690 and 1870, of which more than two-thirds were British.

At the end of February I was very sad to hear of the death of my brother-in-law, Basil Watts, with whom, with his wife Sue (Elizabeth's sister), I had shared a happy relationship for fifty years. We attended a moving service in Twickenham and all had lunch together afterwards, seeing a number of other members of the family. On the following Monday we went to stay with Angela's parents near Guildford, for it was particularly important to spend a day examining Clive Rouse's collection at Billingshurst for the last time before the sale on the Wednesday. Clive had never minded about damage, believing, in my opinion rightly, that it was the history of the piece that was most important. In the event we were able to acquire some 180 pieces at the sale and our restorer was provided with months of work, while many collectors were delighted to find examples of services which, even after restoration, would otherwise have cost them far more had they been perfect.

Apart from a leisurely weekend in London at Brown's Hotel to celebrate our tenth wedding anniversary, we enjoyed three or four visitors a week in April, and it was always nice in spring and summer to take a walk round what was now an almost mature country garden and fast-growing woodland of some three acres. Throughout 1997 and '98 I had worked to complete the last major project, and this had occupied some time every weekend and many summer and autumn evenings. The mowing of the orchards and lawns, including one on which it was just possible to play croquet, was largely now left to Tony who spent twelve hours a week here.

Over the last century a three-foot high and substantial boundary 'dry-stone' wall running for almost two hundred yards along the bank beside our field and above the lane to Castle Combe had slowly subsided, so that it lay as rubble, largely covered by brambles and nettles. It took two years of work to retrieve all the stone and rebuild the wall some two to five yards from the lane on firmer ground. There was no need to acquire more stone, for the remains of a farm building now lost among roadside trees provided further material, and it was possible to construct another three-foot wall from the existing stone, the centre containing all the rubble too small for the outer facing. I hope the result will stand for a century or two, but I was amused by an American friend from the west coast who stood staring for a minute or two at the completed length, hardly believing that I could have undertaken such a task. 'Why David,' he said, 'in California we get Mexicans to do such work.' But it was very satisfying to complete the work myself, probably never achieving more than two yards in any one day.

*   *   *

We were a little more 'adventurous' on our holiday in France this year, and after two days in Paris during which we had dinner with Arnaud and Veronique, and John and Monique Crick, took a train to the south and a car from Cahors to the undisturbed valley of the Lot, staying in the early mediaeval village of Saint Cirq Lapopie. It stands on an unspoiled rock face above the river, inhabited today by people undertaking crafts of past centuries and provided a stay of great beauty. A day at Rocamadour was far too short (and luckily relatively tourist-free) with its history of receiving English pilgrims including Henry II and Simon de Montfort, Blanche of Castille and Saint (King) Louis IX (whose image decorated a few pieces of the Chinese porcelain found in the Vung Tau cargo).

After a few days at our favourite spots in the Dordogne, we drove north to the valley of the Loire, not omitting to spend a few hours in the museum at Limoges so that we could see their display of porcelain. Here was a different world of the 15th to 19th Centuries, where ancient castles had largely been replaced by the magnificent chateaux built after the reigns of King Henry (IV) of Navarre and from Louis XIII onwards. We stayed in comfort in a small privately owned chateau on the Loire near Amboise and spent our days at Cheverny, the gardens at Villandry, the moated fortress at Azay-le-Rideau, the magnificent chateau at Chaumont and that at Amboise, where Leonardo da Vinci spent his last years, dying there in 1519. Although 'lost' in times past, we were able to motor from Tours to Orleans and on to Gien, where we found an excellent porcelain factory and bought a set of modern plates in a style reminiscent of the China Trade. Eventually we left our car in Tours, reaching home by train after a final evening in Paris.

Next day it was fun to have Becky McGuire of Christie's, New York, and her husband to tea, with more visitors most days through May and June including Norman and Kathy, and Graham Beck and his wife, Lida Lopes Cardozo-Kindersley (Graham had been a vital link in the Heraldry Exhibition in New York nearly fifteen years before). A visit by a group from the mid-west travelling under the guidance of Susie Mammel attended a lecture which I gave for them in Bath, and June saw almost daily visits at the time of the

London antique fairs. There was more time to write in July, although I had to struggle to keep to my self-imposed schedule.

In early August we had a welcome break and stayed a night with Frank and Patricia Herrmann in Essex before driving north to Chillingham Castle, on the moors some twenty miles south of the Scottish border and home to the famous herd of cattle, where we arrived in the evening and stayed the night with Humphry and Katherine Wakefield. Humphry had long been involved with art and antiques, and I had first met him in New York in the 1970s when he was the director of Mallets. His wide knowledge and even wider contacts had led him towards the field of fine reproductions of furniture and paintings, choosing as the originals exceptional pieces in private homes he knew. (Among his lesser-known achievements were the Freedom of Kansas City, and honorary citizenship of Houston and New Orleans.) After a fascinating morning spent touring the castle, ending on the roof looking down over the distant landscape and formal gardens which Humphry had recreated, we had to be on our way again.

We drove north through Coldstream and spent a pleasant weekend with David Perth, on the Saturday driving over to have tea with Lord Balfour of Burleigh, recently retired from many of his directorships, where we much enjoyed meeting his wife, the author Janet Morgan, whose biographies of Richard Crossman, Agatha Christie and Edwina Mountbatten had been very successful. More fun even than finding pieces of two 'new' Bruce services I didn't know, was visiting the elaborate tree house Lord Balfour himself had built in a huge tree on the lawns and watching him and his wife swinging from long ropes in the trees as if they were Tarzan and Jane! I was to have a lively correspondence with him over the Bruce porcelain, which he kindly said I could photograph so that it should be in Volume II. But on Monday we had to head south again for a busy week.

The following weekend Angela set off to the south-west of Ireland to spend a week with her sister's family who had taken a cottage there, but I was left with ample supplies of supermarket fish pies and other packets to last me the week and many instructions as to how I was to cope with such essentials as vegetables.

*   *   *

As the volume of manuscript work was mounting and ready to be translated from the handwritten pages to some form of database by Angela, who would also be reading through the text, the problem of publishing ourselves assumed a more important role in forward planning. Two concerns in particular were:

the conversion of probably more than two thousand transparencies, prints, polaroids and various internet downloads into co-ordinated scans for printing, and the preparation of the layout and editing of the formal text.

The illustrations had been assembled over thirty years from many sources and were of varying quality, although about 80% were photographs taken by the author. The problem of editing and layout raised many questions: principally, how much we could undertake ourselves, and how to obtain the technical know-how so that what we did undertake could be integrated into the printing and publishing which was to follow. On this most important front I had been encouraged by my renewed contact with Roy Davey, whom I had known well at Arnold and who had recently retired as a senior director of Harper-Collins and was now an independent publishing adviser. I had already established that Fabers, who had published the first volume, would raise no objection to such a plan, and Roy was to introduce me to a small organisation under the control of Mike Blacker and suggested that they could turn the whole manuscript into print-ready copy for Heirloom & Howard to publish.

During the next twelve months we were to plan and develop a system of coding so that all illustrations would only print against the matching text, each finding the other automatically. It was possible to devise a layout system which would ensure that entries in their sections could also be grouped by style. This tailor-made database was put together by an independent expert, Roger Shapland, and not only ensured the order and cross-matching but later provided an index which grew as the work proceeded, as well as ensuring an alphabetical index of mottoes, each cross-referenced to the relevant service, and an analysis of the location and occupation of owners of armorial porcelain from the text – both important appendices. The contrast with my experience thirty years earlier in hand writing and arranging every name, style, motto and other analyses could hardly have been greater.

None of this was achieved without many revisions and adjustments as our ideas developed, particularly when the scanning from widely different sources produced at first unacceptably different results, and editorially when the transcription of appendices and other material in tabular form proved too complex for an outside source without an unacceptable level of inaccuracy and had to be taken over by ourselves. But as the author struggled to keep to his self-imposed schedule (and his cool) we were able to make steady progress and even adapt already completed sections to incorporate the steady flow of new material which turned up each month. This was planned to continue throughout 2000 and 2001 and was to be complete by early summer of 2002, while the everyday work of Heirloom continued.

In the event we managed to keep to our schedule, but there were some changes in management and control. Mike Blacker's company was unexpectedly integrated into the newly-created Third Millennium Publishing Company and we agreed at that stage that we had learned so much that it would be possible to continue the publishing work ourselves, producing all the copy ready for the printer (although who this would be was not decided). All this seemed to make sense, for not only did it save explaining very complex arrangements to a new team, but we could employ Roger Shapland ourselves and have total control over the production of the book, albeit at the 'cost' of considerable extra work for ourselves. This was agreed amicably, and instead of handing the database to a third party so that it could be set in Quark ready for the printing machines, Angela took a crash course in transferring and editing all the text into Quark herself, mastering this under Roger's guidance, so that there was no third party between Heirloom (newly a publisher) and the printer.

*   *   *

The last autumn of the millennium passed quickly, but included a visit from Peter Brown from Fairfax House, York, who had asked to borrow some porcelain and whose series of exhibitions and catalogues on porcelain and eating in the 18th Century have opened a new field. I also lectured rather closer to home than usual at the Holburne Museum in Bath in early October, and it was fun, as always, to have Bill Sargent from the Peabody to stay a month later. But the most exciting journey of the autumn was a flight to Portugal for a seminar and a trip to Spain. For reasons best known to the scheduled airline, it was far cheaper to fly to Lisbon and travel to Madrid by train than to fly direct to Madrid returning via Lisbon, so we took that route and had a comfortable overnight journey arriving for breakfast at our hotel in Madrid. It was our first visit and we took the opportunity of seeing both the Prado and the Thyssen Bornemisza Museums, much enjoying our day there. We met Antonio and Cristina Diez de Rivera early in the evening for dinner, first introducing them to Cristina and Manuel Alabart with whom we had cocktails in their rooftop apartment with panoramic views over night-time Madrid. Manuel was at the time the Spanish ambassador to Malaysia, whom we had met on a number of occasions and who was a keen collector of armorial porcelain.

Next morning Antonio and Cristina collected us in their car and we drove across Spain, westwards towards Portugal, stopping for lunch at Talavera (where inevitably the conversation turned to the Napoleonic Wars). We continued by way of some magnificent hill-top castles towards Badajoz and the Portuguese border where, after crossing, we stayed at Estremoz at a delightful *pousada*. These luxurious and historic former 'rest houses' are found throughout the country, this particular 14th Century castle bearing the name of its patron, Saint Queen Isabel, who died in 1336. The whole journey was a very interesting and comfortable experience, rendered more so because of the detailed commentary of Antonio, formerly the Director of Spanish motorways and bridges. Later that day we were able to join other members of the symposium in Vila Viçosa, where we toured the Ducal Palace, before arriving at the Sheraton Hotel in Lisbon where we were to meet a number of other lecturers, seven of whom had lectured two years earlier at *The China Circle*.

The symposium itself was organised by the Portuguese Society *Amigos de Oriente*, in which Jorge Welsh played a leading role, and was held within walking distance of our hotel at the magnificent Gulbenkian Foundation, still under the direction of Dr Gulbenkian (nephew of Nubar Gulbenkian, the famed financier, widely known as 'Mr 5%'). The lectures were spread over three days, and among other engagements we had provisionally arranged to have lunch on the Tuesday with a collector, Dr Espirito Santo Silva, whom we knew but had not previously met, before my own lecture in the afternoon (although he was not quite certain he would be able to return in time from a journey to New York).

After the morning lectures, I was signing some copies of my recent books and was giving a newspaper interview when approached by a charming Portuguese gentleman, who listened to the end of my interview and without introducing himself said, 'I'm so glad to meet you. Let us go and have lunch at my favourite restaurant across the road.' This we did, walking across the Museum gardens and discussing the symposium. During lunch we paused after ordering the main course, and our host said, 'It is such a pleasure to meet you and I wanted to present you with a book I have written myself – but of course it does not compare with your own work on the early Chinese export trade to Armenia.' There was a pause as he smiled across the table, and thinking as quickly as I could, I had to reply, 'I have a dreadful feeling that I am not who you think I am, and that you are not who we think you are! Are you Dr Espirito Santo Silva?' 'No, no,' he said, 'I am Dr Gulbenkian – are you not Professor John Carswell?' After we had all recovered from the unexpected turn of events (later learning that the receptionist at the seminar had told him that Professor Carswell was 'giving an interview', which had given rise to the mistake) the rest of a very friendly lunch passed in interesting conversation and we walked back to the Museum. Following my afternoon lecture, John Carswell, who was in the audience, came up and said, with no little irritation,

'You kidnapped my guest for lunch – I have been waiting to have lunch with him for ten years ...'. It was not until after we met at a reception at Jorge Welsh's gallery that evening that I was able to explain that I had thought our host was someone else who had arranged to take us to lunch that day, and that in fact he had 'kidnapped us'! It went some way to assuaging his obviously very considerable annoyance about the affair, and when we met at another symposium in Lisbon two years later we were even able to laugh about it. (On returning home I wrote to Dr Gulbenkian and sent him two of my books, receiving in reply a number of his, with a very pleasant letter.)

One of the most remarkable displays of porcelain in the world is the 'blue and white ceiling' now in the French Embassy in Lisbon, which is formed by a fine design of 16th, 17th and 18th Century blue and white Chinese porcelain attached to the ceiling of a whole room. The French Ambassador had very kindly invited participants in the symposium to a small reception so that he could show us this remarkable sight. It is not easily forgotten. On the final evening we all had an exceptional reception and dinner at the Espirito Santo Silva Foundation, and there was no doubt that the whole affair was one of the best organised and most enjoyable symposia I had attended in some thirty years of lecturing, not least because of the number of interesting events outside the lectures, including several private visits to museums.

Before flying home we made one final journey by train towards Estoril where my nephew, Toby, was teaching English, to senior school pupils during the day, and business executives and their associates in the evening. He had done this in at least eight European countries, and now lives comfortably in his own house in Hungary. Our meeting in Sintra was delayed by an hour because of an accident on the railway line, after which we were invited to walk about a mile along the track to the next station. It was a new experience on the railways, but seemed to work.

Arriving home again, much of the last month of the 20th Century was spent writing, although Garter, who always spurred me on and who I had already asked to write a foreword to Volume II, came down for a long weekend. It was also the closing month of the political tangle concerning the now rather contentious Dome, built at Greenwich (at enormous cost) to welcome the new millennium. To my pleasure, my fifteen-year-old granddaughter, Jenny, was one of the children selected from the west of England to serve on one of a number of 'consultative committees' to make clear their points of view. She had favoured greater emphasis on local initiatives, but at one of her committee's last meetings with a junior minister he had announced that free passes would be given to families visiting with their children during a limited period. Jenny was able to ask Lord Falconer, 'That is nice, but have you

In Manor Farm kitchen with Sophie and my eldest grandchild, Jenny.

Oscar Husum looks Sophie's bronze head in the eye.

thought that it is the cost of rail fares from places like Cornwall that is by far the greatest cost for such families?' It was clear that the minister had not, but by the end of the month he had made fares part of the deal.

I'm delighted that Jenny, my oldest grandchild, is now at Napier University in Edinburgh studying photography, which I hope will enable her to find an artistic career and which, together with some considerable talent at acting (and a willingness to take some part-time work to pay her way), will provide a good background for an interesting life in the new millennium.

But on the 31st December 1999, as the fireworks lit the night skies at West Yatton, and those less fortunate who had been invited to the Dome queued to get security clearance, I was able to feel that I had been glad to have been part of the 20th Century, and was looking forward to the 21st.

CHAPTER 29

Collectors, Collections, Museums and Sales

The new century started with a flight to New York to attend the sales at Sotheby's and Christie's, and where a surprise dinner party at Khalil Rizk's apartment in Park Avenue awaited us. A very special day was spent at Rhinebeck for my 72nd birthday, having lunch at the Beekman Arms and greatly enjoying the journey by train along the Hudson river – as beautiful in January as it was in the summer months. But disaster nearly struck when we discovered that the train returning us to New York from Buffalo was severely delayed by snow and ice, and we were only just able to reach Khalil's apartment in time for an excellent supper with other old friends including Tish Roberts, Margi Gristina and Bill Sargent – and, to my great surprise, a special birthday pudding with candles (though I was not aware that he knew).

For the rest of our stay we were the guests of John Andrew at Grace Church, for two years the Rector of this exceptional church in Gothic style in Lower Manhattan, where the rectory in the same style still maintains a substantial garden in front and was attached by a passage to the church itself. It was an unusual experience staying in the very elegant and comfortable 19th Century rooms of the rectory, just yards from Broadway. On the last afternoon of our stay we enjoyed having tea with Mildred Mottahedeh in her apartment looking south over the United Nations buildings. She was a little slower than when I saw her last, but seemed well as she discussed her plans for the next few years and as usual her latest ideas (including a plan to develop frozen bananas as a new type of ice cream!). As the light faded over the skyscrapers of southern Manhattan, the magnificent view from the 17th floor was lit by a fine sunset and it was easy to understand why, with her achievements and her view, she was a focused 91. We left, as always, with a kiss as she saw us to the lift.

Three weeks later her obituary in *The New York Times* read in part:

> … In 1929, the couple founded Mottahedeh & Company in Manhattan, which rose to prominence as one of the most prestigious firms in the reproduction of porcelain, producing some 1,500 different items for more than 3,000 stores from Tiffany's to small gift boutiques. The company also reproduced pieces in the collections of museums like the Metropolitan and the Museum of Modern Art in New York and the Musée des Arts

At home at United Nations Plaza, New York.
Mildred with a cabinet of early Chinese porcelain.

The view from Mildred's apartment on the 17th floor,
looking down the East River with the United Nations building in the foreground.

Décoratifs in Paris for sale in their shops. Mottahedeh reproductions have graced the White House as well as the reception rooms of the State Department in Washington …

… the Mottahedehs began acquiring Oriental porcelains, ivories, jades and bronzes, amassing one of the world's finest private collections with some 2,000 pieces. In his foreword to 'China for the West', an authoritative publication on the Mottahedeh collection, Nelson A. Rockefeller, a friend and fellow collector of Chinese export porcelain, described the collection as 'utterly fabulous, an artistic and cultural treasure without comparison in its field'.

A member of the Baha'i faith, Mrs Mottahedeh served for many years as the first Baha'i representative to the United Nations. With her husband, she founded a series of primary and secondary schools in Uganda and maintained four village development projects in Maharashtra state in India that served as training facilities in agricultural techniques, public health services and the development of local handcrafts.

It was almost thirty years since I had first met Mildred. She was as understanding, generous and amusing as she was creative and dynamic. She certainly influenced my life and we shall not often see her like again.

*   *   *

The spring at West Yatton was as busy as ever and we enjoyed a day's visit from Osmund Bullock, who had often helped Heirloom at busy times in the past when, as an actor, he was 'resting'. His interest and knowledge of heraldry and porcelain always made for a productive meeting of minds. Every spare minute was still occupied with Volume II, but in mid March we set off again to America for a brief holiday, in part at the invitation of Leo Hodroff and Pamela Copeland.

It was particularly relaxing to be able to adjust to American hours with Malcolm and Joan Sterrett at their delightful 18th Century farmhouse, now encircled by modern Bethesda. Malcolm is a friend with an interesting collection and a particular knowledge of social and maritime history and the China Trade, but who had spent some years as a special advisor at the White House and knew Washington from the inside, while Joan had long been on the committee of the Washington Antiques Show. We were also able to visit the State Department Rooms again, with their fine collection of antiques largely gathered together in the time of Clem Conger. It was particularly interesting to be able to spend a morning at Mount Vernon with Mal and Joan (which Angela had not been to before) and visit various museums, while we were also able to have lunch in the House Dining Room with Rodney Frelinghuysen following a long tour of the buildings, joined by their labyrinth of underground corridors. In the evenings we enjoyed what was for us something of a social whirl, with a particularly nice dinner party given by Joan and Malcolm and another with Judi and Ed Eckenhoff, who has a legendary collection of Chinese tankards. It was also good to see Jim and Nancy Flather again, whom I had known for many years, one evening at the Sulgrave Club.

For our last two days in Washington we moved the comparatively short distance from Bethesda to stay as the guest of Angela's cousin, Noble McCartney (a retired lawyer who she had never met before) at the Chevy Chase Club. Noble had lived in America all his life, the grandson of Angela's great-grandmother, Virginia Dreher, a talented Shakespearean actress who had been brought up in Kentucky but played on Broadway a number of times and twice visited England in productions at Drury Lane. It was interesting to discuss our different backgrounds as we lunched and dined at the Chevy Chase, and fascinating to find how many friends we had in common – Noble having been at Princeton with Peter Frelinghuysen – while Angela wanted to hear more about the American side of her family.

A principal reason we had travelled to America on this occasion had been an invitation from Leo Hodroff to discuss with him the future of his collection, now almost certainly the largest in the world in the field of Chinese Export porcelain. Having given modest bequests to two well-known museums, but finding that these were not always displayed either in the way or to the extent he hoped, he felt that a collection of this importance and quality should, if possible, be made permanently available to the widest public possible over the foreseeable future. Ever mindful, however, that collections could be displayed briefly and then put 'into reserve', he wanted to find a way in which this fate could be avoided.

We stayed in great comfort at the Breakers Hotel in Palm Beach (having breakfast one morning with Dubby and Susan Wynne who, by chance, were also staying in Palm Beach) but spent most of our time with Leo and Doris, and what evolved from a full day of discussions was to be a blueprint for Leo's future plans, for he and Doris had no immediate family. My own input into the discussions centred round the theme of education, which I felt was the main safeguard of any collection in the future. I felt also that if an organisation could have a bequest which funded not just the porcelain itself but one or more curators, *they* would then ensure that the collection, given over a period, would be displayed to its full advantage and *they* would promote and display that collection and educate the public and ensure its permanent exhibition (if only to enhance their own careers and reputation). My own view also was that the gifts of porcelain should be selective, so that a substantial part would still find its way back into the market to continue attracting collectors, many of whom need the stimulus of acquisition to enhance their interest.

Such an overall scenario seemed to please Leo, but no final decision was made as to which museum should be approached, although a number of options were discussed and such factors as location, management, financial strength and educational record were recognised as important, and Leo said that he would like to visit 'incognito' any institution proposed before a final choice was made. I was, however, given permission to mention the idea, without naming the donor, to one particular museum.

It was, perhaps, fortuitous that I was lecturing at Winterthur in ten days' time, and that Angela and I would be staying with Pamela Copeland, whose own collection of birds and animals of China Trade porcelain was world-famous. Indeed, Bill Sargent's book on the subject had provided a major impetus in Leo's determination to have published *The Choice of the Private Trader*.

*   *   *

Leaving Florida, I had arranged for Philippa to fly in from New Mexico and meet us in Atlanta for what was to be a very pleasant joint holiday lasting eight days, for we very much enjoyed staying first with George and Carol Overend for two nights, and then with Bo and Eileen. Four days later we drove eastwards from Atlanta to the sea and reached Savannah in the afternoon to meet Bo's daughter Elizabeth, and her husband Mark, who had asked us to stay for two nights.

I had not been in Savannah since Jim Williams' death and the huge publicity which had surrounded first the publishing of *Midnight in the Garden of Good and Evil* and then the film (which featured more than one object which Jim had purchased from Heirloom almost two decades earlier). After entering an antique shop to look round, the owner remembered our previous meeting some twenty years earlier and telephoned Jim's sister, Dorothy, now living at Mercer House, to say we were in Savannah. When he handed me the phone, she asked if we could have tea with her and we gladly accepted. It was an interesting and happy meeting, and the years fell away as I looked at the largely unaltered rooms. She found the intense publicity very tiring, and even as we stood in front of the house a tourist bus drew up and a guide with a loudspeaker, spotting Jim's sister, said, '… and there she is.' She told us she had decided to sell up and go, and a sale of much of the contents of Mercer House took place later that year in New York. (I bought a heavily potted Chinese blue and white bowl which had sat for many years in Jim's hall, and keep it for sentimental reasons.)

Next morning the three of us set off for Charleston, which neither Angela nor Philippa had visited before, and we spent two nights in that unique place which held so many sentimental memories of my American ancestors throughout the 18th Century. The delightful Vendue Inn at which we stayed was by East Bay Street, and in the morning we walked a few hundred yards to 101 East Bay where Othniel Beale (my great x4 grandfather) had lived on 'Rainbow Row', and where a plaque outside gave details of his life and the fact that he had been in charge of strengthening the fortifications at Charleston in the early 18th Century, an area still called 'The Battery'.

The next parallel street, Meeting Street, contains many of Charleston's finest houses, and of No. 35 is written: 'This house is believed to have been built in 1720 by the first Lieutenant Governor of South Carolina, William Bull. His son, William, was the first native South Carolinian to receive a medical degree and like his father also served as Lieutenant Governor.' It goes on to say that he married Othniel Beale's daughter, but was forced to leave Charleston in 1776, much against his will but because of his principles of loyalty to his post, and died in London in the 1790s, an exile. His niece and her husband, Colonel and Mrs Stapleton, who accompanied him, lived to see their two daughters married to Bishop Lloyd of Oxford and Admiral Beechey, as related in Chapter 7.

Further down the street, originally laid out in 1672 by the Earl of Shaftesbury (the rivers leading to the sea on either side of Charleston being named Ashley and Cooper after the surnames of Lord Shaftesbury), we visited the church where the Beales and Bulls are also recorded. We had an enjoyable lunch with Katharine Danielson and her mother, Kit, (whose husband had been the director of the Gibbes Museum where I had lectured twenty years before) and in the afternoon walked to the south end of Meeting Street to have tea with Peter Manigault and his wife, following an introduction by Tom Savage of Sotheby's. We were able to discuss the various Manigault porcelain which this merchant family bought in China in the 19th Century and see one service still on display in their dining room.

The time had gone all too quickly, and next morning Philippa had to fly home to New Mexico, while we flew on to Philadelphia for what was to be a very special stay. To our surprise we were met by Pamela Copeland herself in her chauffeur-driven car and drove back to Mount Cuba where we spent the next three days. By any standards, Pamela Copeland was a remarkable lady of great knowledge, understanding and determination. Before we left she gave us a copy of her privately printed autobiography up to the time of her marriage to Lammot Copeland. There is little doubt that she must have been a great support, both when he was President of DuPont and later. I had stayed at Mount Cuba before, when Lammot was alive, but on this occasion we felt the enormous affection of the large staff (including some twenty in the gardens) for someone who insisted that they lived in houses on the estate which many would be pleased to own, and whose children attended, at her expense, the same private schools as her own family.

That evening Pamela's granddaughter and her husband, a vice-president of Sotheby's, joined us for dinner. I was scheduled to speak at Winterthur as the first lecturer in the morning, and it was typical of Pamela to insist on getting up early so that she could 'get a good seat' in the Copeland Theatre at the museum.

After the lecture and lunch we were able to have tea quietly with Leslie Bowman, the Director, and two other associates, and I ran before her the substance of our discussions with Leo, although he remained anonymous. They left little doubt in my mind that Winterthur would welcome such a plan to fund a curator, organising travelling displays backed by a permanent collection, and on our return home I put this in writing to her and received an encouraging letter which was sent at once to Leo. Shortly afterwards he and Doris made an anonymous visit to Winterthur and liked the atmosphere, letting me know that I could now inform them of his identity so that negotiations could begin.

That evening at Mount Cuba there was a delightful dinner party with other DuPont relatives, and we dined by candlelight (with over sixty candlesticks of Georgian silver lighting the room) discussing the celebrations planned for the 200th anniversary of the two DuPont brothers who had settled in this part of Delaware. The next day – our last – we spent most of the morning at the gardens of Longwood which had been opened to the public by the DuPont family. On arrival, Pamela joined the ordinary visitors' queue for tickets, until an embarrassed member of the staff recognised her waiting patiently and we were whisked into the manager's office before touring the gardens. Although over ninety she insisted on walking the full length of the long walk round the lake and gardens, and we then enjoyed visiting the original farmhouse of the estate, which had been sold by William Penn to his Quaker friend George

Peirce, whose descendant had sold it two centuries later to Pierre DuPont in 1905. (It was pleasing to find that the arms of this Peirce family, originally from London, were identical to those on a Chinese armorial service of the 1750s made, in all probability, for one of his English cousins.)

It had been a varied and very enjoyable journey, and we flew home from Philadelphia feeling that the first steps in a major new project had been achieved which, if well executed, could make a substantial difference to the record of the China Trade in the future through the generosity of Leo and Doris.

*　　*　　*

A particularly pleasant evening shortly after our return was a lecture I was asked to give to a group representing the West Yorkshire National Arts Collection Fund who were travelling in the West Country with Martin Arnold, but a better surprise was in store. To celebrate Eileen's 50th birthday, she and Bo had taken a delightful villa in the small town of Maussane near Les Baux in Provence, and with four other old friends of theirs, we were invited for a week. The very substantial 18th Century house belonged to France Louis Dreyfus, whose great-great-uncle had been the ill-fated scapegoat of the French government a century earlier, and had herself been married to Jacques Charrier, once the husband of Brigitte Bardot. Bo and Eileen's other guests were Marguerite and Gerry Lenfest, a generous benefactor of the Philadelphia Museum, and Sue and Ted Van Leer, who live in Lexington, Virginia. Both Gerry and Ted had been at Washington & Lee University and were old friends of Bo, serving on the Board of Trustees with him.

We spent much of Sunday at the attractive village of Isle-sur-la-Sorge which was well known for its regular antique fairs, and both Bo and I were lucky enough to discover things to our taste, including an unusual faience bowl in the same style as a known Chinese armorial one made for an East India captain. That evening we enjoyed a fine birthday dinner at the restaurant Oustau de Baumanière at Les Baux, a mediaeval village over-shadowed by a castle, long the home of a powerful feudal lord who ruled the area.

In the days that followed we visited Arles to see the well-preserved Roman amphitheatre, particularly enjoying the museum, and Nimes where there was a similar amphitheatre and fine Roman temple, all preserved in exceptional condition. It would be difficult to leave Provence without spending a day in Avignon, and Eileen had arranged with one of France's leading chefs who cooked at the principal hotel that our party should spend a morning in his kitchen and learn how to cook fish in exotic sauces, and prepare the other courses of an exceptional meal which ended with an extraordinary dessert of wild strawberries with curry spices! I decided to desert the others and wandered round antique shops, but returned to the kitchen at one o'clock to watch the final touches and share their success at an excellent lunch. We later went as far as the bridge at Avignon would allow and visited the palace, but it was clear that we could spend far longer in that fascinating city.

Angela and I also spent a day wandering on our own, while the others drove down to St Tropez to have lunch with Gerry's son, whose yacht was anchored there. We always enjoyed St Remy (where Van Gogh had stayed in 1889 during a particularly successful season of painting in Provence), spending much of the afternoon at Glanum, just south of the town, which must be one of the best preserved excavated Roman towns, revealing streets, houses, shops and temples over a wide but continuous area, many of the buildings with columns and carvings well preserved, and a mausoleum which is the best preserved of the 6th Century in the Roman world.

But we could only stay a week, and on the last evening Eileen invited France Louis to dine with us (in her own house), completing a holiday made as pleasurable by the company as the *campagne*. All too soon we had to catch the Saturday train from Avignon and managed to reach West Yatton by midnight, although delayed a few hours when the train was struck by lightening and came to an abrupt halt in the countryside.

June brought other friends and groups, while we also stayed at the Oriental Club and I gave a lecture at the Ceramics Fair. Meanwhile no opportunity was lost to garner a few more photographs for Volume II in pursuit of which we drove to Olney in Buckinghamshire to get illustrations of a number of damaged pieces in John Swallow's collection, and on another occasion had tea with Lady Westmorland (whose husband had once been Chairman of Sotheby's) who had some Fane family porcelain I didn't know.

It was already ten years since our first Belmont reunion, and this time Brian and Ginny Walton had kindly offered to give a lunch for the 60th anniversary of the school's sailing to Nassau. We met again many of those who had come to Chris Willy's party a decade earlier although sadly my sister Hazel was no longer with us. In spite of the fact that I had long discovered that I was not a clubbable man, preferring meeting friends on a one-to-one basis where one could exchange conversation within one's joint interests, there was no doubt that the bond formed by our journey to Nassau was lasting and took little account of our later careers – whether oil company executive, RAF, Army, Colonial civil servant, dentist, lorry driver, entrepreneur or businessman – for when we met we thought of each other as we had been sixty years before. Only one boy from those days has remained elusive, for his public school's

Antique shopping with Bo DuBose in Nimes.

Sixty years on – boys of Belmont, Bahamas.
From left, standing: Walton, Poupart, Howard, Horwood, Willy, Prestige.
Seated: Goldsmith (Teddy), Melville, Clifton-Samuel, Peter Burr (son of Max Burr, the headmaster) and Barry Stonehill, who briefly joined Belmont in Nassau.

last record of him twenty or more years earlier was that he had become 'a gentleman of the road'.

Philippa and Thomas both stayed in early September, and as the autumn passed Harold and Joleen Poe also paid us a visit, although sadly Philippa and Brian's marriage had by then reached a dead end. Garter and others stayed for weekends, while we planned for what was to be a week of great interest, coupled with fond memories, in New York as, by an extraordinary coincidence, the final sale of the Mottahedeh Collection and that of Jim Williams' estate were to take place at Sotheby's on consecutive days in mid October. We flew to New York on October 14th and had the weekend to prepare for the many engagements of the coming week at the comfortable and convenient Barbizon Hotel on 78th Street. Sunday was a perfect autumn day and Angela's birthday, and Peter Frelinghuysen had kindly sent a car so that we could join him for lunch at Morristown with Rodney and his family (Rodney these days being increasingly involved in his responsibilities in Congress, although always maintaining his interest in porcelain). We had a perfect peaceful lunch in what must be my favourite dining room with Chinese export vases displayed beneath fine impressionist paintings, and after tea we were driven back comfortably to New York ready for an early start in what was to be a memorable week.

Largely through the energy of Tish Roberts, who had known Mildred well, Sotheby's had arranged a special day of lectures under the title 'Marco Polo to Mottahedeh – China for the West', and after coffee on Monday morning I followed Tish's introductory lecture with my own entitled, 'Mildred and Rafi Mottahedeh and their Porcelain Dream'. John Ayers had kindly lent me a number of slides which he had taken when he accompanied Mildred on one of her Chinese journeys to Jingdezhen to discuss manufacturing techniques and designs with the factories there, while I held a considerable collection of others taken over thirty years in New York and at her home in Stamford, Connecticut, as well as a large number of pieces in the Mottahedeh Collection. It was a sentimental journey laced with some exceptional porcelain. The other speakers in the day-long seminar were Robert Leath (now at Williamsburg), Clare Le Corbeiller (long a curator at the Metropolitan Museum), Bruce Perkins (now President of Winterthur), Kee Il Choi, and the new owner of the Mottahedeh Company.

Next day, after a most enjoyable lunch with Harold and Joleen Poe and some of their family, who were by chance in New York, I spoke again at Sotheby's on a related subject before a special dinner given in Mildred and Rafi's honour by the auction house, at which members of their family were present as well as friends and associates over the years. Mildred would have enjoyed it and was nevertheless there in spirit, for the evening ended with a short and engaging film of Mildred in her New York apartment, showing some of her treasures. The opening was emphatic as she smiled and said loudly, 'IT'S A DISEASE! – collecting is …'.

We were able to have a quick preview of Robert Doyle's porcelain at Christie's the following day, which was to be sold in January, for sadly he had died in the summer. Much of it I knew well, for it had headed west from Hay Hill, and Robert had always been happy relaxing in a room with his armorial porcelain, feeling that he could understand, almost hear, the conversations of its owners long passed (as indeed do I when I see a cup or bowl once used by James Boswell, Sir Walter Scott, William Pitt, or General Burgoyne). In the evening we attended yet another reception, followed by a dinner given by the ever-generous Khalil Rizk at his club for a large gathering of friends on the evening of the Mottahedeh sale.

It was a new experience to find myself bidding at a sale of such world-wide interest with a catalogue for which both John Ayers and I had written forewords, and which included so many pieces that we had found and chronicled over thirty years – then watching while the auctioneer's hammer fell. I had mixed feelings as we managed to secure a small part of the collection (nevertheless totalling £160,000), while an exceptional pair of wood and ivory Chinese figures, one holding a lotus flower (for purity) and the other a tall umbrella, which had once belonged, as part of a set of eight, to Queen Mary, but for the last forty years had sat modestly on the dining room sideboard in Mildred's apartment, were despatched to a new home for $590,000. It was a long day, but one filled with interest and the opportunity to meet old friends, while the next morning we saw some of them again at the Mercer House sale at which many of Jim Williams' possessions were sold.

On our last day we enjoyed lunch with Shirley and Tom Mueller, before flying home with memories of New York as I had known it clouded by Mildred's departure. But on the flight I looked again at one of the many articles about her and savoured two paragraphs in a New York magazine which had been written some years earlier.

> Her life's work to produce museum-quality reproductions has preserved precious designs of antiquity for future generations and made possible and practical the use of them today. But that is only a part of her story. Entrepreneur, expert antiquarian, world-renowned collector, designer, philanthropist, aesthete and enthusiast-at-large, Mildred Mottahedeh is one whose life is an extraordinary strand of experiences, accomplishments and

humanitarian acts. She is a woman defined by her work, as much as her work is defined by her.

What is her secret? 'I'll tell you what,' she begins, in her uncanny way that combines the elegance and authority of an empress with the plain-spoken forthrightness of a diner waitress. 'Everybody is an individual, with a different reason for being in the world. And each one of us has a confirmation to do. A few years ago I was being given an award in Texas, and they made this big, long speech and all that embarrassing stuff, and they asked me to make a speech.' The occasion was to honour her with the International Tabletop Award for Lifetime Achievement. 'And I said, "Thank you for the award. But you should know that the gifts we have are given to us when we are born. Our responsibility is to develop them."'

*   *   *

It was to be a short and busy week on our return, because I had promised first to drive to Powerstock to bury the ashes of my Uncle Arthur who, having been involved in hospital administration much of his life, had left his body, then over 100 years old, to medical research, after which his ashes had sat in a casket for some years on a shelf in the home of my cousin Beatrice, who had died unexpectedly and was buried at the same time.

(After his wife's death, Arthur had lived by himself until the age of 99 in a flat overlooking Bridport harbour. For his hundredth birthday I spent a memorable day with him in his Bridport nursing home. He was remembered by his regiment, who kindly sent a Colonel from Warminster to see him, and when asked who his commanding officer had been, Arthur replied, 'Kitchener's younger brother.' His Oxford College recalled him as their oldest living graduate, and the headmaster of Sherborne School also drove down to wish him well, together with the head boy whose 18th birthday was that same day. Arthur told them that when he was at school, they had had a glass of ale each day for breakfast!)

At the weekend we set off on a much looked-forward-to week in Scotland, where we had arranged to photograph some of the services we had seen on our last trip. We stayed three nights with David Perth at Stobhall (for the first time using a walking stick because he had fallen downstairs and injured his back), taking the opportunity to photograph armorial services at Scone, and the following day various pieces of Murray services at Blair Athol where David had long been a friend of the late Duke, while we also visited Glamis Castle together and had tea with Lady Strathmore. Leaving Stobhall, our route next day took us in a new direction, and having called at Drum Castle to photograph the Irvine service and an exceptional porcelain table top made for the Duke of Somerset, we drove on to see and photograph various pieces of Robertson porcelain at Crichie, where we had tea with Geordie and Patricia Burnett-Stewart, before returning to the Udny Arms at Newburgh where they joined us for dinner.

Next day we drove again to Haddo House for lunch with Alexander Haddo (who has since inherited from his father the marquessate of Aberdeen) who lived with his family in a finely converted former orangery overlooking what had once been an extensive area of vegetables, but was now an expansive garden with a terrace leading down to lawns and herbaceous borders. After lunch we drove once more to Brodie Castle where we had arranged to meet Dr Stephanie Blackden, the resident curator, to photograph the various services there. We had an interesting discussion and tea before setting off again northwards to our destination, Foulis Castle, where Mrs 'Timmy' Munro had very kindly asked us to stay for two nights.

We enjoyed a quiet evening with Timmy, and next day after breakfast scoured the cupboards to discover and photograph examples of the numerous services of Chinese armorial porcelain made for the family (which had so excited Phil Cooke when he had visited Foulis thirty years earlier when shooting in Scotland) before having lunch with Anthony Chamier, Hector Munro's cousin, and his wife Carole. Anthony's Huguenot ancestors had also ordered two armorial services, as well as lacquer and mother-of-pearl, whilst serving in the East India Company, and I had corresponded with him about this for some time after an introduction by Stephen Brockman.

We also had an invitation to call the following day at Dunrobin Castle, some distance north, where Lord Strathnaver and his wife Gillian (who had worked with an old friend, Mike Clough, in the London antique trade) kindly gave us tea and a tour, and discussed a number of treasures including some connected with Garibaldi. It was a coincidence that an ancestor of Alistair Tower had been a friend of the Italian statesman and had interesting documents, and I later introduced them as Alastair Strathnaver was considering a special Garibaldi room at the castle. Next day, after a last comfortable evening at Foulis, we set off south, pausing for lunch at Blairgowrie, and having tea with Robert and Janet Balfour, who had kindly arranged for a fine Bruce armorial punch bowl to be repaired so that I could photograph it. It was good to be able to stay the night with Angus and Kay again at their farm, Archerfield, before we visited Lennoxlove with them on Sunday to find yet another different Hamilton service to photograph in a tantalisingly interesting display of the many Hamilton services (totalling about twenty) which the family had accumulated over the years, and Angus has now reorganised to such effect.

As we arrived back at West Yatton late on Sunday evening, we still felt the glow of a fascinating journey, and had with us a roll of film to be developed which included transparencies of examples of seventeen new services, that I had been able to photograph in ten different homes in Scotland in the last nine days. Many had not previously been recorded outside the families who had owned them for between two and three centuries. It left a thrill of discovery which is difficult to describe but very satisfying, while the kindness and interest of the present day descendants was heart-warming.

But the excitement was not over, for arriving home late after the tiring journey we found a catalogue from Phillips in Bath which included a punch bowl with the arms of Goodwin, but the sale was the following day. Exhausted by the long day, I decided that we couldn't drive into Bath next morning but would bid on the telephone. However, I changed my mind when a friend in London rang early next day and asked me if I would be bidding. We arrived to find an exceptional piece with a *famille rose* painting of a shipping scene inside (which had not been illustrated in the catalogue) and settled down for the lot to be sold, because I was almost certain I recognised the main ship from a contemporary engraving. Although the estimate was no more than £1,000, I found myself bidding to a total of more than £38,000 in order to take it home. When we returned, I found the early 18th Century engraving of the *Royal George* that it was copied from. The bowl soon departed to a new home, but not before a number of photographs had been taken and it became the illustration on the front and back of the jacket for Volume II of *Chinese Armorial Porcelain*, together with the engraving it so accurately copied.

Later in November Bo and Eileen DuBose were again at Manor Farm, and on the Saturday we all had dinner in Bath with Ted and Anne Close who were visiting from Denver, and who they had not previously met. During dinner the conversation turned to the second world war in which both Ted Close (a nephew of Marjorie Merriweather Post) and Bo's father, Beverly, had served in the Navy. Ted told a story of a very near disaster to a major American vessel off the coast of Brazil, when the rapid currents nearly grounded the ship had it not been for the action of a newly-joined officer of the watch waking the captain to tell him that the shore lights seemed much closer than they should be. Bo listened intently, and as Ted finished he said quietly, 'That was my father.'

A few days later some old memories were awakened when Richard Wraxall, whom I had met very briefly in the Coldstream and whose home, Tyntesfield, has more recently been a focus of National Trust interest, came to tea. He wanted to look at a portrait of his ancestor's daughter, Maria Elizabeth Gibbs, by Mrs Hoare of Bath, which I had bought some years before because I thought she looked like Angela. (We had later discovered, in a bookshop in Scotland, that the portrait had been used as the jacket of a book called 'Isabella', written by Mary Crewe, and published by the BBC without knowing whose image it was! I was able to tell a helpful Tracey Smith, the Editorial Manager of BBC Books, that Maria Elizabeth Gibbs was the daughter of Sir Vicary Gibbs, the Lord Chief Justice, and that she had married at an early age a young officer, later General Sir Andrew Pilkington, who fought at Waterloo. Maria Elizabeth's and Isabella's stories were, in fact, sufficiently alike to make the image appropriate.)

At the end of the month we experienced a new type of sale when the German auction house Nagel sold, over a week, in Stuttgart the huge 'new' Hatcher cargo called 'Tek Sing', after exhibiting it at Stuttgart railway station. The numbers dwarfed those of previous cargoes and the rather late date, of the 1820s, all made it an unenviable task, but we were pleasantly surprised to find that for the first time we could bid live on the internet, and were able to land about 350 pieces (just a fraction of 1% of the whole cargo). To those who took part in Stuttgart it must have seemed like the days of the Nanking Cargo, while to us it was but an interesting echo of the past.

*   *   *

The new year of 2001 broke with a lunch party at the Oriental Club for Pat and Robin's 50th wedding anniversary, and I greatly enjoyed meeting many of their friends from those days in Singapore, and a world when that grand port was part of a greater Empire. Later in January we flew once more to New York and stayed six days with John Andrew, still at Grace Church. Although it was an opportunity to have lunch with Henry and Dinah Moog, and visit the treasure-trove apartment of Joy and Erving Wolf for tea (which I hadn't seen for a dozen years or more), the main purpose of our visit was to attend the sale of Robert Doyle's collection at Christie's. Robert had been a friend since the days of my earliest 'porcelain tours' in the late 1970s and, as I had been able to write in a Christie's publication, he was never happier than when he could relax in his drawing room with his armorial porcelain. I don't think that he would have minded us acquiring about ninety pieces of his collection for others interested in the same historical perspective. After the sale Becky

MacGuire hosted a very nice lunch in Christie's board room at which Cary Doyle and her son, Henry, were present, and Cary kindly gave both Becky and me a piece of fun modern porcelain with scenes of the factories at Canton (both pieces in the form of sleeping piglets!). We were also able to spend a delightful evening with Nelson and Jackie Kline, seeing his marvellous collection of fine Yongzheng armorial porcelain, but although we could happily have stayed longer in New York, we had to be home two days later.

Progress on the second volume of *Chinese Armorial Porcelain* required discussions on another front, and at the end of January we had the first of several meetings with Mike Blacker that slowly confirmed our resolve that we should do as much as possible of the editing process ourselves. My own part in this involved writing the entries for the hundred or so new services which turned up each year, amending and incorporating the large addendum in Volume I into its place in Volume II, updating and adding considerable material to the extended appendices, including the part played by Britons living in Sweden (in which Kristina Söderpalm of the Gothenburg Museum was a great support, sending much information from the Swedish East India archives) and writing the new chapters which would provide background to the story. Angela increasingly assumed the role of editor whilst still preparing on the database the material I wrote by hand. Roy Davey also visited us in West Yatton on a number of occasions, while the everyday life of Heirloom continued and we experienced such occasional diversions as a large sale of armorial porcelain in Exeter, followed by an enjoyable lunch with Michael and Anne Pursey. Shortly after this, I spent some two hours on the telephone to Northeast Auctions in New Hampshire to cover the sale of the porcelain of the redoubtable Madeleine Shea who, with her daughter, Pat, had visited us on so many occasions in the past and, as many of the great collectors, had continued collecting with undiminished enthusiasm well into her nineties.

A near week-long visit from Thomas, coinciding almost exactly with his thirty-fifth birthday, gave us the news that after a long estrangement, he and Emma Lavelle (whom we had last seen when she stayed with us in Bath in 1990, and whose father was a doctor in Liverpool) had got together again and hoped to have a child in late November or early December. It was exciting news and with so much else happening promised a happy future for Thomas, who now worked for Stanley Leisure in Liverpool. Shortly after Angela and I set off on a different holiday to France and Italy (although I had to admit to carrying part of my manuscript in a briefcase in case there was time to write, which indeed there was!).

We saw José Manuel and Maria Abaroa in London where we stayed overnight at the Oriental Club, and the following morning caught the Eurostar to Paris, having dinner with Arnaud and Veronique. Next day we took the train to Brive and collected a car (which unexpectedly turned out to be a smart and very comfortable Alpha Romeo) to drive to Figeac, a delightful town on the River Cele in Guyenne. The beautifully restored and converted Hotel du Vignier du Roy (the mediaeval home of the Viceroy of Guyenne) made a perfect centre for touring by car, but we were so captivated by the town itself that much of our time was spent within its walls seeing such sights as the enlarged copy of the Rosetta Stone at the birthplace of Jean Francois Champollion, who first deciphered the ancient Egyptian hieroglyphics.

Aware that there was far more yet to discover, after five days we had to drive away, staying en route near St Remy de Provence and then on to the Hotel La Perouse in Nice, an old favourite where we had stayed in the past, which was unusually sited high up on the rock overlooking the old port of Nice but away from the roar of the traffic. While there we spent a day with Alastair and Nicole Tower at Beaulieu, and another at Monte Carlo with old friends, before catching a train to Como. This journey was not without incident, for as we relaxed into our seats on the train I discovered that I had been the victim of a professional pick-pocket at Nice railway station who had sat next to me while waiting for the train. Fortunately, he only took my wallet (my passport was in another pocket) although he had worked with considerable skill because I was also wearing an outer coat. The first hour on the train was spent on the telephone cancelling credit cards, and the pick-pocket only enjoyed an expensive visit to a supermarket and a gargantuan lunch.

It was our first visit to Lake Como, and the excitement continued, for our taxi was involved in an multi-car shunt on the winding road from Como to Tremezzo. We spent an idle two hours at the roadside while the Italian police investigated the incident at length, and the local villagers brought out chairs and sat round, gossiping and drinking coffee, while the chief of the fire brigade (resplendent in dark glasses, gold jewellery, and a cigarette in his mouth!) asked us to take some photographs for his report.

But the Grand Hotel at Tremezzo, with a sunlit view of Bellagio on the opposite shore, was worth the wait, and we enjoyed five perfect days travelling by lake steamer to many beautiful lakeside villages and small towns, a number of which beckoned us for future visits. It was difficult to know whether we preferred the mediaeval comfort of southern France, or the lakeside leisure of the Italian lakes, but we arrived home on the sleeper from Milan to Paris and the Eurostar to London after a happy two weeks.

CHAPTER 30

Chinese Armorial Porcelain, Volume II – and ...

Earlier in the year it had been a sad shock to learn that Wallace, the only son of Ruthie Watson (who had been such a pillar of strength at the 'Tale of Three Cities' exhibition) had slipped on the bank of the river in Oxford while a freshman at St Catherine's College and had drowned. Ruthie and Teddy, and their daughter Gabriella, were devastated by their loss, but did everything possible to turn this tragedy into an example of what Wallace might have achieved by founding, with the support of many friends, the Wallace Watson Award to encourage undergraduates who loved challenges to scale their own peaks in the future. We attended a moving service at Queen's College Chapel in mid May and were greatly impressed by the undergraduate support and the numbers of his friends who wished to contribute to this fund (which, at the time of writing, has already made its first two awards).

The summer of 2001 saw its usual number of visitors, while I spent every spare moment completing entries and writing chapters for Volume II which, it was now clear, would probably be more than nine hundred pages with certainly over two thousand illustrations. As usual we enjoyed meeting a number of friends at our customary stay at the club for the June Ceramics Fair, but this was somewhat marred this year by a sad incident, for a dealer well known to us later accused me of deliberately breaking an unimportant piece of porcelain after its purchase, so that I had an excuse to return it to him, having in fact found some concealed restoration which he had not made clear on viewing, or on his invoice. Despite two affidavits by reputable experts supporting my view, he unaccountably preferred to go to law rather than discuss it. This affair also revealed the lengths to which a senior London solicitor was willing to go in putting forward a number of totally unsupported lies in favour of her client without any corroborating evidence whatever. (A sad commentary on the integrity of the law.) The whole affair ended with an unreserved apology on his part, but only after two months of unnecessary and unpleasant correspondence which, on our side, was conducted entirely by myself, although it diverted too much attention from more important matters.

It was a welcome relief to go to a large family picnic on the hill enclosure at Old Sarum in Wiltshire, organised by Sophie – the third she had arranged in as many years. The bringing together of over sixty relatives from the North, Howard, Sanctuary, Graham, Shipley and other families under a shady tree within sight of the remains of the ancient cathedral of Salisbury for a summer picnic provided an informal occasion for renewing old friendships, and was obviously enjoyed by those who came from a number of southern counties, London and even Denmark, without any major organisation and with little cost. I was also delighted that, almost ten years after Hazel's death, Richard had again found happiness and we attended his marriage with Joan in Gloucestershire.

It was most interesting to meet Anne Bulley, the author of *The Bombay Country Ships 1790-1833,* with whom I had corresponded, who came to lunch and exchanged thoughts on the officers of those ships. As a result she kindly made available all the information she had assembled on the ships' officers and I was able to present it as an extra appendix in Volume II, finding that almost certainly a number had been the owners of armorial services. The linking of such research, originally undertaken for quite different reasons, is often most useful; indeed, had I had Anthony Farrington's *A Biographical Index of East India Company Maritime Service Officers 1600-1834* (published in late 1999) earlier, I could have saved myself much research!

Later in the week we drove to Norfolk and stayed again with Colin and Annabel McKay. We had had an invitation from Lord Cholmondeley to visit Houghton so that I could photograph pieces of Sir Robert Walpole's service, much of which was still at Houghton after three centuries. A most useful and interesting visit was followed by a dinner with John and Val Guinness at their beautiful 16th Century home, built originally by Sir William Fermor in 1538 and still having its original gatehouse, with a range of armorials displayed on the walls.

July saw Angus and Kay Hamilton to stay, followed by a sad journey to St Albans for the funeral of my cousin Kay's husband, Aubrey Boutwood, a talented and gifted lawyer who had not always found the success which he might have achieved. While Angela went on for a few days in Yorkshire with her sister's family I hurried back to West Yatton to start trawling through the 35,000 images on a microfilm, just received, of all the bookplates of the Franks Collection in the British Museum, which also linked conclusively with armorial porcelain as the exact originals of many of the services made in China. It was to be an added task to compare images for the next three or four months, but provided great satisfaction as one discovered many additional names and precise identifications just in time to include the information and complete another appendix.

In late August we had our first visit from Ron Fuchs, the newly-appointed curator of the Hodroff Collection which was slowly building at Winterthur. It was almost eighteen months since our stay in Palm Beach and discussions with Leo, and rapid progress had been made in financing and appointing a special curator at the Museum and organising a flow of porcelain and its display, so that the groundwork was beginning to develop for a very considerable advance in the exhibition and educational background of Chinese Export porcelain as a whole. Ron, the son of an East Coast lawyer, had always wanted such a challenge in the decorative arts world and seemed an ideal candidate for the position, having taken a post-graduate degree at Winterthur. He was particularly anxious to get to know others in this field so that he could benefit from their experience and broaden his own. It was the first of a number of visits and considerable correspondence, which I enjoyed and wholeheartedly supported, leading to detailed plans for a travelling exhibition of export porcelain from the Hodroff Collection, with a new catalogue written by Ron (to be published in early 2005) for which I wrote the foreword.

It was on Tuesday 11th September that Tony, who was gardening that afternoon and had his radio switched on as he worked, hurried in to tell us that there had been a terrible 'accident' in New York with a plane crashing into a skyscraper. We immediately turned on the television as the story unfolded and the world became aware of a new world war.

A number of friends stayed in September and October, including Bo and Eileen (who arrived on the 12th and told us that Eileen's brother had been in the canteen at the Pentagon at the time of the terrorist attack, but fortunately was safe), as well as Chris and Susie, and Arnaud from Paris.

In mid October we drove to the Lake District to join Pat and Robin, Thérèse and Paul, and their children Harry and Joanna, staying at a comfortable hotel overlooking Lake Windermere for Angela's fiftieth birthday, visiting Milnthorpe where her Postlethwaite ancestors had lived in the 18th Century and Broughton-in-Furness, where their Postlethwaite kinsmen had employed the young Branwell Bronte in January 1840 as tutor for their two sons. It was just over fifty-six years since I had camped not far away, south of Coniston Water, and heard of the 'new' bomb that had landed on Hiroshima and had introduced the modern age of the atom.

*   *   *

Back at West Yatton we had pondered deeply after Dorothy told us that she would have to leave in order to help her husband, Philip Smith, compile records of his extraordinary work in bookbinding. We had advertised for someone to replace her with only moderate confidence in success, but were surprised to have received more than twenty replies, which we had narrowed to a small number of interviews, and a week later were able to appoint Rebecca Wise. She had served in the Army, and had lived and worked in Germany and Hong Kong where her husband had been stationed, and later been an assistant to a professor at the University of York. Nearly two years on, we are all very happy with the choice.

It was particularly nice to see Norman and Kathy again in November, for Norman had flown over from Nassau for his well-deserved investiture as a Companion of the Order of St Michael and St George, and we had dinner together at the Oriental Club, while on the Monday I flew to Lisbon to lecture once more for the 'Amigos do Oriente' Seminar which again was organised with considerable care and was a pleasure to attend, meeting many of the friends from the previous occasion two years before.

It was very exciting to hear that Thomas and Emma had had a baby daughter, Lydia Jane, on 6th December and we looked forward to seeing her early in 2002. The year ended with Angela's family for Christmas, but with no-one to stay in January (although various friends including Rupert Tower, Alistair's son, spent the day with us) I had set my sights on the manuscript going to the printers at the end of the year and there was much to do. But very sadly the end of the month was thrown into disarray with the terrible news that Lydia had died during the night in her sleep after just six weeks. I was able to catch a train to Liverpool next day and stay for a night with Joe Lavelle, Emma's father, and his wife Sheila, and see Lydia before the coroner's advisors were to examine her and eventually allow a funeral to take place. Even in a world of sudden death one does not imagine that such an unexpected tragedy can strike so close. I could only hope that my visit to see my seventh grandchild in some way comforted Thomas and Emma to a small degree. It was not for some weeks that almost all the family were able again to travel to Liverpool by train to attend a comforting service and cremation, followed by a reception for family and friends.

The sudden shock of such an event made one more aware of the good fortune that had attended most of the lives of my other children and grandchildren, all of whom were capable of making a clear and independent path in life. Sadly Philippa had recently suffered the loss of her partner of several years, Al Guilford, who died unexpectedly on Christmas Eve 2001 of a heart attack. Al, who had won a scholarship to Yale, ran a small computer business and was an author. Notwithstanding this, her children, Gareth and Elizabeth Poe, are developing fast, and while Gareth is intelligent but easy-going and expects to go to university in 2004 (although the football field seems to be as interesting to him as the academic field), Elizabeth, with a sharp mind, could easily be a success at whatever she really sets her mind to with a little application and discipline.

Sophie had followed an artistic career since leaving university which sometimes linked itself to unusual employment, as when for two or more years she worked in a high security prison teaching art to long-term repeat offenders as part of a government programme to break their cycle of crime. (It was a symptom of ill-planned bureaucracy that although this scheme showed definite signs of success resulting in a significant fall in re-offending, it was wound up for 'financial' reasons, even though the long-term cost of prisons for those who did re-offend was greater than the cost of education – albeit to a different branch of government.) But Sophie, although continuing to teach, later developed her commercial talent in founding Eden Sculptures, a business providing a very wide range of sculptural designs for garden centres, not only in Britain but in America and Europe, while her daughter Jenny is now at university. It is not yet clear what course her talented son Alfie will follow, for although he enjoys studying history and art, and has thought of the law as a career, as a teenager he is probably most involved emotionally at present as a successful rugby player in his age group in Bristol.

For a considerable period, Jo followed the path of social welfare after taking her degree in philosophy at Edinburgh University. For a while she was a part-time advisor in 'Citizens' Advice' and later the secretary of the Bristol branch of the charity 'Nightstop' which rescued teenage children from sleeping rough in the streets and organised alternative accommodation through a large group of volunteer families until a better path could be planned for their future. Moving to St Ives in Cornwall with her partner, David Scott, in 2002 to be a Community Development Officer in West Cornwall covering Penzance and Lands End – an area she had loved as a child – proved a happy change, and her children, Danny and Charlie, the youngest of my grandchildren, are quick-witted and flourish in their new environment, greatly enjoying their swimming and the amateur theatricals which are a feature of artistic St Ives. They have an excellent springboard for the future.

Thomas, who after his adventures while at Stowe decided not to complete his degree course in Hispanic Studies at Liverpool University at the end of two years, developed a strong interest in catering and wines. He later found a cause which greatly stimulated him in the uncovering of thirteen miles of 19th Century tunnels, created by Joseph Williamson under Liverpool, and was for a while Chairman of 'The Friends of Williamson's Tunnels' while later being Chairman of the Edgehill Neighbourhood Council. Remaining in Liverpool, he has been able to rebuild his life after Lydia Jane's tragic death.

*   *   *

February saw renewed attention to finalising the scanning of all the varied illustrations for Volume II and it became increasingly clear that when the work was completed by June, and the illustrations could all be printed in page order because the database would ensure this, it would still be necessary in perhaps two hundred cases or more to make further minor adjustments so that colour values were consistent on each page spread, most of which would include six illustrations.

We had planned another visit to America in mid March and flew to Washington to stay three nights with Malcolm and Joan Sterrett in Bethesda. We spent a particularly interesting morning at Hillwood, the former home of Marjorie Merriweather Post, and enjoyed lunch another day with Angela's cousin, Noble, at the Chevy Chase Club. Joan organised an excellent dinner at which we met again the Eckenhoffs and the ever-enthusiastic Bruce Perkins, now Chairman of the Board of Trustees at Winterthur, while another guest was Mark Leithauser, with his wife, who had designed 'The Treasure Houses of Britain' exhibition which had been such a success in the '80s, and was to do the same for the upcoming exhibition at the National Gallery of Art in Washington celebrating the 50th Anniversary of Winterthur as a museum (sponsored by Linda Kaufman, whose husband George had recently died but who had been a friend over the years).

Taking the train down to Charlottesville, we were met by Tom Litzenburg who drove us to Lexington and had arranged for us to stay in the comfortable university guest house. We had dinner with Tom and his son Timothy that evening, discussing his book to be published in 2003 on the Reeves Collection of porcelain at Washington & Lee (of which I had read the manuscript and had written the short preface). Next day we were able to walk round the university campus before having lunch with Elizabeth and Larry Boetsch, the acting President of Washington & Lee, and Tom Litzenburg and his associate, Holly Bailey – a lunch at which Jim and Celeste Whitehead were also present (Jim having managed the Reeves Center from its gifting until his retirement; indeed, his recent book *A Fragile Union* tells the story well).

Although very anxious not to appear to interfere in matters which were not my responsibility, I could not disguise the fact that my own feelings were that the University itself might give greater recognition to the Reeves Collection (as their collection of China Trade porcelain was known) which occupied a separate building on the campus. I felt it might also be possible to utilise the collection as an academic asset and to integrate it more into mainstream college life by using this clearly well-exhibited facility as an additional focus in the teaching of the decorative arts – one of the university's principal courses. If this could also be supported by the recent good fortune of

Leo Hodroff discusses his plans for the future in the Hodroff Gallery
at Winterthur, Delaware.

Winterthur in this field (and there were obvious links as the Chairman of the Board at Winterthur was also a Washington & Lee alumnus) and Tom's new book which provided very full historical details, all this would give added stimulus to the story of the influence of Eastern design on Western decorative arts and illuminate perhaps the earliest pattern of trade in the newly independent America. In correspondence, I had the feeling that Larry Boetsch was not unsympathetic to these ideas, although there were obviously many factors which needed to be taken into consideration which were no business of mine and he was shortly to be leaving his post, as indeed was Tom, on his retirement the following year. That evening we had a very pleasant dinner with Ted and Sue Van Leer whom we had last seen with the DuBoses in Provence.

As Tom drove us to collect a hire car in the morning we hoped that our visit to Lexington would be as helpful as it had been interesting. Angela drove the six hours north to Wilmington, Delaware, and we arrived at the Inn at Montchanin near Winterthur, in time for dinner and an early start next day. This began with a near disaster, because as we drove from the Inn to return our hire car and go on to Winterthur one wheel collapsed and we were rescued by Ron Fuchs who came to pick us up. It was to be an important day, for a meeting was scheduled with Leo and Doris Hodroff; the Director, Leslie Bowman; other Winterthur executives, and ourselves, to chart the way forward and agree a policy over a travelling exhibition and its catalogue. This followed a tour of the display of Hodroff porcelain already on view in their galleries. Undoubtedly progress had been made but there were numerous points of detail yet to negotiate. In the evening we had dinner with Leslie Bowman and her husband at their home, the other guests being Leo and Doris, Pat Halfpenny (well known for her scholarship in the English porcelain field) and her husband, and Ron Fuchs.

With a day free of meetings and lectures, we went the following morning by commuter train to Philadelphia, although we nearly didn't make it for the ticket office said emphatically that all foreigners had to show a photographic driving licence or passport (which we did not have with us) before buying a ticket to 'prove' we were not terrorists. After some argument, and a long queue forming behind us, we were let off with a severe warning. In Philadelphia, at the kind invitation of the very helpful Donna Corbin, we saw all the Chinese porcelain in the Museum – both on display and in the basement reserve collection – revealing two or three 'new' services which we were able to photograph, and after lunch with her spent some time exploring the city and its historic architecture.

The following day I lectured at the Winterthur Ceramics Conference, meeting Robert Leath among many old friends. In the evening there was a gala dinner and we particularly enjoyed having conversations with Mary and Bill Bridges and other friends, including Robert Copeland. But the all too short visit was over and on Saturday after lunch Ron drove us to the airport to catch the evening flight to Heathrow – by luck upgraded to a comfortable business class – reaching home in time for lunch on Sunday.

Still in pursuit of porcelain, we motored to Warwick Castle to photograph two exceptional pieces of armorial services, one of which had belonged to the now extinct Earls of Leicester. It was a piece of a service of which I knew, but had not been able to locate until a friend, Peter Dakin, spotted it on display at the castle. We thought it was the last piece of porcelain we should be able to add to the almost complete manuscript, but photographs and emails continued to arrive for some months yet, while technical advances made it possible to go on adding more discoveries and adjusting entries until final pagination had taken place.

*   *   *

In the last week of April we took the Eurostar to France and stayed for two happy days with Francis and Catherine Lesur at Hardelot, a now thriving resort south of Calais well-known for its golfing facilities which he and his family had done much to develop over the last century. Francis had long shared our enthusiasm for armorial porcelain and inevitably we found two or three more 'new' pieces which he had discovered since we had last stayed. But it was only the first stage of our journey, for we took the train to Paris two days later and were met by Arnaud and Veronique who drove us to L'Orient to visit the museum at Port-Louis. The museum contains a very well-displayed collection of Chinese Export porcelain, with considerable comparative material arranged with engravings and models covering the history of the French East India Company, certainly a 'must' for anyone who has time to make the journey and wander round the Citadelle. The friendship we had developed over the previous decade, and Arnaud's interest in the China Trade, made our journey to Brittany so much more fun, but after two nights, and dinner with Veronique's brother and sister-in-law, we had to hurry back to Paris to catch an afternoon train to Lausanne.

We had chosen this route, carrying a spare suitcase, because an old acquaintance, who had long collected porcelain but had now retired to Lausanne, had asked us to visit him and take away some armorial pieces. The Hotel Mirabeau made a pleasant overnight stay and we left next morning by train to Milan, laden with a full suitcase. This time we reached the Grand

Hotel at Tremezzo without incident and once more much enjoyed five days on the lake, taking a steamer each day to Bellagio and other villages along the shore, while a rainy day spent in the hotel provided time to work on one of the chapters, not all of which had yet been written.

We had decided to hire a car in Como to drive to the Metropole Hotel in Beaulieu-sur-mer on the Riviera, where we spent an evening and had dinner with Alastair and Nicole before continuing along the coast and north to Aix-en-Provence where we were to stay for the last five days of our holiday in France.

*　　*　　*

As June approached, a flurry of friends came to lunch or stayed before we set off to the Ceramics Fair in London. We were not to know it, but it was the last time that the Fair was held at the Park Lane Hotel where it had been now for sixteen years, and it was particularly exciting that on this occasion there was a small display of Chinese Export porcelain from the Hodroff Collection at Winterthur – a loan exhibit which attracted much attention, and a first indication here of the major plans that were stirring in America.

The cut-off day for new material added to Volume II had been planned for 1st July, but the great flexibility provided by the database made it possible to continue to add services after this date and in fact to within three weeks of handing the whole book to the printer in the new year. Our scanners, Prudence Cuming in London, had completed their work on time, although not without some problems. Thereafter every new addition was scanned into the manuscript 'in house' and close support from Roger Shapland made us increasingly confident that we could complete all the pagination and layout ourselves. The final decision to do this had only recently been taken, and as the tempo increased, Angela decided to cancel a trip to Italy in order to learn how to use the new Mac computer. Taking instruction from Roger, she was within a month able to turn the manuscript into Quark (virtually printer-ready material). As entries turned into pages and final colour adjustments to the illustrations were completed, work on the pagination could take place section by section, using the database for both Volume I, which had been prepared by Rebecca, and Volume II, as the basis for the joint index. It was, of course, now particularly important not to add any further new services without adjusting both the pages and the index already in Quark, and also the database. This sometimes required as many as a dozen changes for a single additional entry. But we had been right to do it ourselves, with Roger's encouragement and indispensable help, particularly as it enabled me to include almost six additional months of new material (some thirty-five services).

It was, however, a relaxation to see some more friends during September and October: David Rose from Washington, Arnaud, Rosemary and Mike Gomez, George and Carol Overend and the Welds, but by November our most frequent guest was Roger to oversee and 'sign off' the final scanning and pagination. This did not stop us driving up to Ashbourne in Derbyshire for three nights' rest at the very comfortable Callow Hall to celebrate Angela's birthday with Pat and Robin, and on the return journey spend an extra night at Rode Hall in Cheshire, the home of Richard and Anne Baker Wilbraham. Richard was not only the heir to more than one interesting service, having a life-long interest in porcelain (although English rather than Chinese), but his son, Randle, was married to my second cousin's daughter, Amanda Glossop, who was an artist. Our journey was a very welcome break, but we needed to be home for a busy last week in October.

Even at this late stage, it was still exciting to be able to drive to Lewes for the sale of the collection of Dennis Cowell's porcelain at Gorringes, amongst which we had found yet more unrecorded services. Dennis had long been a dealer and collector of Chinese export porcelain before he retired and had particularly liked armorial coffee cups, of which there were a number. On our return we were pleased that Steve and Mary Lynn Marks would be staying; he too had been at Washington & Lee and we had a number of mutual friends.

As November came and went our most frequent guest was still Roger and it was most exciting to see whole sections of Volume II printed out in a form which would qualify for the term 'final proof'. My only 'spare time' away from West Yatton was another visit to London University to examine a candidate for a fellowship or doctorate after her submission on an interesting theme covering the widespread distribution of Chinese prints for export in the late 18th and 19th Centuries. My co-examiner on this occasion was Dr Patrick Conner, the author of a biography of the painter, Chinnery, and other work on China Trade artists.

In early December we had a day-long discussion with Roy Davey which followed up an earlier preliminary meeting in July with the leading printers, Butler & Tanner, who gave us an extensive tour and explanation of their work in Frome, which had been their home for a century. I enjoyed driving through Frome, for near the top of the hill stood the fire station, with outside a life-size bronze statue of a fireman – the sculptor having been Sophie. Butler & Tanner had quoted us for printing and distributing Volume II and while the figures were clearly well in excess of anything we had expected from Hong Kong (or Eastern Europe) their quality, reliability, management accessibility, and distribution and warehousing ability, for books which were likely to be

Munson Campbell looks on as Phil Cooke, then with the largest collection of armorial porcelain, holds a favourite dish with the arms of Pierson of London.

Another boar's head to show Chris Weld in the library at home.

despatched in small quantities or single copies over many years, made them a sensible choice. The individually packed books would weigh five kilograms each, and any thought of despatching from West Yatton would have caused impossible storage problems. The idea of a specially designed bookplate signed by the author, which could be posted separately with an invoice, also greatly helped in avoiding unpacking and repacking books. Roy's visit, however, enabled us to discuss a wide range of marketing plans, for unlike an established publisher with agents world-wide, we would have to try to achieve sales through our own mailing list and similar initiatives. However, fortified by these plans, and with help from more than one friend in America, particularly Henry Moog and Lawrence Bradshaw, we were able to draw up a schedule and design leaflets to inform a wide range of those who might be interested, remembering always that Fabers had taken a dozen years to sell a similar number of the first volume of *Chinese Armorial Porcelain* in the 1970s and '80s.

December passed quickly with not an hour to spare, except for Chris and Susie, who stayed the weekend before Christmas en route for Lisbon. The manuscript was ready in the first week of January and was delivered to Butler & Tanner on the 24th as planned, illustrating and providing histories for 1,380 services which had not appeared in Volume I (an average of 46 services a year over the thirty years since Volume I was complete at the close of 1972, although the rate of discovery had probably doubled in more recent years). The long term plan of republishing Volume I in colour is still progressing slowly, and, at the time of writing, pieces of a further 150 armorial services for the British and American markets have been found, for history never stops revealing itself.

January still had time for an interesting visit to London with an invitation to a livery lunch with the Blacksmiths' Company, whose Chinese armorial bowl we had recently found and which was shortly to be seen in print. As work on the book progressed, Heirloom had not been allowed to lie dormant and has, over its thirty years, found homes for more than thirty-six thousand objects, the great majority with varying degrees of armorial or other historic interest. In many cases this has enabled pieces which have been sold, discarded, or have otherwise lost their identity and strayed, to be returned to the families for which they were once made, something which was always the aim of the author when starting the business in Hay Hill in 1973. In more recent years, working from Wiltshire, this has been achieved largely by producing illustrated catalogues which go out to a circle of friends, collectors and clients two or three times a year. In this we have been greatly aided by Clare Bradley, who has been our porcelain restorer most of the time at Manor

Farm, and Stephen James of Prudence Cuming Associates (whose studios are still across the road from Hay Hill) who has photographed for us in London, Bath and the country, with intelligent skill.

*   *   *

It was something of a surprise to be told by my oncologist, Ed Gilby, in my new year check-up, that my latest blood tests showed a falling level of white blood cells which, if continued, would threaten my immune system. There was no way that I could have guessed this was happening had it not been for the tests, but it had to result in a careful future regime of 'screening' visitors to see if they had colds or other infections, and I was advised that I should definitely no longer fly because of the unrestricted circulation of air in flight which could contain germs, and that I should also restrict rail journeys to a minimum and have a course of injections to boost the white blood cells if I was likely to be in a crowded environment. As further tests were done over the next two months I was finally diagnosed in May as having myelodysplasia which could develop into leukaemia if the situation worsened, but it had little effect on how I felt although my now daily antibiotics caused some extra drowsiness (and if for any reason I had to have 'reinforcements' it made me exhausted) – which was frustrating for someone who had been able to fill the 'unforgiving minute' for so long. But it was made more tolerable by the long-term support of our GP, Robin While, by the kindness of all the nurses at the Bath Clinic, and by my haematologist, Charles Singer, whose more optimistic outlook echoed my own.

We continued to meet friends with a cheerful warning, and as the weeks passed carried on normally with visits from Mrs Buhler from Texas, Nuno de Castro from Brazil, John Ayers, and Richard Ford from Indiana, who was a strong supporter and Trustee of the American Museum in Bath. At the same time we said farewell to Bill McNaught, who had done so much in twelve years to make the American Museum the success it is today, and whose company we had enjoyed on so many occasions.

Although the long-awaited official publication date for the new book was in May, we had sent out some thousands of leaflets before that date and were pleased by the response as preliminary orders came in and were transmitted to Butler & Tanner who were now able to despatch. It had perhaps not been the best of times to send out our publicity material as the war in Iraq gathered pace, but we felt it made little difference, and were particularly grateful for the support of the Buddy Taub Foundation in California which offered to pay half the cost to any American Museum that ordered a copy. This, and other marketing initiatives, ensured a steady flow of paperwork to the despatch department at Butler & Tanner.

In late May we decided to return to a comfortable private hotel overlooking Talland Bay, near Looe in Cornwall, where we had stayed ten years previously, and we used it as a base to relax and visit various country houses open to the public and drive to St Ives to spend a day with Jo and her family. She now had her interesting new job as a 'community development officer' in West Cornwall, a post which required judgement as to whether local applications for financial support for small industries merited financial help. Driving in our own car was largely risk-free and the hotel provided us with a very pleasant and conveniently secluded suite with doors on to the garden and overlooking the sea. We also enjoyed a visit from my nephew Nick, now a Rural Dean, a Canon of Exeter Cathedral and Rector of St Andrews, Plymouth, and a very busy man – something I felt I understood. Despite his own pressures of work, he has nevertheless found time to read through this manuscript and make helpful comments on its general interest and links with family history.

After a life of giving little thought to the risks that attended travelling in more than eighty countries, with only the occasional anti-malarial jab, it was difficult to appreciate any apparent risk in travelling to London by train and visiting antiques fairs. But fortified by another course of injections, we stayed again at the Oriental Club at the time of the Ceramics Fair in 2003 and much enjoyed the company of a number of friends.

Sotheby's had very kindly offered to put on a reception, lecture and launch party for the book at Olympia in June, after a special viewing of the Wingfield Digby Collection (a name I knew so well in the 1950s). Alastair Gibson allowed us to invite many old friends and relatives to listen to a short lecture on Chinese armorial porcelain. I didn't then know if it would be the last lecture that I would be allowed to give, after speaking in the past in ten countries, and thirty-five states in America, but was particularly pleased to see many faces I knew so well from Scotland, Wales, Ireland and Cornwall, France, Belgium, Holland, Sweden, Portugal and of course America. It was like lecturing to many audiences all rolled into one, in a long, happy past.

A busy summer passed, with the highlight being Sophie's wedding to her second husband, Nigel Shipley; the ceremony on a perfect June day, followed by a boat trip and lunch with all the family on the banks of the Avon. Heirloom continued to play the role it had now played for thirty years of providing the perfect introduction to so many who were interested in Chinese Export porcelain, and who over the years became friends, while I thought it was about time to make amends for my idleness nearly seventy years earlier when I

Pat and Robin Postlethwaite with my nephew, the Revd Nick McKinnel, before the service to celebrate our 15th wedding anniversary.

With Angela in Castle Combe after our 15th wedding anniversary lunch in 2004.

wrote 'Resolved to keep a dairy' – but did nothing. This book is the result, although it probably would not have reached this point without Angela's constant encouragement and help, and was completed on our 15th wedding anniversary.

If history, whether of the long or more recent past, and personal events teach anything, it is as much a perspective for the future as a study of the past. We have all taken a part in it, however insignificantly, and I have been particularly fortunate in having the opportunity of enjoying four lives – in a traditional manufacturing trade, in marketing educational books, as an antique dealer and as an author. Perhaps, too, I feel that the time will one day come when another poem by Rudyard Kipling would also be appropriate:

When Earth's last picture is painted and the tubes are twisted and dried,
When the oldest colours have faded, and the youngest critic has died,
We shall rest, and, faith, we shall need it – lie down for an aeon or two
Till the Master of All Good Workmen shall put us to work anew.

Index

Page numbers in italics denote illustrations